Porno Chic and the Sex Wars

Porno Chic and the Sex Wars

American Sexual Representation in the 1970s

EDITED BY

Carolyn Bronstein
and Whitney Strub

University of Massachusetts Press

Amherst and Boston

ISBN 978-1-62534-226-3 (paper); 225-6 (cloth)

Designed by Sally Nichols
Set in Palatino Linotype
Printed and bound by Sheridan Books, Inc.

Cover design by Sally Nichols
Cover art: Copyright © Peter Berlin, *Self-Portrait in Black Leather,*
c. 1970s. Hand-painted vintage gelatin silver print. Courtesy ClampArt,
New York City.

Library of Congress Cataloging-in-Publication Data
A catalog record for this book is available from the Library of Congress.

British Library Cataloguing-in-Publication Data
A catalog record for this book is available from the British Library.

Contents

Acknowledgments

T HIS BOOK BEGAN AS a conversation over coffee in Chicago in 2011, when the editors met in person for the first time. It turned serious after a meeting with University of Massachusetts Press editor Brian Halley at the Berkshire Conference of Women Historians, where it became obvious that he valued serious scholarship on the history of sexuality and regarded pornography as an important component of this burgeoning field. With his thoughtful editorial guidance, and the addition of a roster of talented contributors, these conversations evolved into *Porno Chic and the Sex Wars*. Our collective thanks begin with Brian, and everyone at the University of Massachusetts Press, for their steadfast support of the project and for recognizing the importance of bringing marginalized areas of study into full view.

Our thanks are also due to our wonderful contributors, whose intellectual range and commitment to fresh approaches have made these essays come together in ways that illuminate new themes. Film preservationist and contributor Joe Rubin also offered images, and fact checking that saved us from several errors; for any that remain, we take the blame. Friends and colleagues helped shape this book in various ways. These include Rick Perlstein (who first told us about each other's work), Mireille Miller-Young, Amy Tyson, Claire Bond Potter, Michael Bowen, Jeffrey Escoffier, and Stephen Patrick Johnson. We thank our anonymous reviewers, and Lynn Comella, for useful and constructive feedback.

Coediting is an intensely collaborative process, and we recognize our fortune in becoming a productive and good-humored interdisciplinary team; each of us thanks the other for editorial and intellectual support, and for a valued friendship. Carolyn thanks Dean Salma

ACKNOWLEDGMENTS

Ghanem of the College of Communication at DePaul University, her colleagues in the College of Communication and the American Studies program, and Susan Lewis of the Charles Deering McCormick Library of Special Collections at Northwestern University. She is grateful to the DePaul University Research Council for providing generous financial support for this project, including grants that underwrote the costs of reproducing numerous photographs. She also thanks John, David, Lauren, and Adam Tapper. She wishes that the historian James L. Baughman had lived to see this volume's publication, and misses his intellectual guidance and friendship. Whit thanks his many friends in the Rutgers–Newark History Department and American Studies and Women's and Gender Studies programs, in particular Christina Strasburger, Georgia Mellos, Rabeya Rahman, Tim Stewart-Winter, and the supportive administration at Rutgers–Newark. He thanks the Rutgers–Newark History Department and the New York Public Library's Frederick Lewis Allen Room for institutional support of the project. A Phil Zwickler Memorial Fellowship at Cornell University, a Martin Duberman Visiting Fellowship at the New York Public Library, and multiple Rutgers University research council grants underwrote much of the thought and work that went into this book. Michael Burand is long overdue for thanks, which are hereby delivered, with affection. Whit thanks Robert Pollard and the cuddly cat Creamsicle for inspiration, and he also has a lot of gratitude, admiration, and love for that Mary Rizzo character.

Finally, we want to thank the scholars upon whose work this collection builds, and particularly those makers and users of pornography who pushed against legal and cultural boundaries in the 1970s to create space for more inclusive sexual representation. For many, this genre has provided an important outlet to challenge sexism, racism, classism, ableism, heteronormativity, and gender binarism, as the essays in this volume collectively show. In tribute to these efforts, we hope that a progressive sex positivity becomes central to every vision of social justice, and may this book, in what it critiques and what it celebrates, provide some historical scholarship toward that end.

Porno Chic and the Sex Wars

Introduction
WHITNEY STRUB AND CAROLYN BRONSTEIN

WHEN THE SOCIALLY CONSERVATIVE Seymour Levov, protagonist of Philip Roth's 1997 novel *American Pastoral,* sits for Thanksgiving dinner with his family and friends in 1973, conversation at the table quickly turns to *Deep Throat*. Roth, a novelist with a sharp eye for historical detail, was seeking to recreate the daily conversational texture of the era, but more than that, he shrewdly read the subtexts of such conversations. Levov's daughter, Merry, had set off a bomb in a post office several years earlier to protest American involvement in Vietnam. The explosion left one person dead, and Merry went underground to avoid police capture. Levov recoils from the conversation in disgust, but even through his emotions he recognizes that "*Deep Throat* had never been the real subject anyway." Rather, the film and the emotions it inspired stand in for what Levov sees as the ravages of the late 1960s in both his home city of Newark and the nation at large, the "wantonness and betrayal and deception," as well as the "mockery of human integrity, every ethical obligation destroyed."[1]

For Levov and millions of Americans in the early 1970s, the proliferation of newly visible hardcore pornography unleashed precisely this affective response, one intimately bound with the ghosts of the youth counterculture, the black civil rights movement, the urban upheaval of the late sixties, the confusions of the Vietnam War, and the other explosive conflicts of the era. "All of this moral anarchy: all of it felt linked," the historian Rick Perlstein writes.[2] Few things could seem more anarchistic than public approval of naked, larger-than-life bodies engaging in graphic fornication on movie screens in public space; the public and private spheres themselves had been dramatically reconfigured.[3] Adding to the emotional impact, sexually graphic films were no longer restricted to rundown theaters in shady urban locations or suburban theaters on the wrong side of the tracks. By the early 1970s, even conventional theaters in small cities were screening exploitation films by directors such as Russ Meyer and Radley Metzger, making the reality of a sex-infused culture inescapable for most.

Yet for millions of other Americans—and perhaps often the *same* Americans—the emergence of hardcore porn signified a form of progress, a tangible repudiation of a repressed and repressive past. Openly attending a film like *Deep Throat,* talking about it over Thanksgiving dinner, watching its star Linda Lovelace chat up Johnny Carson on late-night television, and reading serious reviews of X-rated films in the nation's most prestigious newspapers were all ways of embracing the sexual revolution and participating in the new, freer sexual culture. The hippies and undergrads, with their long hair and free love, and their battles against paternalistic single-sex housing regulations on the nation's campuses, could have proclaimed themselves the frontline soldiers of the sexual revolution.[4] The hip, young urban professionals who were courted by Hugh Hefner's *Playboy* and Helen Gurley Brown's *Cosmopolitan* also had claim to this title through their participation in a radically redefined sexual culture at the office and a vigorous nightlife that might have included iconic 1970s key parties and swinging.[5] But increasingly, there were ways for middle-class, married, suburban—even conservative Christian—men and women to participate. Liberation was everywhere, visible at newsstands plastered with images from *Penthouse, Hustler,* and *Oui;* on movie theater marquees advertising sexually explicit films such as Bernardo Bertolucci's *Last Tango in Paris* (1972) starring American actor Marlon Brando; and in the decade's most popular television sitcoms, such as *Three's Company, Charlie's Angels,* and *The Love Boat.*[6]

This tension, and this iconography—of free love 1960s philosophy transmogrified into the blaring, in-your-face, commercialized phenomenon (that helped to harden many women's attitudes toward pornography)—tends to dominate the historical memory of the 1970s. Despite important recent historical work showing, for instance, how the loss of faith in political institutions and professional authorities fortified a national sentiment that "the family" served as a crucial site of stability for the project of American empire, and how economic downturn revolutionized women's participation in the labor force, the era remains mired in a broader metanarrative of the vacuous, narcissistic "Me Decade"—the lasting label that author Tom Wolfe, never the most generous of writers, gave it in 1976.[7] Of course, as Andreas Killen observes, this label also reflected Wolfe's perspective as a straight white man, for whom the rise of political rights movements centered on questions of race, and sexual and gender equality seemed self-indulgent and trivial. Indeed, this was the decade of which it was famously said that "nothing happened."[8] Mention the 1970s and you may be subjected to a string of frivolous cultural detritus, reducing the politically and culturally significant decade between the Great Society and the Reagan Revolution to the intersection of disco, bell-bottoms, pet rocks, and encounter groups. Pornography fits neatly into that list, often dismissed as an artless and crass expression of human sexuality as opposed to a significant public record of political and cultural struggle.

Yet much is lost in this characterization, where the rough, gritty edges of a film such as *Saturday Night Fever* (1977) are replaced by a reductive campiness that smooths over the film's raw gender and ethnic nerves. A film about social class, economic recession, sexual violence, and racial tensions flaring between second- and third-generation Italian Americans and a vocal new generation of Latino immigrants and Puerto Ricans becomes remembered as a story of white polyester suits, silk shirts unbuttoned down-to-there, and the performance of a crowd-pleasing Hustle. When it comes to pornography, likewise, the iconic shadows of *Deep Throat* often cover the complex roles porn played in seventies culture, where a particular iteration of publicly screened narrative smut followed the earlier underground market of stag films and loops and preceded the privatized video (and later, internet) market of the 1980s and beyond. Film historian Eric Schaefer has noted that the technological development of 16-millimeter film facilitated the rise of the hardcore feature, and other structural conditions likewise assisted in its emergence: legal change, evolving social mores, and downtown urban decay, but also feminism, gay community formation and pride, and racial fetish and resistance, as well as such emerging counterpublics as transsexual and later transgender individuals, with their creative energies around producing and sharing expressive media, as Nicholas Matte illustrates in this collection.[9]

Though historians have shown an increasing interest in the 1970s, and film and media scholars have devoted considerable attention to porn since the publication of Linda Williams's landmark *Hard Core* in

1989, a disconnect remains that has obstructed a richer understanding of the place of porn in the seventies.[10] Histories of the decade have often taken a bifurcated approach to "culture" (e.g., disco, popular music, television) and "politics" (e.g., Watergate, the presidential election of Jimmy Carter, the oil embargo). Historians do relatively little close examination of pornography and its impact on American social life, despite its constant, pervasive presence in the cultural and even material urban landscape. One reason for this has to do with the ephemeral quality of the historical evidence; libraries and archives preserved very little period pornography compared to mainstream cultural artifacts, such as blockbuster films *Rocky* (1976) and *Taxi Driver* (1976), Stephen King's horror classic *Carrie* (1974), or Andy Warhol's iconic pop art. The white polyester suit that John Travolta wore as Tony Manero in *Saturday Night Fever* is valued at more than $100,000 and currently resides in the Smithsonian.[11] The touring museum exhibit *David Bowie Is* presents a retrospective of the artist's life and performances, including such period stage costumes as the Ziggy Stardust bodysuits (1972) designed by Freddie Burretti; Kansai Yamamoto's asymmetric knitted jumpsuits for the Aladdin Sane tour (1973); and black-and-white photos of Bowie shot for the cover of the *Heroes* album (1977). By contrast, film preservationist Joe Rubin points out in this collection and elsewhere that the classic sex films of the 1960s and the 1970s are disappearing daily due to the chemical breakdown of celluloid, and the absence of financial and institutional resources dedicated to their preservation.[12]

Another reason for the lack of historical scholarship on pornography involves professional respectability, namely, the historian's need to produce work that is suitable for publication in academic journals and that intersects with both established and emerging work in the discipline. Today, porn studies has taken life as an entire field of inquiry, which is a promising development, but its works tend to privilege the contemporary industry and questions around sexual desire, identity, and agency. It is rare for scholars in this area to engage in the sort of rigorous historicization that characterized, for instance, studies of Shakespeare in the wake of New Historicism.[13] The affective texture of porn as encountered in daily life, and as affected by the economic, cultural, and political environment so richly (if problematically) conveyed by Philip Roth, remains largely absent from porn studies. So too does a more fine-grained sense of what porn looked like beyond the infamous titles that form its canon—the inescapable *Deep Throat*,

Behind the Green Door (1972), *The Devil in Miss Jones* (1973), and *The Opening of Misty Beethoven* (1976), in effect—a quartet that emphatically does not represent the genre but rather its glossier, up-market variant. The period work of directors such as Herschell Gordon Lewis (*Black Love*, 1971) and Matt Cimber (*Black Is Beautiful / Africanus Sexualis*, 1970), both of which offer a significant window into the representation of women and men of color in pornography, rarely appears in scholarly analyses. Indeed, only with the publication of Mireille Miller-Young's *A Taste for Brown Sugar* and Jennifer C. Nash's *The Black Body in Ecstasy* (both 2014) have scholars afforded us a substantive examination of the history of black women and pornographic representation.

The scholarly gap here in effect cedes historical understanding to other narratives, from the facile Golden Age nostalgia of popular films such as *Boogie Nights* (1997) to the nightmarish dystopia proffered by the feminist antipornography movement—each of which had some semblance of truth, mixed with other reductive elements. The essays here offer a corrective to such accounts, situating a broader reckoning with pornography, including both print and film manifestations, within the complex currents of the 1970s, a decade of both continuity and rupture when it came to politics and culture. *Porno Chic and the Sex Wars* seeks to complicate and enrich the dominant existing narratives, which bookend the decade with the sociologically driven President's Commission on Obscenity and Pornography's hearty endorsement of (heterosexual) pornography as a social good in 1970, and the ascension of the most powerful organization of the feminist antipornography movement, Women Against Pornography, in New York City in 1980–81. The essays in this collection look beyond these iconic moments to ask both what constituted pornography, expanding our perspective beyond the typical mass-market films and magazines to include lesser-known forms, and what pornography *meant* to its producers and consumers in a variety of contexts and forms. Some of the chapters celebrate victories, such as the emergence of a vibrant gay porn genre that constructed same-sex desire as normative and pleasurable, or the ways that pornography performers such as the black actress Desiree West and the gay porn star Peter Berlin sought pleasure, subjectivity, and agency in their own pornographic representations. In other cases, we highlight what mainstream pornography often failed to achieve—namely, robust, diverse, sexual discourses that spoke in a sustained way to audiences other than the industry's bread-and-butter-customers, heterosexual white men.

In hopes of both building on familiar narratives and staking out new ground, we have asked our authors to explore fresh interpretive spaces and lesser-known dimensions of porn in this period. These essays offer novel insights and unexpected twists, even to those well versed in the larger frameworks of pornography in the 1970s. Instead of analyzing *Hugh* Hefner's role in the industry, Elizabeth Fraterrigo asks: How did feminist daughter *Christie* influence the trajectory of *Playboy* and the company's business model? Instead of describing how religious conservative Christians mounted an attack on what journalist Pamela Paul has called a "pornified" American society, Gillian Frank shows how evangelicals created their own pornography to support the traditional heterosexual family and provide a suitable way for conservative Christians to participate in the new sexual culture.[14] Instead of focusing on the controversial images produced by child pornographers in the 1970s, Greg Youmans investigates how the panic around child porn seeped into the work of gay filmmakers and quashed their ability to represent dimensions of youth sexuality and create authentic coming-of-age narratives. These types of new spaces and new questions are the hallmarks of these essays; each one seeks to explore a less familiar aspect of the 1970s pornographic terrain.

As editors of this collection, we have written about pornography from many angles already, with a great deal of emphasis on obscenity law, new technologies, feminist activism, citizen discomfort with pornography, marginalized audiences, and the political mobilization of the so-called New Right.[15] Our goal here is not to retrace these steps but rather to offer new work that complicates some of these topics while also opening up previously unexplored areas of study. Thus, the methods in these pieces range widely from close textual analysis of pornographic materials to biographical studies, industrial perspectives, political investigations regarding free speech and the nature of feminism, and sexual memory. We hope historians will take interest in the textual studies, and film and media scholars in the more historical pieces, leading both groups to a more holistic understanding. Instead of offering a stable definition of "pornography"—always a term enmeshed in sexual politics, law, and other variables—we believe the essays here show that only through both macroscopic attention to social and political change *and* a closer scrutiny of the texts deemed pornographic themselves can we really understand the cultural meanings of *pornographies* during this pivotal decade between an ostensible sexual revolution and the consolidation of a self-declared Moral Majority.

For students and readers new to this historical terrain, let us briefly lay out some context for understanding American culture and politics in this period. Debates over free speech and the First Amendment provided one crucial backdrop to the emerging visibility of pornography in the 1970s. The first significant federal law against obscenity in the United States had been the 1873 Comstock Act, passed at the behest of New York City smut fighter Anthony Comstock. For the next several decades, he single-handedly drove crackdowns across the nation, empowered by his permanent appointment as postal inspector. Comstock's targets ranged from sexy "French postcards" to erotic novels but also included marital sex manuals and information about contraception and abortion sent through the mail.

This outright attempt to keep sex linked to procreation faltered in the face of early twentieth-century social change. The rise of urban amusement cultures such as Coney Island, an increasingly sexualized mass media driven by the new motion picture industry, and changing gender roles as young single women sought employment and enjoyment in a rapidly urbanizing nation led to a modernization of sexuality. By the time of his death in 1915, Comstock was often seen as a Victorian relic. Yet the obscenity laws he had spent his life enforcing outlived him, and the U.S. Supreme Court avoided clarifying the relationship between obscenity and the First Amendment until the 1957 *Roth v. U.S.* case. In this landmark ruling, Justice William Brennan reached two fundamental conclusions: that obscenity was *not* protected by the First Amendment (meaning it could be criminalized), but that "sex and obscenity are not synonymous." Instead, obscenity was *only* that material that "deals with sex in a manner appealing to prurient interest"—a somewhat vague standard, but one that folded a great deal of increasingly graphic material into the realm of constitutionally protected free speech.[16]

Roth thus played a central role in fueling the so-called sexual revolution of the 1960s. While the precise legal contours of obscenity were constantly revised over the course of the decade, the clear and undeniable trajectory was toward greater legal protection for sexual explicitness, and fewer grounds on which material could be declared obscene. We can chart the limits of the law as they expand: novels such as D. H. Lawrence's *Lady Chatterley's Lover* and Henry Miller's *Tropic of Cancer* at the start of the sixties; more adult imported films such as Louis Malle's *The Lovers* (1958) and *I Am Curious (Yellow)* (dir. Vilgot Sjöman, 1967); then exploitation and grindhouse films showing topless women lining Times Square, full-frontal nudity, and, by decade's end, such fleeting innovations as "split beaver" viewing booths in adult shops. Finally, right around 1970, hardcore pornography, featuring graphic, unsimulated sex in small storefront theaters, was visible across urban (and sometimes rural) America.

These changes coincided with transformative shifts in the United States' politics, economic structure, gender politics, and more. Regardless of how one precisely defines "the seventies," it was a period of seeming decline, marked by the failure of U.S. imperialism in Vietnam, the beginnings of economic deregulation, deindustrialization, and the shift from a unionized industrial labor market to a service-sector economy of increasing worker vulnerability. Fears of a corporate oligopoly dominating the national media were evident in the paranoia of such hit films as *Network* and *All the President's Men* (1976). While the strident antiporn moralism of Richard Nixon moved to the national political back burner in the wake of Watergate and the near-disintegration of the Republican Party, new think tanks, megachurches, and computerized direct-mail technologies set the stage for a conservative moral resurgence, one already at play in the STOP-ERA movement associated with conservative activist Phyllis Schlafly, and singer Anita Bryant's path-setting antigay activism in the Save Our Children campaign of 1977. As federal policy redistributed tax money from the northeastern Rust Belt to the growing southwestern Sunbelt, companies such as Wal-Mart pushed for faith in both God and the free market, while rising political star Ronald Reagan offered simple, soothing narratives about family values and Horatio Alger–style individualism that replaced the newly complicated discussions of American foreign policy with reassuring parables that resonated with many voters. This "pivotal decade," as historian Judith Stein calls it, commenced the shift from factories to the financial sector that gave birth to neoliberalism and, ultimately, the catastrophic failure of capitalism in 2008.[17]

Sexuality, too, remained fraught across the seventies, with a series of unresolved tensions sustained in uneasy coexistence. Gay and lesbian rights and visibility expanded enormously, even as a protracted antigay backlash rose up in south Florida and spread rapidly. Feminism and reproductive rights also grew, alongside a sweeping antifeminism that prevented the Equal Rights Amendment from entering the U.S. Constitution. And while U.S. immigration policy formally barred homosexuals, in practice the state did not deport a single gay Marielito during the Cuban boatlift that brought the decade to an end in 1980.[18]

Pornography linked to these shifts in myriad ways, and it is into this new cultural landscape that the essays in this collection delve. Pornographic films loom large over the historical memory of the 1970s, and the early essays here offer multiple perspectives on hardcore history. Whitney Strub's essay situates smut in the so-called urban crisis of the 1970s, which opened doors to both pleasures and dangers, distributed unequally across lines of gender, sexuality, and race. For the predominantly male directors of straight porn, the decline in urban surveillance and regulation wrought by disinvestment and white flight allowed adventurous guerilla location shooting that made evocative use of urban space. At the same time, the story of the city told by straight porn paralleled that of the racialized media depiction of imperiled whites in a dangerous "urban jungle." Instead of offering critique, straight porn films often reveled in the threats to women that saturated this imagined lawlessness. In contrast, gay male porn of the decade took a different tack; for gay men, urban decay meant increased opportunity for visibility, and gay porn films envisioned the city—its subways, parks, and alleys—as an erotic grid of desire, linked to the ethos of the nascent gay liberation ideology. Thus hetero porn reflected the influence of the urban-crisis framework, while gay porn exposed its heteronormative underpinnings.

The 1970s were a transitional time for pornography, poised between the underground black market of earlier decades and the streamlined corporate industry that solidified in the 1980s as video technology supported massive expansion. *Deep Throat* remains the iconic embodiment of the porno chic moment, the film that transformed hardcore porn from the shameful back-alley pursuit of desperate, solitary, trench coat–wearing men (as the mythology of the times had it) to something hailed by college undergrads, married suburbanites, and celebrities alike as a cultural rite of passage into the urbane sophistication of the sexual revolution. *Deep Throat,* male students at Michigan State University gushed in response to female student protest, was "a valuable contribution to art."[19] Yet, as corny and aesthetically impoverished as that film was, Laura Helen Marks reminds us in her essay of the varied, frequently talented, and ambitious work occurring within the financial and generic constraints of the hardcore feature, which was not yet a standardized cultural form. *Deep Throat* was the blockbuster adult film of the decade, without question, but dozens of porn auteurs were at work throughout the 1970s, creating bodies of work that sought to join personal visions of sexual liberation with aesthetic innovation.

Focusing on the body of work produced by adult film actor and director Shaun Costello, Marks reveals films that ranged from grim violence to impish comedy, complicating any effort to reduce pornography to a homogenous genre. She concentrates her analysis on Costello's 1975 film *The Passions of Carol*, a surprising adaptation of Charles Dickens's *A Christmas Carol* for a sexually liberated era. In a close parody of the literary classic, Costello critiqued the commodification of sex for profit, taking on porn barons such as Bob Guccione and Hugh Hefner, whose slick glossies and market orientations seemed to Costello to rob the sexual revolution of its emancipatory potential. As San Francisco pornographer and theater owner Artie Mitchell (of the infamous Mitchell Brothers) stated in a 1974 interview, "Our early motivation was almost a hundred per cent, you know, in it for the money."[20] In *The Passions of Carol*, Costello romanticizes a more innocent vision of free love outside of the marketplace as a liberating touchstone of human experience, a vision shared by director Wakefield Poole, whose *Boys in the Sand* (1971) depicted a community of gay men on Fire Island exulting in their sexuality, engaging in beautifully shot hardcore and interracial sex acts. Continuing the theme of innocence, and to represent "Christmas past," Costello depicted adult actors dressed as children playing with dolls and toys—all of whom were involved in explicit sexual activity. By the end of the decade, as Greg Youmans shows in his essay on the child pornography panic, such images were unthinkable, fraught with intense legal danger for filmmakers and viewers alike, and immediately suspect as part of a gay conspiracy to recruit children into a life of perversion.

Just as Marks demonstrates the diversity of approaches to adult filmmaking that were present in the 1970s, Jennifer Christine Nash challenges the dominant narrative that mainstream pornography featured only white performers. Desiree West was the first black porn star, debuting in 1973 and working steadily throughout the decade opposite such well-known male stars as John Holmes. Nash acknowledges that early films were white-dominated, and rife with problematic racial representations, yet through West's career and life, Nash identifies pockets of resistance and opposition to racial stereotypes. Building on personal conversations with West that merge film history and the labor history of the adult film industry, Nash finds more than just the predictable, stereotyped racial tropes. Instead, she reveals unexpected moments in which the Other speaks back to the objectifying lens. Ultimately, Nash offers an important argument about the centrality of racialized desire to Golden Age pornography, noting that adult filmmakers constructed, produced, and circulated a new kind of desire through their portrayals of West's body, setting the stage for how black women would be represented—and imagined—on the pornographic screen in the years to come. In so doing, Nash's work is in conversation with feminist porn studies scholars such as Mireille Miller-Young, who demonstrates in *A Taste for Brown Sugar* (2014) that black women in pornography use their creative work to intervene in, critique, and sometimes expand the relatively narrow landscape of representational possibility for black female sexuality in contemporary culture.[21]

In this transitional era, white bodies, too, bore unstable meanings, as Nancy Semin Lingo shows in her nuanced biography of *Deep Throat* star Linda Lovelace. Revered as the most famous sex symbol of the decade and a powerful beacon of what sexual liberation could mean for women, Lovelace was in the public eye from 1972 on. However, Lingo explains that maximum visibility meant being seen but not necessarily heard, as Lovelace's public voice was constructed to suit others' needs, and was rarely true or authentic to the star herself. Although black women could use porn as a site to occasionally disrupt or destabilize cultural meaning, as "a practice of freedom for a moment, even if it is for sale," as Miller-Young writes, meaning could also be inscribed onto the very bodies of the performers—regardless of their own experiences.[22] Lovelace provides a particularly spectacularized example of this. As Lingo shows, Lovelace was relatively uneducated, raised in modest economic circumstances, and desperate to escape her repressive Catholic schoolgirl upbringing for a chance to live life on a bigger canvas. Abused by her first husband, Chuck Traynor, and male handlers who sought both to have sex with her and earn money off her body, Lovelace suffered recurrent injustices as her fame grew in the wake of *Deep Throat*. Once she became a star, Lovelace was ghostwritten for public consumption over and over again, first presented as an insatiable sex goddess and later co-opted by antipornography feminists, who held her up as a timeless victim of male seduction and proof positive of the physical and psychological harms of pornography.

If hardcore films captured the public's attention and came to stand in for the expansion of the pornography industry as a whole, it is equally true that print culture still flourished in the 1970s and provided millions of readers with messages of sexual liberation and the right to personal pleasure. One of the most important aspects of sexual revolution ideology was its benefits for all—young and old, single and married, gay and straight. Yet even a cursory glance at the dominant products of the 1970s reveals a distinct preference for the heterosexual male point of view, evident in magazines such as *Hustler* and *Penthouse* and even the sexually infused rock-and-roll music of the decade, performed by legendary bands such as the Rolling Stones and Led Zeppelin. In her essay, Carolyn Bronstein analyzes an important alternative experiment: pornography directed toward women, namely, publisher Bob Guccione's erotic magazine for the "new woman" of the 1970s: *Viva*. Taking on *Cosmopolitan* and *Playgirl*, both of which also vied for the attention of the independent, sexually avid woman, Guccione hired talented female editors, including a young, pre-*Vogue* Anna Wintour and women's magazine veteran Patricia Bosworth. Together they sought to create a dynamic publication featuring tantalizing male nude pictorials and high-end, feminist literary content. A true believer in the healthy, liberating power of sex, who claimed at age sixty-nine to still be capable of intercourse five times a day, Guccione wanted to bring a pleasurable, sex-positive experience to adult women readers, as he had for male readers of *Penthouse*.[23] Of course, he also relished the idea of profiting off of the female consumer that advertisers hotly desired.

Yet, for all the promise of a skin magazine for women in this brief moment of social acceptance for pornography, *Viva* failed to hit its mark. Guccione's dogmatic, chauvinistic insistence that he knew what women wanted sexually better than women knew themselves led to numerous editorial missteps. His preference for sexual scenarios that privileged the male gaze and traditional heterosexual and white couplings made *Viva* feel unwelcoming to women of color and to lesbians, as well as limiting to straight white women who wanted to expand their sexual horizons and experience something nonnormative, or what we would today call queer. In addition to reproducing dominant iconography, the magazine ran into trouble with advertisers, who balked at associating with pornography, especially as the political climate turned increasingly conservative over the course of the decade. Struggling to stay afloat, the magazine published far fewer sexual images and cut out male nudes entirely after April 1976, leaving readers complaining that *Viva*'s editors had no idea what erotica for feminist women might look like. Beginning in the 1970s, and continuing through to the present day, feminists question how (and whether it is possible) to create authentic and sexually empowering pornography for diverse groups of women in a culture saturated with heterosexist images of desire. But, in his effort to offer a new resource, Guccione made important contributions toward a more open sexual environment in which women could explore their sexuality. *Viva* is part of the historical continuum of feminist pornography that seeks to prioritize and celebrate "female desire, pleasure, and orgasm" and dispel the messages present in society that for women, "sex is shameful, naughty, dirty, scary, dangerous, or it's the domain of men," as the feminist pornographer Tristan Taormino has written.[24]

The case of *Viva* and the effort to create mainstream pornography for women in many ways runs parallel to the trajectory of transsexual publications, as Nicholas Matte shows in his essay on the creative production of erotic magazines aimed at the transvestite and transsexual consumer. Tracing the history of such little-known magazines as *Female Impersonators* and *FI News*, Matte brings print media into focus as a significant space where sexual identities were negotiated under the duress of ideological and market forces. Like most of society, which privileged the combination of biological sex and socially assigned gender identity that would later be termed cisgender, pornography tended to reify the gender binary. As Matte observes, pornography by and for transvestites and transsexuals remained deeply closeted for much of the 1970s, entangled in the web of normatively ascribed values that forced community members to seek identification and sexual pleasure in magazines devoted to the art of celebrity female impersonation. Better known today as drag queens, female impersonators were men who dressed up in women's clothes, wigs, and makeup to entertain audiences, often taking on the persona of such celebrities as Barbra Streisand, Judy Garland, and Peggy Lee. For fans for whom cross-dressing was part of a private sexual activity or erotic identity, magazines such as *Female Impersonators* served as a meager substitute for the heterosexual man's *Penthouse* and *Hustler*. Over the course of the decade, Matte shows that the magazines—already compromised in their ability to present cross-dressing as a specifically sexual act —succumbed to the same forces of commercialization that drove Guccione's editorial direction away from sexual eroticism and toward advertiser-friendly recipes and fashion features. These were the same commercial pressures that troubled independent directors such as Shaun Costello. The magazines abandoned their political roots in trans liberation and concentrated on advertising and ever-expanding

"personal" classified ads to leverage the economic power of trans consumers—a reminder that when the law failed to discipline pornography, the market often did.

Following Matte's argument that pornography found its way into
every community, and proved constructive (even generative) for its
users, historian Gillian Frank presents compelling evidence of pornography's reach to the unlikeliest of audiences: right-wing women and
men. In his essay on evangelical Christian women's marriage guides,
including Marabel Morgan's best-selling *Total Woman* (1973) and *Total
Joy* (1974), Frank argues that this highly eroticized marital advice literature was a new form of pornography popularized by religious conservatives who sought to find ways to participate in the freer sexual
culture without sin or shame. Evangelical authors fully embraced the
genre and created their own body of erotic literature that supported
patriarchal marriage and likely provided psychological and physical
benefits to husbands and wives. They did so as a response to threats
to the traditional family posed by tantalizing adult films and a sexualized mainstream culture, and as a way to shore up the male ego once
the devastating economic downturn known as stagflation compromised the male breadwinner model. Frank argues that these authors
used Christian-variety eroticism to bolster the institution of marriage
and assure men of their continued virility in the bedroom, if not the
office. Instead of seeing these conservatives only as opponents of the
sexual revolution and pornography, waging a war on filth, as they are
typically painted in histories of the 1970s, Frank argues that we ought
to reassess them as innovative creators of their own sexually charged,
quasipornographic subculture.

Frank plumbs the tension inherent in religious conservatives'
wholesale adoption of marriage manuals that advised wives to
greet their husbands at the door dressed in erotic lingerie and initiate fantasy-based romps. Historian Elizabeth Fraterrigo considers
a similarly loaded question: Could a self-proclaimed feminist run a
magazine and a pornography empire built on the celebration of heterosexual male privilege? Taking daughter Christie Hefner as her
subject, a complex subject who defies easy categorization, Fraterrigo
examines the ways that Christie navigated the political waters of a
growing antipornography feminism during the 1970s and early 1980s
in her role as a high-level Playboy executive and ultimately as president of Playboy Enterprises. Similar to Alex Warner's treatment of
lesbian sadomasochists who vehemently opposed the arguments

of antiporn feminists, Fraterrigo presents Christie as someone who refuted dominant feminist views about the harms of pornography, and argued instead that posing in *Playboy* or working as a cocktail waitress in a Playboy Club could deliver significant career benefits for women. Whether her opinions were rooted in a sincere belief regarding *Playboy*'s beneficial role in the sexual revolution or a more simple desire to protect her father's legacy, Christie defended *Playboy* on civil libertarian and feminist grounds. Seeking to extend the magazine's stated commitment to civil liberties, Christie helped set the agenda for the magazine's charitable arm, the Playboy Foundation, and tried to give money to various women's rights organizations, such as the National Organization for Women (NOW). As Fraterrigo shows, these actions often landed Christie at the center of feminist controversy, navigating difficult terrain as both a feminist (a white, heterosexual, well-educated, and wealthy feminist, which in and of itself made her suspect in some quarters) and an executive of the nation's most famous adult magazine for men.

Leigh Ann Wheeler and Alex Warner also turn to the emergence of antiporn feminism and establish its roots in the cultural and political contexts of the 1970s. Wheeler observes that as sexual speech increased, most of it originating from the male point of view, many women became suspicious of pornography's aims and sought refuge from the constant bombardment of adult material on the streets that made them feel embarrassed and degraded. From the perspective of women who felt themselves under hostile attack from unrestrained, objectifying sexual speech that reduced them to their body parts, the American Civil Liberties Union (ACLU) had an obligation to fight for women's right to be free of sex. However, the ACLU moved in a different direction, privileging privacy, consumer rights, and freedom of expression, all of which worked in pornographers' favor. Wheeler reveals the anger and disappointment of feminist leaders such as Andrea Dworkin and Susan Brownmiller, who believed that the organization's civil liberties paradigm wrongly privileged access *to* over protection *from* sexual expression, whether that expression came in the form of public displays of porn films or magazines, sexual harassment, or unwelcome sexual material in the workplace.

Warner, in turn, shows that the decade's battles over pornography did not always pit women against men. She offers a lesser-known narrative of deep conflict that emerged between groups of women who had very different perspectives on the question of pornography.

Returning to the sexual margins visited by Youmans and Matte, Warner analyzes the pitched battles between 1970s feminists who advocated on behalf of lesbian sadomasochism and sexual diversity, and antipornography feminists who denounced SM as a form of self-imposed patriarchal violence against women. Warner describes the founding of the nation's first lesbian SM advocacy group, Samois, and its members' attempts to educate others about the sexual pleasures and personal empowerment made possible through SM practice. The labeling of such activity as "feminist" enraged some feminists of color and nascent antipornography groups, who argued that Samois was creating a form of pornography (illustrated SM education guides) and promoting slave/master role play that reproduced oppressive, sexist, and racist structures of domination. Warner uncovers the intertwined histories of pornography and sadomasochism, showing how central the issue of lesbian SM was to the formation of an organized feminist antipornography movement at the end of the 1970s and revealing one of the many ways that pornography was actively contested during the decade.

As these battles over porn intensified, their impact reverberated widely through American culture and politics. The issue of child pornography became a significant source of social alarm in the late 1970s as right-wing groups began claiming that pornographers and pedophiles were leading American youth into a lifestyle of gay debauchery, while antiporn feminists identified women and children as vulnerable populations whose bodies were corrupted and exploited in pornography. This era presents great obstacles to historians, who cannot write with much authority about what did or did not exist in the child porn genre because the material has been criminalized, and most of it subsequently destroyed. Using this absence as a point of departure, Greg Youmans asks how the child-porn panic affected the sexualized culture of the 1970s, and in particular, how it limited activist gay filmmakers' ability to depict youth sexuality. From the start, anti–child pornography rhetoric carried sharp homophobic overtones, and conservative activist and singer Anita Bryant's 1977 Save Our Children campaign fused child-protection and antigay sentiment in ways that shaped American political discourse for decades to come. One result was a deeply internalized, preemptive gesture on the part of gay filmmakers to protect themselves from allegations of child pornography by abandoning the representation of young people and their natural sexual desires. Youmans shows that we must read child-porn anxieties as structuring forces even in nonpornographic gay films of the 1970s, from liberal LGBT documentaries such as *Word Is Out* (1977) even to radical, transgressive works such as the German filmmaker Rosa von Praunheim's *Army of Lovers, or Revolt of the Perverts* (1979).

With these cultural and political changes afoot, the pornography industry itself was changing radically as the invention of home video technology reshaped user access to pornography. The introduction of the home-viewing VHS and Betamax videotape player systems in the late 1970s made it possible to consume pornography in the privacy of one's own home, rather than in a public theater, removing one of the greatest barriers for would-be users. Using the trade and consumer publication *Adult Video News* (*AVN*) as a case study, film historian Peter Alilunas shows how its editors sought to protect the industry at a moment of radical change by helping producers, retailers, and consumers create the new landscape of professional video rental stores, with knowledgeable clerks serving confident rental consumers. The change here was technological but also conceptual as pornography moved from gritty, and often risky, urban space to the living room, and the flood of adult movies shot on video rather than celluloid threatened to undermine quality standards associated with the Golden Age of pornography. As Alilunas shows, such transitions require careful cultural mediation, and *AVN* helped usher pornography out of its 1970s realities and into the new corporate world of the 1980s, complete with astonishing economic power and a star system modeled on mainstream Hollywood.

Looking back is also a theme for film scholar Lucas Hilderbrand, who returns to the scene of gay liberation to make an argument about both history and memory. Hardcore porn *was* the gay visual culture of the liberation era, Hilderbrand contends—yet until very recently, little effort was put into preserving gay porn, despite its immense political and cultural importance. Using *Nights in Black Leather,* a striking documentary-style 1973 view of gay urban life as a case study, he charts a cultural arc, from politicized sexual expression to selective memory project. The film stars actor/auteur Peter Berlin as a young, gay German who visits San Francisco and narrates for his friends back home a travelogue complete with flashbacks revealing the city's vibrant sexual culture and his own encounters. In one scene, Berlin describes an SM scene he has enjoyed with a man who prefers to dress in Nazi garb (the homoerotic qualities of men's leather culture often led participants to don military and police uniforms). Yet, in keeping with Alex Warner's discussion of the pro-SM lesbian community, Berlin makes it clear that leather is a sexual aesthetic, and role-playing dominance and submission a form of sexual performance but not a declaration of a right to hold power over others. *Nights in Black Leather* thus celebrates the diversity of gay life in San Francisco and the freedom that Berlin experiences there as he engages in various erotic explorations. Through the lens of this film, Hilderbrand asks what "the 1970s" come to mean in the shadow of Reagan, AIDS, and the gravitational pull of what queer scholars call homonormativity.

Finally, Joe Rubin contributes an afterword that reflects on the question of the preservation of 1970s pornographic films, noting that many of the era's most important works are literally disappearing with each passing day. Indeed, some images in this volume could not be reproduced at their original quality level because of severe limitations in the currently circulating versions. Rubin is a founder of Vinegar Syndrome, an exploitation film–focused preservation company, widely known to online cult-movie and porn communities as the Criterion of smut for its lovingly restored DVDs and Blu-rays, often featuring lavish historical extras in the form of previews, commentary tracks, and other features. Rubin weighs in on the challenges of porn preservation, and reminds us of what the field of porn studies misses when its scholars concentrate their critical attention on only the best-known films and filmmakers of the period, yet lack a broader knowledge of and appreciation for the lost films that constitute a *majority* of pornographic history. Indeed, Vinegar Syndrome, building on work previously undertaken beginning in the 1990s with Something Weird Video and Alpha Blue Archives, has contributed immensely to our knowledge of adult film history, and continues to unearth new chapters of this story even as this book goes to press; its twelve-film Storefront Theatre Collection, vol. 1, released in early 2016, brings such very early 16-millimeter Los Angeles hardcore films as *Homer, the Late Comer* (c. 1970) and *Erotic Point of View* (c. 1971) into circulation for the first time in decades, allowing us to observe more closely the generic conventions of hardcore taking shape.

Rubin is at the forefront of a group of scholars and historians who are arguably building, right now, the Golden Age of porn studies. Because of increasing (if still limited) archiving of pornography, online fan communities, a wealth of publications, and new exhibition, distribution, and oral history projects, the knowledge base for porn studies has grown immeasurably since Linda Williams published

Hard Core in 1989. Vinegar Syndrome and Distribpix have recovered entire previously lost bodies of work, while the *In the Flesh* series that Casey Scott curated at New York City's Anthology Film Archives in 2013 helped spur a broad reassessment of 1970s porn films. April Hall and Ashley West's *Rialto Report*, a meticulously researched blog and podcast, has brought to life the voices of culture workers from the porn industry previously omitted from scholarly treatment by both antiporn feminists, who gravitate toward those such as Linda Lovelace who speak the language of oppression, and feminist and queer scholars, who tend to highlight the voices of politically engaged sex-industry workers from Annie Sprinkle to Buck Angel.

On the *Rialto Report*, we hear for the first time the experiences of such performers as Michael Gaunt, bisexually active in his private life but primarily heterosexual on screen, except for a failed foray into gay porn in which he could not perform; George McDonald, who ambled around late-1960s San Francisco and wound up the first male porn star, appearing opposite Marilyn Chambers in *Behind the Green Door*; and Billy Dee, whose multiracial identity eluded easy categorization and who continued performing even after finding God, bringing his Bible to the set of porn shoots.[25] This wealth of historical material has been matched by an outpouring of memoirs. While porn star autobiographies date back to the dawn of hardcore, the genre was revitalized by Georgina Spelvin's *The Devil Made Me Do It* in 2008, which was followed by engaging and thoughtful books by other performers of the 1970s, such as Serena and Howie Gordon.[26] Some of the most revealing work has come from those behind the camera, or involved in distribution; cinematographer and director Larry Revene's two memoirs, and Robert Rosen's *Beaver Street*, detailing his work on such magazines as *High Society* and *D-Cup*, flesh out less familiar territory.[27] As well, Jill C. Nelson's enormous *Golden Goddesses* tells the life stories of twenty-five women from the adult film industry between 1968 and 1980, in their own words.[28] Alongside the knowledge produced by such online communities as Vintage Erotica Forums, AV Maniacs, and various adult film Facebook groups, which often share advertisements, pressbooks, digitized copies of obscure magazines, and films, this work has generated a far richer, more detailed, and expansive—if scattered—archive than any previous generation of historians could have accessed. These nonacademic historians, such as Robin Bougie of the well-researched *Cinema Sewer* zine, have done more to preserve the history of 1970s pornography than any institutional archive to date.

Porn studies scholars are still struggling to navigate and utilize much of this material, though a recent outpouring of scholarly studies has further refined knowledge of the pornographic past, too.[29] We hope this book can build further bridges, and restore to our memory of the seventies stories that have been overlooked by scholars and fans alike. Collectively, these essays force us to think beyond the iconic moments of porno chic or the mainstream sexual revolution, to recover the more tumultuous, complicated, problematic, and occasionally radical texts that circulated across the 1970s, on screen, by mail, and in newsstands and adult stores. Ultimately, what we see in these essays is an unfolding, partially concealed dialectic between and among culture, sexuality, politics, law, technology, and commerce that shaped expressions of sexuality in the public sphere and affected the presence and proliferation of pornography through the 1970s. This contested pornographic decade ultimately gave birth to the politically conservative and morally outraged Reagan years, and the concurrent maturation of pornography into a streamlined corporate endeavor that has saturated the mainstream ever since. It gave us feminists trying to suppress porn, as well as feminists engaged in both defending and making it. These essays restore what was forgotten when all of these groups laid claim to historical narratives that served their interests and erased the rest.

NOTES

1. Philip Roth, *American Pastoral* (Boston: Houghton Mifflin, 1997), 380.
2. Rick Perlstein, *Nixonland: The Rise of a President and the Fracturing of America* (New York: Scribner, 2008), 113.
3. For an excellent history of these transformative changes, see John D'Emilio and Estelle Freedman, *Intimate Matters: A History of Sexuality in America*, 3rd ed. (Chicago: University of Chicago Press, 2012).
4. For a history of the battle to sexually liberate the nation's campuses, especially the University of Kansas, see Beth Bailey, *Sex in the Heartland* (Cambridge: Harvard University Press, 1999).
5. On Hefner's readers, see Elizabeth Fraterrigo, *Playboy and the Making of the Good Life in Modern America* (Oxford: Oxford University Press, 2009), and Steven Watts, *Mr. Playboy: Hugh Hefner and the American Dream* (New York: John Wiley, 2009); on Gurley Brown, see Jennifer Scanlon, *Bad Girls Go Everywhere: The Life of Helen*

Gurley Brown (Oxford: Oxford University Press, 2009).

6. On television and the sexual revolution, see Elana Levine, *Wallowing in Sex: The New Sexual Culture of 1970s American Television* (Durham, NC: Duke University Press, 2007).

7. Natasha Zaretsky, *No Direction Home: The American Family and the Fear of National Decline* (Chapel Hill: University of North Carolina Press, 2007); Tom Wolfe, " 'The Me Decade' and the Third Great Awakening," *New York*, August 23, 1976, available at http://nymag.com. Among historians, Bruce Schulman conceptualizes a "long seventies" lasting from 1968 to 1984, while Laura Kalman highlights the "short '70s" as the transitional period of 1975–79. Philip Jenkins, by way of contrast, equates the long seventies with a decade-long fallout from the sixties lasting from 1975 to 1986. Bruce Schulman, *The Seventies: The Great Shift in American Culture, Society, and Politics* (New York: Free Press, 2001); Laura Kalman, *Right Star Rising: A New Politics, 1974–1980* (New York: W. W. Norton, 2010); Philip Jenkins, *Decade of Nightmares: The End of the Sixties and the Making of Eighties America* (New York: Oxford University Press, 2006).

8. Andreas Killen, *1973 Nervous Breakdown: Watergate, Warhol, and the Birth of Post-Sixties America* (New York: Bloomsbury, 2006); Edward D. Berkowitz, *Something Happened: A Political and Cultural Overview of the Seventies* (New York: Columbia University Press, 2006), 5.

9. Eric Schaefer, "Gauging a Revolution: 16mm Film and the Rise of the Pornographic Feature," *Cinema Journal* 41, no. 3 (2002): 3–26.

10. Linda Williams, *Hard Core: Power, Pleasure and the "Frenzy of the Visible,"* expanded ed. (Berkeley: University of California Press, 1999).

11. Sam Kashner, "Fever Pitch: How Travolta and the Bee Gees Shook the Night," *Vanity Fair*, November 30, 2007.

12. Alison Nastasi, "Meet the Archivists Working to Preserve Classic Sex Films," *Flavorwire*, February 11, 2015, http://flavorwire.com.

13. New Historicism is a literary theory based on the idea that works of literature or other texts, such as films, should be studied and interpreted through the lens of the major ideas and cultural assumptions of the era in which the text was produced. Every analysis thus takes into account both the context of the history of the author—his or her life and times—and those of the critic who is making sense of the text.

14. Pamela Paul, *Pornified: How Pornography Is Damaging Our Lives, Our Relationships, Our Families* (New York: St. Martin's, 2006).

15. See Whitney Strub, *Perversion for Profit: The Politics of Pornography and the Rise of the New Right* (New York: Columbia University Press, 2011); Whitney Strub, *Obscenity Rules: Roth v. United States and the Long Struggle over Sexual Expression* (Lawrence: University Press of Kansas, 2013); and Carolyn Bronstein, *Battling Pornography: The American Feminist Anti-Pornography Movement, 1976–1986* (Cambridge: Cambridge University Press, 2011); Carolyn Bronstein, "The Political Uses of Lesbian Romance Fiction: Reading Patrick Califia's *Macho Sluts* as a Response to 1980s Anti-Pornography Feminism," *Journal of Popular Romance Studies* 4, no. 1 (February 2014): 1–20.

16. *Roth v. U.S.,* 354 U.S. 476 (1957).

17. Judith Stein, *Pivotal Decade: How the United States Traded Factories for Finance in the Seventies* (New Haven: Yale University Press, 2010); Bethany Moreton, *To Serve God and Wal-Mart: The Making of Christian Free Enterprise* (Cambridge: Harvard University Press, 2009); Rick Perlstein, *The Invisible Bridge: The Fall of Nixon and the*

Rise of Reagan (New York: Simon & Schuster, 2014).

18. Julio Capó, "Queering Mariel: Mediating Cold War Foreign Policy and U.S. Citizenship among Cuba's Homosexual Exile Community, 1978–1994," *Journal of American Ethnic History* 29, no. 4 (2010): 78–106.

19. Marianne Rzepka, " 'Throat' Not Sexist?," *Her-Self: Women's Community Journal* 3, no. 2 (1974): 6.

20. Artie Mitchell quoted in Kenneth Turan and Stephen F. Zito, *Sinema: American Pornographic Films and the People Who Make Them* (New York: Praeger, 1974), 170–71.

21. Mireille Miller-Young, *A Taste for Brown Sugar: Black Women in Pornography* (Durham, NC: Duke University Press, 2014).

22. Ibid., 280.

23. John Colapinto, "The Twilight of Bob Guccione," *Rolling Stone*, October 21, 2010.

24. Tristan Taormino, "Calling the Shots: Feminist Porn in Theory and Practice," in *The Feminist Porn Book: The Politics of Producing Pleasure*, ed. Tristan Taormino, Celine Parreñas Shimizu, Constance Penley, and Mireille Miller-Young, 255–64 (New York: Feminist Press, 2013), 261.

25. See *"Barbara Broadcast:* A Podcast in Four Courses," June 2013, "George McDonald: The First Adult Film Star," September 2015, and "Billy Dee: Porn Again Christian," November 2015, all at www.therialtoreport.com.

26. Georgina Spelvin, *The Devil Made Me Do It* (Los Angeles: Little Red Hen, 2008); Serena Czarnecki, *Bright Lights, Lonely Nights: The Memories of Serena, Porn Star Pioneer of the 1970s* (Duncan, OK: BearManor, 2014); Howie Gordon, *Hindsight: True Love and Mischief in the Golden Age of Porn* (Albany, GA: BearManor, 2013).

27. Larry Revene, *Wham Bam $$ Ba Da Boom!* (n.p.: Hudson Delta Books, 2013), and *Life in a Film Can* (n.p.: Hudson Delta Books, 2015); Robert Rosen, *Beaver Street: A History of Modern Pornography* (London: Headpress, 2010).

28. Jill C. Nelson, *Golden Goddesses: 25 Legendary Women of Classic Erotic Cinema, 1968–1985* (Duncan, OK: BearManor, 2012). See also Mike Stabile's documentary *Seed Money: The Chuck Holmes Story* (2015).

29. Important recent works in porn studies, in addition to others cited in this essay, include Stephen Patrick Johnson, "Staying Power: The Mainstreaming of the Hard-Core Pornographic Film Industry, 1969–1990" (PhD diss., University of Maryland, 2009); Tristan Taormino, Celine Parreñas Shimizu, Constance Penley, and Mireille Miller-Young, eds., *The Feminist Porn Book* (New York: Feminist Press, 2013); Enrico Biasin, Giovanna Maina, and Federico Zecca, eds., *Porn After Porn: Contemporary Alternative Pornographies* (Milan: Mimesis International, 2014); Lynn Comella and Shira Tarrant, *New Views on Pornography: Sexuality, Politics, and the Law* (Santa Barbara, CA: Praeger, 2015); Tim Dean, Steven Ruszczycky, and David Squires, eds., *Porn Archives* (Durham, NC: Duke University Press, 2014); Eric Schaefer, ed., *Sex Scene: Media and the Sexual Revolution* (Durham, NC: Duke University Press, 2014); William E. Jones, *Halsted Plays Himself* (Los Angeles: Semiotext(e), 2011); Jeffrey Escoffier, *Bigger Than Life: The History of Gay Porn Cinema from Beefcake to Hardcore* (Philadelphia: Running Press, 2009); and the journal *Porn Studies*, begun in 2013. Even as this book goes to press, new work continues to emerge; of particular relevance, see David Church, *Disposable Passions: Vintage Pornography and the Material Legacies of Adult Cinema* (New York: Bloomsbury Academic, 2016); Juana María Rodríguez, "Pornographic Encounters and Interpretative Interventions: Vanessa del Rio: Fifty Years of Slightly Slutty

Behavior," *Women and Performance: A Journal of Feminist Theory* 25, no.3 (2015): 315–35; Ryan Powell, "Queer Interstates: Cultural Geography and Social Contact in *Kansas City Trucking Co.* and *El Paso Wrecking Corp.*," in *Queering the Countryside: New Frontiers in Rural Queer Studies*, ed. Mary Gray, Colin R. Johnson, and Brian Joseph Gilley (New York: New York University Press, 2016), 181–202; Shira Tarrant, *The Pornography Industry: What Everyone Needs to Know* (New York: Oxford University Press, 2016).

FILMS

CHAPTER 1

From Porno Chic to Porno Bleak

Representing the Urban Crisis in 1970s American Pornography

WHITNEY STRUB

A N INEVITABLE SCENE FROM the hit 1974 vigilante film *Death Wish* perfectly crystallized pervasive media narratives of urban dread, as two sneering muggers swagger through a subway car, their menace accented by the flickering lights and grinding roar of the tracks. Passengers scurry away, leaving only the placid-looking Charles Bronson, on whom the creeps pull switchblades. The film solicits audience cheers when Bronson nonchalantly draws a gun, blowing them both away.

The scene's inevitability rests on the subway's role as mobile metonym for the much-bemoaned urban crisis of the 1970s. According to the reactionary narrative of *Death Wish* and companion films such as *Dirty Harry* (1971), the crisis stemmed from a breakdown in law and order, as petty bureaucrats and legally hamstrung police left men, women, and children unsafe on city streets, susceptible to the criminal intents of a wide array of muggers, rapists, and murderers. While liberals disputed the causes of the crisis, few in the mid-1970s questioned its existence, as urban public space took on dangerous hues in media representation. Nothing better symbolized the urban crisis than the New York City subway train, rickety, often graffiti-scarred, and—if movies like *Death Wish; The French Connection* (1971); *The Taking of Pelham One Two Three* (1974); and even Woody Allen's *Bananas* (1971) were to be believed—lawless.

Film scholars have certainly noted the role of 1970s American film in propagating ominous visions of the city that "for the most part reproduced and validated the right's discourse on the urban crisis while amplifying the suburban middle-class fears the discourse helped to generate," as Steve Macek writes.[1] For the most part, however, these analyses hew close to the Hollywood mainstream, or the opposition it drew from marginal but reputable sources, such as the independent black films *Killer of Sheep* (1977) and *Bush Mama* (1979).[2] Less recognized are hardcore pornographic films such as Shaun Costello's *Fiona on Fire* (1977), which virtually replicates the iconic *Death Wish* scene, this time on a New York commuter train. Everything from the mise-en-scène to the costuming matches the Bronson film, except this time when the creeps clear out the car, two women are left behind. Instead of a cathartic vigilante killing, what ensues is a brutal rape scene.

"Urban crisis" was a phrase that emanated out of macroeconomic trends such as deindustrialization that had begun as early as the 1950s but grew increasingly visible and even visceral in the wake of the urban unrest that had coursed across the nation in the late 1960s, most notoriously in Watts, Newark, and Detroit. In New York City, the primary base of early hardcore filmmaking, a heightened sense of economic and political crisis suffused the 1970s, as the city teetered on the brink of bankruptcy by 1975, while racial and ethnic tensions swelled. Meanwhile, Times Square, in midtown Manhattan, acted as a virtual open red-light district, besotted with lurid theater marquees promising to test the legal boundaries with ever-increasing explicitness. Indeed, the connection between the so-called urban crisis of the 1970s and the emergence of hardcore pornography is generally understood as a material or spatial one: as downtowns decayed in the face of white flight and disinvestment, the abandoned spaces provided ideal sites for the proliferation of small storefront adult movie theaters and the repurposing of older, now defunct cinemas, resulting in a smutty blight etched across the urban landscape.[3]

Fiona on Fire suggests another angle: that heterosexual smut frequently colluded in the reactionary narrativization of the urban crisis, joining the mass media in promoting images of a lawless urban jungle that reinforced middle-class white fear and hostility to the city. While theorizations of the genre emphasize its utopian formal qualities, in fact heterosexual porn of the era was often markedly *dystopian* diegetically, representationally, and also in its regularized depiction of sexual violence. Shooting guerilla-style and making vivid use of urban locations, 1970s heterosmut offered a vision of the urban crisis in which the erosion of the social contract provided sexual opportunities—but also grave sexual danger for women. From alleys to subways to apartments, city space was presented as rife with threats. In this sense, straight porn reinforced the dominant cultural narrative of the urban crisis being peddled by such Hollywood scare films as *Dirty Harry* and *Death Wish*.

As imbricated as straight porn was with the city, gay male pornography of the decade made even *more* striking use of urban space, but to very different ends. For gay men, any breakdown in a social order partly defined by violent, state-sponsored homophobia was an advance, and indeed, gay porn documented the historical moment in which once-furtive cruising spaces took public shape as affirmations of pride and visibility. From its very inception, gay porn offered a powerful counternarrative of the city. While the straight world indulged its urban anxieties in *Death Wish* and *Fiona on Fire* (fig. 1.1), the early gay hardcore film *The Back Row* (1972) reclaimed the subway car as a site of pleasure and desire. Here, stars Casey Donovan and George Payne drift from the Port Authority bus station, where they cruised one another through sustained eye contact, to the Times Square subway stop. For them, the empty car they enter is no threat but rather opportunity; the two men build erotic tension as they fondle their respective crotches enticingly, before exiting at the Christopher Street stop, delivered to gay-friendly terrain where they continue their erotic flirtation (figs. 1.2, 1.3).

In this essay I analyze the still underexamined body of pornographic 1970s cinema, using both pioneering early films that set the template for the narrative hardcore feature and also representative works from across the decade to show how straight porn often proved complicit in a reactionary cultural narrative whereas gay porn called into question the very heteronormative underpinnings of the "urban crisis" framework. I also suggest that contestations over the periodization of "the seventies" or the "Golden Age of Pornography" might take into account the use of urban space as a useful historical marker; between the secretive smut of earlier years, generally shot inside for legal reasons, and the reprivatized porn of the 1980s that followed the brutal new enclosure movement of the rising carceral state, the documentation, and indeed constitution of, public sex acts as a central historicized marker of this era.

FIGURE 1.1. The commuter car as a site of sexual danger in *Fiona on Fire* (Shaun Costello, 1978).

The Urban Pornotrope

Thomas Jefferson failed to chart the future with his ideal of the agrarian yeoman farmer, but the dyspeptic founding father did set the tone for subsequent visions of urbanism, likening cities to degeneracy, cankers, and sores in *Notes on the State of Virginia* (1787) and calling them "pestilential to the morals, the health and the liberties of man" in an 1800 letter.[4] As the industrial revolution helped spur urbanization, cultural representations played a key role in keeping Jefferson's animosity alive. While cities were indeed sites of crime, poverty, squalor, inequality, and pollution, sensationalized sexual representations often served as one of the most visceral venues for antiurbanism. The penny press itself took shape largely around the 1836 murder of prostitute Helen Jewett; salacious pamphlets such as *Prostitution Exposed* (1839) doubled as exposés and guidebooks; the dime novels of George Thompson and George Lippard mixed class consciousness with lurid reveling in urban debauchery, leading one scholar to term their books, with such titles as *City Crimes* and *Venus in Boston*, "urban pornogothic"; and even reform-minded serious literature such as Stephen

FIGURES 1.2 AND 1.3. The subway system as gay erotic nexus in *The Back Row* (Jerry Douglas, 1972).

Crane's *Maggie: A Girl of the Streets* (1893) used a young woman's descent into prostitution to chart the ravages of the city.[5]

By the time the cinema emerged at the dawn of the twentieth century, these urban pornotropes informed its very development. Early nickelodeon features built on a specifically urban mode of spectatorship. The "white slave" panic of the 1910s coincided with the birth of the modern narrative feature film, with *The Traffic in Souls* (1913) helping shape cinematic grammar even as it depicted New York City's streets as rife with nefarious sex traffickers who sought to abduct innocent white women and coerce them into a life of "iniquity," as the film has it.[6] While graphic stag films also accompanied more socially acceptable movies from the birth of the medium on, their illegality pulled them away from actual city space; the exploitation films whose prurient charge drew audiences all the way into the 1960s, meanwhile, further perpetuated antiurbanism in their various narratives of sin, drugs, and death.[7]

Events of the late 1960s helped solidify what we might call the urban pornotrope, a symbolic fusion of city space and sexual depravity. Liberalization of obscenity law coincided with urban unrest and disinvestment in American cities to open new space for pornography-oriented businesses to take root. Adult bookstores and storefront theaters proliferated as traditional shops moved out and downtowns became economic deserts. But the urban pornotrope was inscribed *textually* as well, most visibly in the grindhouse exploitation films that often depicted a nightmarish Times Square even as they played it. Tawdry works such as *The Sex Killer* (1967) and *The Curse of Her Flesh* (1968) suggested urban chaos driven by dark desires, a sexual noir in which the depravity was linked visually to the stark location shooting that left "sexploitation" films "inextricably tied" to the concrete geography of Times Square.[8]

When hardcore porn moved aboveground in 1970, as liberalized obscenity laws and a relaxation in public sexual mores made even greater openness possible, its pioneering works proved insistently urban. *Mona: The Virgin Nymph*, often regarded as the first hardcore narrative feature film, begins in a city park and moves quickly to a Los Angeles sidewalk, where heroine Mona approaches a passing man with a brazen inquiry: "Do you want me to suck your cock?" The act itself is completed in an adjacent alley. *Tomatoes*, another hardcore front-runner, foregrounds its urbanism as well, opening with a man walking among sleek downtown San Francisco corporate towers

FIGURE 1.4. Urban decay literally enables hard core in *Tomatoes* (Joel Roberts, 1970).

(fig. 1.4). Even the film's opening credits were painted on the sides of buildings and tacked to public bulletin boards. Finally, the New York City–lensed *Bacchanale* featured an apparitional female lead drifting past tenement buildings, their intricate fire escape ladders a surreal geometry for the roving camera.

Not all heterosmut relied on the city; the genre also had its share of escapist fare, pastoral drama, and futuristic science fiction. But so embedded was the urban pornotrope that all three of the definitive "porno chic" films of 1972–73 employed it. *Deep Throat*, the most famous porn film of all time, began with a protracted credit sequence of Linda Lovelace driving through Miami, set against the city skyline. *Behind the Green Door* exuded its San Francisco setting throughout. Despite being set primarily in Limbo en route to Hell, even the existentialist *The Devil in Miss Jones* nodded to New York in its opening suicide scene, where an open window reveals a busy street several floors below as Georgina Spelvin's title character prepares to take her own life. The view of the city street acts as a metaphor for the cold, impersonal world she is leaving behind. As New York exerted a gravitational force on the burgeoning hardcore industry over the course of the decade, the helicopter (or, for the budget-strained, ferry) view of the city skyline practically acted as a geographic money shot over dozens upon dozens of opening credits, providing the "proof" of the urban setting.

This fetishistic insistence on the authenticity of the environs paralleled the location-shoot fixation of the concurrent New Hollywood cadre, in which directors William Friedkin, Martin Scorsese, Brian De Palma, and others relied on real urban space to distinguish their work from the classical Hollywood set-based shoots. Many of these films, mainstream and porn, responded to the perceived urban crisis, but few literalized its metaphors as jaggedly as Shaun Costello's early *Forced Entry*, shot mostly in 1971 and released in 1973, which intercut footage from war-ravaged Vietnam with New York City streets to invoke the "asphalt jungle." The militantly unerotic film features a deranged veteran stalking, raping, and killing the women who stop at his gas station, with startling scenes of sexual violence that suggest a disintegrating social order and ever-present danger, as the villain peeps and invades from alleys, fire escapes, and windows. If such Scorsese films as *Mean Streets* (1973) and *Taxi Driver* (1976) depict "a city where a stable heterosexual urban space has disappeared," as one film scholar suggests, Costello's film extends this theme, albeit escalated far beyond Hollywood's limits of representation.[9]

Forced Entry was unique in its viciousness, but it nonetheless helped set the template for pornographic visions of the city even in milder fare. Certainly pleasure and danger intermingled, but were distributed in highly gendered fashion, with women bearing the overwhelming burden of risk. *Mona* itself led the way on this front; while *Forced Entry* is remembered specifically as violent rape porn, *Mona* presented itself as comedy. Mona's desire drives much of the film, as she pursues men to fellate in her sexual explorations while intending to technically remain a virgin until her impending marriage. Yet the film fits a remarkable amount of sexual coercion into its seventy minutes, beginning with a disturbing flashback to the young Mona learning how to perform oral sex on her father, who snaps, "You know you like it, stop playing games" after she cries, "Daddy, please don't make me do it again."

Back in the diegetic present, Mona learns about the gendering of urban space through force. While deserted alleys seem like opportune spots for her to exercise her desires, attending a small storefront porn theater to "do her thing," as she tells one willing man, results in disaster when her fiancé suddenly storms in. "You cocksucker!" he shouts, pulling her away from her partner. "I'll fix you, you little bitch." From there, the film cuts to a shot of Mona tied spread-eagle to her bed, as her fiancé invites her various partners from earlier in the film to "fix" her. A rape orgy ensues as she whimpers, "Don't fuck me, please," and the film ends with Mona running out of the room to weep in her mother's arms.

Certainly not every hardcore film featured depictions of rape or sexual assault. *School Girl* (1971), one of the best-regarded early porn films, was driven wholly by the desire and curiosity of its protagonist, a college student who decides to undertake research on sexual sub-cultures by answering classified sex ads in the *Berkeley Barb*, a weekly underground newspaper. The student signifies her enthused consent verbally and physically throughout the film's several sex scenes. Yet even taking into consideration such important exceptions, *Mona* and *Forced Entry* in some ways set the poles for 1970s heterosmut—poles that, like sadists and sissies in 1950s cold war sexual politics, really collapsed into one regulatory model, this time of a city dominated by male aggression toward women.[10] Rape might come in the form of grim, violent force, or it might be absorbed into a comedic structure that presented it as benign and laughable, but either way, it was far more present than most surveys of porn outside the feminist antiporn movement have acknowledged.[11] In both variants, sexual violence and coercion were central to the urban pornotrope.

For films that took the *Forced Entry* approach of brutal realism, various alibis strove to narratively justify the graphic representations. In that film, the rapist himself winds up committing suicide after two drugged-out hippie women respond to his assault not with fear but obliviousness, then mockery, undermining his male power. Thus the film is able to conclude on a deconstructive note in regard to masculinity—after wallowing in violence against women for its dura-tion.[12] Director Costello took another approach to depicting rape in the aforementioned *Fiona on Fire* scene, which takes place as a flash-back (the title character is seemingly shot to death in the shower after the film's opening sex scene, though like the 1944 noir film *Laura*, she turns up unexpectedly alive later); the detective investigating Fiona's death interviews his own brother, a pimp, in the back of a limousine driving through Times Square. Having linked Fiona to his brother, the detective assumes she hooked for him. "Worked for me? She paid me," he exclaims, explaining that "she made me set up a scene—I mean, it was weird! It was far-out!" When Costello then cuts back to the rape scene itself, the spectator is unburdened by any qualms that might have come from watching a protracted, violent rape in which Fiona first hides behind the train car's door as the two invading thugs attack another female passenger, before being pulled out and herself assaulted; it is, after all, a staged—and thus consensual—scene (for Fiona, at least—it remains unclear whether the other woman was part of the act or a random bystander dragged into it).

This alibi of the staged rape established as such diegetically or through voiceover found frequent recurrence, from the prostitute employed by police to submit to a violent home-invasion gang rape in *Expensive Tastes* (1978) to the actress Terri Hall "confessing" to her satanic cult leader in *Ecstasy in Blue* (1976) that "I go to the worst part of town" hoping to attract "the crudest, most violent sort of men . . . in alleyways, in cars, in dungeons," as the film's visuals show her walking a poorly lit street, being accosted, dragged into an apartment, and raped. Ex post facto justifications also widely prevailed. In *Sleepy Head* (1973), writer Georgina Spelvin contrives to have her uptight religious sister Tina Russell gang-raped. Russell asks Spelvin to pray for her afterward, not because she was raped but because "I loved it. I loved every moment." In another example, C. J. Laing begins a scene in *Anyone But My Husband* (1975) screaming "Please . . . let me go" to an art gallery owner who has tied her up. By the end of the ensuing sex scene, she has signified her pleasure and enjoyment, eliding the rape with a retroactive consent.

All of these scenes are presented with at least some degree of violence and force. Other contemporaneous heterosmut played similar circumstances for laughs. The San Francisco–based *Pretty Peaches* (1978) features multiple sexual assaults within its 1930s-screwball comedy guise. When the ditzy protagonist, Peaches, crashes her stolen jeep and passes out, one of the two male bystanders who witness the accident has sex with her while she is unconscious; later, when Peaches tries out at a strip club, a gang rape by a group of angry female strippers ensues. Though the scene ends with Peaches crying, its musical cues and director Alex de Renzy's jaunty rhythms encourage audience laughter. This recasting of sexual violence as humor reaches its zenith in another San Francisco film, *Hot and Saucy Pizza Girls* (1979), in which a sexually available pizza deliverywoman on roller skates is accosted on a city sidewalk and dragged behind a fence, to the sound of clucking and the sight of feathers floating up. When she returns to work and tells her boss she was raped, he shrugs, "So what's new?" It turns out to be the work of the San Francisco Night Chicken, whose prowling occupies the backstory of the ostensibly lighthearted farce.

Grim realist scenarios and farcical rape-for-comedy could coexist, as in *Joy* (1977), a seeming inversion of rape tropes. Sharon Mitchell's high school character begins the film by resisting her boyfriend's sexual entreaties, only to face a home-invasion rape in the second scene. The scene begins with brutality but evolves into another sexual awakening, as Joy calls out for more with an assertiveness that drives the second of the two men away. Director Harley Mansfield concretely situates the film in urban space, from the opening "New York City: The End of June" to a visually effective shot of Joy after the rape, leaning topless out of her high-rise apartment window to shout, "I want more!" as the camera pulls back from across the street to pan across a smoggy skyline. The narrative then swerves to the comedic as the insatiable Joy ravishes men across the city, from a married, frustrated businessman in a trash-strewn alley to a nerdy young man on a subway car reading a book on how to pick up women. As newspaper headlines scream "Female Rapist Strikes!" a television newscaster reveals that all other crime in the city has vanished: "No muggings, no murders, no violent crimes," he declares.

As a film directly engaged with the urban crisis, *Joy* plays urban anxieties over crime for laughs in its sexual solution. The humor is asymmetrically gendered, though, with all of the male rapes played for light humor, and then a sudden, jarring return to grim realism when a police officer assigned to the case stalks Joy, drags her forcefully off a sidewalk into an apartment building, cuffs her to a stairwell, and rapes her as she cries, "Please don't hurt me!" This scene is at decided odds with those preceding it, belying the film's (thin) veneer of inverted gender politics by reinforcing the continuity of male pleasure in all of the sexual episodes, independent of the women's enjoyment or consent.

That the rapist cop is the film's sole black male sexual participant further situates *Joy* in the contemporaneous urban crisis discourse, with its consistently racialized sense of urban dangers. While Jennifer Nash shows elsewhere in this volume how black women were able to carve out spaces of subjectification in pornography, black men faced an even greater struggle in some ways, bearing the semiotic weight of entrenched racist stereotypes that went largely unchallenged in the genre. The basic spectrum ran from the "exotic" awe of the magnetically hypersexual black man played by Johnnie Keyes in such films as *Behind the Green Door* (1972), *The Resurrection of Eve* (1973), and *SexWorld* (1978), to such rapists as the one played by Jesse Wilson in *Joy*—curiously, called Barnes by his sergeant in the film but credited more generically as simply "Black Officer" in the credits at the end. In another instance, *Lustful Feelings* (1978) ends with white prostitute Leslie Bovee's violent demise at the hands of two black clients. So thoroughly did racialized fear of urban space permeate the very construction of the urban crisis that *Hot Summer in the City* (1976), set almost entirely in a single, distinctly nonurban, cabin, was able to summon "the city" (Detroit, in this case) through the mere presence of the three black men who kidnap a young white woman and rape her repeatedly while holding her hostage. In its racial economy, "black" connoted "urban," and vice versa.

Not every articulation of white urban anxiety was plotted on a black/white binary grid, though that was certainly the dominant organization of the "crisis." *Oriental Blue* (1976), for example, returned all the way to Orientalist "white slave" fears of the 1910s (recycled in the 1960s for the grindhouse-based *White Slaves of Chinatown* series), opening with a young white woman abducted into Madame Blue's limousine in Times Square and dragged to Chinatown for a life of sex slavery. One scene, with actor Jamie Gillis as a procurer tricking Bree Anthony (as a recent New York arrival straight from Nebraska) into coming with him, so directly echoed a similar scene from the pivotal white-slavery film *The Traffic in Souls* that it might be read as an homage by director Bill Milling. Even with the racial focus shifted, though, the theme of the city as dangerous terrain for white women remained consistent.

In this, heteroporn shared certain affinities not only with reactionary urban-crisis discourse that located danger in a racialized city, but also with feminist analyses of the 1970s. "Rape can be said to be a big-city crime," Susan Brownmiller wrote in her landmark 1975 book *Against Our Will: Men, Women, and Rape*—and porn films seemed to agree.[13] Along with Brownmiller, author and activist Andrea Dworkin helped launch the developing feminist antipornography movement and bring it to national prominence with her 1981 manifesto *Pornography: Men Possessing Women*. This book included painful, visceral, protracted descriptions of pornographic violence against women, and many of the heteroporn films of the 1970s did fit this bill, a reality lost in the subsequent feminist sex wars, during which many of Dworkin's legal, metaphysical, and ideological conclusions about pornography were rightly challenged, but without any substantive returns to the films or other textual landscapes she had traversed in her work.[14]

To be sure, the heterosexual pornography of the early hardcore feature era often had a complex textual richness that the antagonistic Dworkin reduced to simple power struggles, and as Laura Helen Marks points out in the next chapter, the developing scholarly field of porn studies has yet to fully delve into the complicated, often melancholy work of leading porn auteurs such as Anthony Spinelli, Roger Watkins, Roberta Findlay, or Shaun Costello (indeed, Marks moves beyond my comments on *Forced Entry* and situates it within Costello's larger body of work). Still, when it came to depictions of the city in crisis, straight pornography was less radical or oppositional than in sheer congruence with dominant media narratives: the city was a frightful place.

Cruising the Crisis

So central has the city been to both LGBT history and historical methodology that a resultant critique of "metronormativity" emerged in the early twenty-first century to remind citycentric observers that queer rural life existed and persisted.[15] Gay male smut acknowledged this, mostly prominently in director Joe Gage's blue-collar "working man's" trilogy of *Kansas City Trucking Co.* (1976), *El Paso Wrecking Corp.* (1977), and *L.A. Tool and Die* (1979), which canvased the dusty highways, rest stops, and back alleys of America—but, like hetero-porn, the gay hardcore films of the early 1970s hewed overwhelmingly to urban settings.

As a criminalized demimonde, the gay world had long subsisted on coded maps and signals, with cultural texts providing frequent pointers, all the way from the 1784 pamphlet *The Philadelphiad; or, New Pictures of the City*, with its chapter "Misfortunes of a Fop," to the 1933 Hollywood musical *42nd Street*, which hinted at queer spaces even in the midst of conservative Depression-era gender politics.[16] While lesbian pulp fiction played a pedagogical role for numerous female readers in urban geography and subcultural signals, gay men found glimpses of their desired social world scattered across an array of sources. As Martin Meeker notes, the geography-making impetus of these texts played a crucial role in gay community formation, and began to rise in visibility in the 1960s with such events as the publication of Guy Strait's *Lavender Baedeker* in 1963, the first national gay guidebook to bars and safe spaces.[17]

This all transpired against a backdrop of violent, state-sponsored attacks on gay existence, from the psychiatrists who pathologized "deviants" to the police forces who beat, blackmailed, assaulted, and imprisoned them. To the extent that the urban crisis represented a breakdown in this social order, then, this fracture provided increased freedom for queer people, who were now less subject to such surveillance and control. Even liberal observers read the urban crisis through a heteronormative lens, linking gay visibility to the seemingly disintegrating structures of control, as Marc Stein shows in his reading of Jane Jacobs's depiction of a "pervert" invasion of Philadelphia's Washington Square in her classic *Death and Life of Great American Cities* (1961).[18] As the straight, white middle class fled for suburbs specifically designed for procreative heterosexual families, urban opportunities beckoned for gay communities, from San Francisco's Castro to Atlantic City in New Jersey.[19]

Also buttressing the new gay assertiveness over public space was the liberationist bent to gay activism that followed the Stonewall rebellion of the summer of 1969. While the homophile movement had displayed courage and tenacity dating back to the early 1950s, including public protests for gay rights that began in the mid-sixties, gay activism was increasingly informed by both radical youth movements (black power, women's liberation, the student Left, etc.) and countercultural sexual politics that chafed against the constraints of the homophile focus on respectability. The budding currents of the era could be seen in the pioneering softcore short films of Pat Rocco beginning in 1968. Shot across Los Angeles, from Hollywood Boulevard to Griffith Park, Rocco's works demanded gay inclusion in the public sphere, with such daring cinematic feats as a nude man dancing on the normally traffic-clogged Hollywood Freeway in *A Breath of Love* (1969).[20] This stood in stark contrast to the earlier "physique" shorts of Bob Mizer shot largely in his own backyard as a means of evading the prying eyes of antigay police.[21]

Although Rocco rejected the label "pornography" for his erotic films and kept his name away from hardcore explicitness, subsequent filmmakers showed less hesitation. Wakefield Poole's *Boys in the Sand* (1971) and Fred Halsted's *LA Plays Itself* (1972) in some ways constituted the ur-texts of 1970s gay hardcore as much as *Mona* and *Forced Entry* did for straight smut, setting the parameters of the polar but conjoined trajectories of the genre. "Conjoined" because both adopted radical liberationist attitudes toward gay sex, from Poole's relatively uncomplicated celebration of male beauty and desire to Halsted's more obtuse insistence that he was not even a homosexual but rather a "pervert" first, a declaration that shared affinities with the gay liberationist deconstruction of sexual identity itself in such writings as Carl Wittman's "Gay Manifesto" (1970).[22] "Polar," though, because their settings differed wildly, with Halsted fixated on the grimy, smog-saturated streets of Los Angeles, and Poole preferring the pastoral idyll of Fire Island. Though that famous gay resort was, of course, linked to the New York City metropolitan area for which it formed a vacation outpost, on screen it appeared as a place detached from urban visuals from the very first scene, when star Casey Donovan emerges Adonis-like from the ocean waters.

Boys would set the stage for the gay pastoral fantasia; as one film that followed its steps, Jack Deveau's *Fire Island Fever* (1979) declared in its opening voiceover, "It was the night before the night before Christmas in Manhattan. If you hadn't already stuffed two Lacoste shirts into a Vuitton bag and lit out for Key West, chances are you'd wind up at Frank and George's Fire Island Pines Christmas party." As production companies such as Catalina and Falcon brought a factory-line approach to gay porn by the late seventies, pastoral nature settings would increasingly take center stage, a tradition brought into the next century by Bel Ami and others.[23]

Yet it was Halsted's *LA* that ushered in a wave of gay hardcore that engaged directly with the city. Unlike the heterosmut that saw danger in urban decay, Halsted showed a rigorous cinematic eye in his examination of Los Angeles urban space as an opportunity for unleashed perversity. The film, which opened with a shot of a Los Angeles city limits sign, consisted of two extended sex scenes, the first itself a pastoral idyll—in a Malibu canyon on the brink of extinction. As two young men make love gently, Halsted begins superimposing tractors destroying (or "developing") the land over their entwined bodies. Soon he cuts to grittier settings, as a car-based camera pans and zooms across porn theaters, strip clubs, hustlers on corners, and more signs of urban sexuality. In this terrain, sex takes a rougher form, and the film's second half features Halsted himself dominating a willing Joey Yale. As he flogs his young submissive, makes him lick his boots, and subjects him to a demanding disciplinary regime (culminating in an infamous fisting scene, cut from all later home video versions of the film—a rupture in the gay visual archive that Lucas Hilderbrand discusses later in the collection),[24] Halsted frequently cuts back to the sordid cityscape, taking particular visual interest in such sights as the wreckage of a building at a redevelopment site. If *LA Plays Itself* linked urbanism to transgressive sexuality, it did so in a celebratory (if also ambivalent) manner.

Wakefield Poole moved into urban terrain with his second feature film, *Bijou* (1972), the original print now faithfully restored by Vinegar Syndrome founder Joe Rubin, as discussed in the final essay in this volume. From its very first shot, of a construction site adjacent to the Lincoln Center in New York City, *Bijou* too reflects awareness of a city in flux whose redevelopment plays out not just infrastructurally but also sexually in a dialectic with its unnamed protagonist, a worker at the site. Just as the worker constructs the city, it in turn constructs his sexuality with its web of possibilities. Though an early scene reveals him masturbating to a girlie magazine, he later participates in gay sex acts in a mysterious, surreal sex club located on a busy city street. Like Halsted, Poole grounds this ambiguous, fluid sexuality within a concrete urban setting whose constant reconfiguration and regeneration, the film implies, enables the very queerness of its sexual cosmos.

If not every gay porn film aspired to quite the thematic richness of Halsted's or Poole's studies in urban sexuality, many used location shooting every bit as vivid as that of the New Hollywood auteurs to map out a proud sexual geography. The aforementioned *Back Row*, for instance, opens with a montage of Times Square porn theater marquees. Though many of their offerings are heterosexual, the space itself is effectively queered with a pan down from a marquee for the pseudo-documentary *All About Sex of All Nations* to Casey Donovan, facing away from the camera—thus allowing director Jerry Douglas to zoom in on his backside, housed in tight jeans.[25] From there, Donovan goes on to cruise George Payne in the Port Authority. Next, they pursue one another through the subway, into Washington Square, and the Pleasure Chest sex shop before returning to the 42nd Street Cinema, where the ticket taker greets them with an exposed erection that they both casually decline. After Donovan joins two other men for a bathroom threesome in the theater while a forlorn Payne bides his time, the cruisers finally make contact, holding hands and kissing on the Hudson River piers and even making out inside a sidewalk phone booth (fig. 1.5).

Before Stonewall, much of this public affection would have been unthinkable, and even in the early 1970s it required courage in the face of a still-homophobic police force—not to mention the audacity to

FIGURE 1.5. Straight porn marks space that affords room for gay desire in *The Back Row* (Jerry Douglas, 1972).

shoot without the legal protection afforded by the filming permits held by more "legitimate" productions. For the subway scene, Douglas and his small cast and crew of a half dozen boarded a downtown train for Wall Street on a Sunday morning and simply looked for an empty car—another way the specific material conditions of the city in the early 1970s facilitated adult filmmaking.[26] As such, *The Back Row* laid claim to social space in a way reflective of liberationist ideals regarding assertive public gay sexuality. Indeed, for Peter Berlin (discussed later by Lucas Hilderbrand, and featured on the cover of this book), displaying his body in public space, dressed in "tight white pants, showing off that huge organ of pleasure of his," as the narrator of *That Boy* (1974) describes, *was* in many ways the central visual pleasure of his two San Francisco–based hardcore features. *That Boy* situates him very specifically on Polk Street, and *Nights in Black Leather* (1973) airily drifts through fifteen minutes of local scenery before getting around to any sex. These are films about gay men enjoying themselves in public (fig 1.6).

Other films of the era followed suit. The gay porn films rarely

FIGURE 1.6. Gay desire embedded in the streets of San Francisco, in *That Boy* (Peter Berlin, 1974).

reflected naively utopian visions of the city but rather nuanced assessments that recognized the opportunities of urban life without blindly embracing every facet. Jack Deveau's *Left-Handed* (1972) cuts back and forth between metropole and rural periphery in its story of drug running. In striking New York City location shots, sex in the city occurs randomly, spontaneously, and urgently, as when one character walks into a restroom in a city park, long known to be welcoming venues for anonymous gay hookups. Deveau leads the camera in past sexual graffiti that acts as spatial marker to show a man masturbating in a stall and the sexual encounter that ensues. If this is contrasted to the film's more conventionally romantic sex scenes up in forest-ensconced, upstate Woodstock, Deveau refuses to draw hard lines. "It's so different from the people in the city," protagonist-dealer Bob tells a New York friend over the phone, to which the city friend shrugs, "Oh, I was going to have an orgy this weekend; I thought you might like to come." Yet even the earlier "tearoom" sex, as fellatio in public restrooms was called, ended with a kiss, so urban sex is not merely crass and jaded.

Arch Brown's *The Night Before* (1973), another of the first wave of ambitious gay hardcore, does romanticize urban sex, with a montage of breakfast, a couple running in a park, and other tropes straight out of the Hollywood romance playbook—except that in this case, the montage also includes naked cuddling in a cot between its inter-racial black/white couple. As with Halsted, Poole, Deveau, and others, Brown shows a keen eye for the semiotics of urban space, with a spray-painted "Power to the People" sign on a public wall in the opening scene invoking the radical activism of the 1960s that undergirds the film's social world. When the couple walks hand in hand down a New York street, a middle-aged white woman passes by, and Brown's camera stays on her as she turns, holding her ambiguous expression (confusion? dismay? surprise?) in brief freeze-frame; the effect is both to defamiliarize her, as if *she's* the one out of touch with the conventions of 1973, and also to pause and register the larger heteronormative backdrop through which the gay characters stroll. Though a place of possibility, the city is never a place of complete liberation.

Even as the ambitions of early hardcore seemed to recede into more rote sexual workouts by mid-decade (a narrative I would not want to overstate, yet one that corresponds in material terms to hardcore's evolution into an undeniable *industry*),[27] the spatial politics of gay hardcore remained defiant. Even a fairly run-of-the-mill film like Steve Scott's *12 at Noon* (1977), effectively a series of unconnected short loops strung together into a feature, takes on a documentary-like vérité quality when viewed through the lens of its use of space. The opening scene, a mini-orgy in a city park restroom, has no real sound but the ambient background noise of nearby cars passing—whether due to directorial laziness, ineptitude, or perhaps aesthetic precision, it is a remarkably effective aural invocation of the tearoom's exposed liminality between public and private space. When a fourth man steps inside to join the three already at work midscene, after asking, "How's the action?" he volunteers to guard the door—again, a reminder of the dangers that accompany such pleasures. While nothing else in *12 at Noon* matches the risky intensity of that literally criminal opening scene, its other scenes at city parks and bathhouses that became ubiquitous staples of the genre carried significance above and beyond the film's aesthetic limitations. Gay porn continued to chart the staggering erotic density of the gay urban nexus, from alleys (Scott's 1978 *Gemini*) to gas stations (the Glendale-shot *Grease Monkeys* in 1978) to the bars that served as social and sexual nodes in virtually every film, such as *Inches* (1979), in which porn superstar Al Parker and his boyfriend argue over whether the bar scene is too superficial—though Parker finds himself drawn in by its seductive allure.[28]

Porn theaters themselves provided another recurring motif, from *The Back Row* onward. Reflexive views of the theatrical experience ranged from Times Square (Jack Deveau's 1978 *Night at the Adonis*) to Los Angeles' Silver Lake (Tom DeSimone's *Dirty Picture Show*, 1979). In the latter film, one male hustler tells another, "The old Bijou Theater has some of the best action in town," leading him to investigate. When he questions the five-dollar ticket cost at the door, the masturbating clerk explains, "You're not paying for the *movies*." Indeed, sex ensues in the seats, aisles, and restroom of the theater. Given that audiences watched—and reenacted—these films in the very locations where they were shot, the porn-theater movies amounted to not only a proclamation of place claiming but also a radical breaking of the fourth wall rarely achieved by even experimental filmmakers of the era.

Even seemingly apolitical gay porn films carried sublimated political charge, as when John Amero—who, with the straight Michael Findlay, shot a series of gay films that evocatively captured the sights and sensations of Christopher Street, the nearby piers, and other markers of gay city life—included footage of a gay pride march, replete with an "Anita Sucks" sign to offer resistance to the burgeoning anti-gay movement spearheaded by Anita Bryant (and discussed later in this volume by Greg Youmans), in *Killing Me Softly* (1979). William Higgins's *The Boys of Venice* (1979) provides an exemplary model of this mode of tacit politics. Opening with a montage that encapsulates the various California sunshine mythologies, Higgins shows men, women, and children happily strolling the beach, with men walking casually arm in arm alongside straight couples. Eventually two roller-skating men crash into one another, leading them back to one's apartment to treat injuries and enjoy a quick sexual encounter. Later the film follows men hitchhiking and working out in the open gyms on the beach, in between various sex scenes. If it all seems blithely unconcerned with sexual politics, that's in part because Higgins's film reflects the aftermath of a gay victory. Hostile Los Angeles police had fought gay visibility at Venice Beach all the way through a 1974 city council effort to outlaw nude bathing. The battle for space was openly homophobic; one concerned citizen wrote to council member Pat Russell to complain of "homosexuals, prostitutes, and other dregs of humanity" on the beach that year.[29]

By the time Higgins arrived to film *The Boys of Venice,* nude swimming may have been restricted, but the gay presence was undeniable. What appeared to the outraged letter writer as a sign of urban decline amounted, on the other side of the equation, to new visibility and freedom. Indeed, gay hardcore throughout the decade served as a record of these contests over space and legitimacy, as gay men claimed space and then documented and celebrated those claims through smut, and *The Boys of Venice* played sunshine to the Santa Monica noir of John Rechy's contemporaneous "documentary" book *The Sexual Outlaw,* which focused on darker sexual cultures at the beach and pier two miles north of Higgins's California paradise.[30] While these developments were obviously multicausal, resting on a backdrop of years of gay activism, as well as liberalizing obscenity laws and shifts in urban politics and governance, none of these brazen uses of public space would have been possible without the urban crisis and its accompanying "decline" of the city. What the straight, white middle class read as a narrative of threats from poor people of color also contained in its interstices a collapse of the heteronormative strictures that had mandated gay secrecy and privacy. "Come out!" was a battle cry in the sexual politics of the seventies, and gay hardcore shouted it proudly.

Reclothing the City

While debates over periodization remain perpetual in the historiography of the modern United States, the seventies seem easier to close, or at least bookend, than the sprawling sixties—whether it be the election of Ronald Reagan in 1980 or the first official reports in 1981 of a disease that would become the AIDS epidemic, the vast social changes of the early 1980s were undeniably swift, decisive, and devastating. Several historical transitions converged to reshape pornography, not least of which were the two just mentioned. The Reagan administration worked hard to win and keep the Christian Right, especially after the reactionary political movement realized that Reagan's substantive policy priorities lay with economic deregulation and the upward redistribution of wealth; one result was an obviously biased 1986 porn study by the Attorney General's Commission on Pornography and enhanced obscenity efforts by the Justice Department, after years of enforcement laxity under the Carter administration.[31] Meanwhile, the monumentally tragic impact of AIDS—exacerbated immeasurably by Reagan's disregard for those most affected by it—proved shattering to the performers in gay pornography, while infusing the straight porn world with anxiety and periodic casualties as well.

Other developments also helped reshape porn, especially technological advances in home-viewing formats that ushered consumption out of theaters and into living rooms, as Peter Alilunas discusses in his essay in this volume. The video store's replacing the porn theater in turn coincided with broader trends in urban land use, as neoliberal politics began a three-decade (and ongoing) dismantling of the public sphere, with sweeping efforts to privatize space for the sake of business-oriented downtown redevelopment. From the militarized police forces roaming the inner city in Reagan's "war on drugs" that spawned a racialized mass incarceration to even such detailed urban planning gestures as bus stop benches designed to preclude the homeless from resting on them, the 1980s marked a new regime in urban spatial politics.[32] A new conservative "counterintelligentsia" funded by such well-endowed think-tanks as the Manhattan Institute rewrote the urban crisis as one not of economics but rather "values and culture," terms used to displace (while simultaneously reinscribing) race even as poor people of color bore the brunt of urban policy shifts of the 1980s.[33] Even gay activists often joined the calls for "safer streets" as former "gay ghettos" gentrified, invoking the very state powers that had so recently oppressed their own communities.[34]

Pornography reflected these changes. Straight and gay porn both increasingly moved to interiors, as New York city streets began fading from centrality. The sparse Manhattan location shooting often obliquely hinted at the changes underway, as when Carter Stevens's *Bizarre Styles* (1980) opens along the fashion district on Seventh Avenue. In the film, actress Vanessa del Rio's lingerie shop, which supplies both models and prostitutes, faces challenges that hint at the broader business attack on local industry—indeed, Robert Fitch identified the fashion district as a key battleground in the "assassination of New York" by redevelopers eager to drive out economic diversity in the name of real-estate interests.[35] This directly affected porn production in the city; director and cinematographer Larry Revene lost his midtown Manhattan lease in 1982 and, like his frequent collaborator Chuck Vincent, relocated to Queens.[36] The early 1980s heterosmut of director Phil Prince also shifts to the outer boroughs; though *The Story of Prunella* (1982) opens with a typical NYC skyline shot, its action takes place on Staten Island, and *Dr. Bizarro* (1983) begins in front of Elmhurst Hospital in Queens. By mid-decade, Los Angeles' suburban San Fernando Valley had superseded all else as the pornography industry's ground zero, with films shot predominantly indoors, in studios whose deliberately bland warehouse-like exteriors housed an almost wholly interior pornographic visual world.[37] These changes coincided with the "cleanup" of Times Square, as Disney and redevelopment drove out both smut and socioeconomic diversity in order to cater to suburban, international, and wealthy tourists.[38]

Gay porn followed a similar arc, represented well by the films of Fred Halsted. After *LA Plays Itself,* his next major work, *Sextool* (1975), situated itself in a sex club by tracking the geography of Hollywood's Sunset Strip but then largely confined itself to the inside of the club. By the time of *A Night at Halsted's* and *Nighthawk in Leather* (both 1982), Halsted's mise-en-scène had grown even more claustrophobic, shot almost entirely within the interiors of his own short-lived sex club. By the time of the dispiriting *Fast Friends* (1987), brief opening-credit footage of Los Angeles traffic was all that prevented the film from transpiring entirely in bland domestic settings. The 1985 gay porn film *L.A. Boiling Point* perhaps best symbolized the changes in the genre: even its cursory opening shot of the city appeared to be a close-up of a postcard.

The privatization of the city, then, marks a transition away from the pornography of the 1970s, as much as do new modes of shooting on video, big hair and muscles on newly depilated bodies, and the appearance of condoms. With the urban pornography of the seventies went a particular assemblage of pleasure and danger.[39] Gay sex would thereafter lose the carefree political valences of its liberationist incarnation, and under pressure from both a prosecution-happy Justice Department and a well-mobilized feminist antipornography movement, heterosmut would distance itself from the pervasive rape of the first wave of hardcore. A tamer, more disciplined, if arguably not always less misogynist, straight sex would dominate the video era, and many of the seedier urban porn films would go unremembered or omitted from discussion as porn studies took shape as a field of scholarly inquiry. Recovering this rich and problematic cinematic landscape helps us better understand how pornography, far from being marginal cultural territory, operates in tandem with, and opposition to, the powerful discourses of urban crisis that have shaped American politics since the 1960s.

NOTES

1. Steve Macek, *Urban Nightmares: The Media, the Right, and the Moral Panic over the City* (Minneapolis: University of Minnesota Press, 2006), xvi.

2. On black urban counterdiscourse, see Paula Massood, *Black City Cinema: African American Urban Experiences in Film* (Philadelphia: Temple University Press, 2003), esp. 107–16.

3. Thomas Sugrue, *The Origins of the Urban Crisis: Race and Inequality in Postwar Detroit* (Princeton: Princeton University Press, 1996); on New York City in the 1970s, see Vincent Cannato, *The Ungovernable City: John Lindsay and His Struggle to Save New York* (New York: Basic, 2001); and Jonathan Soffer, *Ed Koch and the Rebuilding of New York City* (New York: Columbia University Press, 2010).

4. Thomas Jefferson, *Notes on the State of Virginia, with Related Documents,* ed. David Waldstreicher (Boston: Bedford / St. Martins, 2002); Jefferson letter to Benjamin Rush, September 23, 1800, available at http://founders.archives.gov.

5. Patricia Cline Cohen, *The Murder of Helen Jewett: The Life and Death of a Prostitute in Nineteenth-Century New York City* (New York: Knopf, 1998); Joseph Ridgely, "George Lippard's *The Quaker City:* The World of the American Porno-Gothic," *Studies in the Literary Imagination* 7, no. 1 (1974): 77–94; Donna Dennis, *Licentious Gotham: Erotic Publishing and Its Prosecution in Nineteenth-Century New York* (Cambridge: Harvard University Press, 2009), 22.

6. Tom Gunning, "From the Kaleidoscope to the X-Ray: Urban Spectatorship, Poe, Benjamin, and *Traffic in Souls* (1913)," *Wide Angle* 19, no. 4 (1997): 25–61.

7. Eric Schaefer, *"Bold! Daring! Shocking! True!" A History of Exploitation Films, 1919–1959* (Durham, NC: Duke University Press, 1999).

8. Elena Gorfinkel, "Tales of Times Square: Sexploitation's Secret History of Place," in *Taking Place: Location and the Moving Image,* ed. Gorfinkel and John David Rhodes (Minneapolis: University of Minnesota Press, 2011), 55.

9. Sabine Haenni, "Geographies of Desire: Postsocial Urban Space and Historical Revision in the Films of Martin Scorsese," *Journal of Film and Video* 62, no. 1–2 (2010): 67–85, quoted at 70.

10. Andrea Friedman, "Sadists and Sissies: Anti-pornography Campaigns in Cold War America," *Gender & History* 15, no. 2 (2003): 201–27.

11. For exceptions to this, see Laura Helen Marks's essay in this volume, and also Natalie Purcell's important book, *Violence and the Pornographic Imaginary: The Politics of Sex, Gender, and Aggression in Hardcore Pornography* (New York: Routledge, 2012). My piece overlaps slightly with Purcell's chapter on the seventies, which I came to after writing it, but her entire book is a powerful intervention into a now-stale debate, and deserves attention.

12. Here I would note that the film, approached as a text in a vacuum, can and does yield fascinating, even feminist, themes. Within the material conditions of its theatrical exhibition, however, in a male-dominated space transparently hostile to women, certain hermeneutic strictures might reasonably be inferred. Even Samuel Delany, as he queered the masculinity of Times Square theaters in his personal history of them, acknowledged their hostility to women; Delany, *Times Square Red, Times Square Blue* (New York: New York University Press, 1999). Indeed, while my focus here is on the larger discursive congruences of porn and urban crisis imagery, there can be little doubt that—as any representative sample of hardcore previews will attest—the violence against women was in fact part of

the very appeal of pornography to many male viewers in this era. Its reliance on urban crisis imagery did not, therefore, constitute a *critique* of violence against women.

13. Susan Brownmiller, *Against Our Will: Men, Women, and Rape* (New York: Bantam, 1975), 201.

14. Andrea Dworkin, *Pornography: Men Possessing Women* (New York: Perigee, 1981).

15. Judith Halberstam, *In a Queer Time and Place: Transgender Bodies, Subcultural Lives* (New York: New York University Press, 2005); Scott Herring, *Another Country: Queer Anti-Urbanism* (New York: New York University Press, 2010).

16. Clare Lyons, "Mapping an Atlantic Sexual Culture: Homoeroticism in Eighteenth-Century Philadelphia," *William & Mary Quarterly* 60, no. 1 (2003): 119–54; Leonard Leff, " 'Come on Home with Me': *42nd Street* and the Gay Male World of the 1930s," *Cinema Journal* 39, no. 1 (1999): 3–22.

17. Martin Meeker, *Contacts Desired: Gay and Lesbian Communications and Community, 1940s to 1970s* (Chicago: University of Chicago Press, 2005), 208–17.

18. Marc Stein, *City of Sisterly and Brotherly Loves: Lesbian and Gay Philadelphia, 1945–1972* (Philadelphia: Temple University Press, 2004), 85.

19. Clayton Howard, "Building a 'Family Friendly' Metropolis: Sexuality, the State, and Postwar Housing Policy," *Journal of Urban History* 39, no. 5 (2013): 933–55; Bryant Simon, "New York Avenue: The Life and Death of Gay Spaces in Atlantic City, New Jersey, 1920–1990," *Journal of Urban History* 28, no. 3 (2002): 300–327.

20. Whitney Strub, "Mondo Rocco: Mapping Gay Los Angeles Sexual Geography in the Late-1960s Films of Pat Rocco," *Radical History Review* 113 (2012): 13–34.

21. On Mizer's travails, see Whitney Strub, "The Clearly Obscene and the Queerly Obscene: Heteronormativity and Obscenity in Cold War Los Angeles," *American Quarterly* 60, no. 2 (2008): 373–98.

22. Carl Wittman, "A Gay Manifesto" (1970), available at http://library.gayhomeland.org and widely online.

23. Jeffrey Escoffier, *Bigger Than Life: The History of Gay Porn Cinema from Beefcake to Hardcore* (Philadelphia: Running Dog Press, 2009).

24. On the editing of the film—and for a remarkable examination of Halsted more broadly—see William Jones, *Halsted Plays Himself* (Los Angeles: Semiotext(e), 2011), 39.

25. This moment also points to a tension that would later mount between antipornography feminists and gay men, as the former concentrated on the textual materials saturating places like Times Square while the latter emphasized the queer possibilities afforded by its unregulated spaces. For the classic articulation of this impasse, see John D'Emilio's 1980 essay "Women Against Pornography: Feminist Frontier or Social Purity Campaign?" in *Making Trouble: Essays on Gay History, Politics, and the University* (New York: Routledge, 1992), 202–15.

26. Escoffier, *Bigger Than Life*, 108. On the commentary track for the 2002 Mercury Releasing DVD of *Bijou*, Poole notes that he did obtain proper permits for the film. This would seem to be an exception rather than a norm, though recent work by April Hall and Ashley West at the *Rialto Report* suggests permits may have been more common than pornography's outlaw reputation would imply. See "*Anna Obsessed* (1978): Anatomy of an Enigma," September 2014, and "*The Double Exposure of Holly* (1976): Murphy's Law in Action," October 2014, both at www.therialtoreport.com, for two well-researched examples of straight porn films whose makers claim to have held proper shooting permits.

27. Kevin Heffernan, "Seen as a Business: Adult Film's Historical Framework and Foundations," in *New Views on Pornography: Sexuality, Politics, and the Law*, ed. Lynn Comella and Shira Tarrant (Santa Barbara: Praeger, 2015), 37–56.

28. Jeffrey Escoffier also notes Arch Brown's *Pier Groups* (1979) and Ian McGraw's *Subway* (1980) in his examination of "urban queer realism," "Sex in the Seventies: Gay Porn Cinema as an Archive for the History of Sexuality," *Journal of the History of Sexuality* (forthcoming).

29. J. Edward Gibbons to Pat Russell, July 26, 1974, Pat Russell Papers, box 606057, file: Nudity, Los Angeles City Archives.

30. John Rechy, *The Sexual Outlaw* (New York: Dell, 1977).

31. Whitney Strub, *Perversion for Profit: The Politics of Pornography and the Rise of the New Right* (New York: Columbia University Press, 2011), 198–212.

32. For one brilliant recounting of these transformations, see Mike Davis, *City of Quartz: Excavating the Future in Los Angeles* (New York: Verso, 1990).

33. Alice O'Connor, "The Privatized City: The Manhattan Institute, the Urban Crisis, and the Conservative Counterrevolution in New York," *Journal of Urban History* 34, no. 2 (2008): 333–53.

34. Christina Hanhardt, *Safe Space: Gay Neighborhood History and the Politics of Violence* (Durham, NC: Duke University Press, 2013).

35. Robert Fitch, *The Assassination of New York* (New York: Verso, 1993).

36. Larry Revene, *Life in a Film Can* (CreateSpace, 2015), 99.

37. Darrick Danta, "Ambiguous Landscapes of the San Pornando Valley," *Yearbook of the Association of Pacific Coast Geographers* 71 (2009): 15–30.

38. Alexander Reichl, *Reconstructing Times Square: Politics and Culture in Urban Development* (Lawrence: University Press of Kansas, 1999); Lynne Sagalyn, *Times Square Roulette: Remaking the City Icon* (Cambridge: MIT Press, 2001).

39. It is worth noting that porn would return to the city again in later iterations of handheld, camcorder-based gonzo and other styles, from Rick Savage's *Streets of New York* series in the 1990s through several twenty-first-century internet series. These developments require their own further historicization. For a start, see Peter Alilunas, *Smutty Little Movies: The Creation and Regulation of Adult Home Video* (Berkeley: University of California Press, 2016); and "Rick Savage: New York's Last Porn Star," *Rialto Report*, March 23, 2014, www.therialtoreport.com.

CHAPTER 2

Re-Sexualizing Scrooge

Gender, Spectatorship, and the Subversion of Genre in Shaun Costello's The Passions of Carol

LAURA HELEN MARKS

THE RICH FIELD OF porn studies has made significant strides since its formal inception in the late 1980s with the publication of film scholar Linda Williams's *Hard Core*. Prior to this, the most notable contribution to the field was Steven Marcus's 1964 *The Other Victorians: A Study of Sexuality and Pornography in Mid-Nineteenth Century England*. Between 1964 and 1989, the majority of scholarly treatments of pornography consisted of radical feminist critiques such as Andrea Dworkin's 1981 *Pornography: Men Possessing Women*. However, the field now known as "porn studies," characterized by balanced interrogation of pornographies in a manner detached from the politically fraught antiporn work of the 1980s, fully established itself in the wake of Williams's influential book. Following this groundbreaking book, several exciting works have emerged on genre-specific topics such as premodern histories,[1] feminist and queer analyses,[2] and class-based consideration of erotic appeal.[3] Yet, even with recent expansion of the field signaled by the inaugural issue of the academic *Porn Studies* journal, there has been little in the way of a recovery of the full textual complexity of 1970s porn. In discussions of the 1970s, "porno chic" is typically the focus, and films such as *Deep Throat* (1972), *Behind the Green Door* (1972), and *The Devil in Miss Jones* (1973) tend to stand in as representative of a body of work that in reality is far more dynamic, complex, and unusual than most critics and audiences allow.

One symptom of such an oversight is a simplification of both the object and the reception of these films. Pornography is designed to provoke sexual arousal, the popular assumption goes, yet its functions and scope are far more complicated than standard definitions allow. Pornographic appeal frequently intersects with disgust and conservatism, while the aims of pornographic filmmakers of the 1970s are closely tied to broader filmic goals in line with the decade's cinematic revolution characterized by such mainstream filmmakers as Martin Scorsese and Francis Ford Coppola.[4] Furthermore, individual texts are rarely approached for analysis in porn studies in the same way as in other fields, an indication of the way society treats porn as a monolithic and disreputable genre worthy of study only in terms of what is representative of the genre as a whole (and thus must be taken on in studies of entire histories or subgenres). The important work of critical attention to specific auteurs and films of the 1970s has thus primarily been undertaken by fans and bloggers who write dedicated and well-researched reviews on their sites or for the Internet Movie Database, as well as on podcasts such as the *Rialto Report* and the *Projection Booth*.[5] The 1970s boasts a rich and diverse catalogue of films by auteurs who consistently produced dynamic, transgressive films that deserve academic attention. One entry in this canon is *The Passions of Carol* (1975), written and directed by one of the decade's most important hardcore auteurs, Shaun Costello.

It is not only porn studies scholars who overlook this film. Citing an episode of the 1980s television show *Moonlighting* as the first adaptation of Charles Dickens's *A Christmas Carol* with "a female consciousness," Paul Davis, author of the preeminent *Lives and Times of Ebenezer Scrooge*, adds in an endnote, "In describing 'Moonlighting' as the first feminist *Carol*, I also dismiss the inevitable pornographic adaptation of the seventies, *The Passions of Carol*."[6] In dismissing *Passions* on account of its genre, Davis disregards an important entry into the canon of *Carol* "culture texts." While Davis evidently recognizes *Passions* as potentially feminist, and certainly inevitable, he resists interrogating either implied claim. Davis is onto something, though. The inevitability of hardcore appropriations of canonical literary works, and the complex gender politics of hardcore film, means that *Passions* is a text worth exploring.

As an adaptation of the *Carol*, *Passions* disrupts and renders explicit desires and sexualities that are only implicit in the original text; as a pornographic film, *Passions* disrupts the spectator's expectations of pornography, and complicates the spectator-image relationship. Moreover, the film disrupts and complicates notions of domesticity and femininity present in the original text, disruptions that are mobilized by hardcore's insistence on social transgression, transgressions that can be quite selective in terms of race, gender, and sexual orientation, as discussed below. These disruptions result in an unsettling and conflicted narrative. Indeed, what is particularly interesting about *Passions* is its central paradox as a pornographic adaptation that stays faithful to the social values of its Victorian source text in a decade purported to be concerned with sexual revolution.[7] *Passions* stays true to its Dickensian roots, perpetuating the Dickensian ideal of domesticated femininity, at the same time as it rebels against this ideal by "resexualizing" the repressed components of the original story. In doing so, *Passions* exposes the displaced sexuality of the original story, present in the abundant families, delicious and tempting foods, and a rampant middle-class consumer culture. The commodification of female sexuality, arguably the milieu of pornographic film, is critiqued and depicted as the downfall of Carol Scrooge. This paradox—of a pornographic film that maintains a Dickensian notion of sexuality—aptly reflects the central contradiction of Victorian culture as it exists in the postmodern cultural imagination: a sexually repressed society that is simultaneously sexually perverse.

Gender Politics and 1970s Hardcore

The 1970s are known for a flourishing female-led antiporn feminist movement, thanks to activist authors such as the aforementioned Andrea Dworkin and her frequent collaborator Catharine MacKinnon, and organizations such as Women Against Pornography, all of whom operated primarily in the late 1970s and 1980s.[8] These groups fought what is characterized as a male-dominated, violent pornography industry that exploited women and funded its films via the mob. However, this picture is overly simplistic. In the 1970s, many women were using their newly earned sexual freedom and a cultural environment of radical creativity to create pornography, and often consume it. Indeed, while a feminist response to pornography is largely associated with the *late* 1970s, there had been feminist opposition, critique, analysis, and creation of pornography occurring far earlier.[9] Moreover, "improving porn rather than banishing it emerged as a frequent feminist goal in the years before 1976."[10] Much of this feminist response was part of a reaction to censorship, which historically targets women and LGBTQ artists and audiences.[11]

In 1968, Betty Dodson had her "first one-woman show of erotic art titled *The Love Picture Exhibition*" in which she showed "beautiful drawings of couples having intercourse and oral sex."[12] At her second show, which focused on "masturbating nudes" and featured a "six-foot drawing of a masturbating woman holding an electric vibrator next to her clitoris—an erect one at that,"[13] reactions were less positive, and the gallery refused to show any more of her work. Dodson would go on to experience censorship in 1971 at the hands of a Connecticut district attorney over Dodson's erotic art published in *Evergreen* magazine. This was the same year Dodson began her bodysex workshops, where she taught women about body acceptance, their genital structures, and how to achieve orgasm.[14] Other feminist trailblazers of the 1970s such as Annie Sprinkle, Candida Royalle, Veronica Hart, Kelly Nichols, Sue Nero, Gloria Leonard, Sharon Mitchell, and Veronica Vera were proud feminists who also performed in and created hardcore pornography. These women, excluding Mitchell, would later form Club 90—a sex-positive feminist support group for women in porn that called for "a revolutionary feminization of the industry" designed to eliminate sexist stereotypes and more authentically portray female pleasure and desire.[15]

Women were consuming pornography too. As demonstrated by Eric Schaefer, adult film theaters offered special rates and accommodations for couples and women.[16] Meanwhile, *Playgirl* (1973–) magazine was selling well. In *Passions*, Carol Scrooge is the editor of *Biva* magazine, a sly reference to the attempt by Bob Guccione (publisher of *Penthouse*) to create a porno magazine for women, the subject of Carolyn Bronstein's essay in this volume. Guccione's magazine was called *Viva* and debuted in 1973, ending its publication run in 1979. As a *Time* magazine article from 1973 reports, Guccione's imagined female reader was "lusty, real, indefatigable, down-to-earth, fetching, bright, sexy, uncompromising."[17] *Viva* was for the modern, liberated, mobile woman. Indeed, in a 1973 *Pittsburgh Post-Gazette* article on the release of *Viva* and magazines like it, journalist Jacki King spends as much time discussing the women's liberation movement, the possibility of female desire for erotica, and "loss of inhibitions among women about sex" as she does about the magazine itself.[18] It is significant then that the female editor of *Biva* in *Passions* is portrayed as shrewd, cold, and uncompromising—a seeming condemnation of the effects of sexual revolution in a film that is part of this very same revolution.

Writer/director Shaun Costello is a pioneering pornographic film-maker who made the bulk of his films in 1970s New York City. Director (as well as writer, editor, and performer) of over one hundred adult films between 1968 and 1983, Costello was king of the "one-day wonder"—cheap and grimy films made in just one day.[19] He also made ambitious, small-scale films such as *Midnight Desires* (1976), *That Lady from Rio* (1975), and *Fiona on Fire* (1978) that offer subversive and often violent sexual content. However, Costello is primarily known as a sig-nificant auteur in the "roughie" subgenre, a type of hardcore film in which rape and other forms of sexual violence constitute the narrative. Costello has made several roughies, but it is *Forced Entry* (1973) and *Water Power* (1977) that are the best known of his films—notorious, in fact—and tend to define his career. *Forced Entry* follows a disturbed Vietnam vet played by Harry Reems (of *Deep Throat* fame) as he roams New York City raping women. The rape scenes are not captured in erotic fashion, and the women do not change their attitudes during the rape to acceptance and enjoyment, as is common in many hardcore films of the 1970s. On the contrary, the rapes are brutal and shown to be torturous for the women, while the mental plight of Reems's charac-ter is conveyed through the splicing of Vietnam War footage into these rape sequences. The film ends with Reems shooting himself in the head after two potential rape victims accept his advances willingly and laugh at him. Meanwhile, *Water Power* is darkly comic, bordering on a tonal parody of *Taxi Driver*,[20] yet arguably more disturbing than *Forced Entry*, depicting the activities of the "enema bandit" played by Jamie Gillis as he too roams New York City, raping women and giving them forced enemas. The enemas are shown in graphic detail, contributing to the film's reputation as sick and shocking.

Neither film is known for its erotic qualities. Indeed, reviewers remark on the fact that Costello does not seem to be inviting sexual arousal in either film, but rather disgust and alienation. Belgian film reviewer Dries Vermuelen notes of *Forced Entry*, "This flick makes for a harrowing experience which must've rattled adult audiences' cages back when this played theatrically. It's hard to imagine anyone get-ting aroused over the unflinchingly depicted violations. . . . Such stark denouncement of the turn-on, crucial to the genre, may either seem like the makers shooting themselves in the foot by turning their backs on the entire raison d'être of pornography or an actual attempt to make viewers think about the correlation between cinematic sex and violence and the inherent danger thereof."[21] To be sure, Costello does not seem to have had eroticism in mind when approaching *Forced Entry*. Inspired to make a film after watching action and horror movies, he began to strategize as to how to make a low-budget porn film that satisfied obscenity law's demand for "socially redeeming value":

> Putting a series of sex scenes together would be relatively easy, even for a novice like me, but justifying those scenes with a story line that would give the film redeeming social value would be tricky. So Herb [Harry Reems] and I began an outline about a deranged Vietnam Vet, who brings his war home with him and goes on a rape and murder spree. There would be rape, so there would be sex, and our hero's war-induced psychosis would legally justify that sex. Because he had raped and murdered, he would have to be sacrificed on the altar of morality, and blow his brains out in the final reel. I now felt that I had an idea for a sex film that could be safely distributed theatrically.[22]

As for *Water Power*, Costello recalls that the film "opened to empty houses wherever it played. Theater owners were scared of it, and audiences didn't know what to make of it, and I was not surprised by either."[23] With all this said, *The Passions of Carol*—a festive, heartwarming fable intended to become an annual XXX Christmas event—is an unusual entry into the Costello filmography.

Significantly, and somewhat ironically considering my argument, Costello chose to use the directorial pseudonym Amanda Barton under the logic that "'this kind of light comedy needs a sensitive touch, a woman's touch. . . . You can use it in the marketing. 'Finally, an Adult film with a woman's point of view.' "[24] Indeed, the film was received by some as classy and woman-friendly. Al Goldstein praised the film's "tasteful sex" (along with long-legged luscious women), while Robert Rimmer (writing some ten years later) noted, "Women will like it, too."[25] Dries Vermuelen also reflected in 2008 that the imaginary female director has the effect of "adding class."[26] This strategy of attributing hardcore films to female directors was something of a trend designed to appeal to audiences as offering an unusual or different perspective, inviting a male voyeuristic interest, and also perhaps in part an effort to appeal to a new female audience. Anthony Spinelli, legendary director of classics such as *SexWorld* (1978), *Easy* (1979), and *Talk Dirty to Me* (1980), directed *Cry for Cindy* (1976) under the pseudonym Wendy Lyons and the infamous *An Act of Confession* (1971) as Sybil Kidd. Bob

Chinn, too, of the John Holmes–starring *Johnny Wadd* series (1971–79) reputedly directed the majority (possibly all) of the films attributed to Gail Palmer, including *The Erotic Adventures of Candy* (1978) and *Prisoner of Paradise* (1980).[27] It is also possible that queer and transgressive sexual content could more comfortably be included in a "straight" hardcore film if it were thought to be directed by a woman. This is a persuasive argument when considering another Costello film attributed to Amanda Barton, *Midnight Desires* (1976), which includes a scene in which the characters offer a feminist analysis of rape fantasies, and a "pegging" scene (in which a woman performs anal sex on a man using a strap-on dildo) that the characters break down as a deflected homosexual fantasy. A brief scene of male-male oral sex is also included in *Erotic Adventures of Candy* (1978), which is attributed to Gail Palmer.

The plot of *Passions* is surprisingly faithful to the original story, even incorporating Dickensian dialogue into its 1970s New York City setting. As Costello explains, "I was going through a Charles Dickens phase, starting a new Dickens book the minute I finished the last."[28] In accordance with the genre's love of "porning" treasured cultural texts, Costello was unfazed by producer concerns regarding "the possibility of a backlash against the sacrilege of desecrating such a well-known story, by turning it into smut."[29] Costello wrote a script "closely following the Dickens book,"[30] focusing on Carol Scrooge (Mary Stuart), president of *Biva* publications, a magazine for women that prints pornographic images of men (fig. 2.1). Carol is depicted as being cold-natured and demanding, sexually and economically exploitative of her employees, and entirely focused on her business. After forcing her employee, Bob Hatchet (Jamie Gillis), to work late on Christmas Eve while his family waits at home, she is visited by three spirits: the Ghosts of Christmas Past, Present, and Yet to Come. The spirits offer her visions, sexual spectacles designed to teach her a lesson about the ill effects of her exploitative and selfish approach to sexuality that result in her grim existence as a Times Square hooker. Gradually understanding the error of her ways, Carol finally repents and understands what the spirit of Christmas is all about: love, charity, and good-naturedness. Costello remembers, "I read *A Christmas Carol* and I tried to get as close as I could to the original book and it actually is pretty close—I mean it's a bizarre pornographic version of course, but if you really listen to the dialogue, it's very close to the original Dickens story."[31] Indeed, it is. The plot structure, too, is nearly identical. And yet, simultaneous to this dedication to accuracy,

FIGURE 2.1. Cold, materialistic *Biva* editor Carol Scrooge chides Bob Hatchet for providing "limp dicks" for the magazine. From *The Passions of Carol* (Shaun Costello, 1975).

Costello weaves in imagery and sex acts that subvert the ideologies of gendered domesticity, femininity, and motherhood conveyed by Dickens in the *Carol.*

The Passions of Carol critiques the industrialization and mass consumption of sex for profit, and also subverts and perverts what society (and Dickens, let us not forget) has taught us are natural and beloved aspects of femininity: domesticity, family, childbirth, and innocence. Indeed, the Dickensian "womanly ideal" rests on redemption through domesticity.[32] In this way, Costello, intentionally or not, puts forth a conflicting and unsettling vision: a profit-driven pornographic film ostensibly designed to sexually arouse through the depiction of hardcore sexual acts, that condemns its protagonist for producing the very same thing, and in turn challenges the replication of artificial, socially constructed, and gendered sexualities through the very sex scenes that are purported to disseminate these sexist messages. The result? A funny, disturbing, and at times unerotic romp.

Passions plays with notions of spectatorship and voyeurism in ways that build on narrative elements present in Dickens's novel. Audrey

Jaffe argues that *A Christmas Carol* "associat[es] spectatorial and consumer desire with images of an idealized self," pointing to an existing "emphasis on visuality, whether literary or cinematic, [that] promotes spectatorship as a dominant cultural activity."[33] *Passions* positions Carol as both spectator and spectacle: she is both sexual object/subject for the audience, and sexual object/subject for herself, placing her in a dual position. She is both a spectator and spectacle; subject and object. The same can be said for Scrooge, who both watches himself, and is "watched" by the reader. The "inevitability" of a hardcore *Carol* is perhaps related to the sense of spectatorship and voyeuristic participation incited by Dickens's novel, an invitation that lends well to the physically participatory nature of hard core.[34] Jaffe posits, "If, as I argue, Scrooge's sympathetic self emerges from his relation to representation, such is also the implied effect of the reader's relation to the scenes of *A Christmas Carol*, given the text's explicit analogy between Scrooge's activity and the reader's."[35] Jaffe adds, "Spectacle depends on a distinction between vision and participation, a distance that produces desire in a spectator."[36] In other words, the delicate balance between involvement in and distance from the visions offered up by Dickens generates desire and pleasure. This desire is arguably the primary voyeuristic purpose of pornography, yet with pornographic film the relationship between spectator and image is complicated due to a lessening of the "distance" Jaffe refers to. Pornography involves a physical reaction and participation that other genres do not share to the same degree. The "apparent lack of proper esthetic distance," as Williams puts it, renders pornography too visceral, too close, and subsequently has "too simplistically been allied with a purely sadistic fantasy structure."[37] While Dickens is working within a Victorian literary framework that obscures explicit sexual activity, *Passions* is able to render the "spectacle" Dickensian in its faithfulness in establishing desire through spectatorship, but subversive and disruptive through its resexualization of the original text. Sex is the driving force behind not only the plot of *Passions* but also behind the desire and participation of the viewer. In perhaps unsettling ways, the spectatorship and desire of the original text becomes a subversive sexualized voyeurism.

Porning the Victorians

The primary goal of pornography, as Laura Kipnis explains, is transgression of social norms: "Like your boorish cousin, its greatest pleasure is to locate each and every one of society's taboos, prohibitions, and proprieties and systematically transgress them, one by one."[38] Furthermore, pornography is a form of "political theater. . . . [it] is a medium for confronting its audiences with exactly those contents that are exiled from sanctioned speech, from mainstream culture and political discourse. And that encompasses more than sex."[39] Indeed, pornography has a strong tradition of mimicry and "speaking back" to the legitimate mainstream, dating back to its earliest recorded origins[40] and continuing in various forms through to the rash of porn parodies of the twenty-first century.[41] Following the sexual revolution and several small obscenity law cases in the late 1960s and early 1970s, the first hardcore feature films were made and released to theaters.[42] *Mona* (1970), *Boys in the Sand* (1971), and *Deep Throat* (1972) signaled the beginning of the porno chic era, and filmmakers quickly turned to mainstream and canonical works for inspiration.[43] Williams notes of the first hardcore feature films of the 1970s, "Hard-core narratives went about imitating other Hollywood genres with a vengeance, inflecting well-known titles and genres with an X-rated difference,"[44] while Cindy Patton argues that the porn videos of the 1980s and 1990s "represent sex" in ways that Hollywood refuses to: "Clearly, their contingent relation to Hollywood's sexual elisions provides an erotic and humorous critique of the mass media's role in invoking but never delivering the sex."[45] While some films owed a debt in name only, such as *Boys in the Sand* (a riff on the stage play *Boys in the Band,* though the film itself bore no resemblance), many films directly parodied Hollywood film and television. *Gums* (1976) was based on *Jaws* (1975); *Lipps & McCain* (1978), on *Butch Cassidy and the Sundance Kid* (1969); *SexWorld* (1978), on *West-World* (1973) and *Futureworld* (1976); *Hard Soap, Hard Soap* (1977), on the television show *Mary Hartman, Mary Hartman* (1976–77); and even *The Opening of Misty Beethoven* (1976), on *My Fair Lady* (1964), which itself was based on George Bernard Shaw's *Pygmalion.*

Pornographers of the 1970s were not only interested in contemporary rip-offs, however. They also turned to material of the nineteenth century for inspiration. Part of this interest is due to the fact that nineteenth-century literature was (and is) in the public domain, and thus filmmakers could lift entire chunks of prose from famous novels for pornographic purposes without legal complications. There are other, more complex reasons for this interest, however. Constituting what Marie-Luise Kohlke calls "neo-Victorian sexsation," the Victorian is used by postmodern audiences in part to "extract politically incorrect pleasure from what has become inadmissible or ethically *unimaginable* as a focus of desire in our own time. We thus enjoy neo-Victorian fiction at least in part to feel debased or outraged, to revel in degradation, *reading for defilement.* By projecting illicit and unmentionable desires onto the past, we conveniently reassert our own supposedly enlightened stance towards sexuality and social progress."[46]

It makes sense, then, that the 1970s—a time of sexual revolution and a new frontier for artists in Hollywood and porn alike—would draw on the Victorian era as a way of casting their progressive sexual politics in even greater relief.[47] In addition, the Victorians boast a booming pornography trade, as well as canonical novels such as Bram Stoker's *Dracula* and Robert Louis Stevenson's *Strange Case of Jekyll and Hyde* that are infused with sexual energy. In this way, the Victorians could serve dual purposes all while being painted as hypocrites. This is evidenced in the 1970s adaptations of Victorian pornography (*Autobiography of a Flea* [1976], and *The Naughty Victorians* [1975]) alongside adaptations of classic novels (*Dracula Sucks* [1979], *The Erotic Dr. Jekyll* [1976], *Alice: A XXX Musical* [1976], *The American Adventures of Surelick Holmes* [1975], *Portrait of Dorian Gay* [1974], and the *Dorian Gray* adaptation *Take Off* [1978]).[48]

While there are minor, implicit references to race in *The Naughty Victorians, Take Off,* and *Alice: A XXX Musical,* only recently has neo-Victorian fiction, pornographic or otherwise, strayed from canonical constructions of whiteness and directly interrogated colonialism and race in the nineteenth century.[49] While postcolonial critique is certainly a core aspect of the neo-Victorian project, efforts remain relatively minimal, and postmodern commentary on the Victorian tends to maintain a landscape devoid of people of color, highlighting hypocrisies and missing "truths" through a project devoted to issues of gender and sexuality—as if this can be separated from issues of race. At the same time that *Passions* plays with the gender and class expectations of Dickensian ideology, it balks at interrogating the race and class politics of Dickensian England that are also key to constructing this femininity. In addition, *Passions* adheres to a heteronormative framework, in keeping with both Dickensian fiction and heterosexual pornographic representation, though it offers the requisite girl-girl couplings expected of "straight" hardcore pornography. The 1970s New York City of *Passions* features no people of color, which is perhaps reflective of the state of the porn industry at that time[50] but is also representative of a broader failure to approach sexual revolution and women's liberation through an intersectional lens. *Passions* is significant for being set in 1970s New York City, as well as for updating Scrooge's profession to that of pornographic magazine editor, and his sex to that of female—gestures that signify a response to a new era in terms of both capitalism and gender politics, while also obscuring sexual and racial diversity.

A Christmas Carol operates within a discourse of desire, but obscures the explicit and sensual sexualities of the domestic household. Desire and sexuality exist in displaced forms, manifested in voyeurism, consumption, and the fetishization of Christmas rituals that serve to reinforce the promotion of middle-class ideals of domesticity, the private sphere, and proper female sexuality. Christmas went through a transformative experience in the nineteenth century, moving away from antecedent pagan rituals to become "the major celebration of the family in Victorian culture."[51] Through Victorian discourses, not least of which were Dickensian literary discourses, Catherine Waters argues, Christmas became "arguably the most successful vehicle and expression of middle-class cultural hegemony."[52] The Victorian, some might say Dickensian, Christmas had significant ramifications for the role of the woman in the private sphere. The shift away from a pagan community celebration toward a private, family celebration created an exaggerated domestic role for the middle-class white Victorian woman at Christmas-time. The newly domesticated Christmas rituals, such as decorations, private family dinners, and Christmas trees, "generated the need for female industry within the home, requiring planning, purchasing, arranging and cleaning. It thus contributed to that formation of the private sphere—of the domain devoted to the reproduction of everyday life—so central to the rise of the middle classes."[53] In *Passions*, however, Carol Scrooge is not the domestic wife of the private sphere, and is cast in a negative light as a result. She is the new woman of the 1970s—industrious outside of the home, in stark contrast to Mrs. Hatchet (Kim Pope) who awaits her working husband at home. Furthermore, Carol's business—pornographic magazines for women—represents an era in which female sexual autonomy was a major aspect of the feminist movement. On a narrative level, then, *Passions* replicates the Dickensian ideal of the domestic housewife. On a subnarrative level, however—in the form of sexual acts and imagery—*Passions* expresses ideologies far more radical and subversive to the Dickensian ideal, perverting ideals of motherhood, domesticity, and virtue.

The following analysis focuses primarily on three sex scenes from

Passions: first, Carol, Billy, and Barbie of the Past; second, the Hatchets' sex scene of the Present; and third, the "Times Square Hooker" sex scene of the Yet to Come. All three scenes are demonstrative of the paradoxical nature of the film in the sense that the film ruptures ideals of femininity and resexualizes the original Dickensian scenes in often disturbing ways, while at the same time encouraging and maintaining a decidedly Dickensian perspective of gender and sexuality that the original *Carol* conveys. The adoption of such conflicting influences highlights the complexity of postmodern pornographic use of the Victorian, as well as shows that a particular Victorianism, imagined as a distant past, in fact continued to animate erotic imaginaries of the 1970s and served to emphasize an imagined radical present. In the following analyses, I interrogate content from both novel and book in an effort to detail the complex navigations Costello conducts in adapting book to film. Many pornographic adaptations draw from what Paul Davis calls "culture texts"—texts that have become unmoored from the actual substance of the original book, circulating as ideas and images that can be borrowed or referenced without reading the original novel. *Passions,* however, is an adaptation of the novel in a traditional sense, faithfully reproducing the dialogue, substance, and tone of Dickens's novel. For this reason, I approach *Passions* with attention to both novel and film in an effort to untangle the conflicted nature of Costello's efforts.

Christmas Present

The Hatchets' sex scene is a re-visioning of what for many readers, not to mention Dickens himself, constituted the heart of the Carol. Over the course of a century, fans—particularly those of the Victorian period—have regarded the Cratchit Christmas dinner as the centerpiece of the *Carol,*[54] embodying the domestic family ideal. Positioned in Dickens's text among a plethora of consumable visual images, the Cratchit Christmas dinner serves as the climax of a steadily building onslaught of mouth-watering temptations for not only Scrooge and those he watches but for the reader also. Just as the Ghost of Christmas Present sat upon a throne of food himself,[55] the contents of the market that he presents to Scrooge appear to flirtatiously offer themselves up to the passersby, as well as to the reader: "There were ruddy, brown-faced, broad-girthed Spanish Onions, shining in the fatness of their growth like Spanish Friars, and winking from their shelves in wanton slyness at the girls as they went by, and glanced demurely at the hung-up mistletoe. . . . there were Norfolk Biffins, squab and swarthy, setting off the yellow of the oranges and lemons, and, in the great compactness of their juicy persons, urgently entreating and beseeching to be carried home in paper bags and eaten after dinner."[56] The desirability of the food on display is only compounded by the personification Dickens employs in their description. The agency of the edibles operates in much the same way as a pornographic image, "entreating and beseeching" to be consumed for the pleasure of the eater/spectator. Operating as part of the relationship between spectator and spectacle, these scenes are rendered all the more appealing in their distance and unattainability, an erotic distance that operates in tandem with their urgent entreaties.

The Cratchits are a happy family of abundant children that are "everywhere at once,"[57] and very much a family unit: "Mrs. Cratchit made the gravy . . . hissing hot; Master Peter mashed the potatoes with incredible vigour; Miss Belinda sweetened up the apple-sauce; Martha dusted the hot plates."[58] Rather than being expressed through sex and sexual desire, the sexuality of the Cratchit family is displaced onto the family Christmas dinner, lovingly prepared and offered up by Mrs. Cratchit: "At last the dishes were set on, and grace was said. It was succeeded by a breathless pause, as Mrs. Cratchit, looking slowly all along the carving-knife, prepared to plunge it in the breast; but when she did, and when the long expected gush of stuffing issued forth, one murmur of delight arose all round the board, and even Tiny Tim, excited by the two young Cratchits, beat on the table with the handle of his knife, and feebly cried Hurrah!"[59] The desire, anticipation, and satisfaction (not to mention violence) presented in these scenes arouse the desire of not only the Cratchits but also the reader.

Passions combines the imagery of consumption in these scenes of the Cratchit Christmas and adapts them into one sex scene between Bob and Barbara Hatchet designed to replicate the idealism of the traditional middle-class reproductive family. Within the hardcore project of nonreproductive, nonmonogamous sex, and in a genre that typically avoids acknowledging the existence of minors, the scene is riddled with complications. Situated as a private moment in domestic space, the Hatchets' lovemaking is presented as an idealistic spectacle to the cold and exploitative Carol Scrooge. It is significant that Tiny Kim, the stand-in for Tiny Tim, while absent is figuratively present as her crutches rest against the table behind her parents while they make love under the Christmas tree—an inclusion that Vermeulen describes as "heartbreaking."[60] The presence of children completes the Dickensian vision of a

FIGURE 2.2. The Hatchets kiss and make love by the Christmas tree, with visible signs of marital domesticity. From *The Passions of Carol* (Shaun Costello, 1975).

loving family, and yet in a hardcore feature film the crutches are a perverse detail. The Hatchets verbalize their love for each other, and the traditional lesson Carol is to learn is that "they're happy because they love each other and it's Christmas!" While the metaphorical presence of Tiny Kim renders the scene subversive in terms of pornographic conventions, another act of disruption is occurring through the foregrounding of marriage as the true symbol of love and "Christmas spirit." As she grasps her husband's penis, the camera lingers on Mrs. Hatchet's wedding ring, a feature rarely seen in pornography, a genre that typically resists the traditional Christian conventions of marriage, love, and sexuality in favor of the sexual liberation from social norms. In combining an affirmation of marital values with an explicit scene of sexual intercourse beneath the family Christmas tree, the scene simultaneously subverts and reaffirms the traditional Dickensian values of privacy, monogamy, and domesticity (fig. 2.2). The centrality of Tiny Kim's crutches completes the family Christmas at the same time as they unsettle the pornographic scene.

The centrality of childhood in this scene corroborates not only the importance of childhood to the Dickensian Christmas and Victorian domestic space but also the connections between childhood, family, and sexuality. James R. Kincaid highlights the ways in which "childhood" has become intimately connected with sexuality in the face of societal efforts to suppress these connections: "By insisting so loudly on the innocence, purity, and asexuality of the child, we have created a subversive echo: experience, corruption, eroticism."[61] Hence, through a system of binaries, the symbolic figure of the child has become an integral part of our understanding of adulthood and sexuality. *Passions* takes Dickens's allusions and carries them to their graphic conclusions, creating what is arguably the most disturbing scene in the film: that of Christmas Past. However, while the scene disrupts and resexualizes the *Carol's* implicit sexualities, it also, much like the Hatchet scene, reinforces and maintains Dickensian notions of female sexuality.

Christmas Past

In Dickens's original *Carol*, the Ghost of Christmas Past shows Scrooge visions of his childhood, followed by a vision of a former sweetheart, Belle, at the moment of her giving up on their love. Belle tells Scrooge, "I have seen your nobler aspirations fall off one by one, until the master-passion, Gain, engrosses you."[62] Scrooge's former sexual passion for Belle has been usurped by monetary passion. Soon after this scene, observing a now-aged Belle enjoying time with her husband and children, Scrooge observes the happy family and vaguely acknowledges his voluntary abandonment of a sexual relationship: "And now Scrooge looked on more attentively than ever, when the master of the house, having his daughter leaning fondly on him, sat down with her and her mother at his own fireside; and when he thought that such another creature, quite as graceful and as full of promise, might have called him father, and been a spring-time in the haggard winter of his life, his sight grew very dim indeed."[63] Watching Belle's beautiful daughter by another man, who potentially could have been Scrooge, Dickens subtly makes the connection between sexual activity and the happy, vibrant, domestic family. Significantly, it is Scrooge's acknowledgment of the lack of this energetic, sexual vibrancy of youth in his life that disrupts his gaze and causes "his sight [to grow] very dim indeed."[64]

Scrooge is not the only admiring observer. Also present as desirous spectator is the narrator, whose voice intrudes on the predominantly anonymous narrative. In an ambiguous passage, childhood and adulthood are figured together as the narrator watches the same beautiful daughter that might have been Scrooge's, remarking,

> As to measuring her waist in sport, as they did, bold young brood, I couldn't have done it. . . . And yet I should have dearly liked, I own, to have touched her lips; to have questioned her, that she might have opened them; to have looked upon the lashes of her downcast eyes, and never raised a blush; to have let loose waves of hair, an inch of which would be a keepsake beyond price: in short, I should have liked, I do confess, to have had the lightest licence of a child, and yet to have been man enough to know its value.[65]

Not only does this passage point to the way in which desire is created in looking and not having, but it also suggests that sexual desire is linked to childhood abandon. The juxtaposition of these childhood and adult desires are adapted in *Passions* in the Christmas Past scene, fusing childish desires and sorrows with adult passions. While Scrooge's sexual passions are usurped by monetary capital, Carol's passion is for sex *as* monetary capital. Building off a successful feminist movement, sexual liberation, and relaxation of obscenity law, the pornographic landscape of the 1970s trades in nonprocreative sex as a commodity. Carol trades in sex also, and yet her greed and exploitation are presented as destructive to others and ultimately herself. At the same time, the imagery used in the Christmas Past sequence is radical in its perversion of sexual and gender norms.

The Ghost of Christmas Past presents Carol with a vision of herself as a child, playing with Billy and Barbie, two childhood friends. The scene is played out by adult actors dressed in children's clothing, and in an oversized room, making the actors appear smaller than they are. When Carol enters, she is carrying a large, long-haired doll that Barbie wants to play with. Carol pulls the doll away, telling Barbie that she can play with the doll, but "first you have to do something for me," adding, "everything has its price." The price for playing with the doll, Carol explains, is kissing her "all over," and subsequently the three of them engaging in various sexual acts. The doll is immediately figured as a commodity, as is sex through the monetary value Carol ascribes to it. Consequently, the doll and sexuality are positioned as items of exchange and commerce.

While Ebenezer Scrooge's exploitation of his workers consists of low wages and a lack of human feeling for the poor, Carol Scrooge literally screws her workers out of a fair wage. As her maid comments to her boyfriend, "She's got lots of playboys, and I bet they don't get paid much anyway. Just what she calls 'fringe benefits.'" Similarly, in this childhood scene of the Past, Carol exploits her friends, bullying and blackmailing them into giving in to her sexual demands. Significantly, it is Billy—the film's version of Belle—who is most prominent as the victim of sexual exploitation, a gendering that is uncommon and regarded with skepticism by a culture that persists in viewing women as always passive victims and men as always active not-victims. Positioning Carol in this way reinforces the corruptive nature of commercial sexuality, especially when controlled by a woman.

Carol, in the opening moments of the scene, is centered between Billy and Barbie, facing the camera as she snaps, "I want to see what you two look like. Take off your clothes." With language rooted firmly in childish sexual exploration, but tinged with adult exploitation, the viewer is reminded of the commodities at stake through Carol's bare chest and the positioning of the doll, legs spread, seated directly behind Carol's head in the center of the shot. This visual connection between sexuality, childhood, and commerce is made even more explicit as the camera cuts to a lingering shot of the doll, and Carol states in childlike language, "Okay, Barbie, I want you to kneel down and make Billy's pee-pee hard. Put it in your mouth, and be very nice" (fig. 2.3).

As the scene progresses, and *Carol of the Bells* begins to play, the imagery becomes more complex. Quick cuts back and forth between a cross-stitch rendering of Raggedy Ann giving Raggedy Andy oral sex, and Carol performing the same act on Billy, reemphasize a sexualizing of childhood and a nostalgia for childhood, creating another layering much like Dickens's layering of the real and the representation, of Scrooge and the reader. The scene takes a darker turn as the film cuts to a shot of the doll transformed: lying on her back, eyes closed and hair in disarray, the camera pans down to her dress sleeve, where it is revealed that her arm is missing. This imagery is mirrored by the following shot of Carol, who is also lying on her back, eyes closed, as the camera pans down to where the doll's arm is being used by Barbie to vaginally penetrate Carol, fist outward. This surprising image—an image in a chain of images that are collectively unsettling—situates Carol visually as a victim of her own sexuality as well as the ruiner, not the guardian, of childhood innocence. The doll, a lifeless embod-

FIGURE 2.3. Young Carol paralleled with a child's doll in flashback. From *The Passions of Carol* (Shaun Costello, 1975).

iment of sexuality, childhood, and commodity, has been "ruined" or "soiled," and, by implication, so have Carol and her victims. Furthermore, the viewer, as sexual participant / voyeur, is engaging in a visual "raping" of childhood and nostalgia. These uncomfortable juxtapositions are complicated further through the visual connection between the sexual insertion of the doll's arm and the moment of childbirth. When the arm is pushed all the way in, so that all that can be seen is the hand, it is suggestive of a child being born, and another doubling occurs: the arm is entering Carol, while visually it appears to be exiting her. This, in turn, renders sexually explicit what is only suggested in the original text. The comfort of mentally separating childhood/childbirth and sexuality, despite the intimate relationship between the two, is shattered. So too is the notion of a private, healthy, nurturing, and procreative feminine sexuality represented by Mrs. Hatchet in the previous sequence.

Yet, paradoxically, the Dickensian obfuscation of female desire in the *Carol* is fully in operation during this unsettling scene. The textual narrative and imagery suggest that Carol's sexual independence results in exploitation, ultimately to the detriment of herself, but also by extension to childhood, family, and society. Carol's exploitation of her friends in childhood is shown as a lesson, a component in a lifestyle characterized by sexual independence and pleasure seeking. In other words, Carol's sexual autonomy, which in turn becomes Carol's commercial product, is shown to damage others, and result in the raping of innocence.

The scene operates as a narrative tool, rather than solely as a sexual stimulant. Peter Lehman notes that "the hard-core feature's diegesis has little or nothing to do with its display of sexual attractions."[66] To be fair to the genre of hard core, Lehman's claim does not apply across the board. Still, in *Passions,* narrative and sex merge together often in contradictory and jarring ways. The Christmas Past scene in particular is disturbing in its ambiguous meditations on childhood sexuality, rendering it a failure in a stereotypically pornographic sense.[67] Indeed, the director himself has commented of his film, "It was big, it was noisy, it was colorful, it was funny, but there was one thing it wasn't; it wasn't sexy."[68] However, as a resexualization of the original Dickens text, this scene, and the film in general, succeeds. Spectatorial pleasure, then, is disrupted. The "ecstatic excesses"[69] experienced by the spectator aurally are disturbed in the scene of Christmas Past, as the "inarticulate cries of pleasure in porn"[70] are absent, covered up by the incessant, violent punctuation of *Carol of the Bells.* Visually, the "almost involuntary mimicry of the emotion or sensation of the body on the screen"[71] is also ruptured, as the multiplicity of unsettling images presented in quick edits makes mimicry and identification difficult and disturbing in itself.

Christmas Yet to Come

Completing this trilogy of disruptive scenes is the "Times Square hooker" sequence of Christmas Yet to Come. Mirroring the original *Carol*'s visions of the future in their intention to shock Scrooge into finally learning his lesson, *Passions* offers a similarly disquieting conclusion, though with a gendered component that reemphasizes the dangers of commodity sex culture controlled by women, and compounds Carol's resolve to change. Shown scenes of herself as a cheap Times Square hooker, Carol is horrified by what her actions might lead her to become. The hooker scene of *Passions* replaces the scenes of Scrooge's death, the plundering of his home and deathbed, and Tiny Tim's death, equating these gendered conclusions in whorephobic fashion. While *Passions'* vision of the future seems to offer a resexualized and subversive alternative to Dickens's dark and somber visions, it is through the sexualization of this scene that *Passions* both disrupts the *Carol* and remains faithful to the gendered notions of sexual morality present in Dickens's original text, a sexual morality that persists to this day.[72]

The image of the third spirit is significant to discussions of the gaze and visuality, as this spirit is the only visitor whose face is hidden. In the *Carol,* while the spirit is intimidating in its black-cloaked, silent appearance, it is the ghost's privileged position as holder of the gaze and Scrooge's vulnerability in not being able to return the gaze that disturb Scrooge the most: "It thrilled him with a vague uncertain horror, to know that behind the dusky shroud, there were ghostly eyes intently fixed upon him, whilst he, though he stretched his own to the utmost, could see nothing but a spectral hand and one great heap of black."[73] The spirit's unreturnable gaze positions Scrooge as the feminized object, yet here again is a doubling, as Scrooge is able to remain privileged subject as he watches the representations of himself that the spirit presents him with.

Quite removed from the bustling, festive streets of Past and Present, Scrooge is taken on a tour of "an obscure part of town, where Scrooge had never penetrated before, although he recognised its situation, and its bad repute."[74] Immediately figured as a privileged "penetrator" of these dark, winding streets, the descriptions that follow are established within a class-based framework. These streets of desire and consumption are a far cry from the desire and consumption of the other working-class characters, such as the Cratchits and market workers: "The ways were foul and narrow; the shops and houses wretched; the people half-naked, drunken, slipshod, ugly. Alleys and archways, like so many cesspools, disgorged their offences of smell, and dirt, and life, upon the straggling streets; and the whole quarter reeked with crime, with filth, and misery."[75] The "life" exhibited by these streets is not the domesticated, family-orientated life of the poor Cratchit family; these streets represent wild, untamed, exposed, and filthy consumption of a sort not compatible with Dickens's ideal private family space. These streets do house a form of privacy, but the privacy of these rotten districts is a different kind from that which Dickens promulgates: "Secrets that few would like to scrutinize were bred and hidden in mountains of unseemly rags, masses of corrupted fat, and sepulchres of bones."[76] In opposition to the sexuality of the domestic family ideal, these decayed private spaces are presented as embodying human desires untouched by the managing hand of middle-class, domestic guidance, and most certainly home to the dreaded prostitute.[77]

Similarly, Scrooge's gravestone represents the moral decay that will be the result of his refusal to participate in the unselfish pleasures of domesticity and family: "Walled in by houses; overrun by grass and weeds, the growth of vegetation's death, not life; choked up with too much burying; fat with repleted appetite."[78] Scrooge's body lies in overfed, overconsuming soil—fat with, yet stifled by, the mass of corpses stuffed into the earth. Like the soiled streets he traversed to get there, the graveyard is representative of the wrong kind of life, the wrong kind of consumption, a consumption that has strayed too far from the containment of the domestic family ideal. It is fitting, then, that a critical component of Scrooge's rehabilitation is the narrator's promise that, having learned his lesson, he went on to be "a second father" to Tiny Tim.[79] Fulfillment of the prescribed paternal family role, then, is one of the guarantees that Scrooge's life will not lead to such rotten spaces as the ones described above.

Passions takes the implicit sexuality of these scenes and adapts them into a single scene that exposes the "secrets that few would like to scrutinize." In doing so, *Passions* appears to be subversive in its voicing of such private sexual deviancy that, through its presumed intention to arouse, stands in direct opposition to the privacy of Dickens's domestic ideal. However, *Passions* remains faithful to the original text's intention to teach its protagonist a lesson, and so the sex scene is designed to repulse. Just as Scrooge is confused by the apparently irrelevant visions the spirit shows him, so Carol dismisses the vision shown to her as "just a cheap hooker picking up some creep" (fig. 2.4). Gazing down at the hooker and her trick, Carol remains unaware that this hooker is Carol herself until a light shines on the hooker's face, showing a future Carol, aged, caked in gaudy makeup, and grotesque. Carol pleads, "My God! Spirit, tell me it's not true! Please, it just can't be true!"

Carol's repeated cries of horror are intercut with the sex scene, which is unscored, dimly lit, and clinical. Carol of the future soaps the trick's penis; the sex acts are done in a perfunctory manner; and Carol's pleasure and encouragement are clearly fake as she gasps lines such as "Come on daddy, give it to mommy" while also complaining, "You sure take a long time." The scene repeatedly cuts back to Carol the horrified onlooker, reemphasizing her position as both sex-

FIGURE 2.4. Carol turns tricks in the Times Square of Christmas Yet to Come. From *The Passions of Carol* (Shaun Costello, 1975).

ual object and privileged holder of the gaze. This cutting back and forth between horrific spectacle and horrified spectator creates a disruptive rhythm similar to that of the scene of Christmas Past. Yet the scene is further complex in its positioning of hooker and trick: Carol the hooker is active and dominating, snapping as they enter the hotel room, "Take 'em off! Let mama see what you look like." In turn, the trick nervously tells her, "Look, uh, I don't want you to think I do things like this. I got a family." This relationship, too, is reminiscent of that of Billy and Carol from the Past, positioning Carol's "raping" of childhood innocence alongside her turning tricks as a hooker. Both scenes depict sexual exploitation of the male character juxtaposed with the sexual ruination of the female as if these positions were interrelated. The point appears to be that female sexual autonomy, especially in the context of commodity culture, has dire implications for men. Additionally, this final sex scene suggests a degree of recompense for Carol's sexual independence in both her profession as president of *Biva* and in her private sexual life that is outside of the monogamous, domestic space of the Hatchets. In this respect, it is significant that the sex scene ends with Carol telling the trick, "You know, honey, you're a rotten fuck." As the camera pans back in silence, Carol and the trick sit staring at each other, his flaccid penis still in her hand. The room feels desolate and cold, reflecting Carol's future composed of a lack of sexual fulfillment rooted in the commercial pollution of sex.

The scene does not simply teach Carol a lesson in curbing her sexual independence; it maintains a Dickensian ideal of private, monogamous, domestic, and reproductive sexuality. Just as Scrooge adapts to a life of paternity, so Carol must adapt to a life in which she submits to patriarchal notions of institutionalized, domestic female sexuality. In this respect, it is important that the last sequence is the only one in which the participants use a condom, a practice that is presented as clinical and devoid of intimacy. This further promotes the Dickensian notion that sexuality is healthy when it is a component of a child-bearing, domestic space. Outside of these spaces, just as in the *Carol*'s fetid London streets, this sexuality and the life it exists among and produces is rotten.

THE JARRING AND CONTRADICTORY NATURE of this unusual film stems from Costello's attempt to merge a Dickensian moral tale with a genre that, for all its contradictory and politically incorrect gender politics, ultimately does rest on ideals (or promises) of sexual independence and freedom from social mores. *The Passions of Carol* creates a series of doublings as it uses the visuality of the original *Carol* to reconcile desires implicitly present in Dickens's text. Davis regards the "essential desire of [*A Christmas Carol*]" to be "to transcend the contradiction of innocence and experience."[80] This desire is taken to its explicit conclusion in *Passions*, drawing together several suggested but sexually stifled elements in Dickens's *Carol*, and in Dickensian and Victorian literature in general: spectator and image; childhood and adulthood; innocence and sexuality. What is significant is that it is the film's pornographic sequences, and the spectator's expectations of and participation in this genre, that enable this resexualization to occur, while at the same time rupturing the spectator-image relationship. It is thus an interesting, and in practice disturbing, paradox that *Passions* is able to remain faithful not only to the marginalized sexualities of the *Carol* but also the transgressive instinct of the hard core genre, as well as the Dickensian promotion of the gendered domestic ideal of sexuality.

Rather unexpectedly, *Passions* has much to say about Dickens, *A Christmas Carol*, and Victorian gender politics, possibly at the cost of its own eroticism. However, "eroticism" is a complicated term to untangle. Indeed, the conflicts and contradictions in *Passions,* and the dissonant pleasures these conflicts produce, reflect a diversity and perversity present in 1970s hard core that is frequently overlooked in favor of a monolithic anti or pro-porn position that attempts to homogenize this body of film into a more workable mass of generic texts. In fact, while *Passions* and other neo-Victorian hardcore films rhetorically distance themselves from the regressive past, much of the complexities of supposedly liberated 1970s hard core are characteristic of hardcore fictions of the nineteenth century. The erotics of pornography rely to a great extent on puritanical sexual politics that create boundaries to cross, a crossing that generates a salacious and thrilling sense of social transgression. The resexualization and perversion of the supposedly hypocritical and repressed past in the 1970s imaginary is brought into stark relief as a tantalizing fable through *Passions,* a fable that, in a broader sense, is arguably deployed in all postmodern pornography.

NOTES

1. See Walter Kendrick, *The Secret Museum: Pornography in Modern Culture* (Berkeley: University of California Press, 1987); Lisa Z. Sigel, *Governing Pleasures: Pornography and Social Change in England, 1815–1914* (New Brunswick, NJ: Rutgers University Press, 2002); Julie Peakman, *Mighty Lewd Books: The Development of Pornography in Eighteenth-Century England* (London: Palgrave, 2003); and Lynn Hunt, ed., *The Invention of Pornography, 1500–1800: Obscenity and the Origins of Modernity* (New York: Zone, 1996).

2. See Linda Williams, *Hard Core: Power, Pleasure, and the "Frenzy of the Visible"* (Berkeley: University of California Press, 1999); and Thomas Waugh, *Hard to Imagine: Gay Male Eroticism in Photography and Film from Their Beginnings to Stonewall* (New York: Columbia University Press, 1996).

3. See Laura Kipnis, *Bound and Gagged: Pornography and the Politics of Fantasy in America* (Durham, NC: Duke University Press, 1999); and Constance Penley, "Crackers and Whackers: The White Trashing of Porn," in *Pornography: Film and Culture,* ed. Peter Lehman (New Brunswick, NJ: Rutgers University Press, 2006), 99–117.

4. See Peter Biskind, *Easy Riders, Raging Bulls: How the Sex-Drugs-and-Rock 'n' Roll Generation Saved Hollywood* (New York: Touchstone, 1998); and Jon Lewis, *Hollywood v. Hard Core: How the Struggle over Censorship Saved the Modern Film Industry* (New York: New York University Press, 2000).

5. As a scholar of pornography, I am thankful for the thorough and dedicated work of Dries Vermeulen on imdb.com, where he writes informed articles about individual films simply for the purposes of education and appreciation, as well as the writings of the blogs *The Gore-Gore Girl: XXX through a Feminist Lens, Mondo*

Heather, Moon in the Gutter, Cinema Head Cheese, Cinesploitation, The Rialto Report, and *House of Self-Indulgence.*

6. Paul Davis, *The Lives and Times of Ebenezer Scrooge* (New Haven: Yale University Press, 1990), 233. Davis's phrasing is interesting in that it suggests that pornography has some intrinsic relationship with feminism. Whether he perceives this relationship to be a positive or negative one remains ambiguous, as Davis does not elaborate.

7. Linda Williams observes that *"non-*sadomasochistic pornography has historically been one of the few types of popular film that has not punished women for actively pursuing their sexual pleasure." See Williams, "Film Bodies: Gender, Genre, and Excess," in *Feminist Film Theory: A Classical Reader,* ed. Sue Thornham (New York: New York University Press, 1999), 274. In addition, Marty Klein speaks to the anti-establishment conventions of pornography when he describes the "truth that porn tells us": "Social norms regarding age and beauty, religious norms about godly and ungodly sex, personal fears about acceptance, cultural myths about the human body—all of these are ignorable; none are inevitable. Each of us can triumph over the ways social institutions attempt to control our sexual experience and expression." See Klein, "Pornography: What Men See When They Watch," in *Pornography: Film and Culture,* ed. Peter Lehman (New Brunswick, NJ: Rutgers University Press, 2006), 253.

8. Dworkin was a member of the early antiporn group that ultimately gave rise to Women Against Pornography in 1979, and published her most famous antiporn tract, *Pornography: Men Possessing Women,* in 1981. However, her antiporn activism dates back to the mid-1970s. In 1976 she was involved in the protests against the film *Snuff.*

9. Whitney Strub, *Perversion for Profit: The Politics of Pornography and the Rise of the New Right* (New York: Columbia University Press, 2011), 217.

10. Ibid., 222.

11. Nadine Strossen, *Defending Pornography: Free Speech, Sex, and the Fight for Women's Rights* (New York: New York University Press, 2000).

12. Betty Dodson, "Porn Wars," in *The Feminist Porn Book: The Politics of Producing Pleasure,* ed. Tristan Taormino et al. (New York: Feminist Press, 2013), 23–24.

13. Ibid., 24.

14. Dodson continues to run her bodysex workshops today, together with Carlin Ross. Bodysex workshops are designed to "teach women about sex through the practice of masturbation. It was sexual consciousness-raising at its best." See Dodson, "Porn Wars," 25.

15. Anne G. Sabo, *After Pornified: How Women Are Changing Pornography and Why It Really Matters* (London: Zero Books, 2012), 21.

16. Eric Schaefer, "Gauging a Revolution: 16mm Film and the Rise of the Pornographic Feature," in *Porn Studies,* ed. Linda Williams (Durham, NC: Duke University Press, 2004), 378–87. Linda Williams also notes her attendance at adult theaters during the 1970s in *Screening Sex,* recalling, "In this era, before very many feminists had decided that pornography was a primary cause of objectification of women, my friends and I dared ourselves to watch and thus, by implication, to watch ourselves watch." See Linda Williams, *Screening Sex* (Durham, NC: Duke University Press, 2008), 125.

17. "Viva *Viva?,*" *Time,* September 24, 1973, 64.

18. Jacki King, "Women's Sex Mags: Not Just Hit or Ms. Propositions," *Pittsburgh Post-Gazette,* November 6, 1973, available at http://news.google.com.

19. In comparison to these one-day wonders, *Passions* is quite ambitious. Still, Costello attempted to make it on a shoestring budget and in just four days. Costello recalls his pitch to the producer: "I told them that my plan was to write a screenplay, closely following the Dickens book, shoot the entire picture on a sound stage which would require building cartoon-like sets, complete principal photography in four days, and bring the entire project in for fourteen thousand dollars, which was only two thousand dollars more than it cost to make any of the three box office bonanzas I had produced for them that year." The production actually ended up taking fourteen days. The excess time and spending meant that the film was not ready for distribution until the spring of 1975. This, together with the fact that Costello chose to screen it in nonporn theaters with the goal of a crossover hit, resulted in a box office bomb. See Costello, "Christmas on Eighth Avenue," *Shaun Costello's Blog,* http://shauncostello.com.

20. Costello regards *Waterpower* as "the funniest movie I ever made." See Costello, "Waterpower," *Shaun Costello's Blog,* http://shauncostello.com.

21. Dries Vermeulen, "Porno Shock," Internet Movie Database, January 21, 2006, www.imdb.com/title/tt0124596/reviews.

22. Shaun Costello, *Wild about Harry: A Friend Who Knew Him Well Remembers Harry Reems* (ebook, 2014), 48–49, www.amazon.com.

23. Costello, "Waterpower."

24. Costello, "Christmas on Eighth Avenue."

25. Robert Rimmer, *The X-Rated Videotape Guide I, Revised and Updated* (New York: Prometheus, 1993), 398. Al Goldstein quote from the 1975 theatrical poster for *The Passions of Carol,* www.emovieposter.com.

26. Dries Vermeulen, "Have Yourself a Merry Little Christmas . . . and Mind the Sheets!" Internet Movie Database, April 18, 2008, www.imdb.com/title/tt0127090/reviews.

27. Chinn told the *Rialto Report,* "Actually, Gail Palmer had nothing to do with directing *Prisoner of Paradise,* but since she was a front woman for Caribbean Films and would be making personal appearances and promoting the film, I was more than happy to share the directing credit with her." Evidently, the use of Palmer's name served a promotional purpose. Palmer was a *Playboy* centerfold, and the idea that she directed hardcore features may have offered some form of erotic appeal to audiences. See Ashley West, Jill Nelson, and Bob Chinn, "Bob Chinn: West Coast Pioneer," *Rialto Report* (podcast), August 4, 2013, www.therialtoreport.com.

28. Costello, "Christmas on Eighth Avenue."

29. Ibid.

30. Ibid.

31. Joe Rubin and Shaun Costello, "Audio Commentary," *The Passions of Carol,* Platinum Elite ed., directed by Shaun Costello (1974; New Jersey: Distribpix, 2013), DVD.

32. Michael Slater, *Dickens and Women* (London: J. M. Dent & Sons, 1983), 339.

33. Audrey Jaffe, "Spectacular Sympathy: Visuality and Ideology in Dickens's *A Christmas Carol,*" *PMLA* 109, no. 2 (1994): 254.

34. Dickens is rather unpopular as a source for pornography, perhaps due to the intricate nature of Dickensian plot and characterization. Three pornographic film adaptations of Dickens's texts are in existence at this time, two of which, significantly, are adaptations of *A Christmas Carol.* The third, released in November of 2007, is an adaptation of *Oliver Twist.* It is additionally significant that the *Carol* adaptations are both "straight," while the *Oliver Twist* adaptation is gay. This de-

tail seems to speak not only to the adaptability of the *Carol* but also to the heter-onormative functions within Dickens's original text, as well as the rituals surrounding it that I have outlined above.

35. Jaffe, "Spectacular Sympathy," 255.

36. Ibid., 256.

37. Williams, "Film Bodies," 273.

38. Kipnis, *Bound and Gagged*, 164.

39. Ibid.

40. Lynn Hunt, "Introduction: Obscenity and the Origins of Modernity, 1500–1800," in Hunt, *Invention of Pornography*, 9–45.

41. Pornography's tradition of parody, adaptation, and revision has been recognized and interrogated by scholars such as Kipnis and Penley. In addition, a symposium titled "Erotic Adaptations: A One Day Symposium" was held in January 2011 at De Montford University in the United Kingdom, suggesting that more in-depth and text-specific work is being done on this subject.

42. See Marjorie Heins, "Sex and the Law: A Tale of Shifting Boundaries," in Lehman, *Pornography*, 168–88; and Robin Bougie's introduction to *Graphic Thrills: American XXX Movie Posters, 1970 to 1985* (Surrey, UK: Fab Press, 2014), 4–16.

43. Mainstream culture was a source of parody for pornography prior to the 1970s, with stag films and erotic animation emulating famous characters and actresses such as Marilyn Monroe, and pornographic literature of the eighteenth and nineteenth century borrowing plots from popular mainstream novels. The British publisher Edmund Curll specialized in such literary parodies, such as a porn version of Laurence Sterne's *A Sentimental Journey through France and Italy* (1768) titled *La Souriciere. The Mousetrap. A Facetious and Sentimental Excursion through part of Austrian Flanders and France* (1794) by "Timothy Touchit." See Patrick J. Kearney, *A History of Erotic Literature* (Bath, UK: Parragon, 1982), 53–57.

44. Williams, *Hard Core*, 120.

45. Cindy Patton, *Fatal Advice: How Safe Sex Education Went Wrong* (Durham, NC: Duke University Press, 1996), 132.

46. Marie-Luise Kohlke, "The Neo-Victorian Sexsation: Literary Excursions into the Nineteenth-Century Erotic," in *Probing the Problematics: Sex and Sexuality*, ed. Marie-Luise Kohlke and Luisa Orza (Oxford: Inter-Disciplinary Press, 2008), 346.

47. Laura Helen Marks, "Behind Closed Doors: Pornographic Uses of the Victorian," *Sexualities* 17, no. 1–2 (2014): 159–75.

48. Literature from other eras has also been borrowed for pornographic purposes, though no era has proved more popular than the nineteenth century, which persists as a popular inspiration today. For example, Pauline Reage's 1954 novel *The Story of O* has been adapted several times, the most notable version of which is Gerard Damiano's *The Story of Joanna* (1975). In addition, Chaucer's *Canterbury Tales* were made into *Ribald Tales of Canterbury* (1985), while the plays of William Shakespeare have been parodied dozens of times, as documented in Richard Burt's *Unspeakable ShaXXXpeares: Queer Theory and American Kiddie Culture* (New York: St. Martin's, 1998). Voltaire's *Candide* has also proved popular with pornographers, serving as inspiration for the *Candy* (1978–1988) and *Pretty Peaches* (1978–1989) series. These films emerged soon after Terry Southern's 1970s erotic update *Candy*, a novel that was not in the public domain. Aside from the use of the name Candy, the novel was not explicitly invoked. A similar strategy was employed with the recent *Dracula XXX* (2012). The styling of the film invokes Francis Ford Coppola's 1992 film adaptation, yet the DVD box includes a disclaimer that demonstrates the

degree to which copyright affects what pornography does and does not exploit: "This is a parody movie based on the classic Bram Stoker book. . . . This movie is not sponsored, endorsed or approved of in any way by Columbia Pictures Industries, Inc., Francis Ford Coppola, or any other person or entity associated or affiliated with them."

49. For literary examples, see Barbara Chase-Riboud's *Hottentot Venus: A Novel* (Random House, 2003), and Belinda Starling's *The Journal of Dora Damage* (London: Bloomsbury, 2006).

50. See Mireille Miller-Young, *A Taste For Brown Sugar: Black Women in Pornography* (Durham, NC: Duke University Press, 2014), for a thorough history of black female performers in adult film, and Celine Parreñas Shimizu's *The Hypersexuality of Race: Performing Asian/American Women on Screen and Scene* (Durham, NC: Duke University Press, 2007) for a history of Asian and Asian American women in adult film. 1970s porn, much like many other media forms, featured comparatively few women of color.

51. Catherine Waters, *Dickens and the Politics of the Family* (Cambridge: Cambridge University Press, 1997), 62.

52. Ibid., 63.

53. Ibid., 68.

54. Paul Davis notes that at public readings of the *Carol*, Dickens focused on the Cratchit scenes, "which he left largely uncut." The high point for audiences, Davis explains through several first-hand accounts, was the Cratchit Christmas dinner (57). Catherine Waters concurs, "The Cratchit Christmas dinner is the most celebrated of Dickens's domestic set-pieces, and contains all the essential ingredients for a happy Dickensian home." See Davis, *Ebenezer Scrooge*, 76.

55. Charles Dickens, *A Christmas Carol*, in *Christmas Books* (London: Oxford University Press, 1954), 39.

56. Ibid., 41.

57. Ibid., 44.

58. Ibid., 45.

59. Ibid., 45–46.

60. Vermeulen, "Merry Little Christmas."

61. James R. Kinkaid, *Child-Loving: The Erotic Child and Victorian Culture* (New York: Routledge, 1992), 4.

62. Dickens, *Christmas Carol*, 34.

63. Ibid., 36–37.

64. Ibid., 37.

65. Ibid., 36.

66. Peter Lehman, "Revelations about Pornography," in Lehman, *Pornography*, 97.

67. It is important to note that, contrary to popular wisdom, pornography is not solely designed to arouse pleasant sexual feelings. Many pornographic films of this era featured bizarre, unerotic, or even downright disgusting sex scenes. Much has been written about the overlap between desire and disgust, and pornography is a privileged site of this comingling. See Kipnis, "Desire and Disgust," in *Bound and Gagged*. Furthermore, pornographers have consistently made hardcore films about the porn industry, presenting complex visions that reveal the conflicted feelings writers and directors have about the films they create. See, for example, *Skin Flicks* (dir. Gerard Damiano, 1978), *Raw Talent* (dir. Larry Revene, 1984), *Fade to Black* (dir. Paul Thomas, 2001), *Pretty Girl* (dir. David Stanley, 2003), and *Throat: A Cautionary Tale* (dir. Paul Thomas, 2008).

LAURA HELEN MARKS

68. "I Wrote and Directed This Movie," Internet Movie Database, February 28, 2006, www.imdb.com/title/tto127090/reviews.

69. Williams, "Film Bodies," 270.

70. Ibid.

71. Ibid.

72. Whorephobic and antiporn sentiments have increased in the last few years especially, alongside an increasingly vibrant sex worker rights movement. An irony of *Passions,* as I have outlined here, is that at its heart it is a whorephobic, antiporn porn film.

73. Dickens, *Christmas Carol,* 58.

74. Ibid., 61.

75. Ibid.

76. Ibid.

77. Judith R. Walkowitz, *City of Dreadful Delight: Narratives of Sexual Danger in Late-Victorian London* (Chicago: Chicago University Press, 1992).

78. Dickens, *Christmas Carol,* 69.

79. Ibid., 76.

80. Davis, *Ebenezer Scrooge,* 209.

CHAPTER 3

Desiring Desiree

JENNIFER C. NASH

> *Memory's false as anything, spliced in the wrong parts,*
> *queerly jumping. But better than forgetting.*
>
> —Elizabeth Spires

Being Undone, or Introductions

WHEN I BEGAN WRITING my first book, *The Black Body in Ecstasy: Reading Race, Reading Pornography*, I made an early decision about the scope of my argument. Though I was regularly asked about the performers whose bodies populated the pornographic screens that I theorized—who they were, the conditions of their labor, and how much they were paid—I always emphasized that my interest was in the kinds of racialized representations their bodies made possible and pleasurable, not in the intricacies of their biographies.

The year that my book was published, I was drawn again to one of the films I had written about at length: *SexWorld* (1978). Why, after so many years of screening this film, was I still captivated by it? Some of the appeal came from its elaborate narrative—a pornographic spoof on Michael Crichton's *Westworld* (1973)—and its unrelenting obsession with racial fantasies. But there was something else about the film that captivated me: Desiree West. West was the film's star, the black female actress who played the role of Jill, and her performance made visible the messy erotics of racial hyperbole. Yet after so many years of writing about *SexWorld*, and about West's performance in the film, I realized I knew little about her career, one that spanned the genre's Golden Age. I also realized that there was no scholarly work that attended to the totality of her career, or to her importance as hardcore's first black female star. This piece, then, began as an attempt to archive and analyze West's long and understudied pornographic career, to place *SexWorld* in the context not only of the genre's history but in the context of West's career.

In the course of researching this article, something else happened: I began to correspond with West.

When I first told West about this article—a scholarly attempt to archive her work—she expressed concern that academics' investment in her work was a kind of exploitation. How was it, she asked me, that her story was being told and that she had not been invited to participate in its telling? A few days later a provocation arrives via e-mail: "Who do I talk to?" West tells me that she wants to be able to talk about what she "really thought and was feeling at the time." This is what I have always wanted, I realize. I want to ask her to remember. I want her to definitively settle the questions that remain after many months of trying to construct an archive of her work: How did she come to participate in *SexWorld*? How did she understand the film's messy narratives? What was the trajectory of her career? And why did she stop performing?

But when we talk a few days later, and I ask her about *SexWorld,* she says simply, "I never saw it." I quickly discover that the film's compli-cated racialized plot is unfamiliar to her, that she never saw Johnnie Keyes—the Golden Age's celebrated black male star—perform the role of what Linda Williams terms the "African savage."[1] Indeed, West seems to have forgotten that he was in the film until I describe his absurd costume, his erect black penis hanging out of a white leotard, his face painted with "African" makeup, a bone necklace around his neck. This is how memory works, of course. If I hadn't willed Keyes from her memory's recesses, he would never have been part of how she recalled the film and its meanings. Quickly, I realize that I am telling her a story I assumed she would be telling me.

Memory's false as anything. A line from an Elizabeth Spires poem that I haven't read for many years comes to me when I talk to West. I began writing this chapter searching for the truth of something. Indeed, this chapter emerged from an archival impulse to create something com-prehensive, and I assumed West would hold a kind of definitive truth. It turns out memory is entirely imperfect, perhaps no more "reliable" than the fan archives I encountered online. What West tells me about the film is that she showed up to cater the event and then ended up starring in the film—a detail I would never have discovered if I hadn't talked to her—but it takes her a minute to remember the director's name (she calls him Sam Weston, though he also used the name Anthony Spinelli). In discovering what West *doesn't* remember—the names of films or their story lines—or what she *couldn't* even know—actors were rarely privy to full scripts—I also learn that the films that have preoccupied me, what I have always called "West's work," simply are not that important to how West narrates her life.

But better than forgetting. What this chapter is, then, is a story of me combing through multiple archives, using West's voice as a guide, and trying to heed her question: How is this story being told without her? Or, to ask it another way, what is obscured by West's absence from scholarly conversation? Here, I do not mean to privilege biography over theorizing representation; instead, I am interested in how the absence of attention to how West was represented both on-screen and in the archive has produced significant gaps in "porn studies" scholarship. This chapter, then, is my attempt to weave together my readings of West's films (many of which she never saw), her story, a fan archive, and an internet archive, to construct something that does justice to a career in what is now termed the "adult entertainment industry." It is also marked by the recognition that I can never master this archive. West performed in pornography at a time when it simply was not archived consistently or comprehensively. As she tells me, she performed in myriad films whose names she never knew (or perhaps forgot), and she rarely, if ever, knew what the film's story would be. Indeed, her genuine surprise now is that there is a West archive, that fans continue to circulate information and rumors about her, and that so much of her work is shared by fans who use message boards as locations of trading information, misinformation, and images.

There is something else, though, that I have learned in the process of writing this chapter. In *Precarious Life,* Judith Butler reminds us, "Let's face it. We're undone by each other. And if we're not, we're missing something. . . . One does not always stay intact. It may be that one wants to, or does, but it may also be that despite one's best efforts, one is undone, in the face of the other, by the touch, by the scent, by the feel, by the prospect of the touch, by the memory of the feel."[2]

I am undone by her.

It is not that corresponding with West changed my article's argument, or forced me to reconceptualize the archive. It is that I feel bound to her in a way I never did before, bound by the intimacy of words typed on a screen and sent, by the way she has generously offered me what she can remember, in all of its messiness, never attempting to collate or organize it for me. I am undone by the question she asks me at the end of our conversation: "How old are you anyway? You sound *so young.*" I could be her daughter, she could be my mother, and this realization touches me in some ineffable way. We are not friends, and despite having seen her again and again in the midst of a series of practices that many of us would consider exceedingly intimate, I do not know her, but we are strangers in the midst of an intimate conversation.

And perhaps she is undone by me.

Imagine it: you are sitting in your office when you receive an e-mail from an unknown woman who claims to be a professor at a university far from where you are sitting. She tells you that she has written a book about pornography, and that it includes a chapter on a film you starred in, a film you never actually saw. Perhaps this film is something you try not to remember, perhaps it is something you are conflicted about, perhaps it is something you have simply forgotten about in the midst of a life spent doing both extraordinary and ordinary things. The book arrives wrapped in the promise of academic credentials and institutional legitimacy. And perhaps what is most striking are the pictures, the pictures of your young body naked. Your young face. A hairstyle you haven't worn in thirty years. What would it be like to receive this unanticipated, and perhaps even uninvited, visit from an earlier self?

Golden Pleasures

During the 1970s—pornography's Golden Age—the genre was reinvented. In place of the "primitive,"[3] anonymously produced, short black-and-white pornographic films that marked moving-image pornography's early days,[4] the so-called stag era, the Golden Age ushered in an era of elaborately plotted, narrative-driven feature-length films that consciously effaced the boundary between the pornographic and the mainstream in an effort to escape the label "obscenity."[5] Films such as *Deep Throat* (1972),[6] *Behind the Green Door* (1972), and *Debbie Does Dallas* (1978) attracted audiences of men and women who, according to Linda Williams, were viewing pornography as a way to stake a claim to "sexual citizenship" at a time when pornography was emphatically mainstream.[7]

If the Golden Age was the era when pornography became mainstream, it was also the moment when the genre turned its attention toward representing a more diverse array of bodies in pleasure. After the relative absence of black bodies from the pornographic screen during the stag era, the Golden Age saw pornographers turn their attention toward representing both black men and black women—though rarely together—in pleasure.[8] In some ways, pornography's investment in representing black bodies in pleasure, particularly in interracial narratives, was not a surprise. The Golden Age began only a few years after Hollywood tamely brought interracial desire on-screen with *One Potato, Two Potato* (1964)[9] and *Guess Who's Coming to Dinner* (1967), and coincided with blaxploitation's obsessive investment in representing certain kinds of interracial sex, namely, between black men and white women.[10] Yet in many ways, the Golden Age's investment in interracialism was a rupture with cinematic representations of interracial intimacy; during the Golden Age, the pornographic screen included myriad representations of black women and white men having sex. During this epoch, there was *one* black actress on whose body Golden Age pornographers perfected their investment in a new form of interracialism: Desiree West. In other words, the Golden Age's newfound investment in representing black female / white male interracial sex was made possible because of West, the era's sole black female star.[11]

Despite West's vast body of work—films including *SexWorld* (1978), *Expectations* (1977), *All Night Long* (1975), *Teenage Madam* (1977), *Coming Attractions* (1976), *Most Valuable Slut* (1973), *Meter Mades* (1974), *Ceremony: The Ritual of Love* (1976), and *Vista Valley PTA* (1981)—scholars have largely ignored her. This scholarly silence surrounding West has contributed to a narrative in which actress Jeannie Pepper is described as hardcore pornography's first black female star despite the fact that her career began only in the early 1980s,[12] and to a body of scholarship that focuses on the era's other stars, including Marilyn Chambers, Johnnie Keyes, Vanessa del Rio, and Linda Lovelace, but ignores the place of black women in Golden Age meaning making and visual politics. This scholarly inattention to West's work reinscribes her relegation to "supporting" roles (and, in fact, wholly obscures the labor—corporeal and representational—of women of color who have struggled to reach star status in an industry fundamentally shaped by race).[13] Reading pornographic texts *for* supporting characters like West—characters who were often significant to pornographic meaning making in an era that was preoccupied with narrative, yet were removed from film credits—is instructive for learning about the production and circulation of racialized desires and pleasures on the pornographic screen. "I'm Linda Lovelace," West sarcastically informs John Holmes after he lists what he has to offer ("rather pleasant smile, nice big blue eyes, fourteen-inch cock") in *Tapestry of Passion* (1976), aligning herself with the iconic porn star discussed by Nancy Semin Lingo in the next chapter. Yet racial difference was impossible to avoid in the film's discursive economy: "And with a bitching tan, too," Holmes responds.

If this chapter is, in part, a project of recovery, it is also invested in understanding the representational logics that were produced *on* West's body. In other words, I argue that the racialized pornographic narratives that have become familiar were practiced on West's body during the Golden Age, that her body was a kind of laboratory in which strategies of racialized-sexualized pornographic representations were perfected. In making this claim, my contention is *not* that the ways that West was represented is identical to how black female pornographic protagonists were represented in later eras. I recognize that representational tropes are mobilized in historically and technologically specific ways, and that pornography is an endlessly malleable genre whose meaning-making strategies and narrative preoccupations shift.[14] Instead, I am invested in understanding how during the Golden Age, for the first time, pornography systematically produced for its spectators—staged for its fans—a desire *for black women*, so that "desiring Desiree" was necessarily a racialized project. I seek to interrogate and archive the visual and narrative strategies deployed to produce and circulate that desire.

Archiving Desiree

For "porn studies" scholars, the archive can be a fraught space, especially for scholars who work on the Golden Age, the Silver Age, and the contemporary moment in which the archive often consists of evershifting websites where fans post pictures, video stills, and clips.[15] This popular archive, though, is often speculative, marked by conjectures about actors. For example, David Jennings insists that "Buxom Desiree West" was a "Black Panther porn star,"[16] and numerous fan websites describe West either as "a combination of black and Asian"[17] or as possessing "vaguely Asian undertones."[18] These conjectures— West as Black Panther and West as part Asian—circulate as truths without an interrogation into why West (or Golden Age spectators) might have produced mythologies of her radical racial politics or her racial exoticism.[19]

If fans produce one West archive, pornographic production companies offer another. Alpha Blue Archives has released *Double D Soul Sister: A Desiree West Collection* (2004), and the nearly two-hour DVD is an attempt to collect and circulate West's work. Yet this compilation collects clips from various films featuring West—rather than offering the viewer access to the full movies themselves—resulting in a collection of decontextualized scenes that make understanding the historical and representational moment in which West was represented nearly impossible. The clips are introduced without indicating which film they are from, and they are presented in a seemingly random order. (Indeed, in this chapter when I reference films from *Double D Soul Sister* that I have not been able to identify, I refer to them as *Unnamed*). My own interest in archiving West, then, is a response to these more haphazardly constructed archives. I seek to collect information about West to help construct a scholarly archive of an understudied and trailblazing pornographic performer, and to develop a more complete understanding of the trajectory of her career over the course of the Golden Age, a career shaped by technological shifts and pornographers' conscious productions of racialized desires and pleasures.

In 1973, Desiree West (posing under the name Pat Lee) was featured in *Players Magazine*.[20] *Players* was a popular black men's lifestyle magazine, "a cultural digest for the modern, heterosexual, or, as the cover states 'progressive' black American male instructing him on not just sex with his black female partner, but situating him in a larger dialogue on current events, sports, politics, literature, arts, and music."[21] It was also a sex magazine that offered "a type of alternative to *Playboy* magazine—a forum in which to focus solely on the black female body."[22] In the *Players* spread, West is rendered as exotic and domestic—strange and familiar—simultaneously. In one image, West wears an Afro wig and a lacy bolero jacket that is open and frames her breasts (fig 3.1). Her head is lowered coyly, and she flirtatiously holds a long peacock feather, which seems both an act of modesty and an act of revelation, as the feather calls attention to her breasts. She sits on a richly textured quilt, next to a small stuffed animal. Here, West is represented both as a shy child—the stuffed animal and the downward gaze all signify a childlike timidity—and as an exotic specimen whose household space is filled with sensual curiosities, including lushly textured fabrics and stuffed animals. This pairing of the domestic and the exotic is mirrored in another image from the *Players* spread in which West is kneeling on yet another richly colored exotic bedspread; behind her are accoutrements of exotica—tropical plants, pillows in lushly colored cases, butterflies, shells, rocks. West is at once in a setting that is deeply familiar—the house—but a familiar setting rendered mysterious and unfamiliar.

If these images are preoccupied with representing black female sexuality as both unusual and familiar, they also present black women's bodies and longings as comical. In yet another image, West lies on her bed with her legs spread, petting a tabby cat whose eyes are closed in pleasure. The cat, then, becomes the object of sexual attention, as he is stretched along West's naked body. Moreover, the pornographic connection between the pussycat and West's own "pussy" lend the photograph a kind of comic charge, and yet again, West is both the gentle and innocent child playing with her cat and the exotic woman whose spread legs undo the image's investment in innocence.

From her spread in *Players* came a nearly decade-long career in hardcore films. In the early 1970s, West appeared in a number of low-budget, poorly shot, thinly narrativized films that looked more primitive than most feature-length Golden Age films. In films such as *Most Valuable Slut, Meter Mades,* and *Coming Attractions,* West's name is absent from the film's credits, and she plays the role of a supporting character. Indeed, West's presence on-screen enables the film to represent certain kinds of interracial desire, but to establish that desire as a secondary part of the larger pornographic narrative. In *Meter Mades,* for example, West and two white women are San Francisco meter maids. After a long day giving out parking tickets, they walk into the Line Up Bar to have cocktails. As the three women chat, discussing how they were "really out to get people," the black male bartender flirts with West. Within minutes, the three women are having sex with three men in the bar; interestingly, though the bartender is black, he is paired not with West but with one of the white women, and West has sex with a white man. The logic of interracialism, then, insists that West and the bartender *not* be paired to heighten the eroticism—and perhaps also the taboo—of the sexual scene. Though West is instrumental to the film's depiction of interracialism as a particular kind of pleasurable sex, she is also very clearly a "supporting" character, one who has few lines and whose labor goes uncredited.

Similarly, in *Coming Attractions,* a film that chronicles the adventures of a white heterosexual couple as they embark on a cross-country road trip, West plays another uncredited role that enables the film to represent the erotics of interracialism. When the couple arrives in Las Vegas, they decide to spend an evening gambling. At the end of the night, they return to their hotel room exhausted and intoxicated. The

FIGURE 3.1. Desiree West, performing as "Pat Lee," poses in *Players Magazine* 1973.

man is awakened by a loud knock on their door, and West—playing the role of a room service waitress—enters to deliver an expensive bottle of champagne. The man realizes his girlfriend is still asleep, and he invites West to enjoy the champagne with him. She responds that the hotel does not permit staff to drink with guests; though he insists, she quickly leaves his room. The white man then closes his eyes and begins to imagine West. What unfolds is an interracial oral fantasy scene: as the man's lips are tightly secured around the champagne bottle, West's lips are wrapped around his penis. West's body, then, enables a kind of interracial sex scene sufficiently transgressive to be represented as fantasy, as outside of the film's other "realistic" sexual scenes.

Anthony Spinelli's *SexWorld* marked a dramatic shift in how West was represented; no longer a secondary character who provided the film with a surprising interracial "sexual number," West's performance constituted the film's narrative spine. The film, a pornographic spoof on Michael Crichton's science-fiction-meets-Western *Westworld*, depicted a sex resort where visitors would have their secret fantasies unleashed by the resort's trained staff and expert use of technology. As proof of the resort's power to arrange anything, the film centers on a sexual encounter between West, who plays the role of Jill, a SexWorld guest, and Roger, a white man who insistently reveals his discomfort with black women, and with the idea of interracial sex. Roger's sexual encounter with Jill is, as is the pornographic tradition, transformative, and as Jill insists on her body's racial and sexual distinctiveness and merit, Roger moves from a position of racial disgust to a place of interracial desire. When the film ends, Roger is shown begging the resort's owners for one last evening at the SexWorld mansion and, ostensibly, one last evening with Jill. What is significant about West's role in *SexWorld* is that, unlike her other roles, the interracial encounter here is central to the film's narrative, and to how the film represents SexWorld's capacity to unleash hidden desires, secret longings, and untapped wishes. In other words, West's body becomes fundamental to showcasing the white male protagonist's transformation, and to making visible how two very differently situated SexWorld guests might both enjoy the resort and its promise to unleash secret or repressed desires.

If *SexWorld* marked the apex of West's career, curiously, a few years later, she vanished from what would later be termed "the adult entertainment industry." In 1997, more than fifteen years after her last film credit, West was inducted into the X-Rated Critics Organization Hall of Fame, but she did not attend the ceremony. The fan archive has been preoccupied with West's disappearance, with fans circulating theories about West's disappearance. On one website, a fan reports, "I heard that VV PTA [*Vista Valley PTA*] effectively ended Desiree's porn career. Apparently she got into a violent row with Juliet Anderson on set and as a result [director Anthony] Spinelli used his connections to ensure she never appeared again in a feature movie. This story came from the movie's cinematographer, a guy who filmed many 'Golden Age' movies, usually under the name 'Jon Fontana.' "[23] West narrates her departure from pornography differently: the decision was motivated by technological shifts. Starring in Golden Age films offered a kind of privacy, as those films were screened only by audiences who actively sought out opportunities to view pornographic films. But with the emergence of video technology, pornography suddenly seemed easily accessible and ubiquitous. For West, it no longer seemed possible to have a life performing that could be cornered off from the rest of her existence. It was these concerns about privacy, she tells me, that spurred her decision to stop performing (fig. 3.2).

In many ways, the "Desiree archive" indexes larger shifts in the Golden Age's representation of black female bodies and its investment in interracial intimacies. In the early years of the epoch, interracialism constituted one of many "sexual numbers" that a film contained, or it was a way of articulating a film's climax, a strategy for representing the most transgressive—and potentially most pleasurable—kinds of sex. Nowhere is this more evident than in the era's classic *Behind*

FIGURE 3.2. Desiree West in *SexWorld* (Anthony Spinelli, 1978).

the Green Door, which concludes with its white female protagonist, actress (and Ivory Soap model) Marilyn Chambers, having sex with black actor Johnnie Keyes, whose face is painted with tribal makeup and who wears a bone necklace. It is the sight of the white female body penetrated by a representation of the "African savage" that constitutes the film's narrative and sexual climax, deploying interracialism generally, as well as a vision of interracialism in which pure white femininity encounters savage black male sexuality, as a kind of titillating conclusion. Yet a few years later, interracialism was no longer a secondary pornographic narrative or a climatic sexual act; indeed, thanks to West, interracialism became central to film's narratives, with Golden Age films both producing and marketing circuits of racialized desire.

Representing Black Desire(e)

If this chapter has endeavored to construct a West archive, one attentive to her critical role in Golden Age films and to the Golden Age's shifting racial politics, I also argue that understanding West's work is essential to understanding the strategies hardcore developed and perfected for representing black female flesh. Indeed, during this era, West's body became complicated representational terrain, a space where racial fictions were inhabited, performed, played with, disrupted, and even exploded. In tracing the representational strategies that pornographers deployed to represent West's body and pleasures, my contention is not that these strategies were adopted wholesale and simply repeated in later pornographic films. Instead, I am interested in how West's body was the location in which pornographers came to imagine and represent both black women's desires *and* desires for black women. In other words, "desiring Desiree" came to be a representational logic that would inform how black women were represented on the pornographic screen during the Golden Age and in the decades that followed. In this section, I trace the development and circulation of three representational motifs that were produced on and through West's flesh: race as a site of pleasure, performance, and play; a preoccupation with black women's labor; and the production of the pornographic predecessor of the "interracial buddy film."

If West's films allowed pornographers to construct a visual and narrative vocabulary for desiring black female flesh, it also made visible the ways that black female bodies could perform racial hyperbole and excessively stage racial fictions for their own pleasures. In considering these pleasures, I am invested both in erotic pleasures in blackness, as I argue *SexWorld* makes visible, and in social and political pleasures in blackness, as I argue *Vista Valley PTA* makes explicit. In other words, West's performances make clear how a genre that mobilizes racial fictions—constantly producing and circulating fantasies of black women's sexual difference—also produced space for black women to name the workings of racialization, to relish in racialization, and to engage in inflicting racialization on white male protagonists (and possibly white male spectators).

The notion of race as a terrain of play is at its most visible in *SexWorld*. As proof of SexWorld's status as a sex resort that can "arrange" anything, the film's narrative centers on Roger, the resort's white male guest. The SexWorld staff determines that Roger needs to be challenged and orchestrate an interracial sexual encounter between Roger and Jill, an encounter that ultimately transforms Roger.

What unfolds between Roger and Jill is a sexual encounter marked by their verbal, racialized sparring. When Jill first enters Roger's room, he presumes she is the maid and brusquely asks, "What do you want? Are you here to clean up the room? Well, if you're gonna clean up, clean up!" to which she replies, "Clean your wet cock when *we'se* done, sir." As the encounter unfolds, Roger insists that he detests black women, and mobilizes racial stereotypes—the idea of black female subservience, black female alterity, and black women's inherent difference—to articulate his disgust. Rather than refute these stereotypes, Jill inhabits them, hyperbolically performing black female sexual subservience and excess in full grammatical incorrectness (as in "Clean your wet cock when *we'se* done, sir"), *and* hurling her own stereotypes back at Roger (at one point she urges him to "prove his spigot ain't no bigot").[24] This kind of racialized sexual banter becomes a terrain of sexual play for them both, with each inhabiting stereotype and deploying it, mobilizing it and relishing it, even as their distinctively raced bodies make the meanings—and consequences—of this play different. As the sexual encounter unfolds alongside their constant banter, it becomes clear that the racial play they are involved in is what gives the scene its erotic charge; race, then, provides a kind of lexicon for naming and claiming pleasures, even as it is also a space of violent stereotype.

If *SexWorld* reveals blackness as a locus of eroticism for its black female protagonist, *Vista Valley PTA* shows that the pornographic

screen can represent other kinds of black pleasures, namely, the pleasures in naming so-called difference, and the pleasures in deploying
racial logics and frameworks to interpret social and sexual encounters. In *Vista*, one of West's last films, a seasoned teacher is sent to a
troubled Vista Valley High School to transform it. She quickly dis-
covers that what seems to be an ordinary high school in an ordinary
suburban town is actually rife with sexual tension and perversion.

The film illustrates these perversions through the figure of a student's father. The father—a devout Christian—regularly visits prostitutes. The viewer is introduced to him when he visits West, who
plays the role of an unnamed prostitute. As he enters her apartment,
she tells him, "Come on in, honey, don't be shy. If you want privacy,
you better close that door!" When he hands her twenty-five dollars,
she chastises him, "You know, honey, twenty-five dollars ain't gonna
buy you nothing fancy." She leans back on the bed and begins to take
her clothes off, at which point the client begs her, "Don't take them
all the way off, please." He shyly communicates that he simply wants
to masturbate while watching her undress. As the scene unfolds, he
clutches a roll of toilet paper in one hand and his penis in another,
and the camera cuts between her fingers moving in and out of her
red underwear and his hand on his penis. Clutching the paper, he
ejaculates. As soon as he does so, she jumps up and exclaims, "Okay,
honey, let's go. I had a good time, you had a good time, let's go!" Yet
rather than simply leaving, the man grabs West's hair and shouts,
"You must repent, please forgive me, poor child." As he throws West
onto the bed, the two begin to hit each other. Ultimately, she pushes
him away and chases him out of her apartment and down the stairs of
her building while he shouts something inaudible about the "hand of
God." Finally, she screams, "Fucking asshole, what's the matter with
you? Damn white boys will drive you crazy!"

If this scene is about the sexualization of black female bodies, it is
also an investigation of the sexual perversions that lie at the heart of
white heteromasculinity. In other words, as West explains, the scene
reveals something about "damn white boys," their perversions and
thwarted desires, and the violence they can inflict on black female
flesh. The scene treats the client as sexually confused: he prefers to
masturbate rather than to have sex with West, and his clutched toilet
paper roll serves as a comic reminder of this curious decision. If the
sexual encounter establishes a curious white male heterosexuality,
the moments after—in which the client repents and proselytizes—

reveal his shame in his own longings and desires. The next scene only entrenches and deepens the film's investment in a kind of perverse white masculinity. Moments after yelling at West, the client returns home and barges into his daughter's room. As she covers her breasts in modesty, he grabs her and says, "There's nothing to be ashamed of in front of your father." He buttons her blouse while flirtatiously rubbing her breasts reminding her, "You're a very beautiful girl." *Vista Valley*, then, depicts heteronormative white masculinity as a kind of perversion, one that is humiliated by an encounter with a black female sex worker but perfectly comfortable with an intrafamilial sexual encounter.

If the previous scene is notable for its construction of white masculinity as sexually odd, it also represents West making sense of the violent encounter *through the lens of race*. In other words, the client's sexual oddities *and* his violence are understood as something intrinsic to "damn white boys." Her exclamation—a critique of the violence "white boys" inflict on black women—is interesting as it reveals that the Golden Age's investment in racial fictions was not limited to representing hyperbolic and excessive black female flesh. The epoch also crafted and circulated images of degraded, humiliated, perverse, or feminized white masculinities (it is possible to understand this investment as coinciding with blaxploitation's investment in representing white male effeminacy).[25]

In other words, the era was preoccupied with understanding sexual pleasures, practices, and longings through the lens of race, and with representing sexual performances as racial performances as well. Ultimately, during the Golden Age, pornographers made their investment in race and racial difference apparent, and West often functioned as a body that made visible how black bodies inhabit blackness, play with blackness, construct racial difference, and embody racial pleasures.

If West's work suggests the Golden Age's investment in racial performance, it also indexes an ongoing pornographic interest in tethering black women to labor. West works in these films—as a domestic worker, as a meter maid, as a truck driver, as a room service waitress, as a secretary—and generally labors in subservient positions. Golden Age pornography's incessant investment in connecting black women to labor suggests not only that the films constructed black female subjectivity as synonymous with laborers but also that black female labor is sexualized. In so doing, the films reveal that all of black women's labor is a kind of sex work, and show that black women are sexualized at work, so that their labor is understood—particularly by white male employers and customers—as a signal of sexual availability.

Nowhere is the sexualization of black women's nonsexual labor more visible than in *Unnamed #1* (from *Double D Soul Sister*), where West plays Gladys, a secretary whose white male boss has "some things on his mind." When Gladys urges him to see her "psychiatrist friend," he instead asks Gladys if he could instead "get a little relief" and reminds her "I'm just uptight because I feel horny." "Anything for the company," she responds, and soon Gladys is on her knees, performing fellatio on her employer. When the sex is over, Gladys quickly stands up, fixes her hair, hooks her bra, and asks, "So how about my raise?" "What?" her boss asks, and she repeats it, "My raise!" It is only when he promises to adjust her salary that West graciously excuses herself from his office. In this scene, West's labor as a secretary is intimately tethered to her sexual labor (and indeed the film suggests that her work "for the company" is always both administrative and sexual, that her very job description includes sexual servicing). Indeed, West's performance suggests the multiple forms of sex work that black women perform at a time when their bodies and labor are treated as available, and in which their bodies and their labor are conflated.

Like *Unnamed #1*, *Ceremony . . . Ritual of Love* conflates black women's domestic labor and sexual labor. In *Ceremony*, West works as a maid for a rich white family; she is also, the viewer learns, involved in a sexual relationship with the family's white male gardener. This ostensibly private relationship, however, becomes public when the family's daughter catches West and the gardener having sex, and reports what she has seen to her mother. The mother, rather than confronting the couple, decides to watch them have sex, and to order them to perform certain sexual acts while she sits nearby pleasuring herself. West's work as a domestic laborer, then, bleeds into a form of sexual labor when her employer makes use of her body, compensating her at the end of the scene with a pair of black panties. In both *Unnamed #1* and *Ceremony*, West's place in the film's narrative is explained through labor, as if black women could appear on the pornographic screen exclusively through the legible role of laborer. Moreover, it is West's status as a laborer—as a secretary and as a maid—that is represented and imagined as inherently or intrinsically sexual. To be a black working woman on the Golden Age screen is to be sexually available.

Finally, West's films produced an early laboratory for developing what would be later termed the "interracial buddy picture." Generally, scholars conceptualize the interracial buddy film as a movie centered on white male / black male friendships. As Melvin Donalson notes, these films "confirm that men of all races share positions in the dominant power scheme, which intrinsically promotes principles of heterosexuality and sexism" and "function as a keeper of America's collective conscience—the repository for fears, guilt, and hopes—the interracial buddy film creates a world where that conscience can find a peaceful balance, that is to say where conflicts can find resolutions."[26] Indeed, the interracial buddy formula made famous in films such as *In the Heat of the Night, 48 Hrs., Another 48 Hrs., Training Day,* and *Rush Hour* often featured crime-fighting interracial buddies whose partnership reveal that racial problems can be overcome through friendship, camaraderie, and shared phallic power.

Yet the Golden Age was a critical predecessor of the "interracial buddy film" and offered a distinctive articulation of interracial partnership, severing it from its insistence on interracial friendship predicated on shared phallic power. Instead, in the Golden Age version of the interracial buddy film, it is black women and white women who forge friendships—and often erotic friendships—that both demonstrate the possibilities of interracial alliance and ultimately enable and facilitate white women's sexual pleasure.

In *Unnamed #2* (from *Double D Soul Sister*), West and her white female friend are in a luxurious summerhouse. The two quietly discuss a white man West has picked up as he floats naked in an outdoor pool. West confesses that she no longer remembers the man's name, but promises to introduce her friend to the man. When the man enters the house wearing a bathrobe, he quickly removes it, and then invites West to swim with him. West quickly responds that she is unable to join him because she has just "set her hair." He then indicates that he will ask the white woman to swim with him, and West intervenes, facilitating an indoor sexual encounter among all three. She quickly and seductively strips in front of the white man, ostensibly performing the labor of arousing him, and then she has sex with him while her friend watches. The scene then unfolds as a traditional ménage à trois and concludes with the man ejaculating over *both* women's breasts, a signaling of the racial unity the sexual encounter has made possible. In other words, West's bond with her white friend enables a sexual encounter that connects black and white bodies.

Nowhere is the logic of interracial friendship more apparent than in *Ceremony*, which features *two* interracial erotic female friendships: between West (who plays the role of a maid) and her employer, and between West and her employer's daughter. The film begins with a nervous bride, Nikki, and her excited mother chatting; Nikki's wedding is hours away, and they quickly discuss the final preparations. As the mother quells Nikki's anxieties, she shouts for their maid to come and assist Nikki with her clothing. West enters Nikki's room dressed in a maid's costume and asks, "You rang?" When the mother leaves the room, West turns to the bride and says, "They sure got you into a lovely outfit," and then pulls at the hem of her own costume, laughs dryly, and asks, "Ain't this the shit?" West then asks Nikki if she has everything she needs for the wedding—something new, something borrowed, and so on. When Nikki reveals she does not have something borrowed, West reaches into her pocket and produces a small lacey black bundle—what the viewer later learns is a pair of black underwear—and says, "They were a gift from an appreciative friend." Here the film reveals that West and Nikki have a friendship that Nikki's mother is unaware of; the two poke fun at West's silly maid's costume, and it is West, not the bride's mother, who soothes Nikki in the anxious moments before her wedding. It is also an erotic friendship, of course, as West's gift to the nervous bride is a pair of panties, underwear that the viewer later learns was used in a sexual encounter with Nikki's mother.

The scene then unfolds as a flashback. Years earlier, West and Tim, the family's gardener, were having sex when Nikki caught them. Nikki ran downstairs and reported that she had caught the maid and the gardener having sex. Her mother stormed upstairs, ostensibly to confront the couple. Instead, when she arrives, the sex act has concluded, and West quietly voices that she is not fully satisfied after simply performing fellatio on the gardener. Nikki's mother sits in a chair near the bed and scolds the gardener for "leaving a woman unsatisfied." She insists that the gardener pleasure West, and she sits next to the copulating couple, watching them, at times instructing them, and always pleasuring herself. At the end of the scene, she gives West her "beautiful panties," precisely the panties West gives Nikki on her wedding day.

In *Ceremony*, interracial friendships—between West and her employer, and between West and Nikki—are necessarily erotic relationships. The first friendship, West's relationship with her white female employer, both enables her sexual pleasure and requires her to perform sexual labor for her boss's pleasure. West's labor, then, unleashes and enables white women's sexual desires. Yet the second friendship is one in which the black panties—passed from employer to employee, and then from employee back to employer—are a kind of sexual gift, one that is imagined to facilitate Nikki's sexual pleasures as a married woman.

Crafting the Archive of Racialized Desire

In this chapter I endeavor to make a reparative archival intervention, carefully tracing Desiree West's Golden Age career, and argue that a set of pornographic representational tropes were developed and perfected on West's body. In other words, during the Golden Age, pornographers constructed, produced, and circulated a certain kind of desire—a desire *for* Desiree West—one that had not previously been represented on the pornographic screen. In so doing, West's body set the template for how black women would be represented—and imagined—on the pornographic screen in the years to come.

If I make a claim about the importance of racialized desire to the pornographic archive, and about the centrality of racialized pleasures to Golden Age pornography, I also make a claim about the archive itself. The archive is a complicated location for "porn studies" scholars, but it is made no less complicated by talking to those who participated in the pornographic labor we study, document, and analyze. Indeed, what I learned from talking to West is that even how we study pornography now is a historically situated academic practice. My own practice of understanding these films *as* narratives is far removed from West's own experience of participating in the production of these films. What I also learned from talking to her is that her experience is far closer to the *Double D Soul Sister* model of producing pornographic archives: she remembers participating in a series of scenes, and has little knowledge of the larger narratives the films sought to circulate or produce. This revelation does not, of course, aspire to problematize the practice of archiving pornographies; instead, what crafting this chapter alongside talking to West revealed to me is that for "porn studies" scholars, archival questions will never fully be settled as we seek to understand the "truth" of a genre whose films remain underdocumented, even for those who participated in the production of those films.

NOTES

1. Linda Williams, "Skin Flicks on the Racial Border: Pornography, Exploitation, and Interracial Lust," in *Porn Studies*, ed. Linda Williams (Durham, NC: Duke University Press, 2004), 300.

2. Judith Butler, *Precarious Life: The Powers of Mourning and Violence* (New York: Verso, 2006), 23.

3. Linda Williams, *Hard Core: Power, Pleasure, and the "Frenzy of the Visible"* (Berkeley: University of California Press, 1989), 60.

4. For more on the stag era, see Al Di Lauro and Gerald Rabkin, *Dirty Movies: An Illustrated History of the Stag Film, 1915–1970* (New York: Chelsea House, 1976); Linda Williams, " 'White Slavery' versus the Ethnography of 'Sexworkers': Women in Stag Films at the Kinsey Archive," *Moving Image* 5, no. 2 (Fall 2005): 107–34.

5. In the wake of *Miller v. California* (1973), which defined the obscene as materials that cultivate "prurient interest" and lack "redeeming" scientific, artistic, or cultural importance, pornographers labored to produce films filled with "redeeming" narratives.

6. Linda Williams reports that by 1973, when the New Mature World Theater in Times Square was closed, over a quarter of a million people had screened *Deep Throat*. Williams, *Hard Core*, 100.

7. Linda Williams, *Screening Sex* (Durham, NC: Duke University Press, 2008), 127.

8. There are significant—and well-documented—exceptions to the absence of black bodies on the pornographic screen. Williams, for example, offers a close reading of *KKK Night Riders* (ca. 1930s), a film that represents a Klansman (who remains hooded for the duration of the film) breaking into a black woman's house and raping her. The sex, which initially appears forced, is quickly transformed into something pleasurable for both the black female protagonist and, of course, for the hooded Klansman. For Williams, the film is significant because it makes clear the shortcomings of feminist engagements with agency in the context of the "stag film," a term that she argues "says too little about the historically determined, coercive context of black female and white male sexual interactions depicted here under the very sign of a white supremacy designed to reassert the race-and gender-based prerogatives of white men." Williams, "White Slavery," 126.

9. This film was produced by Sam Weston / Anthony Spinelli, who directed *Sex-World*.

10. *Shaft* (1971), *Sweetback* (1971), and *The Mack* (1973), for example, all contain interracial sex scenes between black men and white women. For more on blaxploitation, see Mikel J. Koven, *Blaxploitation Films* (Harpenden, UK: Kamera, 2010); Novotny Lawrence, *Blaxploitation Films of the 1970s: Blackness and Genre* (New York: Routledge, 2008); Christopher Sieving, *Soul Searching: Black-Themed Cinema from the March on Washington to the Rise of Blaxploitation* (Middletown, CT: Wesleyan University Press, 2011); Yvonne D. Sims, *Women of Blaxploitation* (Jefferson, NC: McFarland, 2006); Joe Wlodarz, "Beyond the Black Macho: Queer Blaxploitation," *Velvet Light Trap* 53 (2004): 10–25; Stephane Dunn, *"Baad Bitches" and Sassy Supermamas: Black Power Action Films* (Urbana: University of Illinois Press, 2008).

11. As Mireille Miller-Young notes, "There were few black and Latina women in golden-age hardcore films of the 1970s, but according to my research there were thousands who appeared in other erotic venues such as magazines like *Players*, *Playboy*, and *Eros*, in the U.S., and *Femme Souillee, Inhalt, Emanuel, Whitelady, La Cousine*, and *Samy* in Europe (especially France, Germany, the Netherlands, Brit-

ain, and Spain)." Mireille Miller-Young, "Hip-Hop Honeys and Da Hustlaz: Black Sexualities in the New Hip-Hop Pornography," *Meridians: feminism, race, transnationalism* 8, no. 1 (2008): 288.

12. Pepper's first feature was in 1982.

13. There has been an increasing popular interest in the adult entertainment industry's racism. See, for example, Keli Goff, "Is the Porn Industry Racist?," *Root*, www.theroot.com.

14. I write more about this historicized approach to pornography—what I term "racial iconography"—in my book; see Jennifer C. Nash, *The Black Body in Ecstasy: Reading Race, Reading Pornography* (Durham, NC: Duke University Press, 2014).

15. I use the term "porn studies" in quotations, mindful of Linda Williams's critique of the term in *Porn Studies*. See Linda Williams, "Pornography, Porno, Porn: Thoughts on a Weedy Field," *Porn Studies* 1 (2014): 24–40.

16. David Jennings, *Skinflicks: The Inside Story of the X-Rated Video Industry* (New York: Authorhouse, 2000), 63.

17. The Internet Movie Database notes of West, "Her exotic looks—she appeared to be a combination of black and Asian—and spectacular body guaranteed her steady employment in the business, although she never reached the level of stardom that, frankly, she should have." See "Biography" on the Internet Movie Database website at www.imdb.com/name/nm0498317.

18. One website notes, "Porn Star Desiree West was one of the first black porn starlets. She had a full, curvaceous body with huge, firm breasts and a very pretty, wide-eyed face that had vaguely Asian undertones to it from certain angles. Desiree West's voluptuous good looks set the stage for the sexual fireworks that she invariably provided to each film she sexed in. She was one of the first 'wild women' of porn, always ready to push the sexual envelope with her nymphomaniacal need for raw, passionate trysting." See "Desiree West" entry on *1980's Classic Porn* at www.1980classicporn.com/tag/desiree-west/page/2/.

19. When I spoke to West, she identified herself as half Asian and half African American.

20. When I spoke to West, she noted that posing in *Players* brought her more visibility than performing in moving-image pornography.

21. Ariane Renee Cruz, "Berries Bittersweet: Visual Representations of Black Female Sexuality in Contemporary American Pornography" (PhD diss., University of California Berkeley, 2010), 71.

22. Ibid., 70.

23. See "Desiree West" folder on *Vintage Erotica Forums*, http://vintage-erotica-forum.com/t7242-p8-desiree-west.html.

24. Indeed, when I asked West about her memories of the film, she indicated that she was encouraged to perform a hyperstereotypical blackness, and was told that her "accent" was not "Black enough" for the role.

25. I write more about constructions of white effeminacy in blaxploitation, and blax-porn-tation, in *The Black Body in Ecstasy: Reading Race, Reading Pornography*.

26. Melvin Donalson, *Masculinity in the Interracial Buddy Film* (Jefferson, NC: McFarland, 2006), 11.

CHAPTER 4

Making Sense of Linda Lovelace

NANCY SEMIN LINGO

"**D**OCTOR, I DON'T KNOW why it is, I just don't enjoy sex," said Linda Lovelace in the 1972 pornographic film *Deep Throat*. This troubling complaint and her subsequent "medical" diagnosis of an improperly located clitoris, found at the base of the throat rather than its usual anatomical spot, were the basic plot elements of the film credited with reshaping American sexuality. Featuring scenes that venerated graphic and extensive oral sex, *Deep Throat* became an immediate sensation. Four decades later, it is still considered the most successful and high-impact adult film of all time.

More than just a phenomenal box office success, reputed to have earned more than $100 million worldwide, *Deep Throat* had an immeasurable impact on American life, especially sexual culture and politics. *Washington Post* reporters Bob Woodward and Carl Bernstein referred to their secret informant on the Watergate burglary story as "Deep Throat"—a pseudonym not only referencing the popularity of the film but also bringing levity to the enormity of an investigation that culminated in the fall of the Nixon administration. But even more important than its permanent entry into the political lexicon, *Deep Throat* is credited with altering American sexual mores. It became, arguably, the most important statement about American sexuality since the first Kinsey Report in 1948. As the film spread around the nation, and Lovelace appeared on major national magazine covers and late-night talk shows, ordinary couples discovered a new way to talk about their sex lives and their sexual desires. In the wake of *Deep Throat*, Americans spoke more openly about sex.

The success of the film also catapulted its star performer, a young unknown named Linda Boreman, into superstardom. The public was eager to learn more about this new celebrity, reinvented as Linda "Lovelace" by her Hollywood handlers, and she gave interviews to men's magazines such as *Playboy* and *Esquire,* as well as to psychiatrists and pundits who were eager to analyze this unusual public persona. At first, Linda seemed to possess a singular, clear voice that promulgated the importance of sexual pleasure, insisting that sex was less obscene than America's continuous involvement with violence and war. The unpopular conflict in Vietnam, at its height at the same time that *Deep Throat* premiered, gave weight to a simple message much like the 1960s mantra "Make love, not war."[1] Linda became a significant symbolic representative of the social and political currents that gave shape to 1970s America.

And yet, the hypervisibility of Linda's sexualized body muffled her voice. Throughout her life and career, others consistently spoke for her, from porn filmmakers to autobiographical ghostwriters to anti-pornography feminists. The result was to crowd her out of the narrativization of her own life, leaving her a tabula rasa to be inscribed with each new interpretive moment in the sexual revolution and subsequent feminist sex wars. As such, making sense of Linda Lovelace becomes an exercise in sad irony, as the foremost female symbol of the sexual revolution also reflects the limitations women faced in claiming cultural authority over their own stories. Phrased another way, the mythology surrounding Linda the porn star has made it nearly impossible to recover Linda the woman, despite her very public life.

Becoming Linda Lovelace

Linda Sue Boreman was born on January 10, 1949, in New York City, the youngest of three daughters in a middle-class family. Her father worked full-time and her mother stayed at home. Linda described her formative years as positive—she received a "good upbringing."[2] As a teenager, she tagged along behind her older sisters and learned to lip-sync to popular songs and copy the latest fashion trends.[3] During her high school years, the family moved to Davie, Florida, a small bedroom community outside of Miami. Linda befriended another recent transplant to the area, a fellow sophomore named Patsy Carroll.[4] Linda was a year older than Patsy, and she retained a New York accent, which made her seem sophisticated in her new friend's eyes. Linda was a teenage rebel, the first girl at school to roll up her regulation-length shorts during gym class and show more leg.

Bored with the constraints of high school, the girls spent their time at local hangouts, where they met older men attracted to their youth and good looks. They were fond of the armory and the bowling alley, both of which featured live music on weekends. Patsy and Linda approached the managers of the bowling alley and asked if they could perform as go-go dancers and accompany bands onstage. Though they were never paid, they were given a costume allowance that paid for miniskirts and hip-hugger bell-bottoms. They sewed short halter tops and wore low-heeled, midcalf boots with side zippers.

School was never a priority for Linda, and she welcomed graduation and the chance to move away from her parents' supervision. Patsy recalled that Linda was an average student, applying only a minimum effort to get by in most of her senior courses. She had little ambition to attend college. After high school, Linda moved north to help an older sister run a boutique near White Plains, New York. In September 1970, while driving to New York City on a buying trip for the store, she was involved in a head-on collision. Linda was rushed to the hospital and prepped for emergency surgery. Her sister was one of the first family members to arrive, and on seeing Linda lying on a gurney, she felt an initial sense of relief. Her injuries did not seem serious at all. But once she approached, she realized Linda's chin had split wide open and her teeth were missing. Linda also sustained a lacerated liver and multiple broken bones.

The accident left Linda incapacitated, with no choice but to return to Florida to recover at her parents' home. The carefree young woman bound for the big city was now scared and self-conscious about the fresh scars that covered her body. This vulnerability paved the way for an older man, Chuck Traynor, who posed as a successful nightclub owner, to win Linda's trust. Eager to reestablish her independence from her parents, Linda moved in with Traynor following a brief courtship. Soon, Linda realized the limits of Traynor's accomplishments; his club was faltering, and he supplemented his income by prostituting the waitresses.

In the fall of 1971, the club failed, and Traynor suggested that he and Linda move to New York City. They relocated to the Times Square area, a hub for adult sex-related businesses and prostitution, where Traynor sold X-rated photographs of Linda that generated a modest income for them. However, Traynor soon learned that more money could be made filming loops—brief sex films that ran an average length of eight to ten minutes. Inexpensive to produce, they could be cranked out quickly and sold to local distributors. Linda performed in these sex loops, and Traynor also began prostituting her, often forcing her to perform a sexual technique that he bragged he had taught her. Called "deep throating," it involved taking an entire erect penis into one's mouth and throat. Linda excelled at it.[5]

During this period, Linda did not speak out against the repeated indignities Traynor subjected her to; instead she tried to distance herself psychically from the abuse. Traynor insisted that she film an assortment of loops that catered to extreme sexual proclivities. Two notable examples include *The Foot,* which shows Linda masturbating with the aid of a foot that suddenly appears on screen, and *Dogarama,* which shows her copulating with a German shepherd. The loops marked a low point for Linda on an emotional level, symbolizing Traynor's domination and her belief that she could not escape his control.

The loops caught the attention of hairdresser-turned–adult film director Gerard Damiano, who was impressed with Linda's "deep-throat" technique.[6] Through their mutual connections in the tight-knit Times Square adult entertainment crowd, Damiano sought out Linda and Chuck. He thought that Linda's skills could serve as a useful plot device in an entertaining adult film that featured graphic sex scenes but also a real story line. Damiano wrote the dialogue for the screenplay that would become *Deep Throat* over the course of a weekend. He peppered the dialogue with witty one-liners and humor, which set it apart from other sex films of the time, and increased its appeal for mainstream America. His finished project, with the working title "The Doctor Makes a House Call," was just twenty pages long, but this was wordy compared to other adult film scripts of the time.[7]

The main focus of the film is a woman named Linda, who confides to a friend that she has never experienced orgasm. When various remedies fail, she visits a doctor. Actor Harry Reems examines Lovelace and announces his diagnosis: "Your clitoris," he states, "It's deep down in the bottom of your throat." Devastated by the news, Linda begins to sob, and Reems attempts to calm her, telling her that a clitoris in the throat is better than none at all. He then suggests a therapeutic regimen of house calls in which Linda engages in a variety of sexual encounters. They discover that the "deep throat" oral sex technique makes the elusive "bells and whistles" go off for Lovelace, and she is thrilled to experience true sexual pleasure at last. This was the basic plot of *Deep Throat*, but Damiano was satisfied that it gave sufficient attention to Linda's fellating skills.[8]

The shooting lasted just a few weeks. The *Deep Throat* cast and crew relocated to Florida, and the environment on set was relaxed and loose. Linda seemed to be excited about the film, perhaps because the group setting meant less one-on-one time with Traynor. Drugs, alcohol, and sex were plentiful. "The actors, the actresses . . . the technicians, the cameramen, the soundmen. . . . it was party time," recalled Damiano. Many first-time performers were used in *Deep Throat* to keep costs down, so humor and drugs were an effective means of making every-one feel comfortable. "It was just one giant party, the whole making of the movie. Even for the crew," said Reems. "I'd be having sex in front of the cameras, and literally I would see other actors or crew members having sex behind the cameras, while they're shooting." Damiano remembered that Linda joined in the revelry. In what has become one of the most controversial scenes in the film, Linda inserted a hollow glass dildo into her vagina and Coca-Cola was poured inside. When Damiano called out, "That's a wrap!" Linda laughed and used her pel-vic muscles to shoot the dildo across the room, where it fell and shat-tered. Everyone burst out laughing but Damiano, who was relieved he had not been injured by "a flying missile."[9]

Damiano would later surmise that the biggest challenge Linda faced during the filming was Traynor's jealousy. Lovelace, he thought, was simply too popular with the cast and crew. Traynor was brood-ing and angry seeing Linda surrounded by admirers, and he created problems on the set. This became especially troublesome the morning that Linda was scheduled to shoot the doctor visit scene with Reems. Approaching Damiano, Linda confided, "I won't be able to do it good. Chuck is so jealous. So if I really get into the scene, he's going to be mad at me." Damiano dispatched Traynor to Miami on the pretext that he needed more film. "That was the only problem we had," said Damiano. "Not that she didn't want to do the movie. She was upset about not being able to do it well."[10]

Once filming concluded, Damiano readied the film for release. *Deep Throat* had a running time of sixty-two minutes, and contained approximately a dozen sex scenes. In Damiano's estimation, it was a decent piece of pornographic fare, but nothing extraordinary. Neither Damiano nor the cast members expected *Deep Throat* to be a global hit.

To them, it was just another porno film that was perhaps a bit more entertaining because of its plot lines and humor.

Reviewers cited Reems's comedic performance as the doctor as the acting highlight of the film, but his style was due in no small part to Linda's acting skills—or lack thereof. During the filming, only ten to fifteen minutes of rehearsal time was typically allotted before scenes were shot. This was not enough time for Linda, who had no professional acting experience and often fumbled her lines or forgot them completely. In frustration, Reems developed his character as a madcap doctor, largely as a reaction to Linda's monotone readings.[11] The flatter her voice became as she read her lines, the more he exaggerated his own. The end result became something of a roman à clef for the sex hygiene genre—a group of films that in the past often played on fears of sex and disease but in the 1970s adjusted to changing social mores and now offered a humorous, affirmative vision of sexuality.[12]

The Politics of Pleasure

Set against the backdrop of the sexual revolution and second-wave feminism, *Deep Throat*'s plot reflected and contributed to the growing debate about the nature of female sexuality. In the late 1960s, a contentious debate had begun over women's rights to sexual pleasure and the seat of the female orgasm, which had long been thought to be vaginal. The sex therapists Phyllis Kronhausen and Eberhard Kronhausen recalled the experience of one frustrated patient in their 1964 book, *The Sexually Responsive Woman*: "My husband tells me that he doesn't think I have a clitoris, or that it is buried too deep. Sometimes I wonder myself whether I have a clitoris."[13] *The Sensuous Woman*, a popular 1969 how-to sex manual for women, suggested that women ought to fake their orgasms to keep their (male) partners happy.[14] Anne Koedt, a radical feminist activist, countered these male-centered frameworks in her 1968 essay "The Myth of the Vaginal Orgasm," in which she stated that the clitoris was the anatomical locus of female sexual pleasure. Men, she warned, were happy conspirators perpetuating the vaginal "myth" because the vagina was the "best stimulant for the penis," and they wanted to protect their sexual enjoyment and their access to reproduction.[15]

Linda's story line in *Deep Throat* brought a touch of levity to all this confusion. But more importantly, it provided a space to address significant political questions about female pleasure and desire (fig. 4.1). That Linda's filmic voice was a male invention, predicated entirely on the phallocentric trope of fellatio as the crux of her own access to orgasm, was undeniable, and reflected the circumscribed nature of Linda's public persona. Yet her desire to have sex on her own terms and her steadfast pursuit of sexual pleasure and the experience of orgasm was also an affirmation of women's sexual rights. By locating the clitoris in the back of Linda's throat, *Deep Throat* acknowledged the bewilderment many women were experiencing around the question of orgasm and how best to achieve it. As film historian Linda Williams points out, pornography relies on visible evidence of orgasm, which is typically accomplished in male "money shots." Female genitalia provide little actual proof of orgasm, but faces are highly expressive; director Damiano focused on the look of ecstasy coming over Lovelace's face, as it demonstrated orgasm by visibly expressing pleasure and happiness.[16] Despite the absurd plot and anatomical reroute, *Deep Throat* was one of the first contemporary films to openly explore a woman's desire for sexual satisfaction—and without the punitive consequences faced by the earlier *Mona* (1970), as discussed in Whitney Strub's essay. In practically all adult films, a basic formula emerged in which women existed primarily to serve male fantasy and pleasure. *Deep Throat* offered a twist—a female lead seeking sexual satisfaction for herself. The film allowed for the possibility that women had the right to demand sexual pleasure and, in fact, that a woman's exploration and desire could take precedence over that of her male partner. Linda validated this important idea in multiple post–*Deep Throat* interviews. In a September 1973 interview, when asked whether her performance was genuine, Linda replied, "Right! It's me, and that's what I can do, and how I really am."[17] She told a reporter for the *Washington Post* something similar: "In most porno films, people are not enjoying themselves, looking at the ceiling. I'm enjoying it one hundred percent."[18]

Linda's average good looks and youthful sincerity may have also endeared her to some skeptical female audience members. With freckles and a girl-next-door appearance, she brought a wholesome sweetness to *Deep Throat*. In the 1970s, male adult film actors were cast primarily for their ability to maintain an erection, but they also needed to possess average looks. Male audiences needed to believe that the sexual fantasies depicted on screen were potentially available to them, and not reserved for chiseled, muscular, good-looking men.[19] Linda served this same function for female audience members. She did not resemble the typical buxom blonde *Playboy* centerfold model.

FIGURE 4.1. Linda Lovelace receives a medical exam from Harry Reems in *Deep Throat* (Gerard Damiano, 1972). The film was applauded by some critics for foregrounding a woman's sexual desires. Photo: Getty Images.

Her average appearance, scars and all, made it easier for viewers to feel a connection. Damiano specifically wanted Linda for his film because of her talents *and* her looks. "I felt she was . . . very natural looking, if not accomplished," he later remarked, "and I thought that was her charm. . . . She wasn't Tallulah Bankhead. She was somebody that you could relate to . . . if you met her, you could talk to her . . . I think that was part of . . . what I tried to maintain . . . that she was accessible."[20] In other words, Linda's discovery of her own sexuality gave women attempting to make sense of the sexual revolution some hope of discovering and fulfilling their own desires.

Yet the very metaphor of the girl next door rested on an imagined suburban geography that was deeply, if often silently, racialized—suburbia itself had been an explicitly racial postwar project—and Linda's onscreen performance embodied a whiteness so pervasively assumed as a norm that it went unaddressed at the time. While women of color in pornography confronted the "hypervisibility of race" in the 1970s and beyond—ranging from Vanessa del Rio's always-accentuated Puerto Ricanness to the various framings of Desiree West discussed in the previous chapter by Jennifer Nash—Linda partook of a white-

afforded her the opportunity to be openly sexual without

age of racial stereotypes.[21] In this sense, even though Linda

d distinct from the average Playmate, *Deep Throat* built on

d foundations, both the girl-next-door fantasies promulgated

by *Playboy* as well as the overwhelmingly white research base that had undergirded the data that went into the Kinsey Reports, making a great deal of midcentury sexual knowledge in actuality *white* sexual knowledge. Critical race theorists have shown how whiteness maintains its monopoly on "normalcy" precisely by keeping itself invisible. *Deep Throat,* and so much other pornography of the 1970s, reflects precisely that tradition.

Intimate Confessions of a Mass-Culture Persona

Other than the $1,200 she was paid for her performance, which Traynor pocketed, Linda was not reimbursed financially for her role in *Deep Throat.* However, when *Deep Throat* became a hit, Linda emerged as an unlikely star. Journalists clamored to conduct interviews with her, and the public wanted to know everything about her. Linda and Traynor relocated to California in 1973 to exploit her fame and pursue legitimate film opportunities. They hired a personal assistant named Delores Wells to help run the newly created Linda Lovelace Enterprises. Wells processed orders for autographed photos and novelty merchandise such as key chains and whiskey glasses embossed with phrases such as "Linda Lovelace blows my mind." During that time, Wells worked intimately with Linda and grew close to her. Linda, she observed, enjoyed her newfound celebrity status.[22] This included regular visits to the Playboy mansion, where Linda attracted celebrity admirers, including Warren Beatty, Joe Namath, and Hugh Hefner himself. She entered a sexual relationship with the married entertainer Sammy Davis Jr. that lasted for more than a year.

The success surrounding *Deep Throat* created a set of conditions that enabled Linda to free herself from Traynor's domination and find her voice again. Linda's empowerment was incremental but could be glimpsed in the evolution of her narrative voice in her two largely ghostwritten autobiographies, *Inside Linda Lovelace* (1973) and *The Intimate Diary of Linda Lovelace* (1974). Porn star autobiographies were common in the 1970s, with everyone from early female performer Tina Russell to Marc "Mr. 10 ½" Stevens to Harry Reems delivering casual, ephemeral paperbacks.[23] Jumping on the bandwagon, Linda and Traynor were rumored to receive an advance of $40,000 to $100,000 from Pinnacle Books for the provocatively titled *Inside Linda Lovelace*.[24] A ghostwriter assisted, and the book was completed in less than two weeks. One of the book's compelling features was the inclusion of twenty-two photographs, including one of a scantily clad Linda that folded out to three times the book's size. Traynor concocted most of the responses to the ghostwriter's questions for Linda, ensuring that the book did not accurately capture Linda's voice.

Inside Linda Lovelace presented a woman who saw nothing complicated about the sexual revolution, nor betrayed any seeming awareness of gendered power relations. "This is my story. I lived it, I wrote it and I offer no apologies to anyone," Linda was quoted in the preface. Elsewhere, the book furthered the myth of her hypersexuality. She described a runaway libido that required routine masturbation. Of her teen years, she happily described her stint as a go-go dancer, noting that the audience reaction was encouraging. "They dug me and I dug being dug," she wrote. "I guess it was then that I knew I was an exhibitionist."[25] Darker elements of Linda's life went unmentioned, including a painful, botched breast augmentation surgery and the ignominious loops she had filmed at Traynor's behest in pre–*Deep Throat* days.

Film critic Kenneth Turan complained that the book was typical of an old Hollywood studio biography—giving readers little information, most of which was inaccurate.[26] This first autobiography was so obviously a fluff piece that few trade journals bothered to review it. *Newsweek*, however, validated *Inside Linda Lovelace* by publishing an excerpt in which Linda made a startling confession: she once seriously considered becoming a nun. The feminist literary critic Angela Carter wrote a brief review, correctly assessing that the book had nothing of importance to say except for the abjectly sad picture it painted of its own subject. "She is a . . . prisoner in a cage whose bars are composed of cocks. And she has been so thoroughly duped she seems quite happy there," said Carter, who found the public fascination with Linda disturbing. "Each age gets the heroine it deserves, and by God, we deserve Linda Lovelace."[27]

The next year, Linda published her second autobiography, *The Intimate Diary of Linda Lovelace*. Her new manager, David Winters, hired writer Mel Mandel to compose the book, which was produced in only three days' time.[28] Linda's second book did not fare as well as her first, but it allowed glimpses of more troubling truths than Linda's previous autobiography had afforded. The book detailed her claims about Traynor, whom she had left in late 1973.[29] In speaking of Traynor, Linda noted, "I have been threatened by a man who is very sick. He is full of violence." Linda documented the years of abuse at Traynor's hands, pointing out the bruises on her body that were visible in *Deep Throat* and telling of his stalking her with an M-16 rifle in Hollywood after their divorce. Yet she did not renounce her role in the filming of *Deep Throat*: "Don't get me wrong. I enjoyed doing what I did in *Deep Throat*—it's what happened sexually with Chuck that I hated," she wrote.[30] Much of the rest of the book reinforced Linda's image as an insatiable sex goddess, but her account of abuse (which anticipated and was consistent with her later accounts) jarringly belied some of this public persona. Hidden in plain sight, in the pages of a cheap, instantly forgotten, failed cash-in book, was an authentic kernel of Linda's own voice.

Meanwhile, as a now-single woman with a pressing need for income, Linda agreed to film a sequel to *Deep Throat*. The movie parodied the success of the deep throating phenomenon; its plot involved Russian spies attempting to steal the secrets of Linda's fellating skills. Released in the summer of 1974, *Deep Throat II* bombed. According to actress Andrea True, who also appeared in the film, its downfall was an R rating, which was sought (instead of an X) in hopes of bringing in a large mainstream audience. There were no graphic sex scenes, so adult film audiences were not interested. And Linda did not have sufficient crossover appeal as a movie star to attract moviegoers who were drawn to that year's other releases, including *Chinatown, The Great Gatsby*, and *Alice Doesn't Live Here Anymore*.[31]

Linda turned to new opportunities, and foremost on the list were speaking events at college campuses, where students were eager to discuss the ideas of the sexual revolution. Linda and *Deep Throat* had strong cultural capital among student groups, especially among men of the Left. The idea to visit universities began as a joke in 1973, when Linda received the annual prize from the *Harvard Lampoon* awarded to parody bad performances of popular celebrities.[32] That visit was intended as a lark, but campuses provided a good venue for Linda to speak on sexual freedom.[33] Her views were certainly not original, and she had little intellectual depth, but coming from the most popular sex performer of the day, her words resonated with the audience. In the first six months of 1974, Linda visited twenty-five college campuses. Crowds were receptive, first asking tongue-in-cheek questions and later commenting seriously on what they felt were the real obscenities in American society, particularly sexual repression, capitalism, racism, sexism, and militarism.[34]

In some ways, this period represented the apex of Linda's career. She had gained confidence as a public speaker, and could articulate the importance of sexuality and sexual diversity to a crowd. She was well received when she traveled abroad in 1974 to attend one of the major British social events of the year, the Royal Ascot races. Wearing a black see-through blouse that revealed her breasts and a large sun hat adorned with turkey feathers, her attire caused an international stir. The headline of the *Daily Mirror* cheekily referred to Linda's presence at the races as a "winning double."[35] On the heels of that trip, Linda began filming her next project, the comedy *Linda Lovelace for President*. It was a timely piece reflecting both the aftermath of the Watergate scandal and recent gains made by the women's movement. Shirley Chisholm, a New York congresswoman, had thrown her hat into the presidential ring in 1972, seeking her party's nomination at the Democratic National Convention. This was the first time a woman had been considered for the executive office. Moreover, the *Roe v. Wade* decision of 1973 that legalized abortion, and the proposed Equal Rights Amendment, guaranteeing equal rights for all Americans regardless of sex, further inspired feminists. A movie plot with the premise of a female presidential candidate was very much in keeping with the current political climate. And in many respects, it was the vital companion piece to *Deep Throat*. Linda's "nomination" for president in the 1976 film articulated both the political and sexual ascendancy of women in the United States, voicing the idea that a woman could possess authority in both realms.

Ostensibly, this film might have ensured Linda a permanent place of importance in the 1970s feminist pantheon. But Linda was not able to bring her confident self to the filming; never a talented actress, she delivered her lines flatly and unconvincingly. Her average girl-next-door look, formerly an asset, now seemed plain and frumpy, and at odds with the sophistication required of a presidential candidate. Other mid-1970s starlets such as Jane Fonda and Faye Dunaway had greater allure and star qualities, making Linda seem quaint. Even a promotional campaign in front of the White House featuring Linda in a white lace see-through outfit did little good. After its release in the summer of 1976, *Variety* placed *Linda Lovelace for President* at the number eleven spot, from which it quickly fell into obscurity.[36]

After 1977, Linda's career opportunities started to fade. She wanted to be a serious actress, but she had no legitimate acting talent.

Audiences expected nudity from her at the very least, and they were disappointed when she kept her clothes on. Linda retreated from Hollywood and decided to focus on her new relationship with construction worker Larry Marchiano, whom she had married in 1976 and with whom she would have a son (1977) and a daughter (1980). Marchiano and Linda decided there were few incentives to stay in Los Angeles; her career had stalled, and they were running out of money. They packed up their belongings and moved across the country to make a home in Montauk Point, New York. Marchiano secured occasional construction work, but by 1978, the family was in desperate financial straits. Feeling dismal about their prospects, Marchiano sought advice from family friend and attorney Victor Yannacone.

Yannacone insisted that Linda's real story "had to be told."[37] Linda's son was about to enter grade school, and she felt compelled to document her version of events because she feared he would face ridicule when fellow students realized who his mother was. Wanting her offspring to have a different legacy, and perhaps to generate income along the way, the solution seemed obvious. "If you want to make some money," said Yannacone, "why don't you write a book?"[38]

Focusing on the years of abuse she suffered under Traynor, and her fury at the financial exploitation she had suffered in the wake of *Deep Throat*'s multimillion-dollar box office, Linda set about to finally tell her story. The beatings she had suffered at Traynor's hands left her physically compromised with thrombophlebitis, a swelling condition in her legs. Her breasts had been damaged by shoddy silicone augmentation procedures, leaving her misshapen and unable to breast feed. She spoke now as a wife and mother who wanted to be able to look her children in the eyes without feeling shame.

Ordeal

On March 23, 1980, *Ordeal* debuted on the *New York Times* best-seller list in the number nine position (fig. 4.2). Its revelations attracted significant public attention and discussion. Linda alleged that she had been coerced to film *Deep Throat*; Traynor held a gun to her head off camera and threatened to kill her and her family members if she did not comply with the script's demands. She informed readers that the most successful pornographic film of all time, one enjoyed by millions of Americans, was actually a documentary of force and sexual violence, and tantamount to watching rape.

FIGURE 4.2. Linda Lovelace with her autobiography, *Ordeal*, 1980. Photo: Getty Images.

The account of *Deep Throat* contained in *Ordeal* was hard for many readers to believe. The American public recalled a film that was funny, and a star who had appeared in numerous public venues claiming to be authentically free of sexual hang-ups. For many, *Deep Throat* was the first porno film they had ever seen, and the movie held a special place in the national imagination as a precious expression of sexual freedom. Some could not accept that the laughing, smiling Lovelace they remembered so fondly could be the victim of the heinous crimes described in *Ordeal*.

But another set of readers welcomed *Ordeal* as speaking a long overdue female truth, and antipornography feminists rushed to support Linda. The book was released at the same time that a leading group of the feminist antipornography movement, Women Against Pornography, had begun to garner national attention and influence. Linda became a convenient, if not wholly credible, voice in support of their cause. The woman who was once the world's most famous porn star suddenly became pornography's most vocal and visible adversary.[39] She lent support to the feminist antipornography movement through the 1980s, even as she expressed some ambivalence about her relationship to the American women's movement. Activist Andrea Dworkin called her a feminist, although Linda herself explicitly disavowed the term in her next book, *Out of Bondage* (1986).[40]

This surprising shift earned Linda a great deal of criticism. Pornography industry insiders despised her for attacking the world of adult films that had once brought her international attention. Former adult actress Gloria Leonard considered her an "Aaron Burr" who did a "traitorous turn . . . to the adult industry."[41] Linda's critics outside of the adult entertainment business were no less vociferous. When she went on *The Phil Donahue Show* to promote *Ordeal* in April 1980, she was assured that she would find a sympathetic ear.[42] Instead, Linda was startled to discover an audience that responded harshly—and with disbelief—to her tale of domestic violence. Even Donahue seemed to doubt the authenticity of Linda's account. "There's some difficulty in understanding how you could be so helpless," he explained as he fielded audience comments. This skepticism never really dissipated. In 1997, journalist Fawn Germer interviewed Linda for the *Rocky Mountain News.* She repeatedly questioned why Linda had not escaped Traynor's clutches sooner. "They would drive to get food every night," recalled Germer, "and I said, 'Why didn't you jump out of the car at a stop sign or something?' "[43]

Ordeal had been motivated by Linda's personal and financial needs, certainly, but it also served the interests of the publishing industry. Her coauthor, Mike McGrady, had written *A Dove in Vietnam* (1968), but had also spearheaded the literary hoax *Naked Came the Stranger* (1969), a collectively written smut novel. Feeling that American popular literature had sunk to a new low, he organized a group of journalist colleagues and challenged them to churn out a book with "an unremitting emphasis on sex" with no regard for the quality of the writing. The point was to show the poor tastes of the American reading public by creating a hit based on an appeal to the lowest common denominator—sex—and it had worked, even to the point of being adapted as a hardcore film of the same title by Radley Metzger in 1975.[44] Linda's own attorney pitched the autobiography to a skeptical McGrady by telling him (without much care for Linda's travails), "There's a great story here; I got a huge porn star eating dog food from a can and hiding out"[45] (this referenced the period of time during which Linda sought to escape from Traynor and was forced to stay out of sight for weeks lest he discover her whereabouts and force her to return).

From the inception, then, *Ordeal* had addressed multiple needs: Linda's need to regain control over her own narrative, but also McGrady's authorial instincts, which ranged from committed leftist politics to sensationalized ruses. Even the authorial byline reflected concessions to the marketplace: Linda, who had long since renounced the name Lovelace, and whose now-remarried surname was Marchiano, accepted a credit as Linda Lovelace out of marketing necessity.

IN APRIL 2002, LINDA WAS driving outside of Denver, Colorado, when she lost control of her car and crashed. Rushed to a nearby hospital, she remained in critical condition for nineteen days before her family removed her from life support. She was fifty-three years old. She left behind a complex life story; indeed, it is unclear how to categorize Linda Lovelace and fully understand her relationship to the 1970s and the sexual revolution, although she remains one of its most potent symbols. A victim of ruthless male abuse and humiliation, she was also America's first celebrity porn star who came to represent the shifting sexual mores of postwar America and, later, the pleasures and dangers that sex still holds for women in a patriarchal society.

If this was a problem for the general public, it was an even bigger conundrum for the American women's movement, which had long had an uneasy relationship with Linda and *Deep Throat*. Linda had cast herself as a victim, and in so doing, she raised perhaps the most unsettling question of all: do women ever have control in a sexual exchange, or do they merely misinterpret conditions of powerlessness in prostitution, sex work, and even marriage as agency? Renowned feminists such as Gloria Steinem and Andrea Dworkin rushed to Linda's defense, arguing that she embodied the complex position that patriarchy creates for women, offering the illusion of power but never the reality. By contemporary standards, though, her admissions are incongruent with a modern feminist position; third-wave feminists believe in women's ability to exert control over their environments, and reject the premise of unwavering male control. This essay reveals that over the course of her lifetime, Linda was an authentic figure of the 1970s, struggling to make sense of a rapidly changing sexual environment and a young woman's place in it. Her life story brings up questions about women's bodies, sexual freedom, and agency that defined public life in the 1970s, and are still, to a large extent, unsettled today.

NOTES

1. See David Allyn, *Make Love Not War: The Sexual Revolution: An Unfettered History* (New York: Routledge, 2001), 50; and Beth Bailey, "Sex as a Weapon: Underground Comix and the Paradox of Liberation," in *Imagine Nation: The American Counterculture of the 1960s and '70s*, ed. Peter Braunstein and Michael William Doyle (New York: Routledge, 2002), 306.
2. Linda Lovelace, unpublished interview with Legs McNeil, on January 7, 2001, Denver, CO.
3. Ibid.
4. Patsy Carroll, telephone interview with author, October 24, 2005.
5. Linda Lovelace and Mike McGrady, *Ordeal* (Secaucus, NJ: Citadel, 1980), 100.
6. Their first encounter is now cloaked more in legend than in fact. Perhaps it was at a party where attendees engaged in drug use and casual sex, but Damiano insists Linda and Chuck merely showed up in his office one day seeking work.
7. Harry Reems, interview with Randy Barbato and Fenton Bailey, December 5, 2003, transcript, World of Wonder Production Company Archives, Hollywood, CA.
8. Gerard Damiano, "Deep Throat," script, 1971, World of Wonder Production Company Archives, Hollywood, California.
9. Gerard Damiano interview with Randy Barbato and Fenton Bailey, August 7, 2003, World of Wonder Production Company Archives, Hollywood, CA.
10. Damiano interview.
11. Reems interview.
12. On sex hygiene films, see Eric Schaefer, *Bold! Daring! Shocking! True! A History of Exploitation Films, 1919–1959* (Durham, NC: Duke University Press, 1999).
13. Phyllis Kronhausen and Eberhard Kronhausen, *The Sexually Responsive Woman* (New York: Bell Publishing, 1964), 78.
14. Joan Garrity, *The Sensuous Woman* (New York: Lyle Stuart, 1969), 14.
15. Anne Koedt, "The Myth of the Vaginal Orgasm" [1968], in *Sexual Revolution*, ed. Jeffery Escoffier (New York: Thunder's Mouth Press, 2003), 109. See also Jane Gerhard, "Revisiting the 'Myth of the Vaginal Orgasm': The Female Orgasm in American Sexual Thought and Second-Wave Feminism," *Feminist Studies* 2, no. 26 (Summer 2000): 449–76.

16. Linda Williams, interview with Fenton Bailey, July 8, 2003, transcript, World of Wonder Production Company Archives. See also Williams, *Hard Core: Power, Pleasure, and the "Frenzy of the Visible"* (Berkeley: University of California Press, 1989).

17. Diana Helfrecht, *Daily Girl,* September 1973.

18. "Linda Lovelace: The Merchandizing of Porno-Chic Stardom," *Washington Post,* June 5, 1973.

19. On the physical appeal of men in straight porn, see Emily Shelton, "A Star Is Porn: Corpulence, Comedy, and the Homosocial Cult of Adult Film Star Ron Jeremy," *Camera Obscura* 17, no. 3 (2002): 115–46.

20. Damiano interview.

21. Celine Parreñas Shimizu, *The Hypersexuality of Race: Performing Asian/American Women on Screen and Scene* (Durham, NC: Duke University Press, 2007).

22. Delores Wells interview with Fenton Bailey, July 26, 2003, World of Wonder archives.

23. Tina Russell, *Porno Star* (New York: Lancer, 1973); Marc Stevens, *10 ½!* (New York: Kensington, 1975); Harry Reems, *Here Comes Harry Reems* (New York: Pinnacle, 1975).

24. Kenneth Turan and Stephen Zito, *Sinema: American Pornographic Films and the People Who Make Them* (New York: Praeger Publishers, 1974), 90.

25. Linda Lovelace, *Inside Linda Lovelace* (New York: Pinnacle Books, 1973), 33.

26. Turan and Zito, *Sinema,* 147.

27. *Newsweek,* June 28, 1973; Angela Carter, "Fleshly Matters: Lovely Linda: Review of Linda Lovelace, *Inside Linda Lovelace,*" in *Shaking A Leg: Collected Writings,* originally printed in *New Society* (1974; repr., New York: Penguin Books, 1997), 55.

28. David Winters, interview with Fenton Bailey and Randy Barbato, January 4, 2004, transcript, World of Wonder Production Company Archives; Mel Mandel, telephone interview with author, January 10, 2006.

29. Wells interview.

30. Lovelace, *Inside Linda Lovelace,* 9–10.

31. Andrea True, interview with author, January 4, 2006. True had a part in the film and discussed the reason she felt the film was a failure.

32. "Harvard Lampoon Award Goes to Linda Lovelace," *Nashua Telegraph,* November 30, 1973.

33. Wayne King, "Sex Week at U. of Alabama Stirs Only Token Protests," *New York Times,* March 24, 1974.

34. David Winters, unpublished autobiography, accessed via World of Wonder Production Company Archives, 2006.

35. "Why Linda the Sex Star Made Royal Ascot Blush," *Daily Mirror,* June 19, 1974.

36. Winters, unpublished autobiography.

37. Victor Yannacone, telephone interview with author, August 26, 2013.

38. Ibid.

39. And then, for the most part, Linda faded from the public view. Yet by the end of the next decade, Linda resurfaced once again. In the late 1990s, she began to take part in memorabilia shows during which she autographed *Deep Throat* merchandise and old publicity photos, and in January 2001, she posed in *Leg Show,* an obscure fetish magazine with mostly international distribution.

40. Whitney Strub, *Perversion for Profit: The Politics of Pornography and the Rise of the New Right* (New York: Columbia University Press, 2011), 246.

41. Gloria Leonard, telephone interview with author, August 9, 2004.

42. Mike McGrady, interview with author, September 2, 2004, Lilliwaup, WA.

43. Fawn Germer, telephone interview with author, August 23, 2004.
44. Penelope Ashe (pseudonym), *Naked Came the Stranger* (New Jersey: Barricade Books, 1969); document in Mike McGrady Papers, box 1, Rare Book and Manuscript Collection, Columbia University, NY.
45. McGrady interview.

MAGAZINES/
PRINT CULTURE

CHAPTER 5

Mass-Market Pornography for Women

Bob Guccione's Viva *Magazine and the New Woman of the 1970s*

CAROLYN BRONSTEIN

"THE MAGAZINE THAT YOU hold in your hands is my own newborn child. . . . It was conceived out of a lifelong love-relationship with women . . . inseminated with adoration for their chemistry, respect for their wisdom, and awe for the endless mysteries and complexities of their sex."¹ With that macho opening salvo from publisher Bob Guccione, a reader in October 1973 would have found herself swept into the pages of *Viva,* a new international erotic magazine for women. Guccione, best known as the publisher of *Penthouse* magazine and as an editorial and business rival of *Playboy's* Hugh Hefner, sought to translate his wildly successful adult men's magazine for a contemporary female audience. In short, a colleague recalled, he had "dreamed [*Viva*] up as a kind of *Penthouse* for women," to bring pornography to a new group of users.²

Guccione believed that women deserved and desired the same kind of sexually thrilling reading and viewing experience that he provided men via *Penthouse.* He was not alone in this commitment to women's pleasure; similar ideas were circulating throughout American culture. Candida Royalle, a feminist filmmaker who specialized in erotic movies by and for women and couples, wrote that the women's liberation movement in the early 1970s "embraced sexual freedom and promoted a woman's right to a healthy, fulfilling sex life."³ The blockbuster 1972 film *Deep Throat* espoused a woman's right to orgasm and celebrated its star Linda Lovelace for doggedly pursuing "bells and whistles" in her sexual encounters. Feminist works such as Nancy Friday's collection of female sexual fantasies *My Secret Garden* (1973), and Erica Jong's novel *Fear of Flying* (1973), which endorsed the do-it-if-it-feels-good, commitment-free "zipless fuck," communicated that it was normal and appropriate for women to pursue sex avidly. Even mainstream sexual advice books for couples, such as Alex Comfort's best-selling *The Joy of Sex* (1972), emphasized the importance of female sexual satisfaction. Guccione's concept for *Viva* was thus revolutionary in bringing pornography for women to the corner newsstand, but also very much in tune with key 1970s ideas about women's rights to diverse sexual experiences. Guccione intended to deliver explicit content for women that would encourage their full participation in the sexual revolution and bestow the same privileges that heterosexual men enjoyed.

In executing this vision, Guccione also responded to significant trends that shaped 1970s public culture, including the commercialization of sexuality and the growth of entrepreneurship.[4] He was among the first to recognize the lucrative potential of pornography created for a new consumer market: women. Whereas 1960s activists decried the ills of galloping corporate capitalism, the 1970s brought renewed faith in the marketplace. According to the historian Bruce Schulman, Americans came to the conclusion in the 1970s that capitalism was "not the enemy of doing good but the vehicle for it," and industry was once again regarded as a leading ingredient of a productive society.[5] Entrepreneurs launched new businesses as a means for achieving both personal liberation and cultural revolution, a philosophy that supported the 1976 creation of Apple by Steve Wozniak, Steve Jobs, and Ronald Wayne.[6] As publisher of the sexually oriented magazines *Penthouse* and *Viva*, which debuted in the United States in 1969 and 1973, respectively, Bob Guccione embraced this market logic and successfully sold the sexual revolution to an eager public, amassing a personal fortune worth more than $400 million by the early 1980s.

When it came to *Penthouse*, the formula of offering straight male readers a louche version of cultural rebellion achieved through sexuality and lifestyle fared brilliantly. But with *Viva*, Guccione faced a different set of challenges. From the start, he ran afoul of a powerful and vocal women's movement that insisted on the advancement of an authentic, woman-centered, sex-positive perspective that he was ill equipped to understand or provide. Some readers could never accept a Guccione publication as potentially healthy or empowering for women, just as many feminists in the 1970s vociferously objected to Hugh Hefner's financial and political support for pro-choice and equal pay for equal work campaigns.[7] Some resented the idea that an unapologetically heterosexual male pornographer should be the one to decide what women—queer or straight—would view and enjoy on their road to sexual liberation. They felt, as the editors of *The Feminist Porn Book* (2013) have expressed, that good pornography for women had to be different from the typical male fare, and seek "to unsettle conventional definitions of sex, and expand the language of sex as an erotic activity, an expression of identity, a power exchange, a cultural commodity, and even a new politics."[8]

In contemporary discourse, we might say that a diverse range of readers hoped that Guccione would queer the genre, offering erotic photographs and editorial material that welcomed a range of sexualities, rather than relying on heterosexist, patriarchal constructions. Such content would have explored how sexuality and gender intersect with other aspects of identity, such as race, class, age, and physical ability, to shape highly personal forms of desire. A queer perspective eluded Guccione, but he did try to accommodate a broad range of women readers by joining *Viva*'s presentation of erotic photo spreads and explicit male nudity with contemporary feminist content from well-known activists and writers, including Betty Friedan, Germaine Greer, Nadine Gordimer, Maya Angelou, Molly Haskell, Karen Durbin, and Alix Kates Shulman. To woo advertisers, Guccione and his staff layered in typical features about fashion, cosmetics, celebrities, and health. They tried to respond to the dynamic social and sexual environment by inventing a new kind of magazine for the sexually adventurous 1970s woman. Of course, this experiment owed a debt to Helen Gurley Brown's *Cosmopolitan*, which led the way with an April 1972 nude centerfold of actor Burt Reynolds stretched out on a bearskin rug, his penis artfully covered by an outstretched arm.

America in the 1970s

Novelist Tom Wolfe famously described the 1970s as the "Me Decade," an era in which introspection, political apathy, and an emphasis on lifestyle and personal transformation eclipsed the idealistic 1960s focus on far-reaching political and social change. For many years, this characterization prevailed, gaining traction as influencers such as the historian Christopher Lasch dismissed the 1970s as a culture of narcissism in which material acquisition and consumer comforts were king.[9]

Many historians now contest this vision, arguing that the shift to personal experience was rooted in significant political ferment, and that the search for something authentic and vital in the body reflected a profound loss of public trust in the power and benevolence of institutions and authority. Something meaningful occurred in the 1970s— the decade when it was often said that "nothing happened"—including the development of new modes of self-awareness and self-expression that supported broad-based rights revolutions.[10] In the 1970s, gays and lesbians, racial minorities, people with disabilities, and other marginalized groups demanded recognition and voice; the creation of *Viva* spoke to women's urgently felt need to develop a specifically female sexual subjectivity. Queer theorist Nikki Sullivan has expressed this as the need to set aside the desire to be desired (by men) and instead foreground "a woman's pleasure *as her own*," a revolutionary way of regarding women's sexuality.[11]

Two recent books focus on 1973 (the year that Guccione launched *Viva*) as the decade's pivotal year and a moment of highly original creative production. Andreas Killen argues that three shocks—the end of the Vietnam War, the Watergate scandal, and a stagnating economy— destroyed the national self-image and gave birth to dark undercurrents such as a conspiracy culture and a widespread sense of paranoia. At the same time, a postmodern creative sensibility emerged that infused film, television, architecture, and literature with new energy. Killen deems 1973 "a year of uncertainty and disorientation but also of tremendous vitality and creativity."[12] Media historian Edward D. Miller also treats 1973 as a signal year, one in which "new forms of expressiveness and performance" emerged that allowed the voices of gays, lesbians, and feminists to be heard.[13] Miller points to the major influence of nonfiction media, which included *Viva*, in providing a dynamic space for discussions about gender, sexuality, and identity to take place.[14]

These cultural "shocks" and challenges to the status quo produced a wave of creativity that resulted in highly personal artistic expressions across genres. "The same distrust of the powers that be that undermined traditional sources of authority and fractured public life also spurred creative, personal, highly charged art that addressed just that discontent," Schulman wrote. "The decade's most potent and memorable cultural products raised an upturned middle finger at conventional sources of authority—be they the White House, the record companies, or the Hollywood studios."[15] Schulman cites Bob Dylan, Francis Ford Coppola, and Martin Scorsese as examples of artists whose music and films "assailed, mocked, undercut, and exposed the established sources of authority in American life."[16] Miller adds the rebellious artists David Bowie, Mick Jagger, Andy Warhol, and gay porn auteur Peter Berlin, whose self-portrait is on the cover, and whose work is discussed in Lucas Hilderbrand's essay in this volume. Each of these artists challenged the sexual status quo, using their eroticized male bodies to disrupt established regimes of sexuality, gender, and representation.

The impact of these artists on modern sexual culture is undeniable, yet any analysis of artists or cultural products that diversified sexuality in the 1970s must also consider the decade's most influential pornography publishers. Guccione and his fellow pornography barons, Hugh Hefner, Larry Flynt, and Al Goldstein, flouted sexual authority, especially obscenity laws and puritanical sexual regulations. In the great historical tradition of pornography as political critique, they used the genre to encourage a vision of a sexually liberated and "looser" (albeit heterosexist and patriarchal) way of life, enlarging what was permissible and visible in American culture.[17] Pornographers and sexual enthusiasts such as women's masturbation advocate Betty Dodson and Sandstone swingers' retreat founders John and Barbara Williamson displaced physicians as the experts on sexuality, inaugurating a more "confessional, expressive, and playful" discourse.[18] Adult magazines are rarely held up as canonical art along the lines of 1970s films such as *The Godfather*, *Badlands*, and *American Graffiti*, but pornography was also part of the creative cultural shift that encouraged sexual exploration and greater frankness about multiple forms of desire.

This essay recounts the history of *Viva* as emblematic of social changes that gave the 1970s their distinctive sexual and political character. Certainly, *Viva* was a nod to the power of the women's movement, which disrupted and transformed American culture with a vocal pro-woman and rights-oriented agenda throughout the 1970s. The year of *Viva*'s founding, 1973, was notable for gains in women's rights in both legal and popular culture forums, including the *Roe v. Wade* Supreme Court decision that legalized abortion, and the triumph of Billie Jean

King over Bobby Riggs in a hotly contested "war of the sexes" tennis match. The commercialization of sexuality and a supportive culture for creative entrepreneurship also supported *Viva*'s launch. The magazine initially fed off these new enthusiasms and unfettered energies. Yet, as the 1970s wore on, moving from a period of "porno chic" in the earlier part of the decade to one of retrenchment and greater social and political conservatism at decade's end, the magazine faltered. Indeed, *Viva* absorbed and reflected these changes, becoming far less sexually adventurous as the years passed. The magazine ultimately succumbed to the conservative tide in full force by the decade's end, ceasing publication one year before Ronald Reagan's 1980 presidential election.

Bob Guccione and the Founding of Penthouse

Robert Charles Joseph Edward Sabatini Guccione was a first-generation Sicilian American, born to devout Catholic parents in Brooklyn, New York, in 1930. He grew up in Bergenfield, New Jersey, spending his Sundays as an altar boy. As a young adult, Guccione enrolled in a seminary and studied for the priesthood, but dropped out after a few months. He pursued his dream of becoming an artist, an early sign of his rejection of conventional expectations and desire for personal freedom. Guccione moved to California, where he met his first wife, Lilyan, whom he married in 1949. Their daughter, Tonina, was born in 1950, and the family moved to Rome, where Guccione lived a bohemian life, sketching patrons at cafés and cartooning. He also traveled through Paris and Spain, securing odd acting jobs and painting. After five years, Lilyan tired of the itinerant lifestyle and moved back to California with Tonina, initiating divorce proceedings.[19]

Guccione's second marriage lasted longer than his first, but also ended in divorce. Like his future business competitor and fellow entrepreneur, Hugh Hefner of *Playboy*, Guccione found little contentment in traditional marriage or family life. He met the British cabaret singer Muriel Hudson in Tangier shortly after Lilyan's departure, a period in his life devoted to "rebellion and art" during which Guccione painted, played chess, and smoked pot.[20] He married Hudson in 1956, and the couple had four children over the next nine years. They resided in London, where Guccione was unsuccessful in a series of business ventures. He was the managing editor of the *London American*, a weekly newspaper, which failed. He also started a mail order business and ran a dry cleaning chain. Mounting debt, infidelity, and Guccione's quest to launch *Penthouse* contributed to the end of the marriage in the late 1960s; Hudson took the children and filed for divorce.[21]

Guccione's fortunes began to change when he started publishing *Penthouse* in Britain in 1965 as an adult men's magazine. He unabashedly modeled the magazine after *Playboy,* but featured more explicit sexual content. However, he had trouble attracting investors.[22] In an effort to raise cash by selling advance subscriptions, he sent a color brochure filled with images of half-naked women to mailing lists that specifically included clergymen, nuns, young students, retirees, and wives of members of Parliament.[23] The stunt brought public outrage as well as the hoped-for publicity; Guccione was denounced as a pornographer in Parliament and fined one hundred British pounds (about $250) for sending indecent materials through the mail. But subscriptions, accompanied by cash and checks, flooded in, and the scandal ensured that Guccione sold the entire first run of 120,000 newsstand copies of *Penthouse* in days.[24]

The second issue of *Penthouse* led Guccione to his most significant personal and professional relationship. An item in the magazine made an unflattering mention of twenty-six-year-old Kathy Keeton, a South African expatriate and former child ballerina who was then a star of the Folies Bergère erotic cabaret scene.[25] Keeton's manager complained about the slur.[26] Guccione visited Keeton's backstage dressing room at the famous Pigalle Club in London, ostensibly to apologize, and was impressed to find Keeton reading the London *Financial Times,* surrounded by piles of science books and newspapers.[27] The two began dating, and Guccione hired Keeton to sell ad space for *Penthouse.* Later, she became one of the magazine's top executives, paving the way for her eventual role as associate publisher and, later, executive editor of *Viva.* Guccione and Keeton carried on a committed, but open, relationship throughout the 1970s and 1980s, ultimately marrying in 1990.

Guccione was thirty-five years old when *Penthouse* hit the stands, four years younger than Hugh Hefner and less urbane than his rival. By all accounts, he oozed sex. According to Richard Corliss of *Time,* "Bob Guccione radiated a sleazy, erotic charisma."[28] Mike Edison, a former editor in chief of *Screw,* noted that Guccione was more interested in "raw sex" than Hefner, and wanted to be a participant as well as a publisher. "Like the shutterbug in *Blow-Up,* he swung from the ankles, ready to ball on the floor if no sports car was available for a quick toss," Edison observed.[29] Journalist Patricia Bosworth, the exec-

FIGURE 5.1. American magazine publisher Bob Guccione wears a leather shirt and his trademark gold neck chains as he reviews photographic images for *Penthouse* in his New York City office, January 1, 1974. Photo: Bernard Gotfryd.

utive editor of *Viva* from 1974 to 1976, remembers her first impression of Guccione as "a tall, handsome man, very muscled and bronzed, with a strong Roman nose and thick dark hair . . . wearing a black silk shirt open to the waist, tight black leather pants, and white suede go-go boots." Guccione "jangled" when he walked, his heavy gold neck chains and medallions clanking together in a thicket of chest hair (fig. 5.1).[30] One medallion featured a reproduction of the first *Penthouse* cover. Another displayed a replica of Guccione's genitalia crafted in solid gold.[31] Edison noted that Guccione wore "the brash, uninhibited sexuality of the age on his sleeve . . . his shirts routinely unbuttoned above his navel."[32]

Four years after introducing *Penthouse* in the United Kingdom, its success fueled by the sexual revolution and reliable birth control methods like the pill, Guccione brought his magazine to the United States. He launched in September 1969, famously going "rabbit hunting" and challenging *Playboy* for the market with more sexually explicit photographs and content. By 1970, *Penthouse* was selling more than a million copies a month in the United States, still far behind *Playboy*, at six million. But *Penthouse* was on the move; by the fall of 1973, when Guccione launched *Viva*, *Penthouse* was selling four million copies a month. By

1976, *Penthouse* had largely caught up to *Playboy*, with Hefner ahead by no more than 500,000 copies a year. *Penthouse* circulation rose to nearly five million by the late 1970s.[33] Some industry observers argued that *Penthouse* was at the forefront of the sexual revolution with its "explicit, 'hot' treatment of sexuality—revealing poses, women fondling themselves, lesbianism, fetishism, threesomes . . . ," all of which made *Playboy* seem tame, even quaint, by comparison.[34]

Viva: The International Magazine for Women

Guccione envisioned *Viva*, "The International Magazine for Women," as a sophisticated erotic magazine, a *Penthouse* for women. From the start, *Viva* and *Penthouse* were intertwined. Guccione was the driving force behind both publications, and they shared editorial personnel, an art department, and office space. He told media representatives that *Viva* would be "a bright and sophisticated monthly for women who find *Cosmopolitan* too coy."[35] Taking a page from competitor Helen Gurley Brown, whose magazine sought to provide "a strikingly modern and cosmopolitan definition of womanhood" focused on love, sex, work, money, and success, Guccione imagined his readers as "lusty, real, indefatigable, down-to-earth, fetching, bright, sexy, uncompromising."[36] Keeton sought the "new woman of the Seventies" who was neither a feminist nor a traditional housewife, but "the new woman . . . the woman who is sexually liberated but does not hate men; the woman who wants to live independently, but with her man."[37] Keeton wanted to see *Viva* competing for the readers of *Vogue*, *Cosmopolitan*, and *Glamour*.[38] She and Guccione also desired upper-middle-class readers for the high-end advertisers they would attract.

Keeton exerted significant influence over *Viva*. At first, she appeared on the masthead as associate publisher, second-in-command. Mike Edison claimed that Keeton was only "nominally in charge" because the final authority always lay with Guccione.[39] However, other observers gave Keeton more credit. Author Jerry Oppenheimer, a biographer of *Vogue* editor Anna Wintour, described Keeton as a "bright and ambitious" person who "ran the monthly with a halter top, tight pants, fuck-me heels, and an iron hand in a velvet glove."[40] Keeton's influence over the editorial aspects of the magazine increased significantly after July 1974, when she became executive editor.

The first issue of *Viva* was published in October 1973 (fig. 5.2). Guccione and Keeton sold an impressive fifty-three pages of ads, and

FIGURE 5.2. Bob Guccione embraces a model at the New York City launch party for *Viva*, September 17, 1973. Photo: Ron Galella.

the first printing of the magazine sold more than 80 percent of its one-million-plus copy run.[41] But the early reviews were devastating. *Time* magazine savaged the publication, complaining that an interview with novelist Norman Mailer had been conducted by an old friend who "questioned [Mailer] ever so gently" and ignored the misogyny and sexual violence in Mailer's writings, the most compelling issues for *Viva* readers.[42] *Time* doubted that women would spend a dollar per issue for second-rate material that lacked "wit and focus and sex appeal."[43]

Viva also earned a searing critique from the feminist author and playwright Nora Ephron, who deemed it a "lemon" that reflected Guccione's male chauvinist conviction that he knew what women needed and wanted. Reflecting on the first issue, Ephron was offended by Guccione's characterization of *Viva* as an infant that he had "conceived out of a lifelong love-relationship with women . . . inseminated with adoration for their chemistry," finding his impregnation metaphor intolerably sexist. She deemed it a "dose of male overkill and locker room exclusion."[44] Ephron took Guccione to task for anti-feminist content, which included a recurring column by a male sex researcher that presented men's sexual fantasies and advised women how to best respond to them. When a female staffer reportedly complained that this feature held little appeal for a range of *Viva* readers, Guccione retorted that "he had shown the piece to three girls in his hotel room and *they* found it fascinating."[45] *Screw* magazine founder Al Goldstein has described Guccione as an "arrogant and delusional" personality, and the defensive response to criticism of *Viva* suggests that hubris damaged the magazine from the start.[46]

Beyond Guccione's personal limitations, the editorial team also faced the significant challenge of figuring out how to craft exciting content for a heterosexual female audience unused to viewing naked men for pleasure. Edward D. Miller notes that the eroticization of male bodies in the early 1970s meant that heterosexual women and gay men "had to undergo 'an education of desire' " to adjust to public participation in mainstream sexual culture.[47] Similarly, the editors lacked a familiar erotic language with which to communicate with *Viva* readers. Ephron had derided *Viva* as featuring mostly what straight men found sexy: "These men put their heads together, and decided that what women want in a women's magazine is a men's magazine," she wrote.[48] Indeed, the initial issues of *Viva* featured more female nudity than male, and were overall somewhat sexless and tame, lacking the erotic "dirty" quality that was *Penthouse*'s signature style.

The absence of full frontal male nudity in the first issues of *Viva* struck many as disingenuous for failing to disrupt the sexual status quo. Guccione had pushed the envelope at *Penthouse,* driving Hefner to include more explicit female nudity in *Playboy* via the "Pubic Wars" that went on between the two publishers from 1971 to 1972 as they competed for circulation. Guccione was known for his embrace of the "pink shot," a close-up photograph of the vagina that revealed the labia. At *Viva,* however, he was much more conservative. For the first issue, Guccione commissioned a fourteen-page photo spread and interview featuring the young heavyweight boxer Randy Neumann. This feature, titled "The Fighter," included artistically posed nude photos of Neumann in the gym locker room and shower, but every frontal shot was awkwardly and self-consciously cropped so that his penis was never visible.

A second pictorial essay, titled "The Picnic," featured an erotic Edwardian-era romp between Hilary, "a perfect young gentleman and rake," and his female cousin, Phoebe, enjoying a tryst on the "Peckershire Heath" in the English countryside. In fifteen pages of softly lit photographs, the woman appeared nude, breasts and vagina clearly displayed, but the male model was undressed to the waist only— his pants remained on in all images. The *Time* magazine critic observed that he was "as carefully shielded as Marlon Brando in *Last Tango in Paris.*"[49] Guccione reproduced what film theorist Teresa de Lauretis has called "the standard frame of romance," in which the female body is a sexualized object for male consumption.[50] Had he flipped the pictorial, leaving the woman dressed and the man unclothed for her visual pleasure, Guccione would have disrupted conventional ways of seeing, replacing the controlling male gaze with something new. Following film theorist Laura Mulvey, who popularized the idea of the male gaze in the mid-1970s, Phoebe was held up as a passive erotic object to be looked at, whereas Hilary was the active agent who looked, exercising control over and possession of her body.[51] In this narrative structure, Hilary drove the story (and sexual exchange) forward, and viewers were thus invited to identify with his perspective, not Phoebe's. Neither "The Fighter" nor "The Picnic" delivered the subversive erotic content that Guccione had promised. Both smacked of paternalism in denying women the agentic, voyeuristic experience of gazing at fully naked bodies that heterosexual men enjoyed via *Penthouse.*

Some readers were adamant that they wanted more male nudity. In letters printed in the December 1973 issue, readers attacked the coy pictorials that had appeared in October and November (notwithstanding the possibility that letters printed in *Viva*'s forum might have been written in-house). One reader stated it plainly, "We wanna see more cock! Don't hide it between their legs, let it all hang out! I didn't buy a woman's magazine to see nude women—it's men's bodies I wanna see."[52] A reader in Forest Hills, New York, also clamored for more naked men: "I know I speak for all women when I say I would like to see more of the male anatomy and less of the female form. The male body is beautiful, exciting, stimulating, arousing, and too often hidden from view."[53] A reader from Port Chester, New York, complained about the frontal shots in "The Fighter," and claimed that she had to use a magnifying glass to try to see anything "interesting." She described herself as disappointed and chagrined after spending an afternoon reading *Viva*. "I am a bit tired of all the cutesy-poo shots of guys with strategically placed hands, forearms, towels, motorcycle helmets, etc. that keep it from all hanging out," she wrote. "The long and short of it is that you are copping out if you don't see to it that the male models in your *Viva* pictorials join the same bush league that your Penthouse Pets do."[54] Guccione's bold experiment was failing to address and entice the sexually adventurous "new woman" of the 1970s.

Written for Men, by Men

Along with content, such as the recurring feature on male sexual fantasies, *Viva*'s photo essays, too, revealed the magazine's most urgent problem: the initial issues were created almost entirely by men. In addition to Guccione, the executive editor and the two art directors were male, borrowed from the *Penthouse* team. Most of the features and photographs bore male credit lines; women comprised just eight of the twenty-three contributors in the first issue. A practical advice article on venereal disease had a male author and a (heterosexual) male point of view; the piece encouraged women to be sexually active with multiple partners, but to be sure to use spermicide—a directive that ignored the possibility that a woman's lovers might be other women. The interview with heavyweight Neumann was peppered with male chauvinism that was surely odious to feminist readers. "I'm very chivalrous toward women," Neumann told *Viva*. "I hold them in great esteem, especially the attractive ones." In describing his relationship with his wife, the boxer reported that she gladly accepted his authority. "I'm the boss and she knows and respects it," he crowed.[55] For "The Picnic," Guccione himself may have written the stilted dialogue that supposedly unfolded between Hilary and Phoebe as they disrobed on the heath. "By Jove, Phoebe, how soft, white, and firm your 'Mary Poppins' are, to be sure," he said while fondling her breasts. She responded, "Yes, Hilary, mammaries are the dairy that we all carry about with us."[56] With such laughable content in the first issue, it was no surprise that the advertising pages for the second and third issues fell to thirty-three and thirty-one pages, respectively.

Many readers compared *Viva* unfavorably with *Penthouse,* describing the newcomer as a pale imitation. "Considering how sensational and swinging *Penthouse* is, I thought that you'd really be a magazine for the Woman of the Seventies . . . ," a New York City reader wrote. She complained that the first issue of *Viva* was "stodgy" and demure. "Then I got your November issue. Ugh! More of the same, but even more boring—what are you trying to do, steal the *New Yorker*'s audience from their graves?"[57] A reader's husband asked Guccione if it would take an "earthquake" to wake him up to women's demands for a *Penthouse* of their own. "It's simple—put out a magazine just like your great *Penthouse,* only with male nudes," he advised. "*Viva* missed the boat in not doing this. Wise up!"[58]

Some regular features were worse than dull, even glaringly insensitive to women's issues. Cartoonist Art Cumings, who penned "Balloonheads" for *Penthouse,* created a comic strip for *Viva* called "The Little Hooker." In the November 1973 issue, the Little Hooker is being followed by a male flasher wearing a raincoat and rain hat. He hides behind a tree and then behind bushes, as he pursues her down the street. Finally, the young woman confronts him, yelling, "What are you, some kinda nut? Man, you're sick! Get Lost."[59] They turn away from each other and start to go their separate ways, but both change their minds and turn back around. He flashes her, and she likes it. In the next panel, they are shown having sex behind some bushes, their clothes strewn all around. In the December 1973 issue, the Little Hooker is shown crying to a series of johns with the news that she is pregnant. Each man gives her money without the usual sex in exchange. She confesses to a friend that she is making more money and working shorter hours with this scheme. But, she admits, "I miss the wear and tear." This *Viva* content depicted stalking and street harassment as a sexual turn-on rather than a frightening crime, and characterized a prostitute as a manipulating liar who exploited men for money. Not all of *Viva*'s readers were self-proclaimed feminists, of course, but by the early 1970s awareness of male sexual violence and women's sexual oppression under patriarchy was high.[60] A reader in New York City expressed her frustration with the situation in a letter to *Viva*'s forum. "I saw your magazine and was thinking of writing you a letter on a more intellectual level, but then I thought, 'What's the point?' I am *outraged*. The magazine is written and put together by men, for men."[61]

Along these lines, perhaps no element of the magazine drew as much ire from readers as Guccione's male sexual fantasy column. In each issue, sex researcher Dr. Robert Chartham presented the actual fantasies of men representing a wide range of ages and socioeconomic backgrounds. Chartham offered women a peek into the minds of men such as John D., a twenty-four-year-old advertising executive who dreamed of a special school devoted to teaching young girls how to please men sexually. Chartham analyzed each fantasy and commented on the psychology of its creator, as well as offered advice as to how a woman might best conduct a relationship with this man. He described John D. as suffering from "pseudo-pedophilia" but assured readers that this condition would not negatively affect his ability to enjoy sex with adult women.[62]

Reader response to the feature was swift and negative. A New Jersey reader derided the men's fantasies as "anemic."[63] Others insisted that the magazine ought to pay more attention to women's desires. "We would rather hear about our own fantasies. It would be instructional and a turn-on," a reader from New York City pointed out.[64] Others pointed to Nancy Friday's research to alert Guccione that women had just as many exciting, erotic sexual fantasies as men. A feminist reader in San Francisco penned a sarcastic letter to *Viva* to "thank" the magazine for publishing the male fantasies feature. "If ever there was propaganda for the women's movement, then this is it," she wrote. "You should send these fantasies to every woman who still believes that her submissive place is in the home. If these women realized what was going through the obnoxious infantile minds of the men they consider to be their masters, they would be out of the kitchen in two minutes, and on the road to liberation."[65] Although readers complained bitterly about this feature, Guccione stuck with it for close to a year before instructing Chartham to include some female fantasies.

Let It All Hang Out

Starting in January 1974, *Viva* tried to respond to reader demands for more explicit sexual content. The magazine began including full-frontal male nudity, offering two photo spreads in each issue. One spread always featured a solitary man, and the other showed a man and a woman engaged in sexual play. The magazine emphasized the penis that year, with photographs that treated the organ as a focal point. Many readers responded positively to the new format. "I hope you continue to show men's penises like in the January and February issues," a woman in Maine wrote. "If people are to become free to enjoy their own sexuality and that of others, then *Viva* is a logical place to start."[66]

But even with the new emphasis on male nudity, readers continued to complain that *Viva* did not reflect a true woman's point of view or aesthetic. The predominance of male editors and contributors contributed to the problem. Art Kane was the art director of both *Viva* and *Penthouse,* and he hired internationally famous male photographers such as Helmut Newton, Bill King, and James Moore to produce covers for *Viva.* Kane and Guccione dreamed up a "Pubic Hairstyles" feature for the August 1974 issue (fig. 5.3), which featured a series of eclectic looks for women, such as pubic hair teased up into a Mohawk or shaved and trimmed into a heart shape. Celebrity stylist Paul Mitchell created the "hairdos" and Kane took the photographs. Yet the radical feminist author Andrea Dworkin contributed a fiery article to the same issue that described the horrors of foot binding in early modern China. She compared that practice to contemporary American women's obligations to pluck their eyebrows, remove their body hair, wear girdles and high-heeled shoes, and undergo cosmetic surgery. "The pain, of course, teaches an important lesson: no price is too great, no process too repulsive, no operation too painful for the woman who would be beautiful," she wrote.[67] The irony of juxtaposing Dworkin's essay about the political significance of women's beauty regimes with the photographs of women's coiffed pubic hair seemed to be lost on the editors. But it revealed just how fractured *Viva* was in terms of understanding its core identity, mission, and message.

New Talent Comes Aboard

With advertiser support waning, and no clear editorial direction, Guccione relented and went in search of female talent to produce *Viva.* Over the next few years, Guccione and Keeton began hiring top editors and rising stars from magazines such as *Glamour, Harper's Bazaar,* and *Ms.* in hopes of turning *Viva* into a leading women's publication. One of the most important early hires was Patricia Bosworth, a jour-

THE INTERNATIONAL MAGAZINE FOR WOMEN   AUGUST 74 $1.25

VIVA

WOMEN
ARE
INTO:

TOTAL
FEMINISM

MALE NUDES

PUBIC
HAIRSTYLES

HASH
SMUGGLING

GREAT NEW
FALL
FASHIONS

FIGURE 5.3. The cover of *Viva*, including the "Pubic Hairstyles" feature, August 1974, when eroticism was still emphasized.

nalist with a strong track record in women's magazines. Bosworth first appeared on the *Viva* masthead as executive editor in August 1974, although she had been working as an editorial consultant for *Viva* for five months. Bosworth had just left her job as managing editor of *Harper's Bazaar*, where she had worked from 1972 to 1974, following stints at *Women's Day* and *McCall's*.[68] At first, Bosworth was unsure how to respond to *Viva;* the first issue she looked over with Guccione was "a contradictory mix" of fashion pages, a profile of Broadway producer Joseph Papp, an erotic feature on tantric yoga, a sexy pictorial with nude images of a twenty-five-year-old male musician, and a feature on sex educator Betty Dodson's masturbation workshop in which she taught women how to bring themselves to orgasm.[69] In that same issue, Guccione debuted a new column called "Dialogues by Dr. Eugene Schoenfeld," which featured readers' sexual health and beauty questions. For example, "Tina" confessed that while masturbating with a frankfurter wrapped in plastic, the plastic had separated from the hot dog and had become lodged beyond her reach. She asked Dr. Schoenfeld for removal advice. This dubious content gave Bosworth pause, but Guccione persisted. Of his offer, Bosworth recalled, "He said he wanted a 'really classy editor' to run things and he'd pay well. He wouldn't take no for an answer."[70] She signed on to edit *Viva.*

Keeton and Guccione made another significant editorial hire several years later in Anna Wintour, best known since 1988 as the legendary editor in chief of *Vogue.* Although Wintour does not discuss her time at *Viva,* purposefully obscuring her association with Guccione and pornography, she was the fashion editor beginning in April 1977. She joined the magazine at the age of twenty-seven, after being fired from *Harper's Bazaar* for trying to include more sexually erotic fashion photography in that magazine. Wintour used *Viva* as a training ground for *Vogue,* making a serious name for herself as a talented and innovative fashion editor. She traveled around the world on *Viva* location shoots, from the Caribbean to Japan, and hired avant-garde photographers such as Deborah Turbeville, Patrick Demarchelier, André Carrara, and Shig Ikeda. Wintour introduced *Viva* readers to emerging international fashion designers such as Norma Kamali and Issey Miyake.[71] Keeton also hired André Leon Talley, the African American fashion guru who would later work with Wintour as an editor at *Vogue.*

With talented new editors at the helm, the magazine tried to serve the "new woman" of the 1970s by publishing significant feminist content. This included interviews, research-based features, poetry, and short fiction. *Viva* readers encountered diverse women authors, including the Nobel Prize–winning South African novelist Nadine Gordimer, Maxine Hong Kingston, and Maya Angelou. Under Bosworth's direction, *Viva* published serious investigative journalism about battered women, bisexuality, breast cancer, and custody trends affecting divorced mothers. The magazine featured interviews with leading feminist activists such as Betty Friedan and Barbara Seaman, a women's health expert. "We were aware that times were changing, and we tried to capture the rebelliousness and the energy that kept surfacing in America back then, especially in the women's movement, which by 1975 was at its most transformational," Bosworth recalled. "Women were really attempting to experience love, achievement, and independence on a grand scale."[72]

Bosworth took the magazine in a direction similar to *Ms.*, with hard-hitting stories about cutting-edge women's movement issues. She devoted much of the November 1974 issue to coverage of activism around rape, including an anonymous rape questionnaire, which readers were asked to fill out and send back to *Viva* to help antirape activists gather data about the frequency and types of rape experienced. The issue included an article titled "Twelve Rules of Self-Defense" and techniques that could be used to fight back in the midst of a sexual assault, as well as a detailed state-by-state chart listing rape crisis centers where women could seek help, and antirape groups that women could join. Keeton's "First Word" column that month displayed great sensitivity to the effect of rape on women's lives and the movement's efforts to raise awareness and lessen the stigma for survivors. "There are surprisingly few hard facts and figures known about the crime," she observed. "That's because women have either been too afraid or felt too guilty to talk about their experiences as victims. Until now they have felt helpless and unable to change the situation."[73] Much of the rape issue content was authored by the radical feminists Andra Medea and Kathleen Thompson, the founders of Chicago Women Against Rape and authors of *Against Rape* (1974), a significant book that characterized rape as a form of male violence. Medea and Thompson shared the perspective that any man—one's father, uncle, boyfriend, or boss—was capable of committing rape, and that women had to be on constant alert.

The same issue featured a pictorial essay titled "The Hustler," featuring ten pages of naked photographs of Michael Bassett, a tall, muscular and well-endowed thirty-two-year-old pool player from Las Vegas. The photographs emphasized Bassett's penis. In one close-up photo, he appeared naked, seated with his legs spread wide open. In another, he wore tight velvet pants that revealed a sizable bulge. And, for the first time, *Viva* included a two-page foldout centerfold similar to those in *Penthouse*. The centerfold showed a naked Bassett reading a book, his penis the unquestionable focus of the image. The following month, the *Viva* centerfold was titled "Gold for Guys" and featured a tanned, oiled, naked man draped in gold chains, wearing a Canadian lynx fur coat, open to the front. He wore a gold cock ring around his large penis. The centerfolds lasted only for a few issues— perhaps they were voted out by Bosworth and her team, or criticized by advertisers—but the glorification of the penis seemed at odds with the feminist editorial content such as the feature on rape. In a women's movement increasingly aware of male sexual violence and hostile to the institution of heterosexuality, the penis functioned both as a weapon and as a symbol of oppression *as well as* a source of eroticism. *Viva* was caught in the middle.

Goodbye to All That (Penis)

By its third year, *Viva* was struggling to stay afloat. Advertisers were reluctant to buy space, concerned that the magazine provided an unseemly environment for their clothing, packaged foods, and cosmetics. Starting in April 1976, Keeton tried to save the magazine by changing *Viva*'s direction. She announced in her monthly column that the magazine would cease publishing naked photographs that revealed the penis. "Perhaps most obvious at first will be a change in our erotic photography. With tastes developing so rapidly, it's difficult to predict what is going to interest women, but in our opinion it won't be explicit male nudity. . . . Sensuality will merely be expressed in new and different ways."[74] In August 1976, despite reader complaints, she defended the new policy, arguing that the marketing efforts of the magazine had been "crippled" by the inclusion of male nudity.[75] Keeton and Guccione hoped that this move would turn around *Viva*'s ad sales.

Trouble was also brewing on the editorial side. Bosworth was tired of Guccione's imperious ways and his constant interference. One night, he summoned her after midnight to his Manhattan home, which consisted of two combined East Side brownstones that took up almost an entire city block. Guccione and Keeton's faces were carved into massive marble columns in the foyer, and the home was filled with statues of Moorish slaves, sphinxes, pyramids, candelabras, and a gilt piano previously owned by Judy Garland.[76] When Bosworth arrived, Guccione revealed his new idea: she would become the madam of a brothel located near the Las Vegas airport that catered to rich patrons. "'Guys fly in on their private planes, stop for a little pleasure at the

Viva whorehouse,' he said, all excited, 'then get back onto their planes and zoom off!'"[77] *Viva* sustained a major blow in 1976 when Bosworth quit. Guccione had pressured her to hire an alleged rapist to write an advice-to-the-lovelorn column, and this was the last straw.[78] Without Bosworth's editorial oversight, the articles soon began to look and feel like more typical "women's magazine" pieces, with features like "How to Handle a Tightwad Date" and "Stretch Marks—The Best Cure Is Still Prevention" in the March 1977 issue.

Guccione and *Viva* repeatedly fell out of step with central women's movement concerns. In addition to foisting sexist content on his editors, Guccione's vision for *Viva* was limited by his *Penthouse* sensibility, where sex occurred between men and women, and typically between one man and many women. Under Guccione's direction, *Viva* maintained a steadfast heterosexual orientation, which irked readers who directed their sexual and emotional energies to women. "You really are not doing enough for lesbians," one wrote. "Your fantasy pages are about men and admit to being written in the interest of heterosexual relations. Your photographs show men on top of women and your publisher patronizes us by claiming the magazine as his newborn infant."[79] A New York City reader complained in May 1976 that *Viva* had yet to figure out what erotica for feminist women might look like. "It was a pleasure to read intelligent and interesting articles with an adult, female point of view," she wrote. "But those naked men. Ugh! Women's liberation does not mean ripping off the established men's magazines which capitalize on naked women."[80] A reader from Fort Fairfield, Maine, wrote in June 1974, "I'm not going to demean myself by going ape over cock pictures."[81] These were not prudish responses to sexuality but statements about women's conflicted responses to heterosexist images. Many *Viva* readers desired erotic content that fundamentally shifted the gaze, giving them the opportunity to experience pleasure from a new, exciting, and woman-oriented perspective.

Viva also missed opportunities to highlight diversity and inclusion in its erotic and feminist content. The magazine debuted at a time when ethnic and racial groups sought greater cultural recognition and political power, yet *Viva* addressed itself to a white, middle-class woman. One reader pointed out such shortcomings around race in August 1974: "You have an out-of-sight mag! The only problem is you have no people of color, in other words, 'soul brothers and sisters.' Being black, I know how beautiful it is. So let's get it on and get some color in your life."[82] A twenty-six-year-old black woman from

Oakland, California, wrote that thoughts about race were "nagging" at her after reading each issue: "Since *Viva* is the International Magazine for Women, why are there no pictures of Third World people? I think that there are many beautiful and sensuous brothers and sisters of all races. How about having a few?"[83]

The independent feminist press also raised concerns about *Viva*. Writing in the biweekly Seattle-area feminist newspaper *Pandora*, Dena Dawson expressed dismay that men were publishing erotic magazines for women, specifically *Playgirl*, *Venus*, and *Viva*. She argued that these publications exploited the insecurity and fears of young women living in an era when marriage and motherhood were no longer central goals, whereas being a sexy, "liberated" woman was promoted as the new standard. "What would our real erotic images be like if we were not manipulated into mass culture by Big Brother media?" Dawson asked. "Our taste is what the marketing geniuses make it. And our ideals of male and female beauty become these photographs of young, symmetrical, perfect, anonymous, blank bodies."[84]

By late spring 1978, the situation at the magazine was volatile. Guccione fired executive editor Gini Kopecky and senior editor Valerie Monroe when they refused to place a Penthouse Pet on the cover of *Viva*. The editors argued that it would damage *Viva*'s credibility among women readers as "a more serious magazine, a more literary magazine."[85] As editorial talent dwindled, Wintour was the magazine's greatest remaining asset. She made a name for *Viva* as a serious fashion book and was at that time producing twenty-five to thirty cutting-edge pages per issue, many featuring avant-garde photography. Nonetheless, Guccione announced at a November 1978 staff meeting that the magazine would cease publication due to declining advertising revenues.

Farewell, *Viva*

Why did *Viva* fail? Guccione published the last issue in January 1979, ending the magazine's run after five years and sixty-four issues. That same year, *Penthouse* reached its peak, selling more than 4.7 million copies. Part of the reason for *Viva*'s demise had to do with the challenge of creating erotica for women in a society that has primarily defined sexuality on male terms. Pornography has always been a contested genre for women. Mike Edison has observed that pornography for women is guaranteed to fail.[86] Larry Flynt maintained that men are turned on by visual images, by what they see, whereas women respond to what they read and imagine, an observation that may partially explain the success of the *Fifty Shades of Grey* erotic romance novel trilogy.[87] Al Goldstein of *Screw* believed that women wanted romance more than sex, especially the fantasy of a heroic man riding in on a white stallion.[88] None of these pornographers, including Guccione, really knew what kind of erotic material might appeal to a broad swath of women. Bosworth argued that she pushed to make *Viva* more erotic and less pornographic, but Guccione's macho perspective got in the way. He often substituted his own judgment and story ideas for those of his female editors, most of whom had a better intellectual and emotional connection to the average *Viva* reader than did Guccione. "*Viva* would never be anything but hopelessly schizoid," Bosworth wrote, "its feminist intentions overshadowed by male porn."[89]

Jessanne Collins, a former editor at rival magazine *Playgirl*, which also launched in 1973, reflected on that magazine's demise in a 2013 *Salon* interview. She said that the companies that had run *Playgirl* since the 1970s were "best versed in making porn that appealed to straight men," such as *High Society* and *Hawk* magazines. "They tended to take that formula, sub out the women for these buff dudes, and assume that women would find that that spoke to them," she said. "And it wasn't really that good a product, because that switch-out just doesn't exactly work. Something is lost in translation."[90] *Playgirl* had a longer run than *Viva*, by decades, but it was common knowledge at the magazine and elsewhere that a significant percentage of the magazine's readership was comprised of gay men. In both cases, neither the *Viva* nor *Playgirl* editors could really figure out the *translation*—how to make the mass-market pornography model work for women.

For the 1970s female reader, *Viva* likely provided a new experience: gazing at sexually explicit pictures of men. Even ten years later, in 1982, the appearance of a Calvin Klein billboard featuring a bronzed, nearly nude male underwear model towering over Times Square raised considerable public outcry and discussion. *Viva* hit newsstands years before the contemporary world of internet pornography, which has made naked male and female bodies so commonplace that *Playboy* announced in October 2015 that it would cease publishing nude photographs. Many women did not know how to respond to *Viva*, how to feel good about being boldly sexual in a society that was just beginning to vocalize women's rights to a fulfilling, robust sexual life, and to challenge heterosexism. Some women in the 1970s struggled with worries that desiring penetrative heterosexual sex was antifeminist, thus making subscription to (and enjoyment of) *Viva* a thorny ethical problem. For many, pornography created ideologically uncomfortable territory that was difficult to reconcile with eroticism.

BY THE 1980S, GUCCIONE HAD amassed a $300 million publishing empire, General Media International, which owned *Penthouse*, the popular science journal *Omni*, the music magazine *Spin*, and a health publication called *Longevity* dedicated to prolonging one's life, among other titles. But the bulk of Guccione's fortune came from *Penthouse*, which, Bosworth observed, "remains among the greatest success stories in the history of magazines."[91] In 1982, *Forbes* included Guccione on its list of the four hundred wealthiest individuals. But *Penthouse* suffered financially in the 1990s with the rise of internet pornography (fig. 5.4). To pay creditors, Guccione had to sell off his renowned $150 million art collection featuring works by Degas, Renoir, Picasso, Matisse, and Chagall.[92] General Media filed for bankruptcy in 2003, and *Penthouse* was sold to a private equity firm. In 2007, Guccione was diagnosed with throat cancer, to which he would succumb three years later at the age of seventy-nine. At the time of Guccione's death, *Penthouse* circulation had dropped to 178,000.[93]

Although the history of *Penthouse* is well known, *Viva* has been consigned to the dustbin of 1970s history; Guccione's legacy is wrapped up in the success of *Penthouse*. But in publishing *Viva* and trying to offer women a sexually explicit magazine comparable to what heterosexual male readers enjoyed, Guccione should be recognized as a social entrepreneur, an individual who seeks to bring about dynamic cultural and political change through private enterprise. Bruce Schulman has observed that today's young Americans regard start-up companies as a way to liberate themselves and improve the world, a perspective inherited from their 1970s predecessors. "They pursue a revised but potent version of the sensibility of the Seventies," Schulman writes, "a politics of liberation focused on the marketplace rather than the streets as the engine of social transformation."[94] Guccione certainly published *Viva* with profits in mind, but he was also passionate about providing a sexually adventurous magazine for women that embraced the philosophy of the sexual revolution and the "looser" lifestyle.

Viva might have flourished had Guccione's bold vision not been con-

FIGURE 5.4. Bob Guccione and Kathy Keeton laying out *Penthouse* magazine in December 1993, working closely together in the same offices in which they had selected images and content for *Viva*. Photo: David Montgomery.

strained by a deep-seated heterosexist point of view that defined women's sexual freedom on male terms. Created at first by men who imposed their own views of what the "new woman" of the 1970s might want to see and read, and always overseen by Guccione himself, *Viva* was never truly free to transform the erotic landscape for women. Nonetheless, *Viva* was an iconic cultural product of the 1970s. The magazine began its run in 1973—the decade's "pivotal year" and one of "remarkable cultural ferment" marked by the end of the war in Vietnam, Watergate and the fall of Richard Nixon, and a collapsing American economy. *Viva* ended its run in 1979, the year that "the seventies came crashing down on Jimmy Carter's head" in the form of the Iran hostage crisis, bringing the disco-dancing pop culture frivolity of the decade to a hard stop.[95] *Viva* had long disappeared from the newsstand by the time Ronald Reagan won the presidential election in 1980. Claiming victory in all but five states, Reagan ushered in a new period of political and cultural conservatism at odds with the kind of sexual liberalism, support for personal exploration, and independent feminist spirit that Guccione's *Viva* espoused.

NOTES

1. Bob Guccione, "The First Word," *Viva*, October 1, 1973, 9.
2. Patricia Bosworth, "Postscript: The X-Rated Emperor," *Vanity Fair*, December 2009.
3. Candida Royalle, "What's a Nice Girl Like You . . . ," in *The Feminist Porn Book: The Politics of Producing Pleasure*, ed. Tristan Taormino, Celine Parrenas Shimizu, Constance Penley, and Mireille Miller-Young, 58–69 (New York: Feminist Press, 2013), 59.
4. On greater sexual rights and freedoms, and the commercialization of sexuality, see John D'Emilio and Estelle Freedman, *Intimate Matters: A History of Sexuality in America* (Chicago: University of Chicago Press, 1988); on entrepreneurship, see Bruce J. Schulman, *The Seventies: The Great Shift in American Culture, Society, and Politics* (New York: Free Press, 2001); and on creativity, see Andreas Killen, *1973 Nervous Breakdown: Watergate, Warhol, and the Birth of Post-Sixties America* (New York: Bloomsbury, 2006), and Edward D. Miller, *Tomboys, Pretty Boys and Outspoken Women: The Media Revolution of 1973* (Ann Arbor: University of Michigan Press, 2011).
5. Schulman, *Seventies*, 257.
6. Ibid.
7. On Hefner's political contributions, see Carrie Pitzulo, *Bachelors and Bunnies: The Sexual Politics of Playboy* (Chicago: University of Chicago Press, 2011).
8. Constance Penley, Celien Parrenas Shimizu, Mireille Miller-Young, and Tristan Taormino, "Introduction: The Politics of Producing Pleasure," in *The Feminist Porn Book: The Politics of Producing Pleasure*, 9–20 (New York: Feminist Press, 2013), 9.
9. Christopher Lasch, *The Culture of Narcissism: American Life in an Age of Diminishing Expectations* (New York: W. W. Norton, 1979).
10. For the newer interpretations of the significance of the 1970s, see Edward D. Berkowitz, *Something Happened: A Political and Cultural Overview of the Seventies* (New York: Columbia University Press, 2006); Sam Binkley, *Getting Loose: Lifestyle Consumption in the 1970s* (Durham, NC: Duke University Press, 2007); and Schulman, *Seventies*.
11. Nikki Sullivan, "Smacking My Bitch Up: Queer or What?," in *The Ashgate Research Companion to Queer Theory*, ed. Noreen Giffney and Michael O'Rourke, 435–50 (Burlington, VT: Ashgate, 2009), 436. Italics in original.
12. Killen, *1973 Nervous Breakdown*, 4.
13. Miller, *Tomboys*, 7.
14. Ibid. Additional recent scholarship that considers the role of the media in providing a venue for people to express their individual gender and sexual identities includes Elana Levine, *Wallowing in Sex: The New Sexual Culture of 1970s American Television* (Durham, NC: Duke University Press, 2007), and Susan Douglas, *Where the Girls Are: Growing Up Female with the Mass Media* (New York: Three Rivers Press, 1995).
15. Schulman, *Seventies*, 146.

16. Ibid., 148.
17. Binkley, *Getting Loose*, 3.
18. Ibid., 173.
19. Christopher Reed, "Bob Guccione: Founder of Penthouse, He Made and Lost a Fortune in the Porn Industry," *Guardian*, October 21, 2010. See also "Bob Guccione: Biography," Biography, www.biography.com.
20. John Colapinto, "The Twilight of Bob Guccione," *Rolling Stone*, October 21, 2010.
21. Robert D. McFadden, "Bob Guccione: Penthouse Founder, Dies at 79," *New York Times*, October 20, 1979.
22. Reed, "Bob Guccione: Founder of Penthouse"; see also Colapinto, "Twilight of Bob Guccione."
23. McFadden, "Bob Guccione: Penthouse Founder."
24. Ibid.
25. Kathy Keeton, "Push, Stretch, Strain, and Smile," *Viva*, March 1978, 8.
26. Reed, "Bob Guccione: Founder of Penthouse."
27. Jerry Oppenheimer, *Front Row Anna Wintour: What Lies Beneath the Chic Exterior of Vogue's Editor in Chief* (New York: St. Martin's, 2005), 136–37; Mike Edison, *Dirty! Dirty! Dirty! Of Playboys, Pigs, and Penthouse Paupers: An American Tale of Sex and Wonder* (Berkeley, CA: Soft Skull Press, 2011), 90–91.
28. Richard Corliss, "Penthouse's Bob Guccione: The Dark Prince of Porn," *Time*, October 21, 2010, available at http://content.time.com.
29. Edison, *Dirty!*, 85. The quote refers to Michelangelo Antonioni's 1966 film about a photographer who engages in rampant sexual activity with the young models who frequent his studio.
30. Patricia Bosworth, "The X-Rated Emperor," *Vanity Fair*, February 2005.
31. Edison, *Dirty!*, 155; Bosworth, "X-Rated Emperor."
32. Edison, *Dirty!*, 85.
33. Circulation figures for *Playboy* and *Penthouse* appear in Steven Watts, *Mr. Playboy: Hugh Hefner and the American Dream* (Hoboken, NJ: John Wiley & Sons, 2008), 302. *Penthouse* was never quite as popular as *Playboy*, and *Playboy* saw its circulation climb to an all-time high of seven million copies in 1972.
34. Watts, *Mr. Playboy*, 300, 301–4.
35. "Viva *Viva*?," *Time*, September 24, 1973, 64.
36. On Helen Gurley Brown and *Cosmopolitan*, see Jennifer Scanlon, *Bad Girls Go Everywhere: The Life of Helen Gurley Brown, the Woman Behind Cosmopolitan Magazine* (New York: Penguin Books, 2009), 161; on Guccione's views of readers, see "Viva *Viva*?," 64.
37. Kathy Keeton, "*Viva*'s Woman," *Viva*, August 1974, 6.
38. Oppenheimer, *Front Row Anna Wintour*, 117.
39. Edison, *Dirty!*, 160.
40. Oppenheimer, *Front Row Anna Wintour*, 117.
41. Nora Ephron, "Guccione's Ms. Print," *New York*, October 29, 1973, 68.
42. "Viva *Viva*?," 64.
43. Ibid.
44. Ephron, "Guccione's Ms. Print," 68.
45. Ibid., 69.
46. Quoted in Edison, *Dirty!*, 86.
47. Miller, *Tomboys*, 198.
48. Ephron, "Guccione's Ms. Print," 68.

49. "Viva *Viva?*," 64.

50. Teresa de Lauretis, *The Practice of Love: Lesbian Sexuality and Perverse Desire* (Bloomington: Indiana University Press, 1994), 114.

51. Laura Mulvey, "Visual Pleasure and Narrative Cinema," *Screen* 16, no. 3 (1975): 6–18.

52. [Reader name and location withheld], letter to *Viva*, December 1973, 8.

53. M. S. of Forest Hills, NY, letter to *Viva*, December 1973, 8.

54. V. F. of Port Chester, NY, letter to *Viva*, December 1973, 8.

55. "The Fighter," photographs by Eddie Adams, *Viva*, October 1973, 96, 101–2.

56. "The Picnic," *Viva*, October 1973, 68.

57. L. B. of Jamaica, NY, letter to *Viva*, January 1974, 12.

58. J. F. of Schaumburg, IL, letter to *Viva*, December 1973, 12.

59. Art Cumings, "The Little Hooker," *Viva*, November 1973, 66.

60. On the development of concerns about male sexual violence and exploitation, see Carolyn Bronstein, *Battling Pornography: The American Feminist Anti-Pornography Movement, 1976–1986* (Cambridge: Cambridge University Press, 2011), 26–38.

61. C. S. of New York, NY, letter to *Viva*, December 1973, 9. Italics in original.

62. Robert Chartham, "The Male Sexual Fantasy: A Study of the Erotic Fantasies of Men—Their Meaning, Significance and Contribution to the Human Sexual Condition," *Viva*, October 1973, 122.

63. S. L. of Asbury Park, NJ, letter to *Viva*, November 1973, 14.

64. K. S. of New York, NY, letter to *Viva*, November 1973, 12.

65. J. K. of San Francisco, CA, letter to *Viva*, March 1974, 18.

66. D. H. of Fort Fairfield, ME, letter to *Viva*, March 1974, 11.

67. Andrea Dworkin, "Chinese Footbinding," *Viva*, August 1974, 102.

68. "Biographical Note," *Guide to the Patricia Bosworth Papers, 1932–1984 and Undated*, Billy Rose Theatre Division, New York Public Library for the Performing Arts, http://archives.nypl.org/the/21773. Bosworth was an editor at *Women's Day* in the 1960s, and a senior editor of *McCall's* from 1969 to 1972.

69. Bosworth, "X-Rated Emperor." This was the February 1974 issue.

70. Ibid.

71. Oppenheimer, *Front Row Anna Wintour*, 131.

72. Bosworth, "X-Rated Emperor."

73. Kathy Keeton, "First Word," *Viva*, November 1974, 6.

74. Kathy Keeton, "On Past and Future Changes," *Viva*, April 1976, 8.

75. Kathy Keeton, "First Word: The Last First Word on Male Nudity," *Viva*, August 1976, 8.

76. Edison, *Dirty!*, 157.

77. Bosworth, "X-Rated Emperor."

78. Peter Carlson, "Guccione: Porn King without a Penthouse," *Washington Post*, January 18, 2005.

79. L. H. of Miami, FL, letter to *Viva*, March 1974, 22.

80. B. Fram of New York, NY, letter to *Viva*, May 1976, 14.

81. D. H. of Fort Fairfield, ME, letter to *Viva*, June 1974, 14.

82. V. T. of Los Angeles, CA, letter to *Viva*, August 1974, 12.

83. Harolyane Napir of Oakland, CA, letter to *Viva*, August 1974, 12.

84. Dena Dawson, "What Are Women's Skin Magazines Really Selling?" *Pandora*, May 1974, 8–9.

85. Oppenheimer, *Front Row Anna Wintour*, 145.

86. Edison, *Dirty!*, 160.

87. Flynt as described in Edison, *Dirty!*, 161.
88. Goldstein as described in Edison, *Dirty!*, 161.
89. Bosworth, "X-Rated Emperor."
90. Tracy Clark-Flory, "Confessions of a *Playgirl* Editor," *Salon*, June 15, 2013, www
    .salon.com.
91. Bosworth, "X-Rated Emperor."
92. Corliss, "Penthouse's Bob Guccione." In 1994, Guccione was named one of the
    world's two hundred premier art collectors by *ARTnews* magazine. See Peter
    Marks, "From Bob Guccione, an Exhibition in Shocking Good Taste," *New York
    Times*, February 18, 1994.
93. T. Rees Shapiro, "Penthouse founder Bob Guccione Dies at 79," *Washington Post*,
    October 21, 2010.
94. Schulman, *Seventies*, 257.
95. Berkowitz, *Something Happened*, 219.

CHAPTER 6

The Economic and Racial Politics of Selling a Transfeminine Fantasy in 1970s Niche and Pornographic Print Publications

NICHOLAS MATTE

A MERICAN CULTURE SAW MAJOR shifts in sexual politics and its representations in the 1970s, many of which had to do with pornography. Throughout the decade, commercialized and consumption-oriented sexual representations that would have likely previously been considered obscene or pornographic became common in many forms of media. Porn studies scholars have referred to this ongoing process of mainstream culture becoming more pornographic as "pornification."[1] The establishment of gender identity clinics and the new availability of sex reassignment surgery in the United States also led to greater visibility of trans people in the 1970s, particularly transsexuals, and especially transsexual women. Culturally, the idea was spreading that people who had been assigned a "male" role at birth might openly express femininity or "change sex," in part due to patriarchal concerns about maleness and masculinities. Many representations of trans women and transfemininity, however, were either linked to stigma against sexual deviancy or equated with the overly sexualized trope for which the emergent "she-male" genre of pornography would become known.

Trans-oriented print publications were one of the key contexts in which trans politics and sexual representations were constructed and reconstructed over the course of the 1970s. Recent scholarship in trans and queer studies as well as the history of gender and sexuality has emphasized the important role trans people played in the social and political activism of the sexual liberation movements of the 1970s and the significance of print publications to gay and lesbian communities, politics, and economics.[2] Susan Stryker, Robert Hill, and others have written about the circulation of trans print publications such as *Drag* and *Transvestia* as a form of community building.[3] Similarly, Laura Kipnis has written about transvestite pornography as an extensive form of social self-fashioning in a well-known niche genre market of print pornography.[4] Less attention has been paid, however, to the ways in which the media and commercial sex and entertainment industries have shaped trans people's social, economic, and political contexts, as well as broader representations of transvestism and transsexualism in American culture. Trans-themed pornography emerged more prominently in the 1970s and was due to the active participation of transfeminine people.

Throughout the 1970s pornography was an essential component of sexual representations of transfemininity, transvestism, and changing sex, all of which were structured as much in the dynamics of media, capitalism, and race as they were in gender and sexuality. This chapter provides evidence of the key role that pornography played in trans visibility, including why transfemininity has been fetishized in American culture. It also provides evidence of some of the ways that sexual representations of trans people have been intertwined with, rather than separate from, the mainstream pornography industry. Sociologist Viviane Namaste stresses the fact that many trans women have supported themselves economically in performance and entertainment industries.[5] Historian Melinda Chateauvert points out that identity-based movements have stigmatized sex work and marginalized sex workers such as trans woman Sylvia Rivera, who was a major activist for numerous issues and a sex worker herself during the 1970s.[6] Pornographic print publications in some ways extended the possibilities of doing sex work, and certainly influenced the development of trans communities, politics, and symbolic tropes regarding trans people in American culture and media. It is therefore important to chart this decade's sexual representations of transfemininity in relation to the production and proliferation of pornography as a recognition of the ways in which trans visibility shaped and was shaped by pornography. This may be particularly valuable to understanding how sexual fetishization, gendering, and racialized symbolism informed which representations of trans people would be produced and circulated within pornographic markets during the

1970s. Even though transfemininity has been a long-standing component of pornographic markets, approaches that consider pornography primarily in terms of heterosexuality and homosexuality might inadvertently overlook sexual representations of transfemininity. It should also be noted that because the pornographic marketplace was heavily skewed toward sexualizing "male desires," particularly "for the feminine," the emphasis on transfemininity stood in stark contrast to the dearth of sexual representations of trans*masculinity* in both mainstream and niche pornography at the time. By contrast, a small industry of consumers, editors, readers, advertisers, contributors, publishers, and models all contributed to somewhat of a niche pornography market specializing in many variations of male feminization, (male-to-female) transsexuality, and other variations of what might now be termed transfemininity. In developing a genre based on hegemonic, mainstream cultural sex symbols during the 1970s, transfeminine porn paralleled or perhaps reflected similar developments toward niche market genres in the general porn industry of the time. The unspoken expectation in many trans-oriented publications that transsexualism and transvestism were inherently trans*feminine* established a space for certain types of transfeminine representations, particularly those that were shaped by the economics of pornographic print publications and their sexualized gender and racial formations.[7]

From the late 1960s to the early 1980s, representations and public performances of transvestism and transsexualism went through two distinct but overlapping phases in specialized niche media, fusing liberationist fantasies of transfemininity with the publication of commercialized, consumption-oriented pornography. *Female Impersonators* magazine typified the earlier phase by encouraging readers to admire professional celebrity female impersonators from a distance; to identify as fans, audience members, or "amateurs"; and to contrast themselves with professional female impersonators. Trans people began politicizing transvestism and transsexuality in publications such as Lee Brewster's *Drag* magazine, which catered specifically to trans consumers. But by the late 1970s and early 1980s, the pornographic publication *FI News* began commodifying explicit sexual representations of transfemininity for a wider audience. It fetishized transfemininity as sexy by associating it with a supposed potential to transgress the boundaries of normative social and bodily formations, particularly what would now be called cissexism and sexual racism. In the examples examined here, white transfeminine people were positioned as fantasy characters and caricatures, often in relation to sexist, homophobic, and racist stereotypes, most of which were presented as fulfilling and empowering. Transfeminine people thereby came to represent a significant new marketing opportunity for pornographers. For many Americans, sexual representations of transfemininity in print pornography in turn played a role in fetishizing, gendering, and racializing trans people and expressions.

Cabaret Culture and *Female Impersonators* Magazine in the 1960s

Throughout the 1960s, *Female Impersonators,* a glossy, full-color magazine, enrolled readers in the shared fantasy of transfemininity by celebrating, advertising, and reporting on the world of professional female impersonation. The subjects of the magazine were male performance artists who entertained large mixed audiences in cabarets, dinner clubs, and stage shows. Doing impressions of popular celebrities such as Mae West, Bette Davis, and Phyllis Diller, they sought to flawlessly perform idealized variations of femininity.[8] Many female impersonators worked in the tourist and entertainment industries after having trained in theatrical arts in which costumes, makeup, and other embodiment techniques were all considered part of their profession. The establishments where female impersonators worked were often controlled by mafia club bosses, preferred white performers, and did not tolerate any suggestion of homosexuality or gender nonconformity offstage. Patrons of these shows, held in large mainstream venues, were (assumed to be) heterosexual, as were the female impersonators, who often performed heterosexuality offstage by stressing that their cross-dressing was simply part of an act, not a reflection of their own sexual predilections.[9] At a time when sexual and gender expressions were legally, socially, and economically regulated, female impersonators both maintained and transgressed numerous cultural taboos; it was considered exciting for performers to hint at transgressing everyday restrictions against certain forms of sexual, gender, and homoerotic desire.

In the social and economic context of the entertainment industry, *Female Impersonators* magazine played into a broader discourse of transfemininity that positioned readers as fans or "admirers." Readers' interests in "the art of female impersonation" went beyond that of the casual audience member. The magazine was widely distributed and sold in adult bookshops as well as through a subscription service, but like many similar publications of the time, the magazine itself included very little information about its origins. Every issue had at least one multipage spread featuring text and photographs about a given act, club, or show. Some were based in North America, whereas others took readers on a journey to such places as Australia, Paris, Montreal, and Puerto Rico, all of which were traditional "travel destinations" for wealthy continental North American tourists, and which were home to excellent female impersonator troupes. The magazine published detailed information about upcoming female impersonator shows and enabled readers to privately peruse and enjoy images of female impersonators.

One of the features that distinguished *Female Impersonators* from similar publications was Pudgy Roberts, the magazine's editor, primary contributor, and public face, himself a professional female impersonator. Roberts was positioned in the magazine as offering "insider knowledge" into a specialized world. He frequently informed readers that in addition to his editorial career, he had eight and a half years of experience as a female impersonator. His primary claim to fame was that he was the only female impersonator to have ever been featured on the Johnny Carson show, a tagline he also used throughout the 1960s and 1970s in advertisements for his stage performances.[10] He produced many publications, including numerous magazines and several small books, as well as an "artificial bust" prosthetic piece that he designed as an alternative to the silicone and estrogen injections rapidly becoming popular among performers—an option Roberts felt degraded the skill of illusion at the heart of professional female impersonation. In 1972, one article called him the "first activist" in the "field of female impersonation" and "the leading spokesman for the entire world of mimicry."[11] A great deal of Roberts's public image was hype, however, and he would later recount that he was editor "in name only"; he said he got the publishers "models, suggested articles and such, but they still did what they wanted. They didn't let me have the final say on things."[12] Very little was published about Roberts's background, his personal life, or any other human characteristic outside his expertise in professional female impersonation and his eccentric ambition and persistence. He stood out in part because he was both an artist and promoter, and also because he specialized in comedic acts and illusion. He prided himself, for example, on the fact that he was able to perform as the only female impersonator in a burlesque troupe of cisgender women.[13] He also had a penchant for history and a love of early twentieth-century and European female impersonation. Later in life he ran a small company that hired day laborers to wear various costumes and do street promotions for local businesses, such as a bride-and-groom shtick for a jewelry store.[14]

During the late 1960s and early 1970s, there was always tension between what *Female Impersonators* offered and what readers desired from it. Although readers clearly idolized the female impersonators with whom it seemed they did often in fact identify in their fantasies, Roberts worked against transfeminine readers' growing interests in order to avoid obscenity charges and conform to what was socially permissible. He carefully constructed representations of professional stagecraft as theater, performance art that was distinct from overt sexual desire or gender or sexual deviancy. In doing so, he achieved a certain veneer of respectability for *Female Impersonators* magazine. This emphasis on professionalism, which protected Roberts from running afoul of obscenity laws, had the side effect of reinforcing for readers their limited roles as consumers of the magazine and the shows, always constructing their social subjectivities and transfeminine fantasies in legal, commercial, and profitable terms. *Female Impersonators* offered no encouragement to adopt a transfeminine lifestyle and in fact subtly discouraged readers from living out their personal cross-dressing fantasies or from contacting others who might share them.

Roberts seemed to have made a conscious choice to balance readers' intimate desires against the restrictive legal and social environment by emphasizing the professional and theatrical legitimacy of performers. A complex subtext throughout the magazine hinted at the limits of what could be legally communicated in print and in public. For example, the cover of *Female Impersonators* often indicated that it was restricted from sale to minors. Roberts also explained that he was not able to actively build community among readers because "the legal authorities frown on correspondence or in aiding in making personal contacts." When readers requested an opportunity to meet one another, a plea that often explicitly demonstrated a desire to meet others interested in sharing sexual experiences or fantasies, Roberts responded by encouraging them to "visit some of the places where impersonators appear."[15] Roberts also warned, however, that single men were scrutinized by security guards at female impersonator shows and that female impersonator shows were thus not ideal meeting places. Encouraging readers to admire the skill and beauty of distant celebrity professionals such as Coccinelle and Toni Lee, *Female*

Impersonators represented a dichotomy between transfeminine consumers and professional female impersonators. The risks and possibilities of transfeminization were indeed quite different for the two groups, as were the benefits and rewards. *Female Impersonators* was not only at risk of obscenity charges but was also more focused on becoming a profitable publication rather than on serving or building a united community of transfeminine people.

By the end of the 1960s, *Female Impersonators* magazine began to more explicitly recognize readers' personal and potentially sexualized transfeminine fantasies. Whitney Strub has written that at the time, a "cultural shift regarding sex-themed media transpired in the context of a broader evolution of social mores known as the sexual revolution."[16] In the case of *Female Impersonators,* the relaxed social climate emboldened Roberts to begin printing more explicit materials that addressed readers' desires. For example, he printed a letter from a reader identified as Caroline, who wrote that she "would love to be a professional female impersonator" even though "she recognized that it [was] a far-fetched dream." In an effort to provide transvestite readers with material that validated the practice of sexualized cross-dressing offstage, the magazine featured a cover story with multipage photo spread of two female impersonators, Gypsy and Avis, supposedly "dressing" together in a domestic setting. The magazine presented a fantasy montage of two very beautiful and passable female impersonators cross-dressing in lingerie in their living room (figs. 6.1 and 6.2). The text portion of the feature explained, "This photo session is an exclusive solely done for *Female Impersonators* with the amateur mime in mind, since we have had so many requests by fans of this magazine to pictorially illustrate just how 'it's done.'" The fact that the scene included both a white and an African American female impersonator recognized racial and ethnic differences in transfeminine embodiment practices and likely indicated an effort to appeal to both white and African American readers, indicating the growing importance of interracial sexuality in the context of 1960s American culture.

Even as the magazine expanded its content, *Female Impersonators* was able to maintain respectability by featuring professional impersonators and emphasizing stage shows. For example, while the spread on Gypsy and Avis was clearly staged to support the private fantasies of (likely closeted) transvestite readers, the magazine justified it by explaining that Gypsy and Avis had "the experience of many seasons in the entertainment world and the art of impersonation and disguise."

FIGURE 6.1. The cover of *Female Impersonators* no. 3. Courtesy of Division of Rare and Manuscript Collections, Cornell University Library.

FIGURE 6.2. The art of "making-up" with Avis and Gypsy. *Female Impersonators* no. 3. Courtesy of Division of Rare and Manuscript Collections, Cornell University Library.

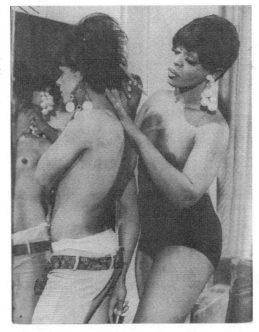

Maintaining its usual overall premise, the magazine told readers that the spread was their opportunity to "see how the professionals do it." Avis and Gypsy, however, also foreshadowed the more explicitly sexual and participatory exhibitionism and voyeurism that would become increasingly prevalent in trans-oriented publications of the 1970s.

The late 1970s saw magazines like *Female Impersonators* fade, with *FI News*, a pornographic newspaper, taking its place. Like an increasing number of trans-oriented publications throughout the 1970s, *FI News* seemed to employ a staff composed almost exclusively of transfeminine people (a mix of transvestites and transsexuals), though staff were not usually the ones profiting from such publications. As the market changed toward more explicit sexual representations, transfeminine staff members of *FI News* were able to continue turning their social experiences and expertise into marketable employment positions by personally representing transfemininity in ways that sold papers. Sandy Mesics, the managing editor and primary voice of *FI News* during the mid-1970s, was a self-described preoperative transsexual from Philadelphia who had previously written for a variety of smaller transvestite publications including *TV Times* and *Image*, both based in Seattle. Like many other publicly visible transfeminine people in the 1970s, Mesics was a social and political activist as well as a celebrity figure and organizer in the transvestite consumer world. She organized drag balls and cross-dressing parties, and had worked as a transsexual counselor at the Philadelphia Gay Alliance and a draft counselor with the Central Committee for Conscientious Objectors.[17]

FI News, short for *Female Impersonator News*, was a newspaper-style publication that circulated at least nationally throughout the mid- to late 1970s and early 1980s. Billing itself alternately as "the only 'heterosexual' transvestite newspaper" and "the only drag newspaper," it was an undated, pornographic publication, with pages of news items, editorials, and fantasy erotica literature, as well as extensive personal classifieds and advertising. It was one of the many publications distributed by Neptune Publications, a mail-order business that sold pulp novels, pornographic magazines, and various sexual goods and services, such as pornographic card decks, dildos, and confidential photo finishing. Annual subscriptions to the paper were available for roughly fifteen dollars, or through various packages in which readers could order a number of Neptune publications together. Originating in Belmar, New Jersey, it catered primarily to consumers in the northeastern, midwestern, and southern United States.

The transfeminine people who worked for *FI News* fused the politicized idea of sexual liberation with a fantasy of increasingly commercialized transvestism. For example, Sussie Collins, a regular contributor, encouraged readers to become more socially involved by becoming more prolific consumers. She wrote that in just six months, she herself had gone from "living the secret life of crossdressing alone" to seeing "more of the transvestite world than I had previously known existed." She, too, focused on the thrill of trans celebrity culture, telling readers she had quickly become part of a world full of people she had previously "always felt were untouchable."[18] Collins urged readers forward with almost missionary zeal, enthusiastically proclaiming her message of personal empowerment via public expression of transfemininity. She wrote, "I'm trying to show you that the TV world is out here and all you have to do is step across the threshold. . . . I want to show you that it is possible to break out of the closet."[19] Her rallying cry, "It's time for the TRANSVESTITE LIBERATION!" provided readers with an imagined social movement in which their enjoyment of transvestism was directly linked to their consumption of media, goods, and services.[20] For readers of *FI News*, "coming out of the closet" was primarily defined as a social and commercial affair, and even if they couldn't become as involved in the transvestite world as Collins had, they could still participate as consumers.

FI News was more explicitly pornographic and geared toward mass consumption and sexualized interpersonal contact than previous trans-oriented publications, however. It featured content that marketed transfeminine people as a fantasy for sale to each other and everyone else. Its extensive personal classifieds section created a marketplace of voyeurism and exhibitionism catering to consumers' desire for a semianonymous venue in which to express both their specific individual desires and their broader desire for supportive social contact. The classified section also provided a forum for escorts and sex workers to advertise to clients in a context in which commercial and noncommercial social and sexual connections were equally acceptable. One ad, for example, from Misty Monroe of Virginia, told readers that she was seeking a "generous gentleman" who wanted to live out his fantasies with a "hot transsexual."[21] *FI News* clearly also catered to consumers who were interested in sexualized fetishistic representations of transfemininity as embodied by transsexual women, and the majority of those advertising services were transsexual women.

As the burgeoning movement for sex workers' rights garnered

momentum and attention in the 1970s, it provided a significant context for newfound radical sex politics based in commercialized sex that sometimes transcended, but often reproduced, the hegemonic gender, racial, and sexual formations of heteronormativity and ciscentrism. Between 1970 and 1978, sex work activists across the country had begun raising money and public awareness for the decriminalization of sex work at large, open, highly publicized events, such as the Whores' Masquerade Ball, Hookers' Balls, and Hookers' Conventions.[22] The 1977 Hookers' Ball in San Francisco raised $93,000 for the leading sex work activist group Call Off Your Old Tired Ethics (COYOTE), which had been founded by sex worker Margo St. James in 1973.[23] Similar groups formed around the country throughout the decade, including chapters of COYOTE in San Diego, New Orleans, Des Moines, and Miami, as well as the Associated Seattle Prostitutes (ASP) and Prostitutes of New York (PONY).[24]

While *FI News* readers may have expected its readers to be familiar with the political purpose of the Hooker's Ball, it depoliticized transfeminine sex work and downplayed differences between sex workers and clients by representing the world of commercial sex as one of mutually enjoyable entertainment and fantasy. For example, *FI News* basically described "the Big Apple's first Hooker's Ball" as another exciting party. The event, it said, which had transpired at the famous Copacabana nightclub in New York "brought out a lot of the city's whores, who partied it up until dawn . . . [including a] group of drag queen whores [who] made their appearance to help the festivities."[25] Sex activist Annie Sprinkle later recalled that the event had attracted hundreds of people, including many johns, photographers, and journalists.[26] It was clear, however, that *FI News'* coverage of sex work was limited to stories that would sell papers, and while it did mention that the event was not as profitable as similar events on the West Coast, it failed to mention that such balls were fundraising ventures for sex work activist groups. It did capitalize on public interest, however. Mainstream media journalist Earl Wilson, for example, noted that the New York Hookers Ball had primarily attracted "sightseers"; although it had been advertised that many celebrities and feminists would make appearances at the ball, it was in fact "50 or 60 real live hookers" who did.[27] Neither Wilson's mainstream media article nor that in *FI News* reported in depth on the role that the transfeminine sex workers played in politicizing and attempting to decriminalize sex work, instead using the event simply as an opportunity for salacious, profitable content.

It was clear that *FI News* prioritized content that could double as commercial advertising for businesses oriented toward transfemininity and sex, a very common feature of commercial media and an evident variation of product placement. In an illustrated article, for example, Mesics took readers on a virtual trip to a sex shop in Philadelphia called Fantasy Island, where she modeled lingerie and posed for photographs, giving readers a tantalizing look into what could be their own experience as potential consumers. Mesics described Fantasy Island as "a tiny shop, but packed with some of the most sexy and sensuous lingerie this side of Paris."[28] Readers were welcome to indulge in voyeuristic enjoyment of her photographs, but the article was clearly an advertisement for the store. Mesics encouraged readers to come in and shop, noting that the owner, Joe, a masculine, friendly-looking man, who also posed for a photo with her, was a cross-dresser, and "really has an idea as to what turns us on."[29] Mesics also reassured nervous potential consumers that the shop regularly catered to cross-dressers from Pennsylvania, New York, and New Jersey, as well as "neighborhood women."[30] For those still too timid (or far away) to go to the store in person, the feature included a mail-in order form to purchase clothing and accessories. By using such multifaceted marketing techniques, *FI News* both capitalized on and commercialized transvestite and transfeminine desire, fusing consumption with the expression of personal gender and sexual desire. Mesics's Fantasy Island feature demonstrates but one example of how sexual representations featuring trans people were gendered and sexualized in ways determined by capitalist consumer economics, and how many trans-oriented publications during the period were framed by the profit motives of producers.

Transfeminine Fantasies of Money, Race, and Power in the Late 1970s and Early 1980s

By the late 1970s, *FI News* publishers also began using race as an opportunity to create profitably salacious content for its consumers. In doing so, publishers often demonstrated hegemonic whiteness by primarily addressing white readers and sexual racism by representing African American people as an exciting turn-on. For example, *Female Impersonator Newsletter,* a side publication of *FI News,* published photographs of a New Jersey event called Jackie's Annual Valentine's Ball, which it described as "a completely black ball" and "a real mind bender," featuring "the best of the Black drag queens."[31] The anonymous author acted as a virtual tourist to the event and provided readers with a racialized narrative that framed the party's black transvestites as both available for readers' consumption and sexually liberated. The author proclaimed that although she was "the only Whitey in the place," she was nevertheless "completely comfortable and really felt like a piece of the scene."[32] Encouraging readers to consider themselves part of the action through their consumption of the publication, the article told them, "This year, you're here too (even though only in pictures)."[33] *FI News* thus presented the "black ball" as an opportunity for readers to experience African American spaces as an entertaining and liberating "escape."

For white readers in particular, the equation of blackness with sexual liberation from mainstream white societal norms reproduced the historically rooted American cultural tradition of white "slumming," though it also clearly represented a sense of transfeminine community bonding that was thought to transcend race, racial divisions, and racial power relations.[34] Coverage of such parties may have appealed or been familiar to some black readers in that it did recognize and glamorize African American ball cultures. But just as transfemininity was increasingly fetishized and commoditized in the creation and representation of transfeminine "characters," the African American people in these stories were included as players in a fantasy world still dominated by long-standing segregations that differentiated many balls as black spaces, and commoditized African Americans as available for the consumption of white readers.

In line with what Carolyn Bronstein has called the 1970s "market manifestation of the sexual revolution," *FI News* began using transfeminine people such as columnist Haley Tiresius to seemingly push the boundaries of sexual taboos and expand the company's profitable sexualized services in pornography.[35] Like Mesics, Tiresius was a hardworking, entrepreneurial, transfeminine person and transsexual woman. Before Tiresius worked for *FI News,* she had been managing editor and monthly columnist at a publication called *Unique Encounters,* a Florida-based sexual contact magazine for swingers. She also ran her own business, Tiresius Fashions, which she advertised in the pages of *FI News.* Tiresius became a regular feature in the paper, however, through her column "Tiresius Knows." Tiresius's work history and social involvement resembled that of Mesics, but her position at *FI News* exemplified the late 1970s' shift to more commercial, fetishized representations of transfeminine people. In the pages of *FI*

News, she was a character designed to titillate and appeal to presumably male consumers' sexual fantasies of white transfemininity.

Tiresius represented a fantasy ideal of white transfemininity as the ultimate sexual pleasure and her character encouraged readers to cultivate their own sexual pleasure and fantasies in ways that commoditized and fetishized male feminization and transfemininity. Although never stated explicitly, Tiresius's name referred to the mythical Greco-Roman goddess who, after experiencing sex as both a male and female, had determined womanhood and femininity to offer the superior pleasure. In contrast to the shame and social stigma that mainstream hegemonic masculinity associated with male feminization, *FI News* introduced Haley Tiresius as "a pre-op transsexual who claims to be quite content being what she is."[36] Her catch phrase "Tiresius knows" was a kind of wink to readers that implied that readers could share her in-depth knowledge of the sexual pleasure of femininity by reading her column and taking part in the consumer culture of *FI News.* Indeed, in her first appearance, she told readers, "Tiresius knows that it is a lot of fun being a girl—if only for part of the time."[37] This reference spoke directly to men who occasionally engaged in cross-dressing as a sexual activity, namely the transvestite consumers who seemed to make up the bulk of the paper's target audience. For them, a "preoperative transsexual" or transfeminine person with a penis could represent the potential fulfillment of their fantasies.

Tiresius also provided important emotional and social support to readers by coaching them through their fears about expressing their transfeminine sexuality and encouraging them to fulfill their desires. Her advice columns urged readers to use the paper's contact ads to find sexual partners. Her motivational pep talks took readers through their fears and constructed their transfeminine gender expressions as being intimately linked to their sexual desires. For example, she wrote, "Don't let yourself begin to believe that no one out there wants to meet you. Don't sell yourself short. If you do, you will end up on the short end! Be specific about what you want, and how what you want includes sex; 'coming out' often involves 'going down.' "[38] Part of Tiresius's job was ostensibly to empower readers who might become sexual consumers and would pay to participate in *FI News'* classifieds and contact club services to do so. By essentially encouraging readers to be sexually explicit in their ads and selling a motivational message of personal sexual liberation from secrecy and shame, she was also generating potential content for the publication that would likely attract another major group of consumers: non-trans people who fantasized about having sex with transfeminine individuals.

Tiresius had become a full-blown icon by the early 1980s, when she appeared as a caricature in a multipage presidential campaign spoof that positioned transsexual politics fully within a pornographic discourse of outrageous content and camp humor, simultaneously widening her appeal to non-trans readers and producing a conservative vision of radical sex politics. The back cover of the issue featured Tiresius as a typically feminine, attractive, slender, demure-looking white woman with long curly blond hair, wearing a corset with garters, her small breasts and (flaccid) penis exposed. Inside the issue, the headline "Transsexual for President" accompanied cartoon-style drawings and an article in which Tiresius boldly declared her supposed intention to run for president of the United States. Her ridiculous promises were evidently meant to be entertaining, and contained elements of both political and economic commentary. For example, she told readers that if elected, she would immediately pass "by fiat" the Equal Rights Amendment, a long-standing feminist goal for achieving gender quality, and that she would guarantee every American a "Piece of Ass Daily" or "POAD." Encouraging readers to focus on sexual satisfaction and sexual objectification, she asked "Do you want a POAD? Are you one?"[39]

FI News capitalized on selling Tiresius and her transsexuality as the antithesis to American sexual conservatism through this exaggerated, satirical, and perhaps utopian fantasy in which a transsexual woman could get rich and become president of the United States by running on a platform of sexual satisfaction. Lampooning American culture and political leaders for widespread and damaging sexual repression, Tiresius promised that daily sex would cure everything from inflation to hunger, and she poked fun at the emphasis on achieving wellness through nonsexual means, such as exercise, writing that jogging "has seduced even our leaders into believing that going in circles is getting somewhere and is to be encouraged . . . [whereas] skillful fucking will exercise every muscle, . . . [will] make for a trim and healthy nation and will stop us from running in circles. We may again achieve vision."[40] Tiresius's spoof campaign was a far cry from earlier and continuing attempts to achieve genuine legal rights for trans people as a minority group.

The satirical nature of her approach to political representation became evident as she announced that her campaign was to be completely profit-oriented. She ridiculed the notion of liberal, democratic political engagement by presenting her satirical strategy for her presidential campaign as being based on economic exploitation. She told readers that "running for president . . . looks like a damned lucrative business to me, which is one of the reasons I'm getting in the race," and that "candidly, about seven of your dollars will be profit, which will go toward furthering my other campaign activities, which will also mostly consist of raising money. Down the road I see mass mailing, bumper stickers, and of course campaign pins, all for profit! In fact, as a campaigner, I promise to do nothing but raise money and spend it on our cause."[41] Furthermore, she encouraged consumers to donate money to her campaign and to buy fifteen-dollar T-shirts that read "Go POAD."[42] Evidently, the campaign was a sexualized socioeconomic critique of a political culture of economic exploitation, even as Tiresius and FI News profited from it in jest. Perhaps more importantly, however, the presidential campaign feature contributed to a broader public discourse in which transsexual political power was presented as a pornographic joke and transfeminine people were considered bizarre, outlandish, and highly sexualized fantasy characters. By the early 1980s, this type of pornographic representation was seemingly disconnected from the genuine discussions about trans people's cultural and political place in American society that were taking place, but certainly influenced the politics of sexual representations of trans people and transfemininity.

Neptune Publications' focus on producing commercially viable representations of transfemininity in the guise of radical sex politics was also typified by Lori Stevens, another white transfeminine character presented as both a real person writing for the publication and a fictionalized fantasy character. Stevens's role was specifically to promote a fantasy of "interracial" sex between white transfeminine consumers and masculine African American male consumers. In the pages of FI News, Stevens appeared as a white, very female- and feminine-looking person, dressed in lingerie that hid her own genitals. She held the exposed penis of a fully dressed, fairly average-looking anonymous African American man in her hand. Beside this photograph was an extensive story describing a mutually pleasurable sexual rendezvous between Stevens and the unidentified man after they reportedly met through her new contact club service. The story marked both Stevens and the man as sexual objects associated with taboo interracial and possibly homoerotic desire, reducing both to their sexual symbolism and implying that such a reduction was mutually pleasurable. The African American man was highly racialized with an excessive dialect. For example, when expressing his fascination with Stevens's penis, he was quoted as saying, "Ah don't wanna take mah hand away," though such phrasing may have also been designed to appeal to the vernacular of consumers of a lower socioeconomic class.[43]

Race, racial stereotypes, sexual racism, sexualized racial taboos, and racialized homoeroticism were all central to the complex gendered and racialized integration of African American men as pornography consumers and to Stevens's representation as a sexualized, sexually liberated white transfeminine person. The article included a very short column of personal ads that was supposed to introduce readers to this new contact club "for getting white tvs together with black studs." Stevens acted as the club's spokesperson and leader. Readers were asked not only to mail in their ads but also to identify themselves as belonging to one of three categories: white bitches, black studs, or white sissy fags.[44] Stevens thus encouraged both white transfeminine readers and (implicitly non-trans) African American men to become consumers of her mediated racialized sexual services and to embrace sexualized and racialized gender categories that were usually considered demeaning but were presented, in this context, as being pleasurable.

The introduction of race as a central component of the transfeminine fantasies *FI News* constructed in the late 1970s and early 1980s can be understood in the context of the contemporary emergence of the burgeoning pornographic genre of "inter-racial pornography." In what Mireille Miller-Young calls "the manufacture and distribution of racial difference as a specialized fetish in hardcore media," the early 1980s saw the mainstream American porn industry expanding dominant racial stereotypes.[45] Neptune Publications, which published *FI News*, became part of this trend when it introduced a new spin-off publication called *IR News*, which stood for "Inter-Racial News." This new publication fetishized "inter-racial" sexual experiences much as *FI News* had been fetishizing male feminization and transfemininity. Both publications encouraged consumers to sexualize and fetishize sexual taboos by transgressing normative expectations of gender, sexuality, and race, and both created unique and problematic pornographic discourses and sexual cultures for the groups they fetishized and targeted as consumers, models, and participants.

Neptune's new interracial transvestite pornography, like other interracial pornography of the time, represented oppressive racial tropes as a potentially empowering source of individual sexual pleasure for both white transfeminine and (implicitly non-trans) African American male consumers. Tapping into deeply psychological and sociocultural symbolism, it reframed the power of gender, sexual, and racial symbolism into something that could be bought, sold, and rendered personally and sexually satisfying. It offered African American men the opportunity to express masculinity, possible racial dominance, and seemingly acceptable homoerotic desire for transfeminine people or femininized white men. This phallocentric fantasy nevertheless also reduced the African American men to their symbolic, racialized penises. Stevens's association of blackness with hyperphallic masculinity stood in stark contrast to the presence of black transfeminine people, who had previously been well represented in *FI News*'s coverage of social events. Likewise, African American transfeminine people, who had previously been more visible in the pages of female impersonator publications, became increasingly marginalized as *FI News* prioritized white transfeminine people and (implicitly non-trans) African American men as groups that could be both targeted as consumer markets and fetishized as commodities for those who derived pleasure from witnessing their enactmentments of racialized gender and sexual stereotypes. The long-standing racist cultural associations between blackness and masculinity, on the one hand, and whiteness and femininity, on the other, no doubt also contributed to the racialized gender dynamics at play in the emergence of "inter-racial transvestite porn" as a genre.

The racial and sexual dynamics of Stevens's "club" not only established a racialized symbolic economy in the pages of *FI News*, it also reflected the extent to which both specialized niche pornography and mainstream, heterosexual pornography established and maintained hegemonic whiteness and racialized gender binaries through the fetishizing of both African American masculinities and white transfeminine sexualities and embodiments. Miller-Young argues that although mainstream, heterosexual interracial pornography did find a market among African American men, "the constant reproduction of interracial sex as both subversive and hegemonic in this genre is really about the sexual desires of white men."[46] Miller-Young's criticism that mainstream heterosexual interracial pornography had black men "perform[ing] roles as studs, coons, criminals, pimps and giant talking phalluses" certainly also applies to Stevens's contact club, *FI News,* and *IR News.*[47] The symbolic exchange was somewhat different in these examples of interracial transfeminine pornography as opposed to mainstream, hetero- and cis-normative interracial pornography, however, not only because of the transvestite content and potentially homoerotic overtones, but also because *FI News* always represented black men as sexually powerful men to be worshipped, typically at the supposed symbolic expense of white males, who were always feminized. Given that sexual enjoyment of white femininity had historically been used to justify white male violence against black men, African American men may have been especially empowered by feminizing white males, and the feminized white males may have indeed constructed their sexual and racial objectification of the African American men as antiracist.[48] The sexual charge probably stemmed from the combined gender, sexual, and racial transgressions at play, and Neptune always insisted on constructing encounters in racial and sexual objectification as mutually pleasurable for all involved. It was evidently carefully catering to many possible ways of capitalizing on the complexities of American sexual and racial, as well as gender desires.

On the surface, *FI News* suggested that a rearticulation of sex, gender, and race between white transvestites and black men would result in greater sexual and racial freedom for all; in reality, it focused on selling white consumers a racialized fantasy of being dominated by black men. Characters such as Stevens absolved white readers of their racialized (and racist) sexual desires. For example, another such fantasy character, "Princess Temptation," was quoted as stating, "Some of my TV's like black dicks and I understand." Furthermore, she wrote, "I endorse the latent feelings of black domination and worship of the black penile organ for happiness."[49] White readers were also encouraged to develop such racialized sexual desires. One letter to the editor testified to this possibility, exclaiming, "I never thought this would happen to me, but it has, I'm a nigger-lovin' white TV faggot and glad of it!"[50] Evidently, such content played an important role in racializing and fetishizing sexual representations of transfemininity and in expanding the sexual racism prevalent in depictions of black (implicitly non-trans) men and black transfeminine people.

FI News advertised its transvestite race porn as having a kind of radically liberal, antiracist sexual politics, billing itself as a more extreme version of the mainstream American media's changing race politics. This tactic echoed that of fairly mainstream pornographers such as Al Goldstein, the publisher of *Screw,* and Larry Flynt, the publisher of *Hustler,* both of whom created pornography that condemned conservative American sexual values in ways that would appear extremely offensive. Laura Kipnis calls this kind of pornography an "oppositional political form."[51] Just as *FI News* had framed Tiresius's presidential campaign primarily as a tirade against American sexual conservatism, it implied that its interracial porn demonstrated a more radical racial politics than mainstream American liberalism. One of its front-page headlines, for example, read, "The American Public Was Ready for 'Roots,' But Are You Ready for This?"[52] The question capitalized on the popularity of the galvanizing 1976 television miniseries that documented the history of African Americans from slavery to emancipation through the fictionalized multigenerational story of former slave Kunta Kinte, played by actor Levar Burton.[53] The 1970s had seen an increasing recognition of African American media representations. Despite the mixed and highly charged political reception of blaxploitation films, black consumers had been revealed as a lucrative market base.[54] *Roots,* therefore, in some ways represented the culmination of 1970s African American representations in mainstream American culture and media. By contrasting its content with *Roots, FI News* positioned its racialized sexual politics as extreme, radical, and controversial. Stevens taunted readers with the idea that "if you're offended, maybe you're not the liberal you thought you were."[55] The idea that readers could express their "radicalism" by consuming sexualized media that used dominant gendered, racialized, and sexual symbolism to fetishize and objectify socially marginalized people for pleasure was a significant turn of events for the politics of trans and racial representations at the end of the decade.

TRANS-THEMED NICHE PUBLICATIONS PROVIDE SIGNIFICANT examples of how representations of trans people and of transfemininity changed over the course of the 1970s. The 1960s and early 1970s had been characterized by distant, secretive admiration of publicly visible, professional female impersonators, while performance venues and print publications featuring them were highly regulated and policed. By the end of the 1970s, however, transfeminine people became represented in pornography primarily in symbolic terms as sexual fantasy characters. Race and racism became increasingly explicit and capitalized upon in pornographic sexual representations of trans people and transfemininity, while the economic factors associated with the pornographic marketplace continued to play a major role in determining trans people's labor, consumption, and social experiences.

For white transsexual women and transfeminine people such as Roberts, Mesics, Tiresius, and Stevens, working in the sex industry provided unique opportunities not only for personal financial gain but also to influence how trans people were represented in American culture, albeit within the limits of a market driven by profit and sexual fantasy. By the end of the decade, transsexual women who could represent more commercially viable fantasy characters became a new kind of sexual norm in pornography and other commercialized sex spaces. These new sex symbols in some ways overshadowed the kind of sexual politics that trans activists such as Mesics had been working toward earlier in the decade, and certainly contributed to political and social divisions among trans people. By the early 1980s, market-driven, mass-produced pornography often fetishized trans women, transfeminine people, and "shemales" as gender, sexual, and racial transgressions.[56] Trans-oriented pornography in the 1970s stood in stark contrast to liberal political efforts on behalf of trans people. In the world of 1970s pornography and female impersonator publications, the sexual symbolism that proved profitable to pornographers was what ultimately informed the sexual representations of transfeminine politics, fantasies, and racialization, and in many cases the economic roles of workers and consumers.

NOTES

1. Pamela Paul, *Pornified: How Pornography Is Damaging Our Lives, Our Relationships, Our Families* (New York: Times Books, 2005); Susanna Paasonen, Kaarina Nikunen, and Laura Saarenmaa, eds., *Pornification: Sex and Sexuality in Media Culture* (New York: Berg, 2007).
2. Martin Meeker, *Contacts Desired: Gay and Lesbian Communications and Community, 1940s–1970s* (Chicago: University of Chicago Press, 2006); Whitney Strub, "Historicizing Pulp: Gay Male Pulp and the Narrativization of Queer Cultural History," in *1960s Gay Pulp Fiction: The Misplaced Heritage*, ed. Drewey Wayne Gunn and Jaime Harker (Amherst: University of Massachusetts Press, 2013), 43–77; Blaine Branchik, "Out in the Market: A History of the Gay Market Segment in the United States," *Journal of Macromarketing* 22 (2002): 86–97; A. Gluckman and B. Reed, eds., *Homo Economics: Capitalism, Community, and Lesbian and Gay Life* (New York:

Routledge Kegan Paul, 1997); Lee Badgett, *Money, Myths, and Change: The Economic Lives of Lesbians and Gay Men* (Chicago: University of Chicago Press, 2003); Alexandra Chasin, *Selling Out: The Lesbian and Gay Movement Goes to Market* (New York: Palgrave MacMillan, 2001).

3. Susan Stryker, *Transgender History* (Berkeley: Seal Press, 2008), 87; Robert Hill, "We Share a Sacred Secret: Gender, Domesticity and Containment in *Transvestia* Magazine's Letters from Cross-dressers and Their Wives, 1960–1979," *Journal of Social History* (Spring 2012): 729–50; Terrence Kissack, "Freaking Fag Revolutionaries," *Radical History Review* 62 (1995): 104–34; Joanne Meyerowitz, *How Sex Changed: A History of Transsexuality in the United States* (Cambridge: Harvard University Press, 2002), 235.

4. Laura Kipnis, "She-Male Fantasies and the Aesthetics of Pornography," in *More Dirty Looks: Gender, Pornography and Power,* ed. Pamela Church Gibson (London: British Film Institute, 2004), 204–15.

5. Viviane Namaste, *Sex Change, Social Change: Reflections on Identities, Institutions, and Imperialism* (Toronto: Women's Press, 2005), 86–102.

6. Melinda Chateauvert, *Sex Workers Unite: A History of the Movement from Stonewall to SlutWalk* (Boston: Beacon Press, 2013), 10.

7. For discussion of transmasculinity and transfemininity, see Alex Iantaffi and Walter O. Bockting, "Views from Both Sides of the Bridge? Gender, Sexual Legitimacy, and Transgender People's Experiences of Relations," *Culture, Health & Sexuality: An International Journal for Research, Intervention and Care* 13, no. 3 (Mar. 2011): 359; Kay Siebler, "Transgender Transitions: Sex/Gender Binaries in the Digital Age," *Journal of Gay & Lesbian Mental Health* 16, no. 74 (2012): 77.

8. Viviane Namaste, "Beyond Leisure Studies: A Labour History of Male to Female Transsexual and Transvestite Artists in Montreal, 1955–1985," *Atlantis* 29, no. 1 (Fall/Winter 2004): 5.

9. Laurence Senelick, *The Changing Room: Sex, Drag, and Theatre* (New York: Routledge, 2000), 365; Mara Dauphin, "'A Bit of Woman in Every Man': Creating Queer Community in Female Impersonation," *Valley Humanities Review* (Spring 2012): 6; Viviane Namaste, *C'Etait du spectacle! L'Histoire des artistes transsexualles a Montreal, 1955–1985* (Montreal: McGill-Queen's University Press, 2005), 28; Namaste, "Beyond Leisure Studies," 7; Michael F. Moore, *Drag! Male and Female Impersonators on Stage, Screen, and Television: An Illustrated World History* (Jefferson, NC: McFarland, 1994); see also Leila J. Rupp and Verta Taylor, *Drag Queens at the 801 Cabaret* (Chicago: University of Chicago Press, 2003); Sukie de la Croix, *Chicago Whispers: A History of LGBT Chicago before Stonewall* (Madison: University of Wisconsin Press, 2012); Nan Alamilla Boyd, *Wide Open Town: A History of Queer San Francisco to 1965* (Berkeley: University of California Press, 2003).

10. Donald Greenhaus, "A Female Impersonator," *Society* 11, no. 1 (November /December 1973): 52–54; Mark Singer, "Talk of the Town 'Positions Available,'" *New Yorker,* July 21, 1986, 21.

11. Pudgy Roberts, "All About Your Editor," *Great Female Mimics* 1, no. 1 (1972): 24–29.

12. Ms. Bob, "Female Mimics Part 3—Pudgy's Challenge," *Transgender Forum,* March 5, 2012, www.tgforum.com.

13. Roberts, "All About Your Editor," 24.

14. Marc Singer, *Mr. Personality: Profiles and Talk Pieces from the New Yorker* (New York: Houghton Mifflin, 1988), 95–99.

15. Pudgy Roberts, Letters to the Editor, *Female Impersonators* no. 2, 69.

16. Whitney Strub, *Perversion for Profit: The Politics of Pornography and the Rise of the New Right* (New York: Columbia University Press, 2011), 147.

17. Phoebe Smith, "Profile: Sandy Mesics," *Transsexual Voice* (1982): 1.

18. Sussie Collins, "We Are Now Monthly!" *Female Impersonator Newsletter* 1, no. 2 (1973): n.p.

19. Ibid.

20. Ibid.

21. Misty Monroe to FI readers, *FI News* no. 54 (n.d.), 14.

22. Nils Johan Ringdal, "Feminism and the Sex Workers' Movement," in *Love for Sale: A World History of Prostitution* (New York: Grove Press, 1997), 369; Chateauvert, *Sex Workers Unite,* 48.

23. Valerie Jenness, "From Sex as Sin to Sex as Work: COYOTE and the Reorganization of Prostitution as a Social Problem," *Social Problems* 37, no. 3 (Aug. 1990): 408.

24. Jenness, "Sex as Sin," 409.

25. "Here and There: First New York Hookers Ball," *FI News* no. 28 (n.d.), 2.

26. Keith Bowers, "Annie Sprinkle Talks about Halloween, Hookers, and Reviving an S.F. Tradition," *SF Weekly*, October 21, 2011.

27. Earl Wilson, "Hookers' Ball was a Boring Assignment," *Sarasota Herald-Tribune*, February 22, 1977.

28. "Our Sandra Models Lingerie," *FI News* no. 38 (n.d.), 5.

29. Ibid., 4.

30. Ibid., 5.

31. "Jackie's Ball," *Female Impersonators Newsletter* 1, no. 2, n.d., 6–7.

32. Ibid.

33. Collins, "We Are Now Monthly!"

34. See Kevin J. Mumford, *Interzones: Black/White Sex Districts in Chicago and New York in the Early Twentieth Century* (New York: Columbia University Press, 1997).

35. Carolyn Bronstein, *Battling Pornography: The American Feminist Anti-Pornography Movement, 1976–1986* (New York: Cambridge University Press, 2011), 63–82.

36. "Tiresius Knows," *FI News* no. 46 (n.d.), 6.

37. Ibid.

38. Ibid.

39. "Transsexual for President," *FI News* no. 48 (n.d.), 24.

40. Ibid.

41. Ibid.

42. Ibid.

43. "Lori Stevens Lets It all Hang Out," *FI News* no. 18 (n.d.), 3.

44. Ibid.

45. Mireille Miller-Young, "Let Me Tell Ya 'bout Black Chicks: Interracial Desire and Black Women in 1980s Video Pornography," in Nikunen, Paasonen, and Saarenmaa, *Pornification*, 37–40.

46. Ibid., 40.

47. Ibid., 35.

48. For critical discussion of black heterosexuality and race in sexual representations, see Jacquie Jones, "The Construction of Black Sexuality: Towards Normalizing the Black Cinematic Experience," in *Black American Cinema*, ed. Manthia Diawara (New York: Routledge, 1993), 247; Kobena Mercer, "Skin Head Sex Thing: Racial Difference and the Homoerotic Imaginary," in *How Do I Look? Queer Film and Video*, ed. Bad Object-Choices (Seattle: Bay Press, 1991), 169–83; Celine Parreñas Shimizu, *The Hypersexuality of Race: Performing Asian/American Women on Screen*

and Scene (Durham, NC: Duke University Press, 2007), 140–63; Richard Fung, "Looking for My Penis: The Eroticized Asian in Gay Video Porn," in Bad Object-Choices, *How Do I Look?*, 145–68; Lawrence C. Ross Jr., "Big Business, Hip-hop, and Porn," in *Money Shot: Wild Days and Lonely Nights Inside the Black Porn Industry* (Philadelphia: Running Press, 2007), 227–37; Mireille Miller-Young, "Interventions: The Deviant and Defiant Art of Black Women Porn Directors," in *The Feminist Porn Book*, ed. Tristan Taormino, Celine Parreñas Shimizu, Constance Penley, and Mireille Miller-Young (New York: Feminist Press, 2013), 105–20.

49. Untitled, *FI News* no. 64 (n.d.), 22.

50. "Our Gal / Sandy Sez: FI News Editorial," *FI News* no. 28 (n.d.), 2.

51. Laura Kipnis, *Bound and Gagged: Pornography and the Politics of Fantasy* (Durham, NC: Duke University Press, 1996), 123.

52. "Black Cocks Invade a Honkey Club," *FI News* no. 35 (n.d.), 11.

53. See William R. Ferris, "Alex Haley: Vicksburg, Mississippi, 1989: Angels, Legends, and Grace," *Southern Cultures* 14, no. 3 (Fall 2008): 6–25; Lauren R. Tucker and Hemant Shah, "Race and the Transformation of Culture: The Making of the Television Miniseries Roots," *Critical Studies in Mass Communication* 9 (1992): 325–36.

54. See Joe Wlodarz, "Beyond the Black Macho: Queer Blaxploitation," *Velvet Light Trap* 53 (Spring 2004): 10; Bill Stanford Pincheon, "Mask Maker, Mask Maker: The Black Gay Subject in 1970s Popular Culture," *Sexuality & Culture* 5, no. 1 (Winter 2001): 61; Yvonne D. Sims, *Women of Blaxploitation: How the Black Action Film Heroine Changed American Popular Culture* (Jefferson, NC: McFarland, 2006).

55. "Black Cocks Invade a Honkey Club," *FI News* no. 35 (n.d.), 11.

56. Jeffrey Escoffier, "Imagining the She/Male: Pornography and the Transsexualization of the Heterosexual Male," *Studies in Gender and Sexuality* 12, no. 4 (2011): 268–81.

CHAPTER 7

"Think about That Special Man Who's on His Way Home to You"

Conservative Women's Sexualization of Marriage in the 1970s

GILLIAN FRANK

"CHRISTIAN SEX HAS EVERYTHING," enthused Anita Bryant in her 1972 book *Bless This House*. "Married sex," she continued, "as with all else God created, is beautiful."[1] Before becoming infamous as an antigay crusader, Anita Bryant participated in what might be called an "evangelical sexual revolution." This phenomenon involved born-again women contributing to the sexualization of American culture as the authors and devotees of best-selling instruction manuals with titles such as *The Electric Woman, You Can Be the Wife of a Happy Husband,* and *The Spirit-Controlled Woman.* In these books, the authors promoted an eroticized version of patriarchal marriage and endorsed a wide range of nonprocreative sexual pleasures, such as sensual massage with scented oils. Reacting to an array of cultural and economic transformations that destabilized marriage as the sole locus of sexual expression in the 1960s and 1970s, these conservative women authors worked to reestablish romance, intimacy, spiritual fulfillment, sexual excitement, and economic stability within its confines. Evangelical advice literature has not previously been characterized as pornography, or as a literary product of the Golden Age of pornography of the 1970s. Yet the sexual scripts that conservative women produced in their prescriptive literature incorporated many elements of the pornographic culture they outwardly disavowed. This body of advice literature should be viewed as a genre of pornography heavily influenced by mainstream 1970s cultural values, adapted for conservative religious sensibilities.

Conservative women produced their sex advice literature in the early 1970s, when American families were experiencing profound social and economic changes. These included an economic recession, the highest rates of unemployment in three decades, an energy crisis, double-digit inflation and a consequent decline of purchasing power, a collapsing housing market, widespread cuts to social services, and new words such as "slumpflation" and "stagflation" to describe these economic challenges.[2] Conservatives continued to maintain that the ideal American family arrangement centered around the male bread-winner, even as tough economic times necessitated two incomes, sending many women in search of paid work. "The economic integrity of the family depends on a wage earner who 'brings home the bacon,'" wrote anti-ERA leader Phyllis Schlafly in 1977, warning of the dangers that ensued when wives joined their husbands in the workforce.[3] This position, which was part of a larger 1970s debate about women's changing roles in the home and the workplace, fueled by a powerful women's liberation movement, raised vexing questions about economic transformations and their effect on women's personal and family lives.[4]

At the same time that economic concerns were rising to the fore, American conservatives found it imperative to address changes in American sexual culture that stemmed from sexual liberation, feminism, and the rise of the gay rights movement. Conservatives were gravely concerned about the increased visibility and availability of pornography, open access to birth control, expanded abortion rights under *Roe v. Wade,* and other legal changes, such as no-fault divorce and Title IX, which prohibited sex discrimination in educational settings. Collectively, these transformations radically redefined the roles and expectations of American women. Against the backdrop of an increasingly sexually explicit popular culture and the rise of social movements that placed sexuality at the center of their legislative and cultural agendas, conservative religious women saw their way of life threatened by profound economic *and* cultural shifts. They bemoaned the erosion of traditional family values, and warned that core American institutions like marriage were under assault. The decline of the family wage and the rise of pornography were interrelated factors that were destabilizing the legal, economic, and cultural conditions that had once supported family life in the postwar period.[5] Remarkably, the response of conservative religious women was not simply to condemn a mainstream popular culture that was, in the words of television historian Elana Levine, "wallowing in sex."[6] Instead, they tried to shore up the institution of marriage—and their traditional position of authority as wives—by integrating the popular new standards of sexual pleasure and variety into Christian marriage. They produced a distinctively Christian conservative sexual subculture that mirrored changes in mainstream American society even as they labeled their marriages traditional.

In this chapter, I trace conservative women's discourse about sex within marriage to explore how they incorporated sexualized popular culture into their own practices while at the same time defending a specific vision of the American family, undergirded by the male breadwinner who earned a family wage. They did so in prescriptive literature that encouraged women to have increased sexual activity and variety within the context of marriage. Sexual expression and experimentation thus became centrally important to the lives of conservative women as they wrestled with new economic arrangements that threatened to undo the gendered moorings of their lives.[7] Conservatives adapted aspects of the sexual revolution's behavioral and ideological changes to support a political campaign that sought to preserve traditional marriage and the economic system that made it possible.

The New Marriage Experts

Rather than simply repudiating an increasingly pornographic public culture, conservative evangelicals channeled these sexual currents into marriage and the home and sought to join an emphasis on physicality with spirituality. This conservative project of appropriating a sexualized popular culture is exemplified by Beverly LaHaye and her husband Tim LaHaye, the pastor of a large Baptist church who established several Christian private schools outside of San Diego. The LaHayes were at the forefront of the religious right by the end of the decade, leading struggles against pornography, the ERA, abortion, and gay rights. But, as they gained followers in the early 1970s, the LaHayes established the Family Life Seminar ministry and brought their message about marriage and sexual pleasure to audiences across the country. These efforts culminated in their 1976 best seller *The Act of Marriage: The Beauty of Sexual Love.* In this book, the authors asserted that the "ultimate objective" of sex "is orgasm for both the husband and wife."[8] The "family values," articulated by conservatives in the 1970s, and which provided a powerful platform for political ascendance through the 1980s, were thus built on the prosexual, proerotica principles of the sexual revolution. At the same time that they claimed to oppose a mainstream culture that supported freer sexual expression and promiscuity—"Flee fornication," urged Beverly LaHaye—conservative women borrowed liberally from this culture to produce explicit sexual materials that instructed women in how to support traditional marriage and the patriarchal family through prolific and varied sexual activity.[9]

One way to understand conservative women's concerns about sexuality, economics, and marriage is through analysis of the popular prescriptive literature of well-known 1970s authors and activists such as Anita Bryant, Darien Cooper, Beverly LaHaye, and Marabel Morgan. Each viewed patriarchal marriage as an antidote to economic and social disorder. These women were part of a cadre of white evangelicals who became a significant presence in American culture and politics in the 1970s.[10]

Although it is not possible to reconstruct exactly how couples appropriated the advice from a cohort of white middle-class evangelicals, the best-seller status of their literature and the media fanfare that greeted it confirms the wide circulation and consideration of their ideas among women from a spectrum of racial and class backgrounds. Features on the *Total Woman* in African American newspapers and the mainstream press marked that celebrity wives from different racial backgrounds took "Total Woman" classes. In keeping with a color-blind worldview that promoted men above women, these pieces did not call attention to racial difference nor did they even list the first names of celebrity wives. Instead, they emphasized men by describing the graduates of Morgan's course as the "wives of Joe Frazier, Alvin Dark, Jack Nicklaus, Bob Griese and other players on the Miami Dolphins, Atlanta Falcons, Green Bay Packers and Washington Redskins."[11] By 1975, more than fifteen thousand women had signed up for Marabel Morgan's Total Woman classes, which were replete with sexual assignments including instructing women "to be prepared for sexual intercourse every night for a week" in a variety of suggested locations ranging from the bedroom to the husband's workplace.[12] Thousands of other women were reported to have attended Darien Cooper's marriage seminars, which she held across the country. The books by authors such as Morgan and Cooper were part of an extensive sexual advice curriculum for adult women and constitute an important site where we can see how conservative women communicated with one another about their fears, their aspirations, and their bodies in a manner that interwove a defense of patriarchy, opposition to the emerging women's rights discourse, and a startling sexual frankness.

This sexual explicitness marked a significant moment of erotic transformation: it celebrated the home as a site of sexual recreation and dovetailed with the sexual revolution's emphasis on explicit sexual literature even as it repudiated those aspects of the revolution that were nonmarital and nonheterosexual. Put another way, conservative women's sexual literature hinged on two unresolved contradictions. First, religious conservative women condemned "cheap, perverted, publicly displayed sex" even as they contributed to the sexualization of American culture. Their texts encouraged risqué sexual activity, such as greeting one's husband at the door in peekaboo lingerie.[13] Second, they intuited that the competitive, hard-driving workplace harmed their families by demoralizing their husbands and sending them home exhausted and unhappy. Yet these same women glorified capitalism by using corporate and consumerist language and logic to idealize their intimate relationships.

Much of the popular prescriptive literature directed at women linked the ideal state of sexual submission to Christian doctrine. The advice literature was organized around scriptural passages that enjoined wives to "submit yourselves unto your own husbands, as unto the Lord."[14] Although there were debates among religious conservatives about what "submissiveness" meant, it was commonly accepted that the male-headed household was the bedrock of true Christian marriage. Marabel Morgan's 1974 best seller *The Total Woman* (fig. 7.1), which instructed women to act out a different fantasy for their husbands' pleasure every night, was the classic text of this oeuvre.[15] Morgan told reporters that she based her book on the very steps that she took to salvage her own once-failing marriage. In terms similar to those used by Betty Friedan in the 1963 classic feminist text *The Feminine Mystique,* Morgan described her unhappiness as a housewife and her troubled relationship with her husband. However, Morgan, in direct contradistinction to Friedan, claimed that her path to liberation did not lay in pursuit of a career but in acceptance of the doctrine of submission because "God planned for woman to be under her husband's rule."[16] In this same vein, Darien Cooper's best-selling marital advice book was cheerfully titled *You Can Be the Wife of a Happy*

FIGURE 7.1. Evangelical Christian marriage advice author Marabel
Morgan at home with her book *The Total Woman*, January 1, 1975.
Photo: Ray Fisher.

Husband. Cooper explained at length that hierarchical gender roles
for men and women within marriage were divinely ordained and the
key to personal happiness.[17] Men, these authors claimed, would naturally respond to submissive women by caring for them, protecting
them, and granting their unspoken desires. This sentiment crossed
denominational lines, and Catholic anti-ERA leader Phyllis Schlafly
concurred in her 1978 book *Power of the Positive Woman* that a marriage
"must have an ultimate decision maker, and that is the husband."[18]

The centrality of heterosexual pleasure to the conservative family values worldview supported the production of numerous sexual advice guides between 1970 and 1980; conservative women created a veritable sex industry. Despite their explicit eroticism, authors disavowed that their efforts were tawdry in any way. Citing the Biblical passage from *Hebrews* "Marriage is honourable in all, and the bed undefiled," conservative women legitimized nonprocreative sexual pleasure within heterosexual marriage; Morgan wrote that she viewed marital sex as something "as clean and pure as eating cottage cheese."[19] Distinguishing between pleasure driven by pornography and that of wholesome marital love, Cooper noted disapprovingly that "some men want their wives to read dirty books or go to X-rated movies to see how they can add variety to their sex life." But she reassured her religious readers that engaging with mainstream smut was not necessary, because loving couples "can provide variety and excitement without such aids."[20] Suggesting tips such as using lighting to create a romantic atmosphere, using different rooms and having "sexual union in a variety of positions," and wearing a new nightgown, as well as enjoining her female readers to explore their husbands' bodies, Cooper sought to produce sexual excitement and variety to keep women and men, but primarily men, happy in marriage. "You must realize that your husband needs the freedom to initiate whatever sexual actions he desires, knowing you will respond lovingly," she wrote. "You can be relaxed in the knowledge that it is God's will for you to meet his needs enthusiastically." She sought, in other words, to rival the tug of commercial pornography on men's desires.[21] The LaHayes also disavowed pornography, claiming in *The Act of Marriage*, a sexual advice book aimed at helping married couples achieve sexual pleasure together, that most Christians were not obsessed with sex and therefore did not need pornography.[22]

Morgan also sought to fire up her married readers' desires. She instructed wives to titillate their husbands with thoughts of what the evening might bring, such as advising them to "call [your husband] at work an hour before quitting time, to say, 'I wanted you to know that I just crave your body!' or some other erotic come-on."[23] Ironically, Morgan's attempts to encourage wives to seek thrilling sexual adventures links *Total Woman* to the other best-selling sexual text that emerged from Miami the year before: *Deep Throat* (1972). Starring Linda Lovelace, this film created what the *New York Times Magazine* described as a "porno chic" phenomenon by popularizing pornographic films among middle-class Americans and validating diverse sexual positions and experiences. In what seems like an equally appropriate defense of

Total Woman, experts testified in court in an obscenity trial that *Deep Throat* had redeeming social value "because it might encourage people to expand their sexual horizons."[24] Indeed, Morgan and her fellow Christian authors emphasized sexual variety, and suggested mutual masturbation, extensive foreplay, and a range of sexual positions for married heterosexual couples to achieve sexual pleasure.

Evangelical literature concentrated on monogamous and heterosexual sex in marriage, whereas *Deep Throat* endorsed a wider range of sexual experiences, described in one obscenity conviction as "explicit heterosexual intercourse, including group sex . . . various scenes of explicit penetration, fellatio, cunnilingus, female masturbation, anal sodomy, and seminal ejaculation."[25] However, these texts converged through an emphasis on sexual pleasure, variety, nonprocreative sexuality, and their respective best-selling statuses. Just as *Deep Throat* was one of the highest-grossing films of 1973, Morgan's *The Total Woman* appeared on the *New York Times* best-seller list for 1974 and spent over two years on the national religious best-sellers lists, bringing erotic Christian sex to millions of homes.[26] Both promised deeply satisfying mental and physical experiences through sex. *Deep Throat* depicted Linda Lovelace's attempts to find elusive sexual satisfaction—she wanted to experience "bells, bombs, dams bursting . . . something"— all of which she ultimately found by performing oral sex on multiple men. "Fireworks will start," Morgan exclaimed to her female readers, when you "fulfill him by giving him everything he wants," a direct instruction for Christian wives to initiate a variety of sex acts with their husbands. "I learned," wrote one of Cooper's readers, who claimed to have become the wife of a happy husband, "that there are no sexual perversions when a wife is satisfying her husband's sexual desires and needs."[27] *The Total Woman* and similar books emphasized that wives could find pleasure by submitting to their husbands and "admiring, accepting, adoring" them and their bodies.[28]

Work-Weary Husbands and Restorative Wives

Within this conservative world, such sexual advice had economic as well as social aims. These texts purposefully eroticized the hierarchical relationships that were fundamental to marriage and the male breadwinner model. By encouraging wives to attend daily to their husband's sexual needs and fantasies, they sought to repair the physical and emotional damage that men sustained in the workplace, giving husbands sufficient strength to return to the office the next morning. Morgan explained to her readers, "At the end of a long day, your husband especially needs your compliments. . . . Put your husband's tattered ego back together again. . . . He needs to be pampered, loved, and restored through food and sex."

Morgan and her fellow authors repeatedly emphasized how husbands returned home from work dispirited and angry, and craving admiration and appreciation. They eroticized the cycle of the workday by encouraging women to spend time on their appearances while husbands were away, and to initiate sexual foreplay immediately on homecoming. Lou Beardsley and Toni Spry, charismatic Bible study leaders who regularly addressed women's church groups in the 1970s, offered Scripture-based marital advice in their 1975 book *The Fulfilled Woman*. Echoing Morgan and Cooper's advice, they wrote that "pleasing your husband is a full-time job and sex is part of it." Therefore they insisted that " 'wives should always be lovers,' too. Run into his arms the moment he comes home to you. Show him how pleased you are that he's home again."[29] A husband needed to be greeted by the "girl of his dreams" who is "feminine, soft, and touchable," Morgan likewise exclaimed.[30] Thus, to counter the monotony of women's domestic labor and men's labor in the workplace, Morgan advised, "You can be lots of different women to him. Costumes provide variety without him ever leaving home." She suggested pink baby-doll pajamas and white boots and going braless (forget about bra burning!) as some of the many options for sexual play in the marital household.[31] "Be a pixie or a pirate—a cowgirl or a show girl," she wrote. One middle-aged husband responded to his wife's kinky costume, according to Morgan, by stating, "This is one of the happiest moments of my life; I just don't want it to end."[32] That these scripts incorporated stock pornographic elements like French maid uniforms was not lost on Morgan's readers. One Illinois housewife wrote to Morgan about her attempts to follow the advice in *The Total Woman*: "I now own some nightgowns and pajamas that would not even be allowed in a[n] X-rated movie. Why? Not for me. I feel very uncomfortable in them but I wear them for him and when it makes him happy, I am more than happy."[33]

Against the grind of men's working life, a woman's appearance and advances were thus meant to raise more than a workingman's sagging spirits; her physical and emotional labor were crucial elements to restoring men's egos and work ethics. Cooper advised women to bolster men's masculinity with a steady stream of compliments: "If you want a manly man, praise him for his physical strength and the ease with which he does manly or difficult things such as opening tight jars, moving furniture, mowing the lawn, and handling heavy equipment."[34] Conservative authors advised wives to be pliant and pliable in recognition of the daily demands of their husband's jobs. Submission to men and invigorating sexual exchanges prevented a husband, in Morgan's words, from becoming someone "who does not do anything but stay home drinking beer in his underwear," but rather a man who was renewed and ready to face the workplace each day.[35] To be clear, the authors did not criticize capitalism, nor did they formulate systemic critiques linking their own malaise with structural forces. Phyllis Schlafly's pronouncement that "the real liberator of women in America is the free enterprise system" was widely accepted.[36] Overall, the texts subscribed to and reinforced the idea that wives had a personal responsibility to help their husbands succeed within corporate culture, and a sexually robust, traditional marriage was key to that outcome.

Conservative women thus registered the harmful effects of capitalism even as they reproduced its structure, both in the demand that men continue to earn a family wage, and in their organization of family hierarchy. The dominant analogy used by conservative religious women to describe the relationship of husband and wife was corporate: that of president to vice president. If marriage was like a corporate system, it was one where women could never be promoted to president. However, promotion was not the point, for as Beverly LaHaye, the founder of the conservative public policy and lobbying organization Concerned Women for America, wrote in *The Spirit-Controlled Woman*, a husband puts his wife "in charge of areas where she functions well. This is a truly liberated woman."[37]However, women who sought to assume leadership roles would turn a family "upside down." Invoking decades of popular psychology that blamed errant mothers for negative social transformations, Cooper warned her female readers, "As homes have become more wife-dominated, there has been a rise in juvenile delinquency, rebellion, homosexuality, the divorce rate, and the number of frustrated women."[38] Even the sexual act itself replicated structures of male domination and female submissiveness. "The very nature of the act of marriage involves feminine surrender," wrote Beverly and Tim LaHaye, who depicted a woman's orgasm as predicated on relinquishing control to her husband.[39] Submissiveness was not the province of evangelical conservatives alone; Phyllis Schlafly, a devout Catholic, also reminded her readers that marriage, like "every successful country and company has one 'chief executive officer.' "[40]

These texts eroticized hierarchical relationships by inciting sexual desires and clarifying the wife's and husband's respective roles in marriage and the bedroom. Making these hierarchies function involved hard work and making men hard, a goal that required conservatives to borrow from the newly liberalized sexual culture. The LaHayes offered women explicit sexual advice along the lines of Alex Comfort's mainstream 1972 best seller *The Joy of Sex* so that they might better manipulate men's bodies to achieve climax:[41]

> Gently massaging the genital region, she should run her fingers over his penis, pubic hair, scrotum and inner thighs. She should be very careful not to put pressure on his testicles located inside his scrotal sac, as this can be quite uncomfortable. With her hand around the shaft of the penis, she should begin massaging up and down. As her motion becomes more rapid, her husband's body will grow more rigid, and she will be able to verify his response to her touch. This motion should be continued until he ejaculates. Before beginning this exercise, the wife should have several tissues on hand to absorb the discharge.[42]

Notably, the authors emphasized variety and suggested mutual masturbation, extensive foreplay, and a range of sexual positions for married heterosexual couples. Although the LaHayes intended their labored prose and practical suggestions to reinvigorate marital sex and reinforce the sexual hierarchy (note the cleanup instructions directed to the wife), one could hardly ignore its potential to stimulate a reader's solitary sexual arousal. Although these texts frowned upon masturbation, the act of reading sexual advice constituted a pornographic pleasure irrespective of the reader's sexual orientation or motivation for seeking out the information.

Sex at Home versus Sex at the Office

In affirming sexual pleasure, the authors of these texts located sexuality firmly within the marital home. This strategic approach addressed a new threat in the early 1970s: sex in the workplace. Evangelical advice manuals fixated on this staple of popular culture—the image of the office sizzling with sex and young pink-collar workers who were actively pursuing sexual encounters as well as careers. Helen Gurley Brown's *Sex and the Single Girl* (1962) and *Sex and the Office* (1964), as historian Julie Berebitsky notes, "radically reworked close to a century of advice to office women" and affirmed secretaries' pursuit of "professional success and sexual pleasure" at work.[43] These books were heralded as ushering in a sexual revolution for women.

In hindsight, we can see that Gurley Brown's texts were not markedly different from the prescriptive literature offered by evangelicals. Both emphasized women's physical beauty, encouraged sexual adventure, and suggested affectations to charm and ensnare men. Critics labeled both sets of texts as encouraging phony and manipulative behavior. The crucial difference was the location of sexuality. Gurley Brown's audience of unmarried female workers terrified conservative women who feared that lusty young secretaries would lure husbands away from their wives, rendering the workplace a site of sexual danger. "All day long [your husband is] surrounded at the office by dazzling secretaries who emit clouds of perfume," warned Morgan.[44] Cooper similarly feared the ranks of "well groomed women in the business world." Beverly LaHaye also worried about secretaries, whom she described as pathetic single women who were "desperately lonely and [who] will pay any price for a period of tenderness." These women would have sex with their bosses, she warned, even when they knew there was "no chance of marriage."[45]

It was not the presence of sexuality that differentiated these two bodies of literature of the sexual revolution, but the location of and context of sex. The antidote for sex in the office (and more broadly for the lure of pornography) was to amplify the amount and kind of sex in the home. Morgan directed her readers to foster intimacy, excitement, and, more importantly, commitment through sexual innovation. In *The Total Woman*, Morgan relayed the story of Connie, who attended her husband's company's annual dinner dance.

> One of the secretaries stopped the show with a most revealing gown. As Connie watched her husband's glassy eyes, she causally asked him, "What would you do if I wore a getup like that to greet you some night?" His reply was a shock to her. "Oh honey," he said, "I'd love it. If I thought you'd be home waiting for me in an outfit like that, the bumper-to-bumper traffic wouldn't bother me a bit. In fact, I might even leave early to beat the traffic!" Connie is a smart woman. She tried it. He liked it![46]

To neutralize the threat of sexually avid women in the working world, Morgan advised wives to replicate the office's sexual allure within the home. However, by casting secretaries as unmoored and predacious, conservative women obscured the pervasiveness of sexual harassment directed at female workers, and absolved their husbands of responsibility for sexual advances, including unwanted advances, they were "lured" into making at the office.

Conservative women avowed that submissiveness to men, kinking up their marriages, and the maintenance of distinct gender roles could act as a shield against various social dislocations, prevent husbands from sleeping with their secretaries, and act as a counterbalance to men's decimating workday experiences. Within this corporatized and sexualized model, evangelical women also expected material rewards for their service. In a very real sense, this system was incentive-based: vacations, clothes, jewelry, cars, flowers, appliances, and, of course, love and tenderness were all promised as rewards for submission.[47] One woman who supposedly took Morgan's Total Woman course claimed: "My husband wasn't even speaking to me when I began, but I did all my assignments. He has never bought me a gift before, but this week he bought me two nighties, two rose bushes, and a can opener!"[48]

Making Ends Meet: Economic Downturn and the Disappearance of the Family Wage

By the end of the 1970s, as anti-ERA forces were victorious in state legislatures, the anxieties unleashed by this political struggle and by broader economic downturns pervaded American life. Increasingly, conservative women sought to resolve these tensions through cultural approaches, such as the celebration of traditional "family values." According to historian Matthew Lassiter, these responses show how "cultural explanations triumphed over economic ones" and represent how conservatives failed to "come to terms with the destruction of a capitalist economy."[49] The emphasis on cultural change gave conservative women license to express anger at working women and anxiety about shifts in the economy that were beyond their control. Conservative women responded to economic transformations in the language most readily available to them: that of family, gender, and sexuality. Their expressions were often aspirational: idealized fictions about what family life ought to be, especially focused on the male breadwinner at a time when the family wage model was rapidly disappearing.

This body of advice literature addressed a multitude of insecurities during a period of economic decline. Many men felt adrift and emasculated by declining wages and the inability to sustain a family on their take-home pay. This condition was apparent to Morgan, who recognized that some female readers would have to go to work to pitch in to pay the bills. "If you're a working wife, he especially needs your reassurance and appreciation, since his masculinity may be threatened by your paycheck," she wrote.[50] This sentiment was not isolated to religious conservative publications. Popular magazines like *Readers Digest* produced articles such as "How to Support Your Husband's Ego" with the aim of helping wives to armor their men "against this intensely competitive world."

In the early 1970s, when the family wage became ever more unattainable, conservative women sought to preserve its underlying ideology. Morgan and her cadre of fellow authors conceded the decline of the male breadwinner model but used their literature to advise women on how to maintain an illusion of a world that had both social and economic order. Left with the task of reconciling a culture that demanded "traditional" domesticity with the stresses engendered by new structures of labor and capital, they turned to role-playing—a practice sexologists William H. Masters and Virginia E. Johnson condemned as a dangerous form of make believe.[51] The fantasy of the happy housewife dressed up in new kinky pixie and cowgirl costumes was the conservative woman's winning strategy throughout the sexualized 1970s.

The legacy of this conservative sexual labor was apparent in cultural battles over gender throughout the decade. In 1979, Chuck Barris, the creator of the hit television shows *The Dating Game* and *The Newlywed Game*, introduced American audiences to his new show, *Three's a Crowd*. This show had a provocative premise: husbands would appear on the show with their wives *and* their secretaries to answer questions to determine "who knew the husband best." Men were asked questions such as "what's the longest your wife has made you go without sex?," "If you and your secretary were planning on having an affair, where would you tell your wife you were going / what excuse would you give her in order to get out of the house?," and "Complete this sentence for us: my secretary always puts her bust too close to my ___." The secretaries and wives would then be called out on stage to answer the same questions. Responses that best matched the man's would be awarded points and the woman with the most correct answers would get a cash prize. These personal queries placed sexual and economic conflict at the center of the show and provoked verbal and even physical fights between the contestants.

The show had a broader significance, however, because it revealed cultural differences between feminists and conservative women over the meaning and practice of women's equality, marriage, and a sexualized commercial culture. Although both groups detested the program, they did so for very different reasons. The National Organization for Women (NOW) called the show "sexist and demeaning," and charged that it encouraged a threat to working women by promoting sexual harassment at the office. The organization mounted license renewal challenges and pressured broadcasters to change their programming. Right-wing women, however, objected to what amounted to public endorsement of "scenes of adultery" and "sexual perversion," and mobilized half a million people to sign pledge cards threatening to boycott the show and the network. For them, the secretary who knew their husbands intimately exacerbated intense concerns about threats to marriage and the family. The encroaching secretary further solidified the belief that these sacred American institutions had to be defended from a degraded popular culture, from "liberated" women who entered the workplace with an unhealthy interest in other women's husbands, and from worsening economic conditions that left even strong Christian families vulnerable.

IN 1977, THE WORLD ALMANAC listed the twenty-five most influential women in the United States. Their selections revealed how the forces of the sexual revolution and counterrevolution ran through the center of American culture. First lady Rosalynn Carter, a devout evangelical Christian, wife and mother of four, topped the list. But NOW president Eleanor Smeal and Shere Hite, author of "The Hite Report," a best-selling survey of American women's sexual experiences, were also included. Anita Bryant, Marabel Morgan, and Phyllis Schlafly also made the list, bringing together some of the most passionate but ideologically opposed activists in the nation.

When the cultural struggles of the 1970s are remembered, right-wing women are typically portrayed as antisexual, antipornography, and wholly opposed to dominant cultural transformations like the sexual revolution. Yet, as this chapter has shown, white evangelical Christian women participated in the freer sexual culture, and adapted elements of the newly prolific pornography to eroticize traditional marriage and gender roles. Marabel Morgan's *The Total Woman* was the best-selling book of 1974. Morgan appeared on the cover of the March 1977 *Time* magazine, was a regular guest on *The Phil Donahue Show,* and made countless mainstream media appearances. Morgan, LaHaye, Cooper, and others created a new genre of erotic religious marital advice literature, and generated a racially diverse market of eager consumers. Often remembered solely for political positions that opposed reproductive rights, gay rights, and pornography, conservative women also contributed to the sexualization of the home and of popular culture in this period. This eroticization, although exclusively heterosexual and marital, placed religious conservatives squarely within and not outside the currents that transformed sexual life in the United States in the 1970s.

NOTES

1. Anita Bryant, *Bless This House* (Grand Rapids, MI: Fleming H. Revell, 1972), 126.
2. "The Recession: Gloomy Holidays—and Worse Ahead," *Time,* December 9, 1974.
3. Phyllis Schlafly, *Power of the Positive Woman* (New Rochelle, NY: Arlington House, 1977), 164.
4. Beth Bailey mapped some of these in a provocative essay on economics and gender in the 1970s: "If women's liberation demanded equality in the workplace, did that mean that women who held jobs were 'women's libbers'? If a great many women who held relatively conservative views about gender roles nonetheless worked outside the home, where did they fit in the angry debates about women's proper roles?" Bailey, "She 'Can Bring Home the Bacon': Negotiating Gender in the 1970s," in *America in the Seventies,* ed. Beth Bailey and David Farber, 107–28 (Lawrence: University Press of Kansas, 2004), 109.
5. In *Power of the Positive Woman,* Schlafly wrote, "Surveying America after our bicentennial, it would be easy to conclude that we may become another of the many civilizations that perished after discarding the moral standards that bound their people together. One out of every two marriages now ends in divorce. Venereal disease has risen to epidemic levels and is one of the most common illnesses of the nation. Abortion, the killing of unborn babies, is our third most popular operation. . . . Militant homosexuals and lesbians are popular lecturers on college campuses and guests on television and radio programs" (140). Her statement represented broader alarm over changing sexual and gender mores.
6. Elana Levine, *Wallowing in Sex* (Durham, NC: Duke University Press, 2006).
7. For general histories of marriage, see Elaine Tyler May, *Great Expectations:*

Marriage and Divorce in Post-Victorian America (Chicago: University of Chicago Press, 1980); Nancy F. Cott, *Public Vows: A History of Marriage and the Nation* (Cambridge: Harvard University Press, 2000); Kristin Celello, *Making Marriage Work: A History of Marriage and Divorce in the Twentieth-Century United States* (Chapel Hill: University of North Carolina Press, 2009).

8. Tim F. LaHaye and Beverly LaHaye, *The Act of Marriage: The Beauty of Sexual Love* (Grand Rapids, MI: Zondervan, 1976), 60.

9. Beverly LaHaye, *The Spirit-Controlled Woman* (Irvine, CA: Harvest House Publications, 1976), 53.

10. Sally K. Gallagher, *Evangelical Identity and Gendered Family Life* (New Brunswick, NJ: Rutgers University Press, 2003); Randall Balmer and Lauren Winner, *Protestantism in America* (New York: Columbia University Press, 2002); Randall Balmer, *Mine Eyes Have Seen the Glory: A Journey into the Evangelical Subculture in America*, 3rd ed. (New York: Oxford University Press, 2000).

11. Bruce McCabe, "The Team Behind 'The Total Woman.'" *Boston Globe*, January 6, 1976; "Classes Help Failing Marriages and Improve Already Good Ones," *Chicago Defender*, June 11, 1975.

12. Marabel Morgan, *Total Woman* (Old Tappan, NJ: Fleming H. Revell, 1973), 127; Barbara Grizzuti Harrison, "The Books That Teach Wives to Be Submissive," *Mc-Call's* (June 1975): 113.

13. LaHaye and LaHaye, *Act of Marriage*, 20.

14. Darien B. Cooper, *You Can Be the Wife of a Happy Husband* (Wheaton, IL: Victor Books, 1977), 83; Morgan, *Total Woman*, 70.

15. Kristin Celello, *Making Marriage Work: A History of Marriage and Divorce in the Twentieth-Century United States* (Chapel Hill: University of North Carolina Press, 2009); Randall Balmer, "American Fundamentalism: The Ideal of Femininity," in *Fundamentalism and Gender*, ed. John Stratton Hawley, 47–62 (New York: Oxford University Press, 1994), 54; Amy DeRogatis, "What Would Jesus Do? Sexuality and Salvation in Protestant Evangelical Sex Manuals, 1950s to the Present," *Church History: Studies in Christianity and Culture* 74, no. 1 (2005): 97–137; Susan Harding, "Family Reform Movements: Recent Feminism and Its Opposition," *Feminist Studies* 7, no. 1 (Spring 1981): 57–75.

16. Morgan, *Total Woman*, 69.

17. I use "submissiveness" as a marked term, for it has changed over time among evangelicals and has been the subject of much contestation within that community and also among scholars who have debated whether submission is simply gender subordination or is, as recent ethnographic studies of evangelical women have shown, also a means of claiming empowerment. See Sally Gallagher, "The Marginalization of Evangelical Feminism," *Sociology of Religion* 65, no. 3 (2004): 215–37; Marie Griffith, *God's Daughters: Evangelical Women and the Power of Submission* (Berkeley: University of California Press, 1993); Julie Ingersoll, *Evangelical Christian Women: War Stories in the Gender Battles* (New York: New York University Press, 2003).

18. Schlafly, *Power of the Positive Woman*, 50.

19. The passage was from Hebrews 16:4. Morgan, *Total Woman*, 111. For further discussion, see Margaret Hardisty, *Forever My Love: What Every Man Should Know about His Wife* (Irvine, CA: Harvest House, 1979), 59–64; and LaHaye and LaHaye, *Act of Marriage*.

20. Cooper, *You Can Be the Wife*, 150.

21. Ibid., 145, 151–52.

22. LaHaye and LaHaye, *Act of Marriage*, 16.

23. Morgan, *Total Woman*, 127–28.

24. Paul L. Montgomery, "Film Critic Says 'Deep Throat' Could Expand Sexual Horizons," *New York Times*, December 21, 1972.

25. *United States v. One Reel of Film*, 360 F. Supp. 1067 (1973 D. Mass).

26. Jennifer Heller, "Marriage, Womanhood, and the Search for 'Something More': American Evangelical Women's Best-Selling 'Self-Help' Books, 1972–1979," *Journal of Religion and Popular Culture* 2 (Fall 2002): n.p.

27. Charlene Dale, "Sex Is God's Gift," *We Became Wives of Happy Husbands*, ed. Darien Cooper (Wheaton, IL: Victor Books, 1976), 161.

28. Morgan, *Total Woman*, 112–13.

29. Lou Beardsley and Toni Spry, *The Fulfilled Woman* (Irvine, CA: Harvest House Publishers, 1977), 60.

30. Morgan, *Total Woman*, 139.

31. Ibid., 94–97.

32. Ibid., 97.

33. Rebecca Davis, "Eroticized Wives: Evangelical Marriage Guides and God's Plan for the Christian Family," *The Embrace of Eros: Bodies, Desires, and Sexuality in Christianity*, ed. Margaret Kamitsuka (Minneapolis: Fortress Press, 2010).

34. Cooper, *You Can Be the Wife*, 39–40.

35. See LaHaye, *Spirit-Controlled Woman*, 74.

36. Schlafly, *Power of the Positive Woman*, 30.

37. LaHaye, *Spirit-Controlled Woman*, 71.

38. Cooper, *You Can Be the Wife*, 62.

39. LaHaye and LaHaye, *Act of Marriage*, 133–35.

40. Schlafly, *Power of the Positive Woman*, 50.

41. Alex Comfort, *The Joy of Sex* (New York: Simon & Schuster, 1972).

42. LaHaye and LaHaye, *Act of Marriage*, 91.

43. Julie Berebitsky, "The Joy of Work: Helen Gurley Brown, Gender, and Sexuality in the White-Collar Office," *Journal of the History of Sexuality* 15, no. 1 (2006): 89–127, quote at 97.

44. Morgan, *Total Woman*, 92. See also LaHaye, *Spirit-Controlled Woman*, 52–53.

45. Cooper, *You Can Be the Wife*, 53; LaHaye, *Spirit-Controlled Woman*, 52.

46. Morgan, *Total Woman*, 96.

47. See Hardisty, *Forever My Love*, 24–26.

48. Morgan, *Total Woman*, 26.

49. Matthew Lassiter, "Inventing Family Values," in *Rightward Bound: Making America Conservative in the 1970s*, ed. Bruce Schulman and Julian E. Zelizer, 13–28 (Cambridge: Harvard University Press, 2008), 16.

50. Morgan, *Total Woman*, 84.

51. William H. Masters and Virginia E. Johnson, "A Warning about Books That Teach Women to Pretend," *Redbook*, March 1976, 68, 70, 72, 74.

CHAPTER 8

"Soft-Core Feminism"?

Playboy, *Christie Hefner, and the Feminist*
Antipornography Movement

ELIZABETH FRATERRIGO

B Y THE EARLY 1970s, *Playboy* was a part of the American
mainstream. When Hugh Hefner launched his publication in the early 1950s, its glossy color photographs of
nude women seemed risqué to some observers, and downright scan-
dalous to others. Its evocative depictions of bachelorhood provided
a marked contrast to the family togetherness of postwar American
culture. By 1960 the magazine reached a million readers each month,
inspiring the creation of dozens of Playboy-themed nightclubs, where
members paid for the privilege of being served dinner and drinks
by women dressed in satin "bunny" costumes. By the early 1970s,
Playboy Enterprises, Inc. (PEI), Hefner's publicly traded umbrella
corporation, produced films, published records and books, owned a
modeling agency and a number of movie theaters, ran a limousine
service, and had a retail line of branded merchandise. PEI also owned
and operated nightclubs, resorts, and casinos within the United States
and internationally, all in addition to publishing the flagship magazine, which then boasted monthly circulation of seven million.

Although the 1970s seemed initially to support the unbridled success of Hefner's "bunny empire," the decade ultimately proved paradoxical and problematic for Playboy's corporate fortunes. As the
decade progressed, both Hugh Hefner and his magazine, no longer
at the forefront of cultural change, became emblematic of the decade's
excesses and exploitations. Consider the November 1976 issue, which

featured an interview with presidential candidate Jimmy Carter, a devout Evangelical Christian. The interview, most memorable for Carter's admission that he had "looked on a lot of women with lust" and "committed adultery in [his] heart," reached millions of potential young voters.[1] *Playboy*'s status as a publication suitable for a presidential candidate seeking a wide reach, however, also signaled that it had lost some of its edge in a changing marketplace. Even as PEI expanded, cultural changes threatened to undermine the company and drive its readers to newer, "fresher" forms of media such as *Rolling Stone* or *Penthouse*. The once hip image of the playboy clad in a silk smoking jacket and sipping a martini in his penthouse seemed stale when compared with the thriving late night discotheque-driven singles scene, fueled by plentiful illegal drugs and a climate of sexual permissiveness. *Playboy*'s brand of sexual titillation—the "girl-next-door" disrobing before the camera—was increasingly challenged by rival upstarts that mocked the comparatively tame sexual display of the "Playmate of the Month."

At the same time that it was trying to fend off competitors and maintain market share, *Playboy*'s ubiquity made it a prominent target for feminists opposed to its packaging of female bodies for male sexual pleasure. For these feminists, the magazine's reputation for serious editorial content was nothing more than a public relations attempt to legitimize its trade in female flesh. Late in the 1970s, as a feminist antipornography movement gained force, *Playboy*'s creators would find themselves caught in a difficult bind: deemed pornographic by critics, ridiculed by competitors dealing in ever more explicit images, and struggling to dissociate the magazine from unsavory hardcore publications like *Hustler*, while these newcomers gradually siphoned away *Playboy*'s circulation.

Within this milieu, both *Playboy* and first daughter Christie Hefner, who eventually came to head PEI, emerged as lightning rods for controversy as highly visible participants in public debates about the era's social and sexual transformations. Did editorial pronouncements about individual rights and reproductive freedom and financial support for women's causes make *Playboy* and its corporate parent an ally of the women's movement? Or were these merely a matter of "spin" and smoke screen, intended to co-opt feminism or deflect criticism? As Christie Hefner presided over the company, critics and commentators asked the perennial question: how could a self-respecting woman, let alone one who called herself a feminist, work for Playboy? Was *Playboy* a brave public voice for sexual liberation, or had it merely paved the way for a spate of harmful, woman-hating pornography? In the late 1970s and into the next decade, antiporn feminists and *Playboy* supporters intent on protecting free sexual expression clashed over the definition and meaning of "pornography." They differed, in other words, not just over what constituted porn but also over the reasons why the industry flourished at this particular moment. Was porn a logical by-product of sexual revolution or a vicious backlash meant to curb women's liberation?

In this essay I seek neither to evaluate *Playboy* as pornography nor to offer a biography of Christie Hefner. Rather, I analyze the commentary and criticism generated by her self-proclaimed feminist identity and Playboy's support for feminist causes as she ascended Playboy's corporate ladder amid an emergent feminist antipornography movement. While Hugh Hefner certainly remained central to Playboy's identity during these years, Christie Hefner's presence further complicated the already contentious relationship between Playboy and the women's movement. Beginning in the mid-1970s, media accounts presented Christie Hefner as an enigmatic character at the crossroads of women's liberation and sexual revolution, interrogating her curious status as "Hugh Hefner's daughter" and eventually as "the feminist in charge of Playboy." By 1982, Christie Hefner was the woman presiding over the company that published the magazine that many critics blamed for opening the floodgates for pornography to saturate American society, and boosting an increasingly powerful porn industry. Both she and *Playboy* were thus central figures in discussions of feminism, sexuality, and pornography from the mid-1970s to the mid-1980s.

Entertainment for Men

Christie Hefner was the first child in Hugh Hefner's life, but it was really *Playboy*, founded in 1953 a year after her birth, that Hefner nurtured from infancy. Shortly after the magazine's launch, Hefner separated from his wife and young daughter. The divorce became final in 1959, and Christie's mother and stepfather raised her along with her younger brother David in the suburbs. For much of her young life, Hugh Hefner would remain a peripheral figure whom she visited a few times a year at his Chicago mansion.

In the meantime, *Playboy's* combination of racy nudes and an editorial package that emphasized the pleasures and material trappings of bachelorhood enticed male readers of the 1950s. The full-color Playmate centerfold set the magazine apart from others containing female nudity, representing a new incarnation of the illustrated pin-ups and "cheesecake" photography that had circulated widely in magazines and calendars in earlier decades. The Playmate also attracted readers to a magazine bursting with consumer possibilities in the form of advertisements and lifestyle features on everything from food and liquor to home furnishings and sports cars. *Playboy* rhapsodized about everything that American consumer society offered, instructing readers to pursue material acquisition as avidly as sexual experience. In both arenas, *Playboy* advised, there was no reason to feel guilty about one's desires. As *Playboy*'s circulation and reputation grew, the editorial package gained further definition. The magazine incorporated serious articles and interviews on social issues such as civil rights, and became known for quality coverage of contemporary political and cultural matters. Hefner also took on the role of crusader, challenging long-standing American sexual mores. In debates, interviews, and editorials, he proclaimed the need to reject conservative sex norms, such as a lingering disapproval for sex before marriage, that were out of step with the ways that most Americans behaved. The disjunction between what was deemed "moral" and what Americans actually did in the bedroom, he argued, caused unnecessary and unhealthy guilt, frustration, and unhappiness.

Keeping Up with the 1970s

During the 1960s, Hefner's editorial series, "The Playboy Philosophy," together with the editorial remarks and content of the "Playboy Forum" positioned the magazine as a standard-bearer in a movement to liberate sexual behavior and expression from the bonds of shame and repression. By the late 1960s, though, *Playboy*'s position at the forefront of change was beginning to falter as the magazine seemed ever more mainstream. Commented a prescient *Business Week* in 1969, "Suddenly the Sexual Revolution made *Playboy*'s winking view of sex look respectable to many readers—and advertisers, too. Perhaps it's too respectable, say a minority of skeptics who think the Revolution may be outpacing *Playboy*—and may leave it behind in the 1970s."[2] Indeed, Hefner himself worried that the monthly "Playmate picture stories," intended to fuel the fantasy of sexual possibility by showing the Playmate centerfold engaged in everyday life, were becoming dull and repetitious.[3] Earlier rivals had tried to copy *Playboy*, but proved no match for the original. But in 1969, Bob Guccione's *Penthouse* emerged from London as a direct challenge to *Playboy*'s vision of the "girl next door." Guccione publicized the entrance of *Penthouse* into the U.S. market with newspaper advertisements depicting the *Playboy* logo in a rifle's crosshairs and proclaiming, "We're going rabbit hunting."

During the early 1970s, *Playboy* was besieged by new competitors amid an expanding adult market and a cultural preoccupation with pornography. "Hardcore" material was increasingly available on newsstands and in movie theaters, and films like 1972's *Deep Throat* were reviewed and advertised in the mainstream press. In what the magazine trade soon dubbed "the Pubic Wars," Guccione pushed at a limit long observed in *Playboy*—the exclusion of pubic hair from Playmate pictorials—by publishing increasingly revealing photographs. Faced with this challenge, Hefner gave *Playboy* photographer Vince Tajiri the go-ahead in 1970 to show pubic hair in the Playmate pictorials—so long as it was treated with "good taste." Notably, *Playboy*'s initial breach of this boundary had taken the form of published pictorials in the late 1960s of black performers Barbara McNair and Paula Kelly. These nude photographs drew recrimination in the African American press for the editors' failure to airbrush the photos in the customary manner reserved for white female bodies in the magazine.[4] *Playboy*'s first full-frontal nude Playmate appeared in the January 1972 issue. Later that year, PEI also launched the more sexually explicit *OUI* magazine to compete directly with *Penthouse*, but this move had the unintended effect of reducing *Playboy*'s own readership.[5] Other competitors such as *Hustler* soon appeared that featured explicit views of female genitalia and a crass, antiwoman sensibility. But even with newer rivals in the market, *Penthouse*'s circulation climbed while *Playboy*'s began an inexorable decline in 1973. Further complicating matters, some advertisers registered concern about *Playboy*'s new pictorial boldness. By the mid-1970s, Hefner conceded defeat, opting to let his rivals compete for the raunchier segment of the market, although he realized that the relative modesty of earlier decades would not return. Nonetheless, *Playboy* would be lumped together with these other publications and forms of sexually explicit content as the critique of pornography launched by both feminists and conservatives emerged in the mid-1970s.

Feminists Critique *Playboy*

From its inception, *Playboy* had endured the opposition of critics. Post office censors in the 1950s had threatened its mailing privileges. In the 1960s, Hefner faced criminal charges for publishing obscenity. Whereas the nude pictorials in the magazine were the primary violation cited by those who deemed *Playboy* obscene, other commentators focused more broadly on its editorial viewpoint. For these critics, the magazine's apparent promotion of uncommitted sex coupled with its celebration of an upscale, consumption-oriented lifestyle amounted to an immoral and socially corrosive form of hedonism. The onslaught of feminist criticism that began in the late 1960s offered a somewhat different interpretation. Many women voiced a similar concern about *Playboy*'s linkage of sex and consumerism, but to feminists the key issue was not a matter of morality. Rather, early New Left–inspired feminist critiques addressed the commodification of sexuality represented by *Playboy*'s centerfolds, the glorification of the idea that women's bodies were legitimate objects for purchase. Other feminists viewed *Playboy* as a powerful symbol of male chauvinism, blaming the magazine and its nightclubs for perpetuating demeaning stereotypes of women. These feminist critiques of *Playboy* were not crafted as an attack on pornography per se; feminist antiporn positions had yet to take shape. Rather, they were part of a broader critique of a sexist society in which media images reduced women to housewives, consumers, or sex objects; female bodies were subjected to an oppressive level of male scrutiny; and pervasive gender discrimination blocked so many avenues for women that posing nude or donning bunny ears could be cast as a decent professional "opportunity."

From Hefner's perspective, Playboy's emphasis on individual rights and sexual liberation meant it had some common cause with the women's movement, although Hefner disparaged some movement activists in private. Playboy's support for abortion rights, which feminists viewed as vital to women's reproductive freedom, flowed naturally from the magazine's commitment to "sexual liberation."[6] Furthermore, Hefner presented the Playmate each month as "the girl next door" who enjoyed sex and received no condemnation for her participation, issuing a direct challenge to the sexual double standard. Hefner was thus taken aback by feminist criticism of his magazine, which only grew more pointed after he called in 1970 for a "devastating piece that takes militants apart." Hefner made clear in a staff memo that he agreed that women should not be relegated to the home nor suffer under a sexual double standard, but he worried that "the militant feminist wants to play a role exactly comparable to the male's."[7] The rejection of conventional standards of femininity, the critique of heterosexuality, and the demands for gender equality put forth by some radical feminists threatened the "complementary"— and typically hierarchical—gender roles long promoted in the magazine. The resultant article, "Up against the Wall Male Chauvinist Pig!," blamed "extremists" for working to "distort the distinctions between male and female and to discredit the legitimate grievances of American women."[8] Soon leaked to the press by a disgruntled secretary, Hefner's editorial directive and *Playboy*'s subsequent article, its first on feminism, only bolstered the view that *Playboy* was an adversary in the fight for women's liberation. Playboy's physical presence on the landscape, from PEI's corporate headquarters and Hefner's mansion in Chicago to the dozens of Playboy Clubs across the nation, provided numerous convenient, public sites to stage feminist protests.

"This Is Hugh Hefner's Daughter!"

Amid this backdrop, Hugh Hefner's daughter entered adulthood and the public eye. Having attended school as Christie Gunn, using her stepfather's last name, she had avoided much of the attention and notoriety that might otherwise have accompanied youth and adolescence as "Hef's" child. When her mother and stepfather divorced, Christie chose to change her name back to Hefner upon induction into Phi Beta Kappa. She had kept in regular though infrequent contact with her father up until this time, but her decision to return to the Hefner surname and her graduation from Brandeis University in 1974 marked the beginning of a closer relationship with him.[9] Christie joined PEI in 1975, serving as a special liaison between Hefner, newly ensconced in his Los Angeles mansion, and Playboy's corporate offices in Chicago. In less than a decade, she became the company's president.[10]

In the years preceding her leadership of an empire built "on female flesh," Christie's mere existence garnered attention from a fascinated media. "This Is Hugh Hefner's Daughter!" proclaimed the headline of a feature published in *Esquire* in December 1973. "Christie is tall, slender, with sparkling eyes and perfect teeth and light brown hair that falls lightly onto her shoulders," began the article in language evocative of a typical description of a Playmate. Indeed, its author pronounced her to be "an ideal choice for a *Playboy* centerfold," but acknowledged that "there is little chance that she would ever apply" for the job.[11] Features and profiles routinely invoked the Playmate pictorial to describe Christie's good looks, while making clear that she was neither a brainless beauty nor a woman whose femininity had been jeopardized by her education or her feminism. "She is attractive enough for a *Vogue* layout. She could be a Bunny. If she dared, she could even be a *Playboy* nude," ran another typical account.[12] One commenter noted that while perhaps she was suitable to model for the centerfold, "comely Christie" had loftier goals.[13] As she ascended PEI's corporate ladder at a pace quickened by the Hefner name, media accounts continued to comment on her looks, intellect, and ambition. The *Boston Globe* described her as both a "look alike of Princess Caroline" and a "brainy Brandeis University summa cum laude alumnus" who "oozes self-confidence."[14]

Writers pondered with a degree of skepticism, however, how Hefner's daughter could so readily accept her father and his publishing empire. "Isn't Christie, who falls into the 'nice woman' category," according to one profiler, "embarrassed by the nudes, the specifics of the swinging life, the suggestive cartoons, the photographic competition with the more frontal nudes of Penthouse and Hustler?" Another columnist observed derisively that Christie had found a way to reconcile her corporate work with her politics, explaining, "Ms. Hefner, you see, is a feminist who considers her daddy's free-swinging Playboy philosophy" to be "the backbone of the women's movement." As for her much-maligned father, Christie portrayed him as a progressive thinker who was still, at the end of the day, a product of his own time. "Hef, like so many American men with a brain," she opined, recognized the validity of the women's movement, but found it difficult to surmount "the remainders of his chauvinistic upbringing that he felt in his gut." Christie construed any lingering sexism or conflict with feminism on Hefner's part as a matter of generational difference, a perspective that some opponents might have dismissed as a convenient rationalization. As for her own relationship with the father who had shared so little of her early life, ultimately it seemed that *Playboy* had brought the two together (fig. 8.1). "At first it was just the business interest that we shared. Now we share everything," she remarked in 1978, the year she became a Playboy vice president.[15]

By 1982 Christie occupied a powerful position in the corporation that published *Playboy* magazine. Her assumption of the PEI presi-

FIGURE 8.1. Christie Hefner with her father, Hugh Hefner, at a Playboy awards banquet, January 10, 1979. Photo: Ron Galella / WireImage.

dency raised a question asked time and again in various ways: how could a feminist "slip into the president's chair at Playboy without a twinge of remorse or the taint of hypocrisy?"[16] The point was not lost on Christie that her perceived status as Playboy executive / corporate porn baron / Hefner's feminist daughter might be construed as a public relations gambit. Of her feminist credentials, another reporter quipped, "The joke around *Playboy* is that if Christie Hefner didn't exist, the public relations department would have had to invent her."[17] "Some people think Christie Hefner is a fraud," she had acknowledged several years earlier. "I'm not a shield for my father . . . I'm very sympathetic to my father's philosophies."[18] A 1982 *New York* magazine feature, "The Princess of Playboy," speculated that a daughter's desire for a father's approval might have clouded her perception. Perhaps, its author suggested, with time Christie would "pass from not having had a father through the stage of thinking he's perfect and agreeing with everything he says."[19] From this perspective, Christie's affirmation of *Playboy* had less to do with any role it played as a liberating force for women and more with a complex, needy relationship with the father who had all but abandoned her as a child.

Whether rooted in a sincere belief about *Playboy*'s beneficial role in the sexual revolution or the result of a complicated family dynamic, Christie's pronouncements about *Playboy* and the women's movement were almost uniformly positive. She made it clear early on that she had no qualms about *Playboy*'s nudity nor could she accept the view that the centerfold pictorials exploited women. She was not wholly uncritical of the magazine, however, telling *Esquire* in 1973, "What I *do* object to is *Playboy*'s contribution to American notions of female beauty. . . . A flawless woman with perfect features, no moles, no birthmarks, no pimples." She continued, "Still, the girls who pose are paid well, and they do it by choice. And the article about each girl tries to present her as a human being."[20] Elsewhere she reflected again on *Playboy*'s promotion of a narrow standard of beauty that few women could attain. Noting the wider culture, however, she explained that *Playboy* was part of that problem but not its cause.[21] Christie had ample opportunity to reiterate such views as she took on more public relations responsibilities at PEI and feminists continued to lambaste *Playboy*. Far from exploiting women, Christie emphasized, *Playboy* paid good wages to the women who chose to pose for the magazine. While some might view it as sexist, it was disingenuous to single out *Playboy* for criticism in a culture saturated with sexist images, including ads that portrayed women as having no larger purpose in life than to fight "wax buildup."[22] Beyond this defense of the centerfold, Christie, as a PEI executive, also trumpeted Playboy's support for women's advancement. "Playboy has been more supportive of feminist politics and philosophies than most other companies I know of—in its attitude toward hiring and promotion of women, through its editorial and financial support of the Equal Rights Amendment and abortion," she asserted. "I'm not the only feminist at Playboy," she further claimed. Feminists worked for the company "because the magazine is a fundamentally liberal and humanistic magazine." In her view, *Playboy* reached "men who are in a state of transition" and reinforced "their liberal instincts" as they grappled with the changes ushered in by the women's movement. Even before the resurgence of feminism, she claimed, *Playboy,* although "edited for men," had stood "for everything we're fighting for now—abortion, contraception information, freedom to choose your own lifestyle."[23]

Christie offered an impassioned case for Playboy's affinity with feminism. Yet how could one separate such assertions from PEI's bottom line and the fact that her financial position was tied to the company's success? As one skeptic put it, "Christie Hefner has an awful lot of economic interests in having the views that she does."[24] Indeed, the fact that she frequently touted Playboy's longtime support of various women's issues bothered many feminists. For them, Playboy's support for high-visibility women's issues allowed the company to neatly sidestep the question of Playboy's role in the sexual exploitation of women. Rather than bolster Playboy's credibility, the fact that a woman who identified as a feminist loudly trumpeted Playboy's support for the women's movement seemed nothing more than a calculated move to silence opponents. Moreover, for some critics, Christie's espoused version of feminism, with its emphasis on individualism and lifestyle, posed little challenge to the status quo. As one critic put it, "Her socially acceptable brand of feminism is as soft-core as the Playboy version of sex that sustains it." Christie seemed to speak "with greater conviction about the Playboy philosophy than about feminist ideals."[25]

Playboy, Feminism, and the Antipornography Movement

The events surrounding one feminist protest in 1974 help to illuminate the diverse perspectives on the magazine and the meaning of Playboy's support for liberal and feminist causes. In August 1974, members of the National Organization for Women (NOW) announced the bestowal of a "Meat Market" award on *Playboy, Oui,* and *Penthouse* for "dehumanizing both women and men." "Eroticism itself is not being objected to," a NOW press release explained, "but instead the denial of human dignity." The event was part of NOW's fifth annual media awards, meant to affirm positive images and condemn negative portrayals of women. In a related move, many of *Playboy*'s notable contributors received a letter from NOW asking them to stop endorsing the "exploitation of women's bodies and male insecurities" by publishing their work in *Playboy*, which only gave "status and prestige" to the magazine. While acknowledging Playboy's support of such issues as abortion law reform, the letter questioned the motives behind this "liberal position," pointing out that "such reforms also contribute to the greater convenience of the playboy, who does not wish to assume responsibilities." Furthermore, *Playboy*'s support of some feminist issues did not make up for or excuse the magazine's negative portrayal of women. "The central message of the women's movement, that women are and should be treated as human beings, is completely ignored, distorted or ridiculed in *Playboy* articles, letters, centerfolds, jokes and cartoons. . . . Whatever function *Playboy* might have played in the past, as a backlash against American sexual Puritanism, has been served and its only function today is to serve as a backlash against the women's movement and women's attempt to achieve a more positive self-image."

Author Joyce Carol Oates was among the group of writers and public figures who received the missive, having published some short stories in the magazine. *Playboy* published her reply. In it, Oates contrasted the "worship of youth, flesh and beauty," which she deemed "fairly innocuous," with "the pathological products of hard-core pornography, which glorify not the flesh but its mutilation." If one compared *Playboy* to "sadistic pornography, in which women's bodies are *not* worshipped but destroyed," she continued, one would find that "anger over *Playboy* and its hedonistic philosophy is possibly misdirected." To Oates, *Playboy* was "astonishingly liberal." She objected to NOW's pitch to get contributors to stop publishing in the magazine, arguing that a democratic society called for open communication in venues that served diverse audiences so that "writers with certain beliefs" might reach others besides those who already shared their viewpoints. Without such access to new ideas, she warned, "change or growth would come to an end."[26]

The exchange encapsulated many of the issues that would trouble feminist activists and organizations for the next decade. NOW's announcement had acknowledged Playboy's support for women's issues but questioned Hefner's motivation and sincerity. Could

Playboy and feminists find common ground? What was at stake for feminists who cooperated with Playboy? Like contributing to the magazine, did accepting foundation money signal endorsement of Playboy, granting legitimacy to the corporation from which those funds emanated? Oates's emphasis on free expression and the distinction she made between *Playboy* and images of sexualized violence also touched on themes that would fuel debate in the second half of the decade, helping to ignite the "sex wars" of the late 1970s and 1980s.

The feminist antipornography movement arose out of two areas of concern, sexualized violence in media and violence against women, in response to the deluge of sexually explicit material during the 1970s. Moving beyond feminist media reform efforts that aimed to eradicate media violence, not pornography, by the late 1970s Women Against Violence in Pornography and Media (WAVPM), founded in San Francisco in 1976, and Women Against Pornography (WAP), initially established as a New York outpost of WAVPM in 1979, had taken the campaign in a new direction. The earlier focus on violent images in mainstream media shifted to sexually explicit images, whether violent or not. Whereas earlier activism was predicated on the belief that media violence perpetuated a cultural climate that tolerated actual violence against women, by the late 1970s, antipornography activists maintained that pornography incited violence against women and that all women were harmed by its existence. Pornography, from this viewpoint, was "antiwoman propaganda," the "ideology of a culture" that promoted violence against women.[27] Although earlier feminist writers and activists had expressed concern about the sexual repression that might result from endorsing censorship as a remedy for pornography, WAP embraced the notion of government intervention to suppress pornography.[28]

Playboy cast its opposition to the emergence of a feminist antipornography movement as another battle against conservative repression. *Playboy* contributor Robert Shea implied that efforts to combat porn detracted from legitimate feminist concerns. "For one wing of the feminist movement, the hot issue these days is not equal pay, job opportunities, day-care centers, the Equal Rights Amendment or abortion rights but pornography," he wrote. Worse, antiporn feminists had not "advanced an inch in their thinking beyond earlier crusading prudes such as [Citizens for Decent Literature founder] Charles H. Keating Jr., and J. Edgar Hoover." Shea acknowledged activists' right to picket and protest, but argued that boycotting retailers selling such magazines as

Playboy was a form of "vigilante censorship" that impinged upon consumers' rights.[29] The publication of *Take Back the Night* (1980), a seminal collection of feminist antipornography writings edited by a WAVPM leader, prompted an editorial titled "The New Puritans." "In the past few months, we've been calling attention to a new kind of Puritanism that is being foisted on us in the guise of liberated feminist thinking. . . . Now comes a book that will serve as the *Mein Kampf* of this new totalitarianism," *Playboy* warned. "In the minds of these women, pornography is no longer an artifact of the sexual revolution—a curiosity or an indulgence. It has become a crime, a conspiracy to commit violence against women."[30] As it denounced antiporn feminists, *Playboy*'s editorial coverage also resisted any attempts to label the magazine "pornography." "Nobody can agree on what pornography is, though nearly all definitions have a negative connotation," explained associate publisher Nat Lehrman. "*Playboy*'s popularity is not based on pornography, hard- or soft-core. All the sexual images we originate are positive. They have no implication of aggressiveness, hostility or exploitation." Another editorial announced, "While Playboy and the Playboy Foundation have always advocated the right to freedom of speech, Playboy Enterprises has never distributed, nor published, sexual material that we (or the vast majority of the public) consider pornographic."[31]

Playboy and its "soft-core" style had been singled out for attack numerous times in *Take Back the Night*. According to contributor Judith Bat-Ata, *Playboy* was "the most dangerous" of pornographic magazines "because it is the leader and the 'philosopher,' precisely as Hugh Hefner likes to claim." *Playboy*'s lack of explicit images, unvarnished sex acts, and violence mattered not. "The hatred of women in *Playboy* is much more insidious and evil than in the other pornographic magazines," Bat-Ata asserted. "*Hustler* is simply the gross exaggeration of *Playboy* and *Penthouse*. It is filled with hate, but at least it is hate you can see. *Playboy* has made its fortune on creating a soft focus for hate."[32] Antirape activist Tracey A. Gardner grounded her discussion of pornography in the historical context of the sexual exploitation of black women in America, while calling upon white antiporn feminists to recognize that women of color faced not just sexism but multiple oppressions. Negative stereotypes about the black female body further shaped black women's views on soft-core pornography. "I know that if any woman of color were to see the brutal and deadly hardcore pornography around, she would be outraged by it no matter what the color of the woman being exploited was," Gardner explained.

"But when you talk about soft-core pornography, it's difficult for a Black woman to identify totally with what white women feel about it." Echoing Christie Hefner's sentiments on the narrow standard of beauty that *Playboy's* flawless images helped to support, Gardner addressed the racial dimensions of American beauty ideals. As an extension of "mass advertising and the beauty market," soft-core pornography was, in her view, "the objectification of white purity [and] innocence"—the "Beauty Queen revealed" who until recently was "by definition white." Gardner explained the impact of messages generated by a dominant culture that prized whiteness: "To little Black, Asian, or Hispanic girls, growing up with dark skin, kinky hair, African, Asian, or Latin features, everything around them—in storybooks and the media, in dolls in stores—announced that something was wrong with them. They could be whores but not beauty queens." Implicitly referencing the whiteness routinely showcased in *Playboy*, Gardner posed the question: "So how does a Black woman feel when her Black man leaves *Playboy* on the coffee table?" Young white women, most of them blonde, comprised the vast majority of models who posed for the "Playmate of the Month" feature. By the mid-1960s, after drawing criticism from the African American press for routinely excluding black women from its pages, *Playboy* had begun to include women of color in the magazine, celebrating their exoticism. In similar fashion, *Playboy* drew attention to the dozens of foreign-born women and "Chocolate Bunnies" employed at Playboy Clubs. Gardner noted the change. "What is beautiful now also includes that which is unusual or exotic, such as women of color. We have started appearing in *Vogue* and in *Playboy*." Gardner expressed ambivalence about this development. "So, Black women have been elevated from the status of whore to 'Playmate.' Now white boys can put them in *Playboy* without damaging the magazine's respectability too much."[33]

In her afterword to the volume, Adrienne Rich pondered the troubling continuum of images that objectified women, from those found in mainstream advertisements and magazines all the way to hard-core publications depicting violence against women. She connected the existence of this material to women's lived experience of exploitation and violence, while also postulating the heteronormative function of pornography. "If its message is a lie about women, that we exist to pleasure and service men and that our deepest pleasure lies in enslavement and subordination, it also affirms the enforcement of heterosexuality for women, the male right of sexual access."[34]

Playboy's feminist antiporn adversaries disagreed with the editors and contributors who defended the magazine not only when it came to defining pornography but to determining its meaning as well. From the perspective advanced in Playboy, the sexually explicit material proliferating on newsstands and in theaters, whether violent or not, was merely an outgrowth of the sexual revolution, a movement from repression to freedom that had helped make possible women's liberation. Antiporn feminists who found objectionable the "healthy" sexuality represented by its airbrushed centerfolds were "antisex" in Playboy's view. From the vantage of antiporn feminists, however, pornography was an antifeminist rejoinder, an attempt to put women who had challenged the status quo back in their place. Playboy played a role in the backlash, having normalized photographs of nude women for a male gaze. "Hefner and his Playboy empire seem comparatively mild," the authors of one Take Back the Night essay conceded. "But we must remember that it was exploitive images of women such as those promoted by Hefner that laid the groundwork for today's atrocities in pornography and media."[35]

Confronting Antiporn Feminists

In January 1981, the San Francisco–based journal Inquiry asked Christie Hefner to review Take Back the Night. Both Playboy and the American Civil Liberties Union (ACLU) subsequently reprinted her critique. Christie began by recounting a grant request received several years earlier by the Playboy Foundation from Laura Lederer, founding member of WAVPM and subsequent editor of Take Back the Night. The foundation ultimately turned down the request, according to Christie, because WAVPM's "stated goals" suggested "a reliance less on voluntarism and persuasion than on state censorship." She found mystifying the shift in perceptions of media violence among some feminists that had occurred in the intervening years. "Somehow, during the past three years, 'women against violence' has become 'women against pornography,'" she observed. Yet, she argued, "the inability to define pornography" remained a fundamental, unresolved problem in the book. Noting contributor Diana Russell's view that pornography comprised "explicit representations of sexual behavior, verbal or pictorial, that have as a distinguishing characteristic the degrading or demeaning portrayal of human beings, especially women," Christie countered by pointing out that "the basic problem of who decides what is degrading or demeaning persists." "In read-ing these essays, you get the strong message that if you don't agree with what some of the authors condemn as pornography," she wrote, "then you've obviously been co-opted by the enemy." She noted Bat-Ada's claim that "healthy, self-respecting females" did not wish to encounter "*Playboy, Penthouse* or any other pornographic magazines" in the local grocery store presumed an exclusively male heterosexual readership for *Playboy* and characterized as unhealthy any female in-terest in porn. Christie wondered what this assertion implied about women who did read *Playboy*. Finally, she made a case for freedom of expression and consumer choice in a free market, comparing *Playboy* to Hollywood films that glorified sexual violence against women. "I agree . . . that the presentation of violence meant to be sexually stim-ulating is offensive and deplorable," she wrote. "In fact, I refused to see [the 1980 popular film] *Dressed to Kill* because the idea of a woman being sliced up was so disturbing and offensive to me. But it never occurred to me that [director] Brian De Palma didn't have the right to make that film." She concluded that "pornographers who make use of violence in their business should be condemned, but not outlawed."[36]

Christie's review of *Take Back the Night* advanced viewpoints shared by other feminists wary of the new direction and tenor of antiporn activism.[37] She also touched on arguments that would gain further definition as other feminist activists, such as those who created the Feminist Anti-Censorship Task Force, organized to oppose antiporn feminists purporting to speak for the women's movement as a whole.[38] Like others, she pointed to the subjectivity involved in delimiting por-nography and denounced censorship as a dangerous, slippery slope. She also expressed concern about what seemed to be the conflation of sexual representations with behavior (i.e., equating images with acts) and registered skepticism about the "common sense" view cited in the book that pornographic imagery prompted violent action such as rape. Others would question further the essentializing nature of feminist antiporn discourses, which drew upon cultural feminists' assertion of distinct "female values" and harkened back to traditional character-izations of women as loving and nurturing in contrast to lustful and predatory men. Such a view cast all women as potential victims of an inherently violent male sexuality. Christie's statements about the ulti-mately idiosyncratic process of identifying porn or determining what constituted "degradation" left room for more diverse forms of sexual expression than antiporn theorists allowed, an issue that soon animated battles between antiporn feminists and self-declared sex-positive feminists.[39] Furthermore, Christie worried about feminist antipornography activists aligning themselves with the "newly powerful new right." Such an alliance would surely be mistaken, she argued, for it would no doubt lead to more than the suppression of violent imagery. The concern seemed justified when the antiporn civil rights ordinances soon proposed in numerous cities cast a wide net in defining the materials that would fall under the purview of these laws.

In Christie's view, as she subsequently explained to *New York Magazine* and the *Washington Post*, feminist antiporn activism sidetracked the women's movement.

> I'm living in a country where the president wants to make abortion a crime, and some segment of the women's movement is suggesting that the major enemy in society is *Playboy*. I think that's crazy. If we don't fight the real enemy, we're likely to lose what we've won in the last decade. If you don't want to look at the pictures, then don't buy the magazine. But don't make the leap from that to saying they're trying to do something terrible to women. Playmates of the Month are paid $10,000 for their work. I don't see how they can be exploited.[40]

In addition to emphasizing issues of choice—to pose in the magazine in exchange for financial reward, to buy *Playboy* or not—she discounted the antiporn movement for promoting a limited vision of healthy sexuality. "I don't think there is a feminist position on sexuality," she explained. "That should be an area people give the widest option for themselves personally."[41]

Playboy's Money

The Playboy Foundation further confounded matters. During the 1970s, the foundation gave money to such groups as the Illinois Women's Political Caucus and the Chicago chapter of the National Organization for Women. Such moves, one journalist noted, were all part of Christie's Hefner's "effort to give the famous rabbit-head symbol new meaning." As Christie put it, "I'd like the rabbit's head to be sort of a Good Housekeeping Seal of Approval for men and women."[42] The Playboy Foundation, she told another interviewer, served as "the conscience of the company."[43] Founded in 1965, the Playboy Foundation functioned, according to *Foundation News,* as "a charitable extension of the 'Playboy Philosophy,' that smorgasbord of libertarian morsels" penned by Hugh Hefner in the mid-1960s. As an extension of Hefner's concern for the individual's "rights as a member of a free society," the foundation supported civil liberties and First Amendment issues. The ACLU and those fighting for abortion rights were prime beneficiaries, as discussed by Leigh Ann Wheeler in her chapter in this collection. Signaling a commitment to women's issues, the foundation appointed prominent women's rights activists to direct its work. It also sought out organizations working on women's rights issues willing to accept its support, an often difficult task.[44]

To accept or decline Playboy support embroiled organizations in an ideologically loaded affair. The question of whether Playboy's provision of funding or other assistance for liberal causes, feminist or otherwise, granted legitimacy to the magazine predated anti-porn feminism, but the stakes became higher, and the debates more intense, during the sex wars of the late 1970s and 1980s.[45] For those who saw links between pornography and violence against women in a culture in which both flourished, Playboy's support for the women's movement caused consternation. "Can Playboy Buy Women's Lib?" asked the feminist newspaper *Majority Report.* This author concluded that just because *Playboy's* representations were damaging to women did not mean its money should not be put to good use. Such a view, adopted by many organizations, justified accepting money from such troubling sources as Playboy as a means of "liberating their funds as reparations." For many, it was a matter of making progress on important goals. Ramona Ripston, executive director of the Southern California ACLU, explained her position: "I cannot accept the notion that *Playboy* is good for women." Yet she claimed, "The good I'm going to do with the money overcomes any feeling that *Playboy* exploits women."[46]

Others rejected this approach, believing Playboy's support for women's issues amounted to nothing more than a diversionary tactic. Some feminists believed the "reparations model" was inappropriate, for it implied an "admission of guilt" and "the expectation that the exploitation will stop," neither of which applied in Playboy's case. Others claimed the Playboy Foundation "targeted feminist groups for funds" in an effort "to defuse the growing antipornography move-ment." "Playboy uses its contributions to our work," asserted law pro-fessor and antipornography activist Catharine MacKinnon, "to transform its position as active oppressors of women into the appearance of being standard bearers of women's equality." Negative comparisons abounded as feminists discussed Playboy's money. One critic referred to Playboy Foundation support as a distribution of "blood money." Another argued that receiving funds from the foundation meant taking dirty money. "We are laundering it just as surely as the Nixon administration laundered their money," she opined. "We help the boys look good while all the time we are the losers." Playboy's support of women's rights in the view of a different activist was "like Mobil Oil giving money to the Sierra Club."[47]

The hardening orthodoxy of antiporn feminism, which brooked no distinction between representations of sexuality and representations of violence and viewed *Playboy* as actively undermining feminism, made the acceptance of funds on the part of organizations such as the Ms. Foundation increasingly untenable. In April 1982, the Ms. Foundation returned to the Playboy Foundation all of the money it had accepted over the previous four years for its reproductive rights efforts, a sum totaling $11,000. At issue, the Ms. Foundation pointed out, was not the personal commitment to women's rights on the part of men and women comprising the Playboy Foundation, but instead the claim that *Playboy* was good for women. *Ms. Magazine* publicized the return of the funds, noting also that Christie's "corporate ascendance" was a "source of ambivalence for many feminists who hate the magazine but like and respect her." The Playboy Foundation asked the Ms. Foundation to reconsider its position, its request accompanied by a letter of support bearing the signatures of numerous foundation leaders from around the country. The letter, which was critical of the Ms. Foundation for rejecting Playboy's money when financial support for women's causes was so desperately needed, also noted that the "the great majority of the profits that create and sustain private philanthropy have been derived from the exploitation of one group or another." The Ms. Foundation stood firm; the Playboy Foundation "recycled" the returned funds, making grants to other organizations that supported women's issues.[48]

The relationship between Christie Hefner, Playboy, and NOW was similarly complex. As evidenced by its "Meat Market" awards and the cease and desist letter sent to *Playboy* contributors, some within NOW clearly viewed *Playboy* as harmful to women. Yet the organization also counted Hugh Hefner, Christie Hefner, and the Playboy Foundation among its supporters in the battle to ratify the Equal

Rights Amendment (ERA). Recognizing a commitment to shared goals, the board of NOW's Legal Defense and Education Fund (LDEF) accepted money from the Playboy Foundation, including funds originally bestowed upon activist Sonia Johnson, who had been excommunicated from the Mormon Church for her part in campaigning for the ERA. Johnson, a recipient of a 1980 Hugh M. Hefner First Amendment Award, attended the ceremony at the Playboy Mansion but announced that as a feminist she declined to accept the tribute. In a personal note to Johnson, NOW LDEF's Muriel Fox praised her for receipt of the honor and acknowledged, "I can understand your feelings about the money." Fox expressed gratitude to Christie Hefner and the Playboy Foundation for the $3,000 gift, the amount Johnson had refused, promising that the funds would go to help the ERA campaign.[49]

The following year, members of NOW's San Diego chapter protested the proposed opening of a Playboy Club in that city. Christie Hefner contacted NOW's leadership, expressing frustration that city officials were holding up necessary permits, an action she believed had been prompted by the negative publicity inspired by the protests. "I don't know quite what to say or do," she wrote. "As you well know, the Playboy ethic—as defined by the editorial positions of the magazine and the 15 year record of the Foundation's support—has been extraordinarily supportive of women's issues." She went on to cite the higher-than-average wages earned by Playboy Bunnies compared to other restaurant and nightclub employees, along with PEI's tuition reimbursement program. Christie acknowledged that NOW's local chapters enjoyed much autonomy. "But, somehow it doesn't make sense to me," she continued, for Playboy and NOW's Los Angeles chapter to have previously cosponsored an ERA fundraiser at the Playboy Mansion, and to get a request to make a personal appearance at a reproductive rights' fundraiser for a Wisconsin NOW chapter, only to receive that same week the "the news that NOW in San Diego is blaming Playboy for violence and degradation against women."[50] The conflict underscored the extent to which the chapter-based membership organization offered no uniform stance on Playboy's relationship to the women's movement. In her response, Fox expressed gratitude for the long-standing support of the Playboy Foundation, which had provided over $15,000 as well as in-kind support over the past four years, before noting that the "relationship between feminists and Playboy is a complicated one, as you and I both understand well." NOW's federated structure, however, meant that action undertaken by a local chapter, so long as not directly contrary to NOW's national policies, fell outside the purview of the national leadership.[51]

Anti-Playboy sentiments on the part of some members did not keep Christie Hefner from seeking assistance again from NOW leadership, asking that they put in a good word about PEI's corporate citizenship in support of the company's bid to renew the license for its Atlantic City casino. Within NOW, though, as leaders struggled to formulate a definition and position on pornography amid the firestorm of controversy fueled by antipornography activism, ties to Playboy and receiving Playboy money became increasingly troubling issues. NOW LDEF had deemed it "acceptable" to take Playboy's money in keeping with its policy to receive corporate funding so long as it was "not obligated to endorse that corporation or its products as a condition of the grant." By 1984, Christie Hefner's membership on the recently activated corporate advisory board of the LDEF and the group's acceptance of Playboy support produced serious misgivings that Hefner sought "political mileage" from these connections, using them to bolster her own and Playboy's feminist credentials. NOW's national board voted to ask her to resign this role and decided to stop accepting Playboy funding.[52]

Antiporn Ordinances and the Meese Commission

As feminist antipornography activists aligned with conservatives in support of proposed laws that allowed individuals to sue porn providers for civil rights violations, Playboy joined forces with such groups as the American Booksellers Association and the Feminist Anti-Censorship Task Force. Together, they challenged the passage in 1984 of an Indianapolis antiporn ordinance on the grounds that it violated First Amendment protections. Christie again acknowledged the "legitimate concern" about "violence in society," and the "special concern" when "violence and sex are linked," but viewed with suspicion conservatives' interest in curtailing pornography, arguing that the Right was "primarily interested in limiting sexual expression, period." Furthermore, she opined, "the trouble with things like the [Indianapolis] ordinance is that they are unconstitutional, and they will always be overturned, and then that becomes the focus," detracting from any meaningful conversations about violence. "Instead of doing a study about that, we wind up with the [Attorney General's] Commission on Pornography, which is not useful at all."[53] Christie's views were born out in February 1986, when the U.S. Supreme Court upheld a lower court's ruling that the Indianapolis ordinance was unconstitutional and violated free speech rights.[54] This major defeat for antiporn feminists, coupled with the vocal opposition of "sex-positive" feminists mobilized against antiporn theory and tactics, signaled the impending demise of an organized feminist antipornography movement.

In July 1986, the Attorney General's Commission on Pornography, known as the Meese Commission, released its findings in a two-volume report that further divided some feminists.[55] The formation of the commission was an example of action on morality issues promised to conservatives in return for their support of Ronald Reagan's successful presidential campaign. Comprised largely of conservatives, the eleven-member body had investigated the pornography industry and its potential links to criminal behavior. Seeking testimony from those victimized by porn, the commission in its final report cast pornography as a dire threat to family values.

The report generated ample criticism, some of it even coming from within the commission's own ranks. In a joint statement, Judith Becker, Ellen Levine, and Deanne Tilton-Durfee, three of the four women who served on the commission, registered their objection to those who profited from "the exploitation of vulnerable people," while at the same time affirming the rights of "all citizens to participate in legal activities if their participation is truly voluntary." These commissioners resisted the characterization of women solely as victims, writing, "We reject any judgmental and condescending efforts to speak on women's behalf as though they were helpless, mindless children."[56] In a separate statement penned by Becker and Levine, the commissions' biases, methodologies, and recommendations also came under fire. Laden with their own personal judgments, the commissioners scarcely agreed on definitions of pornography. With a mandate to assess pornography's "role in causing anti-social behavior," the group also failed to find a common answer to the question of what constituted such behavior. To Becker and Levine, only acts "involving coercion or lack of consent" linked to pornography fell within the purview of the commission, but some of its members included such "private sexual practices" as masturbation or premarital sex. The commissions' public hearings, intended to gather evidence of pornography's harmful effects, likely inhibited the participation of individuals who might have offered positive testimony about their consumption of pornography, they noted. The insufficient funds and time allotted to the commission also hindered its ability to carry out a thorough investigation. Under such circumstances, it was difficult to ascertain the porn market in terms of supply and demand; certainly the materials viewed by the commission "were skewed to the very violent and extremely degrading," resulting in a sample from which generalizations about the larger industry could not accurately be made. The commission's haphazard interpretation of existing social science data and lack of careful consideration of its public policy recommendations also caused serious misgivings. Becker and Levine emphasized their personal concerns about material that eroticized violence and urged the prioritization of "child pornography prosecutions," but given the disturbing nature of the commission's approach to its task, they urged against interpreting the report as warranting a "green light for prosecuting all pornographers."[57]

The issues Becker and Levine raised in their dissenting opinion resonated in Christie's considered response to the Meese Commission, which appeared in *The Humanist* magazine. Christie called the report's broad use of the term "pornography" a "critical flaw," faulting the commission for labeling "everything that has anything to do with sexuality" as "inherently bad." Like Becker and Levine, she questioned the report's selective use of available evidence as well as the conservative definition of "harm" employed by some commissioners when it came to assessing the impact of pornography. "Just think about this," she wrote. "An official government body is telling us that we need to censor material because it might provoke sex between unmarried people. This doesn't give me a lot of confidence in the balance between a safer society and a free society." The report, in her estimation, was "fundamentally at odds with the very mandate given to the Reagan administration—the mandate to get the government out of people's lives." Christie further cautioned that the logic advanced by the report was a throwback, unraveling the gains made by radical feminists who urged that rape be considered a crime about violence, not sexual desire. Intent on curtailing the availability of sexual material, the commission pushed to link pornography to violent action. But such a view would make it possible for perpetrators to claim, "Sexy pictures made me do it," Christie noted, "just like one used to be able to say 'The way she walked made me do it.' " Lest she be misconstrued as "some sort of libertine who is not offended by anything," Christie explained that she opposed the Meese report because she resented "people being

manipulated by others who disapprove of sexually explicit material."
She registered concern "about the quality of life in our society," which
in her view stemmed in part "from tolerating a variety of lifestyles
and mindsets." Furthermore, the "public policy danger and tragedy"
of the report, Christie wrote, is that by presenting "censorship as an
answer," it "misdirects sincere people's attention away from thinking about the real causes of violence and abuse" and recommends
that "scarce resources" be allocated "in the wrong direction." Finally,
despite the negative publicity with which the commission's findings
were received in mainstream media, she noted, "the censorious effects
of the commission's report have only begun."[58]

The final report identified *Playboy* as a "men's magazine," distinguishing it from the producers of more graphic publications and
other visual media. Before the report was even released, however, the
commission's executive director, Alan Sears, notified retailers (including such influential companies as Southland Corporation, owner of
7-Eleven stores) that they would be listed as distributors of pornography in the final report. They responded by pulling *Playboy*, *Penthouse*,
and other magazines from their shelves. To Hugh Hefner, the episode
was reminiscent of the 1950s; he called it "the first successful use of a
national blacklist since the McCarthy era." PEI filed suit, resulting in
a court order for the attorney general's office to withdraw its threat.
But the damage had been done. In Christie Hefner's view, for citizens
who objected to such publications as *Playboy*, the commission's report
seemed to sanction "harassing stores into not selling them anymore."[59]
Indeed, even as feminist antiporn efforts waned, *Playboy* never recovered all of the retail outlets lost in the wake of Sears's ominous letter
and the pickets and boycotts organized by the National Federation of
Decency and Moral Majority.

In the years that followed, as PEI sought profits by continuing its
expansion into cable television, the company faced a familiar conundrum: opposition from critics who objected to *Playboy* regardless of
its difference from hard core competitors, and the continued effects
of that competition on its bottom line. "Many cable operators don't
aggressively promote [the Playboy Channel], fearing activist community groups that find its fare objectionable," *Business Week* explained.
"Ironically, Playboy has been plagued by unusually high numbers
of new subscribers who quickly drop the service as soon as they
realize that explicit sex is deleted from the X-rated movies it broad-
casts."[60] Despite the best efforts of antipornography activists, con-

sumer demand for porn and its production continued unabated in the decades that followed.

CHRISTIE HEFNER SHEPHERDED PLAYBOY THROUGH the tumultuous "sex wars" of the 1980s and moved it into cable television and, later, onto the internet. Under her leadership, Playboy in the 2000s also experienced a period of revitalization, marked by the widespread popularity of the reality television show *The Girls Next Door* and a resurgent interest in the Playboy brand. In 2001, Christie also oversaw PEI's purchase of three cable networks that moved it into the realm of "hardcore" programming.[61] This business decision received modest media attention amid a porn-saturated culture but sparked little recrimination in the absence of a powerful feminist antipornography movement. Christie stepped down as Playboy CEO in 2009, at the age of fifty-six, as the company faced serious economic challenges and slumping sales figures. The proliferation of free sexually explicit content on the Web and the seemingly endless alternatives available to viewers and advertisers presented a formidable challenge for *Playboy*'s survival.

Both Christie Hefner and *Playboy* figured prominently in the debates about feminism, sexuality, and pornography that began taking shape during the 1970s and came to a head in the 1980s. *Playboy*'s existence forced considerations about choice, freedom of expression, and the power of the marketplace. Theorizing pornography necessitated reflecting on *Playboy*'s precedent-setting role in normalizing the consumption of images meant to be sexually stimulating. The possibility of Playboy's support for their organizations and causes also demanded that some feminists engage practical yet thorny questions about how to discern allies from enemies while finding the support needed to sustain their movement. As a powerful Playboy executive, Christie Hefner also defied easy categorization during feminism's second wave: What did it mean to be a feminist—if she could claim that mantel? Scholars today recognize the existence of "feminisms"; these discussions about sexual expression and its connection to women's liberation or oppression point to a multiplicity of viewpoints in terms of definitions, goals, and strategies that underscore the difficulty in unifying and sustaining a movement that endeavored to speak for "women." To some, Christie Hefner, like her father, served as a spokesperson for lifestyle choice, offering a watered-down version of feminism suitable for a consumer society. In a new era, as young women endorsed *Playboy*, Christie Hefner would draw criticism once again as a female profiting from women's embrace of their own commoditized sexuality.[62] Such a critique suggests the extent to which questions about female empowerment, self-definition, and sexual pleasure, all raised during earlier debates about *Playboy* and pornography, continue to fuel contemporary discourses about third-wave feminism.

NOTES

1. "Trying to Be One of the Boys," *Time*, October 4, 1976, 35; David Gelman, "The Great Playboy Furor," *Newsweek*, October 4, 1976, 70; "Bowdlerizing Jimmy," *Time*, October 4, 1976, 71.
2. "Playboy Puts a Glint in the Admen's Eyes," *Business Week*, June 28, 1969, 142, 144.
3. Hugh Hefner to Auguste Comte Spectorsky, January 9, 1967, and Hefner to Spectorsky, Jack Kessie, Vince Tajiri, and Art Paul, December 9, 1968, both quoted in Elizabeth Fraterrigo, *Playboy and the Making of the Good Life in Modern America* (Oxford: Oxford University Press, 2009), 169.
4. The pictorials appeared in October 1968 and August 1969, respectively. For the reaction to them, see Ken Jones, "Screw Playboy!" *Soul*, August 11, 1969, 6.
5. *Penthouse* advertisement in *Chicago Tribune*, September 19, 1969; Guccione quoted in Russell Miller, *Bunny: The Real Story of Playboy* (New York: Holt, Rinehart and Winston, 1984), 179; Hugh Hefner to Vince Tajiri and Art Paul, June 8, 1970, quoted in Fraterrigo, *Playboy and the Making of the Good Life*, 169. On the success of *Penthouse*, see "Bring on the Girls," *Forbes*, August 7, 1978, 75. On circulation battles, see Philip H. Dougherty, "Advertising: Those Illustrated Magazines," *New York Times*, January 5, 1972; Philip H. Dougherty, "Advertising: Risque Magazines," *New York Times*, March 12, 1973; "40-Million Lawsuit Filed by Penthouse against Playboy," *New York Times*, May 25, 1974; Audit Bureau of Circulations, *Magazine Trend Report* (Schaumburg, IL) for 1973 and 1974.
6. For Hefner's surprise over the women's movement, see Gloria Steinem, "What *Playboy* Doesn't Know about Women Could Fill a Book," *McCall's*, October 1970, 76. For further discussion of *Playboy* and the women's movement, see Fraterrigo, *Playboy and the Making of the Good Life*.
7. Fraterrigo, *Playboy and the Making of the Good Life*, 177.
8. Ibid, 178.
9. Christie Hefner's formal employment with Playboy began with a summer job during college as an "assistant bunny mother" for the Boston Playboy Club, which involved chaperoning young women on promotional appearances outside of the club.
10. "Running the Hutch," *Newsweek*, May 10, 1982, 69; "Family Affair," *Time*, May 10, 1982, 98.
11. Roger Ebert, "This Is Hugh Hefner's Daughter," *Esquire*, December 1973, 170–71.
12. Marian Christy, "Christie Hefner, Protecting Playboy and Hugh, Too," *Boston Globe*, January 28, 1978.

13. Sue Roll, "Ms. Hefner: An Empire of Her Own," *Louisville Courier-Journal*, November 30, 1975, Playboy Vertical File, The Kinsey Institute Library, Kinsey Institute for Research in Sex, Gender, and Reproduction Inc., Bloomington, Indiana (hereafter KIL).

14. Christy, "Christie Hefner, Protecting Playboy"; Jim Shahin, "Chronicle Interview: Christie Hefner," *Austin (TX) Chronicle*, September 20, 1985, Schlesinger Library Vertical File for Women's Studies Microform Collection, fiche 310.

15. Christy, "Christie Hefner, Protecting Playboy"; Roll, "Ms. Hefner"; Pat Colander, "Christie Hefner: More Than Hef's Daughter," *Chicago Tribune*, November 30, 1975.

16. Lally Weymouth, "The Princess of Playboy," *New York Magazine*, June 21, 1982, 32–41.

17. Shahin, "Chronicle Interview."

18. Christy, "Christie Hefner, Protecting Playboy."

19. Weymouth, "Princess of Playboy," 41.

20. Ebert, "Hugh Hefner's Daughter," 170–71.

21. "Hefner Daughter Out to End Playboy Image," *Los Angeles Times*, November 30, 1973; Roll, "Ms. Hefner."

22. Cheryl Lavin, "The Greening of an Heiress," *Chicago Tribune Magazine*, March 5, 1978; Bonnie Britton, "Hef's Daughter Speaks up for Playboy," *Indianapolis Star*, January 20, 1978, KIL.

23. Pat Stahl, "Christie Hefner, Soft-Core Feminist," *Majority Report*, October 14, 1978; Weymouth, "Princess of Playboy," 32–41.

24. Weymouth, "Princess of Playboy," 39.

25. Stahl, "Soft-Core Feminist." On Playboy's negative publicity in the mid-1970s, see "Clouds Over Bunnyland," *Time*, January 27, 1974, 34.

26. Playboy press release, August 26, 1974, box 29, folder 52, Records of the National Organization for Women (MC 496), Schlesinger Library, Radcliffe Institute, Harvard University, Cambridge, MA; "Playboy Forum: Misdirected Anger," *Playboy*, January 1975, 60.

27. Quoted in Fraterrigo, *Playboy and the Making of the Good Life*, 302.

28. For the origins of the feminist antipornography movement and its impact on "second wave" feminism, see Carolyn Bronstein, *Battling Pornography: The American Feminist Anti-Pornography Movement, 1976–1986* (New York: Cambridge University Press, 2011); and Whitney Strub, *Perversion for Profit: The Politics of Pornography and the Rise of the New Right* (New York: Columbia University Press, 2011), 213–55.

29. Robert Shea, "Women at War," *Playboy*, February 1980, 87, 184.

30. "The New Puritans," *Playboy*, November 1980, 20.

31. Nat Lehrman quoted in Shea, "Women at War," 92; "Playboy in the News," *Playboy*, March 1981, 26. See also John Gordon, "Women Against Sex," *Playboy*, October 1980, 60–63. Lehrman's statements were in line with those of art director Art Paul, who nearly two decades earlier claimed, "I've never put anything pornographic in the book. I know what pornography is and we have never printed it." Paul quoted in Hal Higdon, "Playboying Around the Clock with Hugh Hefner," *Climax*, February 1962, 13.

32. Laura Lederer, " 'Playboy Isn't Playing': An Interview with Judith Bat-Ada," in *Take Back the Night: Women on Pornography*, ed. Laura Lederer (New York: William Morrow, 1980), 127.

33. Tracey A. Gardner, "Racism in Pornography and the Women's Movement," in Lederer, *Take Back the Night*, 105–14. For characteristics of Playmate models, see

Anthony F. Bogaert, Deborah A. Turkovich, and Carolyn L. Hafer, "A Content Analysis of Playboy Centerfolds from 1953 through 1990: Changes in Explicitness, Objectification, and Model's Age," *Journal of Sex Research* 30, no. 2 (May 1993): 135–39.

34. Adrienne Rich, "Afterword," in Lederer, *Take Back the Night*, 316–17.

35. Megan Boler, Robin Lake, and Bridget Wynne, "We Sisters Join Together . . . ," in Lederer, *Take Back the Night*, 266.

36. Christie Hefner, "By Sex Possessed," *Playboy*, August 1981, 20–22.

37. Ellen Willis, "Feminism, Moralism & Pornography," *Village Voice*, October 15, 1979.

38. For a feminist critique of feminist antipornography activism, see the essays in Feminist Anti-Censorship Task Force, *Caught Looking: Feminism, Pornography, and Censorship* (Seattle: Real Comet Press, 1988).

39. For cultural feminism and antiporn theory, see Ellen Willis, "Radical Feminism and Feminist Radicalism," in *No More Nice Girls: Countercultural Essays* (Hanover, NH: University Press of New England, 1992), 142–44. For discussion of the pro-sex countermovement to feminist antiporn activism, see Bronstein, *Battling Pornography*, 279–308.

40. Weymouth, "Princess of Playboy," 32–41.

41. Lois Romano, "Cristie [*sic*] Hefner, Daughter of the Revolution," *Washington Post*, December 4, 1983.

42. Stephen R. Conn, "Chicago: The Unspoiled Giant," *Town & Country*, September 1978, 122.

43. Stahl, "Soft-Core Feminist."

44. Hugh M. Hefner, "The Playboy Philosophy," *Playboy*, December 1962, 73; Richard J. Margolis, "Personifying the Playboy Philosophy," *Foundation News*, May/June 1983, 28–31.

45. In 1970, for instance, Hugh Hefner hosted an antiwar fundraiser at his Chicago mansion, a move feminists viewed as an attempt to raise the stature of the publisher and his exploitive enterprise. Stationed outside the mansion, feminists urged attendees to provide financial support for the cause but to boycott the party inside. That year, the Illinois ACLU declined a $40,000 Playboy Foundation grant for women's rights issues, though the funding eventually was accepted by the national ACLU board. By the early 1980s, the Illinois ACLU board counted among its members Christie Hefner and Burt Joseph, Playboy Foundation chair. The group also accepted Playboy Foundation money, "happy to have whatever help" was available, according to associate director Kathleen A. Miller. See Margolis, "Personifying Playboy Foundation," 31.

46. Frances Chapman, "Can Playboy Buy Women's Lib?" *Majority Report*, July 22–August 4, 1978, 5; Weymouth, "Princess of Playboy," 38.

47. Deborah Chalfie and Sarah McKinley, "The Politics of Funding the Women's Movement," in "Selected Abstracts from the Second National Conference of the National Women's Studies Association, May 16–20, 1980, Bloomington, Indiana," *Frontiers: A Journal of Women's Studies* 6, nos. 1–2 (Spring/Summer 1981): 71; "Feminists and Playboy Funding," *Women Against Violence in Pornography and Media*, February 1980, n.p., Women's Ephemera Files, Charles Deering McCormick Library of Special Collections, Northwestern University; Catharine A. MacKinnon, "'More Than Simply a Magazine': Playboy's Money (1982)," in *Feminism Unmodified: Discourses on Life and Law* (Cambridge: Harvard University Press, 1987), 137; Bobbe Ross, "All Feminists Pay the Price When Our Purse Strings Are Pulled by Playboy," *Big Mama Rag*, February 1982, 13; Weymouth, "Princess of Playboy," 38.

A resolution that member organizations of the National Coalition Against Sexual Assault had to refuse Playboy Foundation funding was defeated. See Nan D. Hunter, "The Pornography Debate in Context: A Chronology of Sexuality, Media, and Violence Issues in Feminism," in Feminist Anti-Censorship Task Force, *Caught Looking,* 26–29.

48. Margolis, "Personifying Playboy Philosophy," 33; quoted in Romano, "Daughter of the Revolution"; Weymouth, "Princess of Playboy," 38.

49. Muriel Fox to Christie Hefner, July 18, 1980, 91.6, Playboy Foundation, 1974–1987, NOW Legal Defense and Education Fund Papers (MC 623), Schlesinger Library, Radcliffe Institute, Harvard University, Cambridge, MA (hereafter NOW LDEF Papers).

50. Christie Hefner to Muriel Fox and Ellie Smeal, March 31, 1981, 91.6, NOW LDEF Papers.

51. Muriel Fox to Christie Hefner, April 6, 1981, NOW LDEF Papers.

52. NOW Memo, January 11, 1982, NOW LDEF Papers; Lorraine Boreyko to Ms. Bailey, October 18, 1983; Mary Bailey to Muriel Fox, June 20, 1984, NOW LDEF Papers; NOW Resolution, May 1984, 95.7, NOW LDEF Papers.

53. Shahin, "Chronicle Interview."

54. For the anticensorship position, see "Censorship Is No One's Civil Right," *New York Times,* May 27, 1984; Judy Klemesrud, "Bill on Pornography Opposed," *New York Times,* June 14, 1985; Daniel L. Feldman, "What New York Pornography Bill Does," *New York Times,* July 1, 1985; Robert Guccione, "When Foes of Pornography Are Censors," *New York Times,* July 11, 1985. A previous ordinance passed in Minneapolis was twice vetoed by the mayor, who cited the expense the city would face trying to uphold the constitutionality of the law in court. Susan Brownmiller, *In Our Time: Memoir of a Revolution* (New York: Dial Press, 1999), 316–22; Tobias, *Faces of Feminism,* 182–85. On the Indianapolis ordinance, see *American Booksellers Association, Inc., vs. Hudnut,* 771 F.2d 323 (7th Cir. 1985), and Leslie Friedman Goldstein, *Contemporary Cases in Women's Rights* (Madison: University of Wisconsin Press, 1994), 289–92.

55. For NOW's reaction to the report, see Strub, *Perversion for Profit,* 252.

56. Attorney General's Commission on Pornography, *Final Report* (Washington, DC: U.S. Department of Justice, 1986), 1:194.

57. Ibid., 1:195–210.

58. Christie Hefner, "The Meese Commission: Sex, Violence, and Censorship," *Humanist,* January 1987, 25–29, 46.

59. Hugh M. Hefner, "The Blacklist," *Playboy,* July 1986, 3; "Porn Panelist Denies Attack on Magazine," *Sun Sentinel,* July 14, 1986, available at http://articles.sun-sentinel.com.

60. Sandra Salmans, "Profits Again at a Shrunken Playboy," *New York Times,* March 25, 1984; James E. Ellix, "Beyond Bunnies: Rewriting the Playboy Philosophy," *Business Week,* November 14, 1988, 89. In the early 1980s, as Christie Hefner sought profits for the ailing company by moving it into the realm of cable television, Playboy executives mobilized familiar arguments against protestors. "Our material is certainly not pornographic," claimed a Playboy senior vice president in response to protestors who opposed a cable channel's plans to provide Playboy-created content; "Playboy doesn't believe in pornography, doesn't produce pornography and doesn't show pornography." In case that argument failed to persuade, he also reminded critics, "We've been a strong supporter of women's rights." His final plea, "For crying out loud, our company president is a woman," however, was precisely the kind of claim that made some view Christie Hefner's executive

ELIZABETH FRATERRIGO

position with suspicion. "TV Storm Big Surprise to Playboy," *Toronto Globe and Mail,* January 22, 1983.

61. Brian McCormick, "Playboy Testing the XX Factor," *Crain's Chicago Business,* October 22, 2001, 3; Michael Winerip, "No Silk Jammies for Her," *New York Times,* September 27, 2009.

62. Ariel Levy, *Female Chauvinist Pigs: Women and the Rise of Raunch Culture* (New York: Free Press, 2005); Tracy Clark-Flory, "Christie Hefner: Feminist Nightmare?" *Salon,* September 29, 2009, www.salon.com.

POLITICAL
CONTEXTS OF
PORNOGRAPHY

CHAPTER 9

"Handmaiden of the Pornographer," Champion of Free Speech

The American Civil Liberties Union and Sexual Expression in the 1970s and 1980s

LEIGH ANN WHEELER

"I HAVE BEEN DECEIVED BY a bait and switch technique," radical feminist Andrea Dworkin wrote angrily. She felt betrayed after having been recruited into the American Civil Liberties Union (ACLU) in 1975 by a solicitation letter that touted the organization's commitment to women's rights and bore the signature of Ruth Bader Ginsburg. Dworkin, like many other feminists in the 1970s, had hoped that the ACLU would become the legal arm of the women's rights movement. Instead, by 1981, she considered the ACLU "a handmaiden of the pornographers" and denounced it for treating instructions to "rape the women" as protectable speech. The ACLU's "First Amendment absolutis[m]" and blind loyalty to principle had trumped its defense of women's rights, she argued, especially the right to be free from unwanted sex.[1] Dworkin may have overstated her case, but she was right that particular civil liberties principles shaped and constrained ACLU leaders' commitments to women's rights.

The ACLU played an important role in expanding pornographers' rights in the 1970s. In this chapter, I show how and why the ACLU—an organization founded in 1920 to aid conscientious objectors, labor unions, and anarchists—began to defend commercial producers of sexually explicit material, including *Playboy* magazine. By the 1970s, this agenda pitted a number of ACLU leaders against feminists (many of them members of the ACLU) who denounced commercial pornography as sexist, degrading, and harmful to women. Thus, I also argue that the ACLU set in motion a major reinterpretation of the First Amendment, one that would lay the legal and constitutional ground-work for a cultural revolution that would make "porno chic" in the 1970s, draw the battle lines of the next decade's "sex wars," and craft a truce rooted in the First Amendment rights of consumers.

Charting the Course of Freedom of Sexual Expression

Many if not most Americans now take for granted the idea that the First Amendment protects consumers as well as producers of speech. But this idea had gained little legal or constitutional recognition by the onset of the 1960s despite two decades of ACLU efforts to extend the amendment's protections to consumers.[2] That would soon change. In 1961, ACLU attorneys initiated a wave of lawsuits to defend the rights of consumers to read *Tropic of Cancer*, a blockbuster sexcapade by Henry Miller. They did so by representing a wide range of plain-tiffs, including would-be consumers who for the first time claimed standing—or the right to sue—under the First Amendment.[3]

The timing was right; proclamations of consumer rights to media began to show up everywhere. The man who published *Tropic of Cancer*, Barnet Rosset, recruited prominent literary figures to sign a "Statement in Support of Freedom to Read," aiming also to arouse prospective readers to defend their rights. It worked. As one top offi-cial at Bell & Howell wrote, "I haven't read [*Tropic of Cancer*] but I'll be darned if I want a policeman telling me I can't."[4] In the meantime, editorials such as "Who Is to Censor What We See, Hear, Read?" and "Your Right to Read, to Know" began to appear regularly in the press. Pamphlets on "The Right to Read" and "The Students' Right to Read" were published in 1962 by the National Council of Teachers of English in cooperation with the ACLU. Meanwhile, the American Book Publishers Council exchanged the name of its regu-lar newsletter, "Censorship Bulletin," for "Freedom-to-Read Bulletin"; a booklet titled "Freedom to Read" joined the federal government's Public Affairs Pamphlet series; and the emerging homosexual press announced its efforts to "guarantee your FREEDOM TO READ."[5]

Declarations of a right to read received judicial recognition in the first ACLU-initiated lawsuit to defend the rights of prospective con-sumers of *Tropic of Cancer*. In *Haiman v. Morris*, Samuel B. Epstein, chief judge of the Superior Court of Cook County, Illinois, first granted prospective consumers standing to sue on behalf of the "constitutional right to read."[6] His momentous decision—all but forgotten now but declared a landmark case in its day—declared the "freedom to read" a "corollary to the freedom of speech and press." One without the other would be "useless," Epstein asserted. Thus, "the inherent constitutional rights and privileges of the reading public" require the "free distribution and sale" of *Tropic of Cancer*.[7]

The ACLU's consumer approach to freedom of speech allowed it to circumvent the reluctance of commercial producers and distributors to sue by inspiring members of the public, as consumers, to take censorship personally. It also brought public pressure to bear on the judiciary in new ways. After the success of *Haiman*, ACLU attorneys and others brought successful consumer-initiated suits against public officials in South Bend, Indiana; Los Angeles, California; and Montgomery County, Maryland. Moreover, even when ACLU attorneys represented booksellers, distributors, or publishers, they couched their role as one of "defending the right of a free people to choose their own reading matter." The Supreme Court ended the three-year *Tropic* case craze in 1964 when it reversed a Florida court's holding that the book was obscene. The words would come later in Justice William J. Brennan's memorable observation that "it would be a barren marketplace of ideas that had only sellers and no buyers." Meanwhile, John F. Kennedy fortified the relationship between consumerism and civil liberties when he issued what amounted to a Consumer Bill of Rights, complete with presidential support for the right "to be informed" and "to choose."[8]

By the middle of the 1960s, the ACLU's concept of consumer rights had moved to the center of the Supreme Court's First Amendment jurisprudence and received a presidential seal of approval. As a result, the much-touted marketplace of ideas would take on a character that would have been unrecognizable to the First Amendment's framers two centuries earlier. Thanks in part to the efforts of civil libertarians who rode the wave of postwar cultural and political trends in favor of consumerism, the public arena was increasingly conceived of less as a forum for the exchange of ideas and information among citizens of a polity than as a marketplace of buyers and sellers, consumers and producers. No longer a community with aggregate needs, the marketplace hosted individuals with singular claims to speak, to publish, and to access all that was spoken and published.

Consumerism was moving to the center of and animating many

movements, including the civil rights movement. Black citizens directed their consumer power toward political gain at the turn of the twentieth century when Madam C. J. Walker used black women's desire to feel beautiful not only to sell hair and skin care products but also to create jobs for black women and uplift the race. Decades later, in the 1950s, black citizens used consumer power to challenge racial segregation by boycotting public services such as bus companies and sitting in at private vendors, including local lunch counters, that discriminated against black patrons.[9] These civil rights actions show the importance of consumerism in the 1960s while highlighting the extent to which First Amendment–based consumer rights that developed at the same time revolved around products created for and purchased primarily by whites. Thus, when *Playboy* magazine featured its first African American "playmate" in 1965, one wonders whether it was responding primarily to the consumer power of black citizens or to the sexual proclivities of white consumers.[10]

In any case, even as consumer rights gained protection under the First Amendment, they also presented the ACLU with new ideas for membership recruitment. Leaders of the ACLU Illinois affiliate, for example, targeted buyers of *Playboy*, a Chicago-based, nationally circulated magazine confronted with frequent censorship threats mainly because of its nude female centerfolds. "*Playboy* readers," the local affiliate's development director explained, "are 'naturals' for the ACLU." Playboy agreed and allowed the ACLU affiliate to recruit new members using names and addresses from its subscriber list. "Sophisticated people like yourself," one recruitment letter began, "are not afraid to read whatever magazine or book you want to," including one that features "a picture of a divine figure with smasheroo legs." Another acknowledged that "most men who like to gaze at pictures of beautiful women in a magazine . . . couldn't care less about such stuffy business as civil liberties. After all, what has *that* got to do with a divine figure and elegant legs?" Turning to the First Amendment rights of consumers, the letter assured readers that "there are many people—you know the kind—who would do away with pictures of beautiful women" and censor books, movies, and magazines "though you have a right to read these—a right guaranteed by the Bill of Rights of the Constitution of the United States." In a final pitch for membership, the letter pointed out that "a reader who enjoys reading what you enjoy reading about . . . should care enough to join the ACLU," the only organization that defends "the rights of readers, writers, and publishers."[11] Through this recruitment strategy, the ACLU's Illinois affiliate strengthened a growing tendency among civil libertarians to identify freedom and the First Amendment with consumption, adding a new dimension to that equation by treating consumers of *Playboy* as especially laudable individuals whose rights to read represented the vanguard of First Amendment jurisprudence. But the ACLU's deepening affiliation with Playboy and commitment to consumer rights would also have important ramifications for its relationship with the burgeoning women's rights movement.

In the 1970s, the ACLU demonstrated a growing interest in women's rights. ACLU director Jack Pemberton began a sincere effort to address the organization's own history of sex discrimination by acknowledging that his office had underpaid female staff members and overlooked women for high-level positions. "While we are going about the country as busy-bodies attacking other people's faults," he wrote, "we might well look to the consistency of our own practices." Indeed, women made up only seven percent of national board members and were no better represented on the ACLU's affiliate boards. Women were excluded from planning for the biennial meetings, and very few women had ever occupied policymaking or executive positions on the national staff.[12] Pemberton recognized and aimed to rectify these problems, and his successor, Aryeh Neier, worked to engage the ACLU more fully with the flourishing women's rights movement.

Protest movements represented great opportunities for the ACLU because, as Neier explained to a foundation representative, "civil liberties fare best in our society when organized minorities insist on the exercise of their rights." The ACLU could maximize its influence, Neier believed, by supporting grassroots activists who mobilized on their own behalf. He referred to individuals who joined social movements to advance their own interests as consumers, a term that reflected a mindset now central to the ACLU's civil liberties agenda. Identifying the women's rights movement as "by far the strongest and healthiest of today's 'consumer' movements for rights," Neier considered it among the ACLU's strongest potential allies in defending civil liberties. Moreover, he hoped to use the "muscle" of the women's rights movement to advance the ACLU's broader civil liberties agenda. Courts respond to grassroots movements, Neier insisted, and even a conservative Supreme Court will expand individual rights when it feels pressure from "the organized power of a consumer movement."[13]

Accordingly, the ACLU actively recruited prominent women's rights activists into leadership positions. Among them were Wilma Scott Heide, chair of the board of directors for NOW; Suzanne Post, founder of the Kentucky Women's Political Caucus; Brenda Feigen Fasteau, cofounder of *Ms.* magazine and the National Women's Political Caucus; Faith Seidenberg, NOW officer; Margie Pitts Hames, vice president of the Georgia Women's Political Caucus; and Ruth Bader Ginsburg, a Rutgers law professor and future Supreme Court justice. Feminist headliners like Ginsburg drafted and signed ACLU solicitation letters focused on the organization's commitment to women's rights, a tactic that helped to persuade rank-and-file women's rights activists such as Andrea Dworkin to become ACLU members as well.[14]

Under Neier's leadership and the influence of a growing number of feminist leaders and members, the ACLU board voted to make women's rights a priority in 1972. That year it launched its Women's Rights Project (WRP) using seed money donated by the Ford and Playboy Foundations. The Ford Foundation added the ACLU's WRP to a list of organizations it sponsored to challenge sex discrimination, seeing this investment as an extension of its longtime support for civil rights. Playboy officers had a different goal; they hoped that supporting the WRP would help to rehabilitate the enterprise's reputation with feminists and strengthen connections with the ACLU; both had suffered since the Chicago-based ACLU affiliate held a controversial fundraiser at Hugh Hefner's mansion in 1969.[15]

The ACLU, Women's Rights, and *Playboy*

A number of celebrities and local ACLU staff attended the 1969 event hosted by Playboy, but so did several disgruntled affiliate members who also belonged to the newly formed Chicago Women's Liberation Union. Angry that the ACLU would "legitimize Hefner by holding a benefit" at his home—one that included nude swimming at 4 a.m.—the women considered simply boycotting the event but opted instead for guerilla theater. "We could protest both *Playboy*'s portrayal of women as mindless sex objects for huge profits," they explained, "and the ACLU's eager attachment to Hefner, also for money." Equipped with pinups of men in bunny suits, cards showing men as naked "Playmates of the Month," and revealing posters of men with messages like "He's got a nice ass, but he's kind of dumb," the women posted their propaganda around Hefner's mansion before armed guards forced them to leave.[16]

These ACLU women were neither the first nor the last to challenge *Playboy* on feminist grounds. In 1963, Gloria Steinem criticized the enterprise in an exposé written from a "bunny's" perspective. Two years later journalist Diana Lurie published a feminist critique of the magazine in *Life*, and feminists who demonstrated against the 1968 Miss America Pageant in Atlantic City dumped copies of *Playboy* into their "freedom trashcan," while students at Grinnell College stripped in a public protest against Playboy's recruiting on campus. Feminist protests against *Playboy*'s portrayal and treatment of women only escalated in the 1970s.[17]

Hefner fought back, and the ACLU figured prominently in his carrot-and-stick strategy. He hired Morton Hunt to produce a "devastating piece that takes the [feminist] militants apart." "These chicks are our natural enemy," Hefner told Hunt. "The society they want is an asexual one." But even as Hefner attacked "militant" feminists in his magazine, he aimed to bolster his reputation among less radical feminists by advocating and funding more mainstream efforts that advanced the causes of women's rights, especially women's access to sexual expression. The ACLU seemed an especially good bet for the Playboy Foundation. Chicago's ACLU director derided the actions of women who protested the fundraising event as "Bull—." Moreover, the ACLU and its affiliates had long collaborated with Playboy against censorship, and many of their leaders subscribed to, read, and wrote laudatory letters to the magazine. In addition, an Illinois ACLU attorney, Burton Joseph, who assisted in the ACLU's *Tropic of Cancer* cases a few years earlier had just become executive director and special counsel to Playboy and the new Playboy Foundation.[18]

When Aryeh Neier applied to Playboy for funds in 1971, he showcased the ACLU's impressive record in cases likely to appeal to Hefner—sexual civil liberties cases such as abortion, voluntary sterilization, birth control, and "bralessness." Within a month, Neier had the $40,000 he needed to start the Women's Rights Project. Playboy also provided printing services for ACLU pamphlets and manuals on abortion rights and the October 1971 issue of *Playboy* ran a flattering seven-page article praising the ACLU as "the nation's chief defender of personal liberty" and urging readers to join or donate to it. One month later, Hugh Hefner hosted a black-tie benefit at his new west coast Playboy mansion and, with Ralph Nader, Arthur M. Schlesinger Jr., and Jules Feiffer in attendance, raised a reported $100,000 for the ACLU of Southern California.[19]

Playboy deflected some feminist criticism by contributing to the ACLU and women's rights causes, but it could not stop the attacks altogether, as historian Elizabeth Fraterrigo discusses in a chapter that appears in this collection. Feminists disrupted Hefner's television appearances, picketed his mansions and clubs, obstructed his efforts to recruit new "bunnies," and threatened his life. Meanwhile, they debated among themselves whether to accept Playboy money, with some eager to liberate Hefner's funds as "reparations" and others determined to reject it as blood money. Similar disputes emerged over whether feminists should submit to interviews by Playboy staff, allow their writing to be published in the magazine, or accept honors from it. For many feminists, Playboy's contributions to women's rights causes could not make up for the magazine's treatment of women as sexual playthings—literally, things to be screwed, as depicted on a 1972 cover showing a naked woman in the shape of a wine bottle with a corkscrew at the ready. ACLU board member Catherine Roraback protested the ACLU's decision to accept money from Playboy, citing "the exploitative nature of the magazine in its portrayal of women." Also, as other critics noted, Playboy invested in women's rights to birth control, sterilization, and abortion not to empower women but to serve "the convenience of the playboy, who does not wish to assume responsibilities."[20]

Brenda Feigen Fasteau and Ruth Bader Ginsburg, founding codirectors of the ACLU's Women's Rights Project, were, however, more than happy to take Playboy's money. They praised *Playboy* for its reports on reproductive and sexual issues as well as its financial support for efforts to liberalize laws regarding sexuality even though they did not necessarily approve of the magazine itself. Fasteau, a lifelong opponent of pornography, agreed that the magazine "denigrated women," and she criticized the ACLU for holding fundraisers at Playboy clubs and mansions, because these events publicized and legitimized the magazine. But to Fasteau (and, presumably, Ginsburg as well), applying for and accepting money from Playboy to litigate for women's rights seemed a different matter altogether. "I wasn't troubled by it," Fasteau remembered, as long as the ACLU could benefit from Playboy's money without directly promoting the Playboy enterprise.[21]

ACLU feminists debated whether or not to accept Playboy's money in the early 1970s, an era of free-flowing sexual entertainment that had reached unprecedented dimensions. Erotic books and magazines circulated widely, often through the garishly labeled "adult" bookstores that emerged in urban neighborhoods and along the nation's highways. Moreover, the rating system adopted by the Motion Picture Association of America in 1968 led to a new genre of X-rated movies and public exhibitions of what became known as "hardcore." In retrospect, it was pornography's "golden age," the beginning of the era that would make way for *Deep Throat* (1972) and *The Devil in Miss Jones* (1973), shamelessly explicit feature films that found their way into middle-class culture through respectable theaters and movie reviews, including by the *New York Times*.[22] In this context, *Playboy* seemed rather tame, and because support for accepting Playboy funds far exceeded opposition to doing so, Playboy continued to underwrite select aspects of the ACLU's women's rights agenda throughout the 1970s.

But conflicts between civil libertarians and feminists regarding sexually explicit material became sharper over the course of the decade. By the middle of the 1970s, individuals, such as Susan Brownmiller and Andrea Dworkin, and organizations, such as Women Against Violence in Pornography and Media (1978) and Women Against Pornography (1979), were holding conferences, conducting research, and developing theories about the harm pornography posed to women. In 1978, the New York University School of Law hosted "Obscenity: Degradation of Women versus Right of Free Speech," one of the first conferences to address possible conflicts between women's rights and absolutist interpretations of the First Amendment. Feminist speakers included Dworkin, who called pornographic materials "death threats to a female population in rebellion . . . against male sexual authority"—a "new terrorism" designed to degrade women and celebrate violence against them. Brenda Feigen Fasteau, former codirector of the ACLU's Women's Rights Project, also participated even as she insisted that pornography could be combated without challenging the First Amendment. Fasteau recommended either a new tort or creative use of existing "incitement to violence statutes" so that women harmed by pornography could bring legal action against its producers. Other participants considered these suggestions incompatible with the First Amendment. Lawyers who identified themselves primarily as civil libertarians argued that such measures would violate the Constitution. People "should have the right to see and read what they please," one "self-styled 'First Amendment absolutist' " insisted, employing the consumer idiom that had become central to American understandings of free speech.[23] The consumer orientation of First Amendment absolutists was not lost on Dworkin, who criticized the

First Amendment as one that "belongs to those who can buy it."[24] Thus, by the time Dworkin published the scathing letter with which this chapter opened, new tensions emerged within the ACLU as feminist concerns about increasingly ubiquitous and violent pornography confronted the First Amendment rights of consumers that the ACLU had helped to establish.

Feminists and Pornography in the 1980s and Beyond

Feminist activism against pornography dated back to the 1960s, but it took a new form in the 1980s as some activists drafted laws against pornography even as others began to celebrate pornography as a tool for women's sexual liberation. The emerging debate among feminists over the virtues and vices of pornography turned explosive at the 1982 Barnard conference "Scholar and the Feminist IX: Toward a Politics of Sexuality," discussed in the pages of *Feminist Studies* (and by historian Alex Warner in the next chapter). Catharine MacKinnon and Andrea Dworkin took the debate to a new level when, one year later, they unveiled municipal ordinances designed to create a civil rights remedy for victims of pornography, in part by allowing victims to hold producers of the material accountable for the behavior of consumers. The antipornography ordinance provoked determined opposition from Nan Hunter, an ACLU staff attorney, and others who assembled the Feminist Anti-Censorship Task Force to denounce and combat the ordinance as a form of censorship.[25]

The ACLU maintained a strong stance against censorship of all kinds, but it did not escape the "feminist porn wars," which introduced tensions into its efforts to develop a sexual harassment policy in 1983. That year Karen Sauvigne, a veteran of the ACLU's Women's Rights Project and founder of Working Women United—one of the first organizations to focus on fighting sexual harassment in the workplace—made a presentation to the organization's Equality Committee. Sauvigne considered herself "on the free speech side" of the feminist pornography debate, and she tried to distance the movement against sexual harassment from the one against pornography, a tricky maneuver given the overlapping concerns and the prominence of high-profile feminist legal scholar Catharine MacKinnon in each. Sauvigne defined "sexual harassment" broadly as "unwanted attention of a sexual nature in the context of work relationships which make the recipient uncomfortable or deny her opportunity." Unlike criminal law, which tended to focus on the intent and perceptions of the defendant, Sauvigne insisted that sexual harassment be determined by its effect on the complainant. "Men will say it was 'not intended to be harassing,' " she acknowledged, "due to a socialized difference in their orientation to sex and sexuality." But to achieve equality, the law must take into account the different ways that women and men experience the workplace. A friendly exchange indicated that Sauvigne's position was being favorably received until law professor William Forbath objected that a policy against sexual harassment would infringe on the First Amendment. Besides, people interpret sexual messages differently, he argued. A woman joined him, asking if the "the office prude" should set the standards for the workplace. Another wondered whether Sauvigne's goal was an androgynous workplace, and committee member Elaine Spitz maintained that some professional women "would be offended if their sexuality were not recognized."[26]

The issue of "calendar pinups" in the workplace soon dominated the discussion. Committee member Carolyn Simpson argued that pinups threatened women the way photos of lynchings threatened black men. Her claim provoked hostile responses. Spitz asked Simpson if she thought car mechanics should be forced to take down their pinups; Forbath charged Simpson with class bias for assuming that blue-collar men used pinups to intimidate women. Forbath and Spitz insisted that pinups alone, in the absence of "other harassing behavior," should not be considered a form of sexual harassment. But Vicki Been, a recent law school graduate and ACLU staff member, suggested that, whatever the intent of the men who posted them, pinups could create an intolerable environment, especially for a lone woman in a male-dominated workplace. Spitz countered that treating pinups at work as sexual harassment would put the ACLU on the wrong side of "the pornography issue." But others insisted that sexual imagery should be prohibited at work, where employees represented a captive audience. Widespread agreement that antipornography ordinances were unconstitutional provided common ground among them but also increased the likelihood that banning pornography from the workplace would be considered censorship rather than good sexual harassment policy.[27]

In 1984, the ACLU finally adopted a narrow policy against quid pro quo sexual harassment, sharply defined, with no mention of the hostile environment variety that would have included sexual displays in the workplace. The policy defined sexual harassment as "intentional unwanted physical contact of a sexual nature which is clearly offensive" and "intentional unwanted" requests for sexual favors accompanied by rewards or punishments. In a clear rejection of the hostile environment concept, the ACLU policy stated explicitly that it did not apply to "verbal harassment that has no other effect on its recipient than to create an unpleasant working environment."[28] This ACLU policy on sexual harassment privileged the First Amendment over concerns about equality in the workplace.

The ACLU brought its First Amendment–oriented approach into sexual harassment law through its prominent—and internally divisive—involvement in landmark court cases in the 1990s. In *Robinson v. Jacksonville Shipyards,* a district court case that involved "sexually explicit pornography" posted around the workplace, some ACLU leaders suspected that supporters of the plaintiff were using sexual harassment law to advance the feminist antipornography agenda; in the end, the ACLU supported the shipyard against the female plaintiff. But the ACLU and the shipyard were challenged by ACLU attorneys who filed a competing brief that treated pornographic displays at work as violations of sexual harassment law.[29] In *Harris v. Forklift Systems,* the ACLU filed an amicus brief on behalf of the plaintiff, but by focusing heavily on First Amendment rights it came nearly as close to undermining as to supporting the plaintiff's claim—an outcome that angered members of the Women's Rights Project who were not invited to participate in writing the brief.[30]

One year later, in *Johnson v. County of Los Angeles Fire Department,* ACLU factions found common ground on the issue of consumer rights. The case brought the ACLU full circle as it partnered with Playboy attorneys to defeat a sexual harassment policy that denied a firefighter the right to read *Playboy* in the fire station. The ACLU was joined by a new anticensorship organization, Feminists for Free Expression, a group that argued for the right to make "intimate personal decisions such as the choice to read or view sexual materials."[31] The "right to read" figured prominently in the ACLU's brief and in public support for the male firefighter who brought suit. Indeed, no one questioned the "right to read," not even the County of Los Angeles Fire Department responsible for the contested sexual harassment policy. By 1994, the right to read *Playboy* in the workplace trumped concerns about sexual harassment and gender equality—even for advocates of strict sexual harassment law—indicating the extent to which consumer rights now governed popular and judicial understandings of the First Amendment and trumped concerns about gender equity in the workplace.

The ACLU and the Sex Wars

The ACLU helped to set the stage not only for pornography to become chic but also for the sex wars that followed. It did so by collaborating with trade groups and commercial enterprises to position the consumer as a primary client of the First Amendment, thereby bringing to sexual expression the gloss and respectability of constitutional rights and the crowd-pleasing allure of the buyer's choice. Moreover, by establishing in law, jurisprudence, and the broader culture a consumerist approach to the First Amendment, the ACLU heightened public concerns about censorship as well as the sense of violation experienced by consumers denied access to particular media. Henceforth, individual consumer demands, interpreted as an exercise of First Amendment rights, would drive media culture even as collective—pressure group—efforts to reshape media content were recast as censorship.[32]

Playboy figured prominently in this story. Not only did it provide the ACLU with financial support and cooperation; it also became a lightning rod for feminist criticism. As large numbers of women's rights activists joined the ACLU in the 1970s, many objected to events in which the ACLU seemed to promote Playboy and its values. Others criticized the ACLU for accepting money from Playboy, a commercial enterprise associated with sexually exploiting women. To Andrea Dworkin, such behavior rendered the ACLU a "handmaiden of the pornographer"—an organization better represented by a "a woman tied, chained, strung up, and gagged" than its chosen logo, the statue of liberty.[33]

The feminist sex wars derived from a number of different sources, only a few of which are discussed in this chapter. By the early 1980s many feminists believed that pornography was becoming increasingly mainstream. At the same time, other feminists and civil libertarians were reclaiming and celebrating pornography as a means of sexual liberation and a symbol of American freedom and consumer rights. Unsurprisingly, feminists who considered pornography a misogynist instruction manual in sexual violence objected strenuously to the possibility that pornography might come to represent liberation, freedom, and rights. Their efforts to pass civil rights ordinances that would target private uses of pornography had largely failed by the end of the 1980s, but many would continue the fight into the 1990s, in part by using sexual harassment law to keep pornography out of the workplace. In the ACLU and the courts, these sex wars reached a resolution of sorts in 1994 when opposing sides effectively declared a truce by recognizing the right to read at work. Thus, by the middle of the 1990s, consumer rights united ACLU factions that had disagreed over whether pornography in the workplace constituted sexual harassment. Ultimately, by establishing consumer rights under the First Amendment and positioning the consumer as the ultimate arbiter of community standards with regard to sexual material, the ACLU helped to bring pornography even more fully into the mainstream of American consumer culture.

NOTES

1. Andrea Dworkin, "The ACLU: Bait and Switch," *Yale Journal of Law and Feminism* 1, no. 1 (1989): 37–39.
2. For more on the ACLU's earlier efforts to establish consumer rights under the First Amendment, see Leigh Ann Wheeler, *How Sex Became a Civil Liberty* (Oxford University Press, 2013).
3. To gain legal standing, a plaintiff must demonstrate that s/he had been deleteriously affected by censorship in a way that legal action could resolve. Radio industry representatives were among the first to try to expand standing in the 1940s, but they did so to fight a federal regulatory apparatus they loathed. As a result, New Deal liberals viewed the notion of a media consumer's standing with suspicion until, in the 1950s, various groups of radio listeners attempted to claim standing before the Federal Communications Commission to challenge the discriminatory practices of particular radio stations. See Amy Toro, "Standing Up for Listeners' Rights: A History of Public Participation at the Federal Communications Commission" (PhD diss., University of California, Berkeley, 2000), 161–69, 172–73, 175, 178, 180, 220–23. See also Herbert Levy to Alfred A. Albert, July 12, 1954, American Civil Liberties Union-Microfilm (hereafter ACLU-MF), reel 47; "Note: Standing to Protest and Appeal the Issuance of Broadcasting Licenses: A Constricted Concept Redefined," *Yale Law Journal* 68, no. 4 (March 1959): 783–96; Louis L. Jaffe, "Standing to Secure Judicial Review: Public Actions," *Harvard Law Review* 74, no. 7 (May 1961): 1265–314. Relevant case law includes *Martin v. City of Struthers*, 319 U.S. 141 (May 3, 1943), and *Associated Industries v. Ickes*, 134 F. 2d 694 (February 8, 1943). See also Henry Miller, "Defense of the Freedom to Read," *Evergreen Review* (Summer 1959), quoted at length in Jay Martin, "'The King of Smut': Henry Miller's Tragical History," *Antioch Review* 35, no. 4 (1977): 342–67; Clifford Forster to Ernest Besig, September 15, 1952; Herbert Levy to Forster, November 13, 1953, ACLU-MF, reel 47; *Two Obscene Books vs. United States of America*, 92 Fed.

Supp. 934 (October 23, 1953); Henry Miller to Barnet Rosset, summer 1960, quoted in Brian McCord, "An American Avant-Garde: Grove Press, 1951–1986" (PhD diss., Syracuse University, 2002), 88–89, 91–92, 96–96; Phyllis Bellows to Morris Ernst, March 7 and 23, 1961, and Ernst to Bellows, March 9, 1961, Harry Ransom Center (hereafter HRC), Morris Ernst Collection, box 530; Louisa Thomas, "The Most Dangerous Man in Publishing," *Newsweek* (December 6, 2008); Al Katz, "The *Tropic of Cancer* Trials: The Problem of Relevant Moral and Artistic Controversy," *Midway* (Chicago), January 1, 1969, 99–125; McCord, "American Avant-Garde," 90, 95. One of Grove's attorneys, Charles Rembar, explained that *Tropic* ended up in court so often partly, ironically, because the Customs Department and Post Office had lifted their bans on the book, allowing for no "federal criminal prosecution in which the question of *Tropic*'s obscenity might be litigated." Charles Rembar, *The End of Obscenity: The Trials of Lady Chatterley, Tropic of Cancer, and Fanny Hill by the Lawyer Who Defended Them* (New York: Harper and Row, 1968), 168–69. Examples of local *Tropic* cases that involved the ACLU include *Dorothy Upham v. Robert W. Dill*, 195 F. Supp. 5 (June 27, 1961), represented by Ephraim London and Melvin Wulf; Attorney General v. The Book Named "Tropic of Cancer," 345 Mass. 11 (May 16, 1952), amicus brief submitted by the Civil Liberties Union of Massachusetts; *Yudkin v. State*, 229 Md. 223 (July 5, 1962), amicus briefs submitted by the ACLU and the Maryland Civil Liberties Union; *California v. Bradley Smith*, Calif. Sup. Ct. (Feb. 1962), represented by Stanley Fleishman with amicus brief submitted by A. L. Wirin and Fred Okrand; *William J. McCauley v. Tropic of Cancer*, 20 Wis. 2d 134 (May 20, 1963), amicus brief submitted by the Wisconsin chapter of the ACLU; and *Grove Press, Inc. v. Gerstein*, 378 U.S. 577 (June 22, 1961), represented by Edward de Grazia; *Jacob Zeitlin v. Roger Arnebergh*, 59 Cal. 2d 901 (July 2, 1963), represented by A. L. Wirin and Fred Okrand with amicus brief submitted by Stanley Fleishman.

4. First quote from author interview with Joel Sprayregen, January 21 2010; second quote from Charles W. Gray to Elmer Gertz, quoted in Gertz to Henry Miller, February 16, 1962, in Elmer Gertz and Felice Flanery Lewis, *Henry Miller: Years of Trial & Triumph, 1962–1964* (Carbondale: Southern Illinois University Press, 1978), 41; see also McCord, "American Avant-Garde," 102–5; "Statement in Support of Freedom to Read," *Evergreen Review* 6, no. 25 (July–August 1962), reprinted in Alan Kaufman et al., eds., *The Outlaw Bible of American Literature* (New York: Thunder's Mouth Press, 2004), 630–31; Barnet Rosset to Rice, April 5, 1962, HRC–Elmer Rice Collection (hereafter ERC), box 86; Rosa A. Eberly, *Citizen Critics: Literary Public Spheres* (Urbana: University of Illinois Press, 2000), 70, 90–92.

5. "Who Is to Censor What We See, Hear, Read?" *Kalamazoo Michigan Gazette*, January 25, 1961; "Your Right to Read, to Know," unidentified Alabama newspaper December 28, 1962, ACLU-MF, reel 59; "Big Brother Will Read For You," *Portland Reporter*, February 27, 1963, ACLU-MF, reel 61; " 'The Right to Read,' The NCTE Speaks Out on Censorship!," *Modern Language Journal* 47, no. 2 (February 1963): 70–71; Peter Jennison, "Freedom to Read," Public Affairs Pamphlet, no. 344, 1963; "Freedom-to-Read Bulletin," 5, no. 1 (March 1962), ACLU-MF, reel 60; "Audience Unlimited News," May–June 1966, ACLU-MF, reel 64; final quote from *Dorian Book Quarterly* (January–March 1964); see also advertisement cited in Martin Meeker, "Behind the Mask of Respectability: Reconsidering the Mattachine Society and Male Homophile Practice, 1950s and 1960s," *Journal of the History of Sexuality* 10, no. 1 (January 2001): 78–116, esp. 101.

6. First quote from Joel Sprayregen, "Brief and Argument for Plaintiffs-Appellees,"

Haiman v. Morris (September 1952), Northwestern University Archives–Franklyn Haiman Papers (hereafter NUA-FHP), box 11.

7. Sprayregen quotes from "Brief and Argument for Plaintiffs-Appellees,"; Epstein quotes from *Haiman v. Morris* (February 21, 1962), NUA-FHP, box 23; see also Elmer Gertz to Henry Miller, February 22, 1962, reprinted in Gertz and Lewis, *Henry Miller*, 52–54; Grove Press's lead attorney, Gertz, did not initially approve of the ACLU's focus on the right to read. See Elmer Gertz, *A Handful of Clients* (River Grove, IL: Follett, 1965), 231, 256–57; "Tropic of Cancer Wins," *New York Times*, February 22, 1962; Stephen Wise Tulin to Milton Stanzler, December 27, 1961, ACLU-MF, reel 60; Hoke Norris, " 'Cancer' in Chicago," *Evergreen Review* (July–August 1962): 41–66; "Freedom to Read Is Upheld," *Chicago Daily News*, February 23, 1962; Sprayregen to Haiman et al., July 9, 1964, NUA-FHP, box 23, folder 11; Chicago *Daily Law Bulletin*, February 22, 1962, 1; Sprayregen to President, West Publishing Company, March 13, 1962, University of Chicago Library (hereafter UCL)-ACLU, box 32. See also Gertz and Lewis, *Henry Miller*, 28–29, 51–52; Gertz, *Handful of Clients*, 280–81, 301; Eberly, *Citizen Critics*, 91, 102–3n.12; "Suppression of 'Tropic of Cancer' Spreads as ACLU Continues to Fight," February 5, 1962, ACLU-MF, reel 60; Jean Shanberg to Larry Speiser, October 24, 1961, Princeton Mudd Library–National Capitol Area ACLU Affiliate (hereafter PML-ACLU-DC), box 14; Gertz to Henry Miller, February 1 and 15, 1962; Rosset to Rice, April 5, 1962, HRC-ERC, box 86; "Judge Epstein Rules 'Tropic' Is Not Obscene," *Chicago Daily Law Bulletin* 108, no. 38 (February 22, 1962). For more on *Ronsley v. Stanczak*, a companion case, see Wheeler, *How Sex Became a Civil Liberty*, 84. Rosset worked to draw greater attention to the opinion's unique consumer-orientation by recruiting two hundred prominent authors and publishers to endorse the opinion in a "Statement in Support of Freedom to Read" published on the front cover of his *Evergreen Review*. "Statement in Support of the Freedom to Read," in Kaufman *Outlaw Bible*, 630–31.

8. First quote from "Freedom Through Dissent," ACLU 42nd Annual Report, July 1, 1961, to June 30, 1962 (New York: Oceana Publishers, 1962), 5–7; second quote from Brennan's concurrence in *Lamont v. Postmaster General*, 381 U.S. 301 (May 24, 1965). The ACLU filed influential amicus briefs in *Lamont* and *Martin v. City of Struthers*, the two key Supreme Court cases that wrote consumer rights into the First Amendment. See *Martin v. City of Struthers*, 319 U.S. 141 (May 3, 1943). Many legal scholars at the time were unaware of the lower court rulings that laid the groundwork for *Lamont*. See, for example, Michael R. Klein, "Towards an Extension of the First Amendment: A Right of Acquisition," *University of Miami Law Review* 20 (1965): 114–47. Shortly after the U.S. Supreme Court decided *Grove Press*, the Supreme Court of Illinois, to which Morris appealed after his defeat before Judge Epstein, quietly reversed its holding that *Tropic of Cancer* was obscene. See Sprayregen to Haiman et al., July 9, 1964, NUA-FHP, box 23; third quote from "Text of Kennedy's Message to Congress on Protections for Consumers," *New York Times*, March 16, 1962. See also *Jacobellis v. Ohio*, 378 U.S. 184 (June 22, 1964); *Grove Press v. Gerstein*, 378 U.S. 577 (June 22, 1964); Lizabeth Cohen, *A Consumers' Republic: The Politics of Mass Consumption in Postwar America* (New York: Vintage, 2003), 345; "Kennedy Submits a Broad Program to Aid Consumer," *New York Times*, March 16, 1962.

9. Kathy Peiss, *Hope in a Jar: The Making of America's Beauty Culture* (New York: Henry Holt, 1998), 93–94; Cohen, *Consumer's Republic*, 184–91.

10. Carrie Pitzulo, *Bachelors and Bunnies: The Sexual Politics of Playboy* (University of

Chicago Press, 2011), 61–64; Elizabeth Fraterrigo, *Playboy and the Making of the Good Life in Modern America* (Oxford: Oxford University Press, 2009), 138–49.

11. First two quotes from Sandra Silverman to Richard F. Morton, July 19, 1966; see also Silverman to Shel Silverstein, May 4, 1966 and Silverman to Anson Mount, May 4, 1966, UCL-ACLU, box 6. All other quotes from undated drafts and Theodore Berland to Dear Friend, July 15 and 19, 1966, and August 3 and 10, 1966; Theodore Berland to "You know," August 10, 1966, UCL-ACLU, box 6.

12. Quotes from Jack Pemberton to members of the national and affiliate boards, department heads, affiliate executives, July 9, 1970, Sophia Smith Collection–Dorothy Kenyon Papers (hereafter SSC-DK), box 29; Reitman to Executive Directors, October 25, 1972; Charles Lam Markman, "Women and the American Civil Liberties Union," n.d., ACLU-MF, reel 319; Office to Board of Directors, November 20, 1970, SSC-DK, box 30; Nancy Phillips to Dorothy Kenyon, September 5, 1969, SSC-DK, box 14; "1972 Biennial Conference Report of the American Civil Liberties Union," Private Collection–Monroe Friedman. In 1967, the ACLU board consisted of seventy-two men and six women. "New Dimensions . . . New Challenges: 46th Annual Report," July 1, 1965, to January 1, 1967 (New York: American Civil Liberties Union, 1967), 59.

13. Quotes from Aryeh Neier to Eli Evans, March 8, 1973; see also Equality Committee to Board of Directors, November 16, 1971; Aryeh Neier to Louise Noun, October 6, 1971, ACLU-MF, reel 319; Samuel Walker, *In Defense of American Liberties: A History of the ACLU* (New York: Oxford University Press, 1990), 314–15; Aryeh Neier, *Taking Liberties: Four Decades in the Struggle for Rights* (New York: Public Affairs, 2003), xxvi–xxviii, 13. Dorothy Kenyon considered Neier "aggressive and divisive." See Kenyon to O'Hare, September 29, 1970; Kenyon to Neier, January 8, 1971; Marvin Karpatkin to Kenyon, November 22, 1971; Ennis to Kenyon, December 7, 1971; Hayden to Kenyon, December 15, 1971, SSC-DK, box 29.

14. Andrea Dworkin joined the ACLU in 1975, a few years before she began to attain celebrity status as a feminist theorist, writer, and speaker. Pauli Murray to Suzanne Post, February 2, 1973, ASL-PM, box 56; see also Pauli Murray, *Pauli Murray: The Autobiography of a Black Activist, Feminist, Lawyer, Priest, and Poet* (Knoxville: University of Tennessee Press, 1989), 184, 214, 217, 416; Dworkin, "ACLU: Bait and Switch," 37–39.

15. For more on *Playboy* and the women's movement, see Thomas Weyr, *Reaching for Paradise: The Playboy Vision of America* (New York: Times Books, 1978), 225–47, and Pitzulo, *Bachelors and Bunnies*.

16. Quotes from Nancy Moore, Jody Parsons, and Kathy Roberts, "Up Against the Wall, Hugh Hefner," *Chicago Women's Liberation Union News*, January 1970; see also "No Women's Rights in Playboy Mansion," *Hyde Park Herald*, December 31, 1969; author interview with Sprayregen, January 26, 2010; Jody [Parsons] Howard obituary, *Chicago Tribune*, February 7, 2010. Sprayregen believed that Hefner appreciated the publicity incited by the women's protest. See also J. Anthony Lukas, "The 'Alternative Life-Style' of Playboys and Playmates," *New York Times*, June 11, 1972.

17. Quotes from Fraterrigo, *Playboy and the Making of the Good Life*, 174–75. See also Tim Hodgdon, "The Chicago Women's Liberation Union: On the Cutting Edge of Protest against Sexual Objectification," rev. June 6, 2010, CWLU Herstory website, www.cwluherstory.org.

18. Quotes from Fraterrigo, *Playboy and the Making of the Good Life*, 177–79; see also 193–99. Members of the ACLU board and leaders of its affiliates wrote supportive letters to *Playboy* as early as 1960, and *Playboy* praised the ACLU in return. See

Ernst to Editor, *Playboy*, December 1960, 9–10; Nick Landacre to Editor, *Playboy*, August 1966, 145; Jay A. Miller to Editor, *Playboy*, February 1968, 46–47, and April 1968, 66; Harriet Pilpel to Editor, *Playboy*, January 1969, 51; Charles A. Penn to Editor, *Playboy*, October 1964, 65, 166; "Postal Pandering," *Playboy*, January 1968, 61–62; "A.C.L.U. and Abortion," *Playboy*, July 1968, 47. For evidence that many ACLU leaders read *Playboy* regularly, see Larry Speiser to Jack Pemberton, July 24, 1969, ACLU-MF, reel 65, and Speiser to Nat Lehrman, February 13, 1969, ACLU-MF, reel 66; videotaped interview with Burton Joseph, March 30, 2010; Neier to Joseph, February 1, 1971, ACLU-MF, reel 319.

19. Quote from "Women's Rights Cases," February 1971; see also Neier to Joseph, February 1, 1971; "Playboy to Put Up $$ For Lib Gals," unidentified newspaper article, March 10, 1971; Equality Committee to Board of Directors, November 16, 1971, ACLU-MF, reel 319; "Playboy Fete Gains $100,000 for A.C.L.U.," *New York Times*, November 22, 1971; J. Anthony Lukas, "The 'Alternative Life-Style' of Playboys and Playmates," *New York Times*, June 11, 1972; Trudi to Ira and Suzanne, November 3, 1981, PML-ACLU, box 370; Kenyon to Norman Dorsen, April 24, 1970; Kenyon to Neier, February 4, 1971; Neier to Kenyon, February 1, 1971; Kenyon to Karpatkin, November 12, 1971, SSC-DK, box 29; Murray and Kenyon to ACLU Board, September 23, 1970, SSC-DK, box 30; Peter Andrews, "A.C.L.U.—Let There Be Law," *Playboy*, October 1971, 119, 122, 222–24, 226, 228.

20. First quote from "1976 Biennial Conference Report of the ACLU," June 10–13, 1976, ACLU-MF, series 3, reel 2; second quote from Fraterrigo, *Playboy and the Making of the Good Life*, 193 (see also 179–81, 194–204); see also Pitzulo, *Bachelors and Bunnies*; Catharine MacKinnon, " 'More Than Simply a Magazine': Playboy's Money (1982)," in *Feminism Unmodified: Discourses on Life and Law* (Boston: Harvard University Press, 1987), 134–45, 193, 199; J. Anthony Lukas, "The 'Alternative Life-Style' of Playboys and Playmates," *New York Times*, June 11, 1972. Fasteau recalled (and the documentary record confirms) that the *Playboy* grant came with "no strings attached." Author interview with Feigen (Fasteau), June 23, 2010.

21. Quotes from Feigen interview, June 23, 2010; Pilpel, "Contraception and Freedom," *Playboy* (January 1969): 51; Pilpel, "Abortion Laws Challenged," *Playboy* (April 1970): 60; Ruth Bader Ginsburg and Brenda Feigen Fasteau et al., "Equality for Women," *Playboy* (August 1973): 52; Brenda Feigen, *Not One of the Boys: Living Life as a Feminist* (New York: Knopf, 2000), 214–35; Walker, *In Defense*, 305, 338; Ruth B. Cowan, "Women's Rights Through Litigation: An Examination of the American Civil Liberties Union Women's Rights Project, 1971–1976," *Columbia Human Rights Law Review* 8 (1976): 373–412; Margaret A. Berger, *Litigation on Behalf of Women: A Review for the Ford Foundation* (New York: Ford Foundation, 1980); Tracey E. George and Lee Epstein, "Women's Rights Litigation in the 1980s: More of the Same?" *Judicature* 74, no, 6 (April–May 1991): 314–21; Judith Mears to Burton Joseph, October 28, 1975, ACLU-MF, reel 393. Catharine MacKinnon published an essay critical of organizations that accepted *Playboy* donations in 1982. Catharine MacKinnon, " 'More Than Simply a Magazine': Playboy's Money," in *Feminism Unmodified: Discourses on Life and Law* (Boston: Harvard University Press, 1987), 134–45.

22. David Allyn, *Make Love, Not War, The Sexual Revolution: An Unfettered History* (New York: Routledge, 2001), 184–85; Jon Lewis, *Hollywood v. Hard Core: How the Struggle Over Censorship Saved the Modern Film Industry* (New York: New York University Press, 2002), 188–91, 205; Foster Hirsch, "He's Happy in His 'Blue' Heaven," *New York Times*, January 24, 1971; Richard Corliss, "That Old Feeling: When Porno Was Chic," *Time*, March 29, 2005.

23. All quotations from Judy Klemesrud, "Women, Pornography, Free Speech: A Fierce Debate at N.Y.U.: Complex Purpose 'Campaign of Terrorism,'" *New York Times*, December 4, 1978.

24. Quote from Andrea Dworkin, "For Men, Freedom of Speech; For Women, Silence Please" (1979), reprinted in Dworkin, *Letters from a War Zone* (Chicago: Lawrence Hill Books, 1993), 222–25.

25. Carolyn Bronstein, *Battling Pornography: The American Feminist Anti-Pornography Movement, 1976–1986* (New York: Cambridge University Press, 2011), 297–307; "Notes and Letters," *Feminist Studies* 9, no. 1 (Spring 1983): 177–82; "Notes and Letters," *Feminist Studies* 9, no. 3 (Autumn 1983): 489–602; Lisa Duggan and Nan D. Hunter, *Sex Wars: Sexual Dissent and Political Culture* (New York: Routledge, 1995), 29–64, 239–75; author interview with Nan Hunter, November 1, 2010; Donald Alexander Downs, *The New Politics of Pornography* (Chicago: University of Chicago Press, 1999), 95–143; Walker, *In Defense*, 351. Walker credits the ACLU with organizing FACT, but Hunter insists that the ACLU played no role.

26. First quote from Duggan and Hunter, *Sex Wars*, 9; second quote from author interview with Karen Sauvigne, November 14, 2010; all other quotes from Equality Committee Minutes, February 10, 1983, and March 20, 1983, PML-ACLU, box 185.

27. Quotes from Equality Committee Minutes, February 10, 1983, and March 20, 1983, PML-ACLU, box 185; author interview with Mary Ellen Gale, December 3, 2010.

28. First three quotes from ACLU Board Minutes, April 14–15, 1984, Private Collection–Nadine Strossen; all other quotes from excerpt from ACLU Board Minutes, June 1984, PML-ACLU, box 185.

29. *Robinson v. Jacksonville Shipyards, Inc.*, 76 F. Supp. 1486 (January 18, 1991); quote from Joan Kennedy Taylor, "Sexual Harassment and the First Amendment," *CommLaw Connspectus* 4 (1996): 89; author interview with Robyn Blumner, November 29, 2010; Brief of 80 Individual Law Professors and Lawyers in *Robinson v. Jacksonville Shipyards* (August 5, 1992), 5, 7, 18. The Robinson case settled out of court in 1992. Dennis Cauchon, "Harassment, Free Speech Collide in Florida," *USA Today*, November 20, 1991; see also Mori Irvine, "Alternative Dispute Resolutions Symposium: The Lady or the Tiger: Dispute Resolution in the Federal Courts," *University of Toledo Law Review* 27 (Summer 1996): 795–804.

30. *Harris v. Forklift Systems*, U.S. dist. LEXIS 20115 (November 27, 1990); author interview with Jean Baker, December 12, 2010; "Hate Crimes, Harassment Split ACLU," *ABA Journal*, July 1993, 17, 20; ACLU brief in *Harris v. Forklift Systems*, 1992 U.S. Briefs 1168 (April 30, 1993); Susan Deller Ross, "Workplace Harassment," in *Speech & Equality: Do We Really Have to Choose?*, ed. Gara LaMarche (New York: New York University Press, 1996), 109; *Harris v. Forklift Systems*, 510 U.S. 17 (November 8, 1993); Blumner interview, November 29, 2010; Linda Greenhouse, "Court, 9–0, Makes Sex Harassment Easier to Prove," *New York Times*, November 10, 1993.

31. "ACLU Sues for Right to Playboy," *San Jose Mercury News*, December 17, 1993; quotes from Keith Stone, "ACLU, Playboy, Firefighter Sue," and Paul Hoffman, Burton Joseph, et al., "Memorandum in Support of Motion for Preliminary Injunction in *Johnson v. County of Los Angeles Fire Department*," January 10, 1993; last quote from Cathy E. Crosson, counsel for Feminists for Free Expression, amicus brief in *Johnson v. County of Los Angeles Fire Department*, January 24, 1994, Private Collection–Nan Levinson; Janet Gilmore, "Firefighter Contends Magazine Ban Is Unconstitutional," *Daily News of Los Angeles*, June 8, 1994; *Johnson v. County of Los Angeles Fire Department*, 865 F. Supp. 1430 (October 25, 1994).

32. Indeed, by the end of the first decade of the twenty-first century, lead ACLU staff attorney Chris Hansen averred that consumers' rights under the First Amendment are so well established today that the ACLU would readily bring lawsuits on behalf of consumers but rarely needs to do so because such censorship has become so rare. Author interview with Chris Hansen, November 24, 2009. For examples of recent ACLU cases argued in part on behalf of consumers, see *Ashcroft v. Free Speech Coalition*, 535 U.S. 234 (April 16, 2002); and *Ashcroft v. ACLU*, Brief for the Respondents, 542 U.S. 656 (June 29, 2004). Authors of law review articles express frustration at courts' unwillingness to distinguish between producers' and consumers' rights under the First Amendment. See, for example, Dana R. Wagner, "The First Amendment and the Right to Hear: *Urofsky v. Allen*," *Yale Law Journal* 108, no. 3 (December 1998): 669–76; and Geoffrey L. Thomas, "The Listener's Right to Hear in Broadcasting," *Stanford Law Review* 22, no. 4 (April 1970): 863–902.

33. Dworkin, "ACLU: Bait and Switch," 37–39.

CHAPTER 10

Feminism Meets Fisting

Antipornography, Sadomasochism, and the
Politics of Sex

ALEX WARNER

O N A SUNNY AND warm Saturday at the end of April 1982, twelve women donned shirts emblazoned with the name Coalition for a Feminist Sexuality and Against Sadomasochism to picket a conference and pass out flyers explaining the reason for their protest.[1] Given the success of such grassroots feminist activism to date, this scene was not unusual; the fact that the group was protesting another group of feminists, however, was surprising. The Coalition had gathered to confront "The Scholar and the Feminist IX" conference at Barnard College in New York City, a venerable feminist conference that brought together academics and activists around an annual theme. For 1982, that theme was "Towards a Politics of Sexuality."[2]

The Coalition members were staunch antipornography feminists. They criticized the conference's inclusion of organizations that "support and produce pornography," and "promote sex roles and sadomasochism," charging that these groups were "advocating the same kind of patriarchal sexuality that flourishes in our culture's mainstream."[3] They rejected the idea that butch/femme sexuality and sadomasochism (SM) could be healthy or sexually liberating for women, and argued instead that feminists must "analyze oppressive sexual institutions and values as we put forth a sexual politics founded on equality, creativity, and respect for female bodies and eroticism." The Coalition members intended to disrupt the conference and challenge its promotion of "one perspective on sexuality and its silencing of the views of a major portion of the feminist movement," namely the anti-pornography point of view. Finally, the Coalition members expressed dismay, anger, and sadness that "the organizers of this conference have shut out a major part of the feminist movement and have thrown their support to the very sexual institutions and values that oppress all women."[4]

Before Barnard

Within feminist circles, the debates about pornography in general and SM in particular had been developing over the previous decade, sometimes in the legal circles that Leigh Ann Wheeler discussed in the previous chapter and simultaneously within grassroots activism, which is the central focus of this chapter.[5] The central question had to do with whether these sexual practices could be viewed as part of an authentic feminist sexuality, or were necessarily patriarchal, oppressive, or violent. To some feminists, butch/femme sexuality could never be considered acceptable because it involved erotic role play that seemed to re-create unequal masculine and feminine heterosexual divisions. Likewise, SM seemed to reproduce heteronormative unequal distribution of power, where one partner assumed a dominant position and another had subordinate status. The Coalition's critique grew out of feminist doubt that these kinds of sexual arrangements could be empowering for women, as opposed to reinforcing the status quo. Although the critique was not new, and had been building for almost a decade, the strategy of picketing a feminist conference marked an important shift. Indeed, a critical rupture of the women's movement seemed to occur at Barnard that day.[6] But such moments do not appear, fully formed, out of the ether and, while Barnard is viewed within U.S. feminist history as the watershed moment of the Sex Wars, it was in fact the culmination of years of bitter conflict among feminists. Understanding the contours of what took place before Barnard, then, is as critical to understanding U.S. feminism, the Sex Wars, and modern U.S. sexual politics as knowing what happened at the conference itself.

In this chapter, I chart the prehistory of Barnard by mapping out the evolution of second-wave feminist sexual theory during the 1970s and early 1980s, emphasizing the impact of the lesbian SM question. In so doing, this essay adds to a burgeoning body of intellectual history that seeks to understand the development of second-wave feminist sexual politics, and the resulting Sex Wars.[7] In order to add a much-needed and long-ignored complexity to this history, I argue that the Sex Wars were powerfully shaped by debates about lesbian SM, which became inextricably linked to discussions about pornography. Indeed, much of the critique of pornography during the 1970s and early 1980s involved an implicit or explicit critique of SM and its supposed feminist potential.[8]

Since the early days of the second wave, feminists had been struggling to define a sexual ethos that would prioritize women's needs and challenge the existing patriarchal order. For some women, this meant denying sexual access to men and directing one's physical and emotional energies only to women. Other feminists argued that a little-known practice—lesbian SM—offered greater revolutionary potential because it encouraged participants to investigate, problematize, and theorize the nature of power, an experience typically denied women under patriarchy. Throughout the decade, however, other feminist activists, especially those combating violence against women and pornography, argued against this position and insisted that SM reinforced existing power inequities. Both sides were trying to understand and complicate feminist ideas about violence and consent, but their differences regarding SM became a burning focal point. This chapter illustrates how both pro-SM and antipornography feminists' ideas about sexuality formed and changed in response to critiques from feminists on the "other" side. Over time, anti-SM discourse emerged as a core aspect of antipornography feminism.

Between 1978 and 1982, in particular, the issue of lesbian SM moved from the periphery to the center of feminist discussions as antipornography feminist activity increased. Across the nation, feminist groups organized actions to protest media they labeled oppressive to women, frequently pointing to sadomasochistic imagery (e.g., leather, whips, and chains) in advertising and mainstream pornography as the worst offenders. In response, small groups of SM women began gathering to support one another in their sexuality and to educate group members about the practice and theory of sadomasochism. Debate in the feminist press escalated in this period, as activists on both sides shared their opinions. At the same time, women who specifically opposed lesbian SM, in addition to SM or pornography more generally, delineated themselves from the broader antipornography and feminist movements. This increased polarization crippled open dialogues that had occurred during the 1970s, fashioning dichotomous pro-SM and anti-SM rhetoric and camps. By 1982, lesbian sadomasochism had become one of the most divisive issues in second-wave circles. Differing opinions on this complex issue served to harden lines of opposition between antiporn and prosex feminists, which, in turn, became central dividing lines in the Sex Wars and at Barnard. That is to say, to a greater extent than most historians have recognized, SM came to serve as a foundational rupture point for feminists' vision of female sexuality.

Feminist Delineations of Power, Violence, and Consent

From the late 1960s forward, most second-wave feminists agreed that sex mattered. But why and how it mattered deeply divided them. For some, sex—heterosexual and otherwise—was oppressive; it was a force that blocked true liberation, and one from which women needed protection. According to historian Alice Echols, most radical feminists "were convinced that the repression of female desire was central to women's oppression, and sexual liberation essential to women's liberation."[9] Between 1969 and 1971, most radical feminist texts and public conferences linked women's sexuality to their oppression.[10] Indeed, from theorists to organizations, many early advocates of women's liberation agreed that sexual subordination was deeply linked to women's political, social, and cultural status as the "Second Sex." At the same time, other activists insisted that sexuality constituted a crucial site for women's freedom.[11]

These debates over the meaning and purpose of sexuality set the stage for feminist consideration of lesbian sadomasochism. Roxanne Dunbar, a member of the New York–based radical feminist group Cell 16, wrote in 1969 that "sexual 'pleasure' is equal to power and dominance for the man," and that even when females are shown as dominant in pornography, it is "part of the masculine ideology of power."[12] In her 1974 book *Woman Hating*, Andrea Dworkin included a feminist examination of the *Story of O*, a controversial 1954 novel about a sadistic man and his female erotic slave, to demonstrate male hatred of women. She declared, "Sex as the power dynamic between men and women, its primary form sadomasochism, is what we know now."[13] The influential Dworkin positioned SM as antiwoman and antifeminist, which gave credence to this position among many second wavers. By the mid-1970s, there was a growing consensus within the women's movement that sex as constituted under patriarchy was oppressive to women, and that male sexuality was inherently sadistic. Women were sexual victims almost by definition, having been forced into masochism to serve male sexual needs.

At this juncture, practitioners of lesbian SM began to assert their beliefs that their sexuality had liberatory potential, and offered an important means of challenging the patriarchal order. In a 1974 analysis published in *Lesbian Tide,* activist Karla Jay advocated for lesbian sadomasochism, although she admitted that she did not yet know how to resolve the conflicts among competing ideals of fantasy, desire, self-actualization, and antioppression. She called for an open and honest discussion of issues regarding SM, and cautioned her sisters that it was dangerous to unilaterally condemn any particular form of sexuality given how little free space for exploration women had historically been permitted. She pointed out that "the road towards liberation of our deepest selves is hard and long and I suspect that the ultimate definition of what [is] sexist, right or wrong may be as fine as a razor's edge."[14]

Jay's nuanced article, however, stood in stark opposition to bold assertions made by the radical feminist Ti-Grace Atkinson only a few months later at a 1975 meeting of the Eulenspiegel Society, a largely heterosexual SM liberation group formed in 1971.[15] Atkinson's remarks were later widely reprinted under the title "Why I'm Against S/M Liberation," in which she articulated a commonly held feminist assumption that power *itself* was the problem—that power was inherently abusive and oppressive and, thus, women's liberation necessitated both the erasure and evacuation of power. Moving more specifically into the realm of SM, Atkinson claimed definitively that one could not be both feminist and pro-SM. "By no stretch of the imagination is the Women's Movement a movement for sexual liberation," she wrote.[16] Atkinson, along with other prominent feminists, including Dworkin and Kate Millett, theorized that any institution, structure, or relationship that involved an unequal power relationship, even a temporary one, was inherently patriarchal and abusive, and could not be considered feminist. The only way forward for women's equality was to erase power completely, making SM forbidden for feminists.

These claims about violence and power would become even more deeply engrained in feminist theorizing once the issue of rape emerged as a central concern. In 1975, journalist and radical feminist activist Susan Brownmiller published her groundbreaking book *Against Our Will,* which claimed that rape was a crime of male power rather than lust, rooted in men's desire to keep women under male control. Brownmiller's frequently quoted assertion that rape "is nothing more or less than a conscious process of intimidation by which *all men* keep *all women* in a state of fear" became a feminist rallying cry, at least in white, middle-class quarters of the movement.[17] There were serious critiques of her position, however, especially from women of color, for whom the history of rape was deeply intertwined with false accusations and the lynching of black men. Indeed, black feminists, including Angela Davis and bell hooks, argued that Brownmiller failed to acknowledge the role that the rape of black women played in supporting white supremacy. It was unethical, they asserted, for Brownmiller to lump white men and black men together as equally complicit in the crime of rape as if they enjoyed equal rights and privileges in American society. The conflict over *Against Our Will* was emblematic of major tensions that erupted between white radical feminists and women of color in the 1970s as both groups struggled to assert their rights and seek justice.[18]

As a widely read and deeply influential source, *Against Our Will* not only propelled Brownmiller into the role of radical feminist leader, but also contributed to a negative view of sadomasochism among many in the women's movement. On this topic, she wrote that women who endorsed SM had been so damaged by patriarchy that they eroticized their own subordinate state: "Hardly by accident, sadomasochism . . . has been codified by those who see in sadism a twisted understanding of their manhood, and it has been accepted by those who see in masochism the abuse and pain that is synonymous with Woman. For this reason alone, sadomasochism shall always remain a reactionary antithesis to women's liberation."[19] Brownmiller echoed Atkinson's assumptions, and created a theoretical link among pornography, prostitution, rape, and other forms of male violence against women, foreshadowing many hard-line feminist criticisms of lesbian sadomasochism as violence that were to come. Atkinson and Brownmiller also reiterated and built on beliefs about male/female sexuality professed by a variety of second wave feminists. These activists equated men and male sexuality with brutality, dominance, and sadism and, correspondingly, women and female sexuality with submission, passivity, and masochism. Those who accepted these gendered stereotypes concluded that SM and feminism could not coexist, and that freely chosen SM was an expression of violent self-hatred in a society that devalued women.

Yet there were those who did see lesbian sadomasochism as a viable feminist practice and sought to counter the growing assumption of incompatibility. The first published account came from the self-identified lesbian-feminist sadomasochist Barbara Ruth (aka Barbara Lipscutz, aka Drivenwoman). She titled her essay "CATHEXIS (on the nature of S&M)," and published it in the feminist journal *Hera* in 1975. Ruth analyzed lesbian SM through a feminist lens, alternately challenging and reinforcing previously articulated feminist assumptions.[20] She condemned male/female SM for reproducing heterosexual power hierarchies, but insisted that lesbian sadomasochism was a different, positive force because it involved women reclaiming their own power. She also took on the dominant feminist belief that the exercise of power itself was the problem, and theorized instead that SM allowed women the opportunity to script and play with power, delivering tangible benefits for women.[21] Indeed power and trust, rather than sexual gratification through pain, were central to Ruth's analysis of the SM relationship, and stood as the bedrock on which she built her case for a feminist lesbian SM that was liberatory for women.[22] At the close of her essay, Ruth envisioned a nonjudgmental support group for women interested in the pursuit of SM.

In fact, such a group would materialize within several years, encouraged by additional lesbian feminist discussions of SM and its potential benefits for women. In two significant 1976 articles on the topic of lesbian SM, one authored by Ruth and another by an author known as Rosenjoy, two major defenses of lesbian SM emerged. First, these authors expanded on the value of women's explorations of power and trust through SM play. Second, they discussed the "coming out" / closet narrative and the idea that participation in SM could be therapeutic. Far from seeing their participation in SM as evidence of psychological illness, these authors and other feminists who took up the question of SM described it as a way of responding to patriarchal power, managing and healing the damage inflicted on them by dominant male and heterosexual forces.

With this new dimension of the conversation in full swing by the mid-1970s, second-wave feminists began publicly claiming lesbian SM as a *feminist* practice. SM helped them redefine their relationship to power not only in their personal lives but also in terms of larger political power structures that oppressed women, such as capitalism and heterosexuality. These women challenged the common feminist assumption that power *itself* was the problem; rather, they theorized that it was how people (usually men) abused power that should be the central issue for feminist organizing and activism. At the same time, many women experienced SM as useful in allowing them to throw off conventional ideas about how women should emote, behave, and be sexual.[23]

As the debate over lesbian SM made its way through the feminist press, powerful factions within the broader women's movement continued to associate sadomasochism with violence against women. In 1976, many feminists turned their attention to an emerging campaign for social change that had major implications for the SM debates: confronting sexual violence in the media. In response to the brutal film *Snuff*, which was distributed in several cities across the country in 1976, various feminist coalitions formed to protest, and if possible prevent, the showing of, this "porno-violence film whose advertising hypes the dismemberment and murder of a woman."[24] The feminist action against *Snuff* in Los Angeles led to the formation of Women Against Violence Against Women (WAVAW), an ad hoc coalition whose members decided to continue their antiviolence work after *Snuff* was shut down.

In Los Angeles, antiviolence organizing continued throughout 1976 and resulted in two major campaigns. The first was a successful WAVAW campaign to remove a billboard advertising the Rolling Stones' *Black and Blue* album, which depicted a sexually excited, bruised woman with her hands tied above her head and the slogan, "I'm Black and Blue from the Rolling Stones and I love it."[25] Here, feminists targeted an ad with a decidedly sadomasochistic theme, marking this type of sexual presentation as violent, pornographic, and oppressive to women. Later that same year, the group launched a national boycott of the record companies under the Warner Communications umbrella (Warner, Elektra, and Atlantic Records), demanding that they prohibit images of violence against women on their album covers.[26] These activists laid the groundwork for later boycotts against various forms of pornography, and established SM imagery as problematic for both simulating and condoning violence against women.

These broader debates and campaigns about sexual exploitation and representations of violence did not escape the attention of lesbian SM advocates, who worried that the mainstream women's movement was mounting a wholesale attack on SM that threatened their sexuality. In October 1976, a group of twelve women, including the feminist author Pat Califia, the transgender male activist who identified at that time as a woman and as a lesbian,[27] attended a "Healthy

Questions about Sado-Masochism" workshop at the Women's Health and Healing Conference in Los Angeles to grapple with the thorny problem of lesbian SM. The workshop participants discussed their physical, mental, spiritual, political, and sexual experiences with SM, including their feminist politics of trusting in women and remaining open to a wide array of experiences and perspectives as a way of accepting SM. The workshop also offered the first public description of masochism by a lesbian-feminist.[28]

As part of their evaluation of sadomasochism, and in response to WAVAW activity, these feminists pondered the connection between SM sexual play and *actual* violence against women. Confronting their own fears as well as the assumptions and objections of others, they defined sadomasochism as different from violence: the distinction lay in the presence (or absence) of consent. One participant articulated the consensus this way: "There is a bond of trust if you're doing S&M . . . there is a *complicity*, there is a *choice* there." While previous explanations and feminist defenses of SM included numerous references to the role of trust in the exchange, none had specifically claimed *consent* as a critical dividing line. The dialogue about consent that occurred in response to antirape/WAVAW antiviolence organizing helped refine pro-SM rhetoric and logic.[29] Using the concept of consent, pro-SM advocates began to tease out their theories of power—more specifically the value of exercising one's power to consent to a sexual encounter, which made it desirable and distinguished it from a nonconsensual sexual act, like rape, which, because someone's power was compromised, was therefore was violent, abusive, and patriarchal in nature.

Within the workshop setting, practitioners like Califia also emphasized sexual pleasure as a major reason for engaging in SM. Perhaps because the "Healthy Questions" session took place in a room full of women who supported at least a neutral investigation of SM, one woman dared confess that pain was a sexual stimulant. "For me, being bitten really hard or being scratched, or being beaten is a turn on," she confessed.[30] This description of pain as pleasurable was noticeably absent from earlier defenses of lesbian SM, all of which described this practice only as a vehicle for emotional or spiritual transcendence. At the workshop, however, this woman addressed the experience of pain as specifically sexual, opening up new territory in discussions of the physical desire that accompanied SM. What may have been presumed previously—the erotic response to pain—was now openly proclaimed.[31] This was a significant turning point, in that defenders of lesbian SM began to assert women's authority over their own sexuality, and women's rights to fully explore their sexual interests and desires.

The "Healthy Questions" workshop was covered by the feminist press, particularly the *Lesbian Tide*, whose readers vigorously debated the potential benefits of lesbian SM in extensive letters to the editor.[32] One reader offered a new analysis and critique. In "S&M: The Boundaries of Feminism," Susan Helenius challenged lesbian sadomasochists to be more self-reflective about their practice, and insisted that saying it "feels good" was not a sufficient defense for a form of sexuality under public attack. But she also took anti-SM feminists to task and cautioned them about the perils of judging others for their sexual choices: "To section off differences . . . between women on the basis of preferences . . . is to invite defections." Helenius not only joined other *Lesbian Tide* readers in calling for a broader dialogue about the meanings and possibilities of a feminist sadomasochism, but also voiced the first critique of anti-SM feminists as divisive to feminism at large.[33]

By 1977, the debate about lesbian SM increasingly incorporated not only central issues about whether or not SM could be practiced in feminist ways but also the very definition of who could legitimately call herself a feminist. As these discussions intensified in nature and frequency, the issue of lesbian SM took center stage.

Communities: Created and Expanded

In the early summer of 1978, in response to the growing and heated debate regarding the feminist (im)possibilities of lesbian SM, a small but determined group of women organized the first independent lesbian SM group, Samois (pronounced "sam-wah"). The story of Samois demonstrates the centrality of feminist politics in general, and the antipornography movement in particular, to the creation of what I conceptualize as a "poli-socio-sexual" community of lesbian sadomasochists. Moreover this group's development occurred amid the emergence of broader gay rights and pansexual SM movements.

Founded in San Francisco in June 1978,[34] Samois emerged out of Cardea, the all-women but mixed sexual orientation subgroup of the Bay Area SM group the Society of Janus.[35] Feeling that Cardea did not meet lesbians' specific needs, member Pat Califia decided to try to start a specifically dyke-centered support group with two others.[36]

Samois' most significant achievement during its first year was the publication of *What Color Is Your Handkerchief: A Lesbian S/M Sexuality Reader* in June 1979. This informational booklet not only elucidated the group's political philosophies but also launched Samois into the national lesbian-feminist spotlight. Its founding statement described Samois' membership as "a group of feminist lesbians who share a positive interest in sadomasochism" and who "believe that S/M must be consensual, mutual and safe." Samois also believed "that sadomasochists are an oppressed sexual minority" and that "S/M can and should be consistent with the principles of feminism."[37] Samois self-defined as a *feminist* group, which was controversial in itself, and the group also named its central goal as developing and distributing an analysis of SM based on a feminist framework. Within two years of its publication, the booklet earned Samois fame and notoriety among feminists nationally and internationally.

In addition, the group's engagement with local and national U.S. feminist groups helped launch SM into the center of the Sex Wars. Much of Samois' members' time was spent offering public education regarding lesbian sadomasochism within lesbian-feminist and women's communities, but those attempts were often met with strong resistance. Indeed, at any given moment, Samois was embroiled in conflict with one or more women's groups. These conflicts were evident in Samois' efforts to address the concerns of the influential Bay Area antipornography group Women Against Violence in Pornography and Media (WAVPM), which sponsored women's marches through pornography districts, "browse-ins" at "adult" bookstores to scare away male patrons, and antiporn demonstrations.[38] In addition to these grassroots activities, in November 1978, WAVPM held the first national feminist conference on pornography in San Francisco, garnering more attention for an anti-SM platform.

As the antipornography movement became more public in its claims, Samois attempted to challenge some of its assumptions. After the November WAVPM conference, Samois asked for a screening of the slideshow. Califia claimed that WAVPM declined the request because they believed that Samois "glamourized violence against women' " and were afraid that they "would find the slideshow erotic." Members attended screenings designated for other community groups, and were angry to hear SM described as a form of violence against women.[39] According to Califia, "They did not like their sexuality as lesbians being equated with anything male or patriarchal.

Others were angry because we liked some pornography and didn't want to see all of it wiped out." Califia continued, "All of us felt that the picture presented of S/M was biased and distorted."[40]

Throughout the late 1970s and early 1980s, WAVPM organized and endorsed public campaigns that attacked SM as dangerous and anti-feminist. In particular, the organization launched a series of protests against screenings of the film adaptation of *The Story of O.* The first newsletter published by the organization in 1979 outlined the successful campaign by the Rochester, New York, chapter of the sister group Women Against Violence Against Women against a showing of the film at a local university. Twenty-five women used various forms of protest, including leaflets, chanting, and a possible bomb threat. Another article reported a similarly successful protest in Sacramento, California. A third article outlined a planned WAVPM action against the movie in Berkeley. While none of the protests specifically addressed Samois, its membership, or its agenda, the SM group had chosen its name "because it evokes . . . the figure of a lesbian dominatrix in *Story of O."* The membership of Samois likely took these protests personally, given their close connection to the film and its characters.[41]

Attempts by lesbian sadomasochists to control the spread of anti-SM sentiment among antipornography activists faced another challenge when a WAVPM conference organizer moved to New York City in 1979 to help build the newest antipornography group, Women Against Pornography (WAP). Shortly thereafter, WAP organized a national conference in September 1979. About eight hundred women attended, and according to one source, "some 35 percent of them were women who had not previously been active in the Movement."[42] Many rhetorical strategies were employed at the conference that conflated pornography, SM, and actual violence. Yet, when challenged to unpack this assumption, and prove causality, antipornography activists typically attacked the questioner as being sexist or misogynistic. According to the feminist journalists who covered the conference, the WAP position on porn and SM as violence came down to "We just know it's true, we don't have to prove it."[43]

The endemic equation of sadomasochism with pornography, and both practices with actual violence against women, appeared regularly in antipornography rhetoric. In their attempts to heighten public concern about pornography, antipornography feminists critiqued images that incorporated SM as evidence of the connection between pornography and violence. In her *Ms.* article "Erotica and Pornography: A

Clear and Present Difference," Gloria Steinem challenged readers to "look at any depiction of sex in which there is clear force . . . it may be very blatant, with weapons of torture or bondage." This, she continued, was "sex being used to . . . tell us the lie that pain and humiliation (ours or someone else's) are really the same as pleasure."[44] Steinem, like other antiporn activists, explicitly connected SM to violence, and also argued that pain and pleasure were incompatible. Another frequent connection was made between images labeled as pornography and actual violence against women. For example, one activist cited rape, battery, and child abuse statistics (some of them questionable in and of themselves) as though these acts of violence were clearly and undeniably related to the existence of pornography. This "porn equals violent behavior" assumption was adopted by many antipornography activists, and was presented to community groups through slideshow presentations like the one offered by WAVPM.[45]

Antipornography activists viewed women who chose to engage in SM as unwitting victims who participated in their own oppression. Andrea Dworkin, who later worked with Catharine MacKinnon to create an ordinance that made pornography legally actionable as a violation of women's civil rights, explained that masochism was an emotional response to conditions of subordination. "When I'm feeling very powerless, very humiliated," she wrote, "I regress and have sexual feelings about cruel men. Women experience so much sadomasochism that it becomes the only way we can come to sexuality."[46] Here, Dworkin articulated the idea that women who had sadomasochistic desires had internalized patriarchal notions of sex and were re-creating sexist paradigms in the bedroom. Steinem echoed these ideas. "Yes, it's true that there are women who have been forced by violent families and dominating men to confuse love with pain; so much so that they have become masochists," she wrote.[47] These feminists denied masochistic women any sexual agency, treating them as if they were strangers to their own bodies and desires. SM, they claimed, could never be an authentic, healthy sexuality for straight women or lesbians.[48]

Yet not all feminists, even those sympathetic to the antipornography movement, accepted the anti-SM assumptions at face value. Journalist Lindsy van Gelder, writing in Ms., articulated a number of concerns about the WAP slide show presentations. She was concerned that the group's analysis of pornography failed to address the complexities of sexual fantasy, which certainly included SM. In ignoring the reality that many women enjoyed pornography and SM, the movement was treating some of its own members as "brainwashed degenerates," a tactic that "can push women right back into the closet of sexual guilt." She warned that it was "crucial that we aren't tempted into expedient oversimplification or overstatement . . . to protect our own multiplicity of issues, backgrounds, and experiences as women."[49]

Heating Up: The SM Debate Goes National

The April 1980 edition of the *Advocate*, a national gay rights newspaper, revealed mounting tension over the SM issue. An article described the efforts of a Philadelphia bookstore to defend itself against cries of sexism by a local branch of WAVAW. WAVAW was protesting the store's sale of *The Story of O*, claiming that the book contributed to violence against women. A bookstore representative responded that the store offered material for diverse audiences and was trying to meet community demand.[50] That issue of the *Advocate* also included what would become one of the most controversial publications of the Sex Wars, Califia's essay "Among Us, Against Us—The New Puritans," which attacked antipornography feminism.

Califia, operating from an authorial position of lesbian feminism, expressed rising anxiety and frustration with the antipornography movement and its impact on marginalized sexual communities. Califia criticized WAVPM's rhetoric and strategies, calling the group's definitions of pornography and violence "circular and vague," and further charged that WAVPM was "basically a group with a right-wing philosophy masquerading as a radical feminist organization." Labeling some of their positions "absurd" and "awful," Califia also criticized WAVPM for becoming increasingly conservative, and refusing to support other feminist causes, such as gay rights and abortion: "They continue to grow . . . more powerful and more pro-censorship and antisex in their positions." Members of both WAVPM and the larger antipornography movement responded swiftly.[51]

Although WAVPM did not specifically mention Califia's article, organization leaders responded to the article by reworking and reprinting their article, "Questions We Get Asked Most Often," in a July 1980 newsletter. In the four-and-a-half-page article, WAVPM outlined its beliefs about pornography, citing various social scientific studies that claimed that pornography was connected to actual violence against women. WAVPM included SM imagery among the types of pornography that members found problematic, but the group did not directly address the issue of lesbian sadomasochism in any way. Perhaps recognizing how explosive the issue had become in the larger women's movement, the leadership had decided to take a "publicly 'neutral' stance."[52]

This neutral stance was unsatisfactory to at least one subset of WAVPM members, who decided to press forward with their own statement on SM and its harms to women. Four women published a call for submissions to a special forum, "Feminist Perspectives on Sadomasochism." They expressed concern over the influence of Samois, whom they termed a "group of so-called lesbian feminists," and their forum flyer recounted the group's recent activity, including the publication of *What Color Is Your Handkerchief.* The flyer explained that the authors were "interested in receiving manuscripts which [brought] a feminist political and ethical analysis to bear on sadomasochism," and they offered a list of possible topics, including connections between violence and sadomasochism, scrutiny of "community/media receptivity to lesbian sadomasochism," and analysis of Samois' writings. The dispassionate title aside, the flyer content indicated that these feminists were decidedly anti-SM. Indeed, Robin Ruth Linden, one of the original four, would be the lead editor on the anthology *Against Sadomasochism: A Radical Feminist Analysis* published two years later.[53]

Meanwhile, as the specifically anti-SM movement was beginning to coalesce, *What Color Is Your Handkerchief* was selling briskly, supporting Samois' theory that there were many women interested in learning about SM. The group sold two hundred copies between June and September 1979, when a second printing provided two hundred more. In October 1979, the group reported that the booklet would soon be available for purchase at stores in New York, Oregon, Massachusetts, Michigan, Arizona, and Alaska. In their June 1980 newsletter, Samois reported that a third run of five hundred copies had sold out and a fourth printing was planned.[54] Samois' organizing had a profound impact, providing a wide range of women with the information and inspiration to explore and understand lesbian SM.

During the same period, on the East Coast, the feminist newspaper of record *off our backs* was publishing a debate about lesbian SM that mirrored what was unfolding on the West Coast. Califia was also a central player in this conversation, and contributed a scathing critique of antipornography politics and a passionate defense of lesbian SM.

In response, *off our backs* contributors condemned lesbian SM in general and Califia's work in particular.[55] Between 1979 and 1981, similar discussions occurred in the pages of *Lesbian Connection* and *Plexus*, two major feminist publications.[56] Indeed, by 1981, lesbian SM was one of the most prominent and controversial issues within American feminism.

As the debate over lesbian SM continued in the pages of feminist newspapers and journals, a parallel debate was going on in their back offices. Samois leaders were negotiating with these publications to purchase advertising space to promote *What Color Is Your Handkerchief* and the group's forthcoming book, *Coming to Power*. *off our backs*, *Big Mamma Rag*, and *Inciter* (and perhaps other publications as well) asked Samois for more information regarding these books, and most refused to run the ads. Each attributed the refusal to the collective nature of decision making and the inability to arrive at a consensus on lesbian SM as an acceptable feminist practice.[57] This denial of access to the feminist community at large also plagued Samois' interactions with at least one feminist bookstore and with the San Francisco Women's Building when Samois sought to hold meetings there.

The SM debate in regional communities and feminist presses also began to play out a national level. At the 1980 National Organization for Women (NOW) annual convention, anti-SM advocates achieved a substantial victory. NOW reaffirmed its commitment to lesbian rights, but the organization also passed a resolution condemning sadomasochism. Introduced by the chair of the Lesbian Rights Committee, the resolution stated that sadomasochism had, along with other controversial issues such as pederasty and public sex, been "mistakenly correlated with Lesbian/Gay rights" and that it should properly be defined as "an issue of violence, not affectional / sexual preference / orientation." NOW did "not support the inclusion of . . . sadomasochism . . . as [a] Lesbian rights [issue], since to do so would violate the feminist principles" of the organization. In denying the validity of lesbian SM, NOW also declared sadomasochism an antifeminist activity and thereby marked lesbian sadomasochists as being outside of legitimate feminist politics.[58]

Shortly thereafter, in spring 1981, *Heresies* published a special "Sex Issue" of the magazine devoted to questions around sexuality. The issue had taken "almost two years to produce . . . [because of] . . . many disagreements and difficulties, both intellectual and interpersonal," according to the editors. The ninety-plus-page journal included essays and art on wide-ranging topics, from "butch-fem relationships" to stripping, each revealing that feminist understandings of sexuality remained highly contested. The issue also included the by then requisite articles on lesbian SM and pornography, and letters protesting the anti-SM NOW resolutions.[59]

The *Heresies* issue included Califia's essay "Feminism and Sadomasochism," which focused largely on demystifying SM, through emphasizing the centrality of consent and fantasy to SM. Next, Califia outlined the major objections to SM and offered an explanation of how each particular objection was based on false assumptions.[60] Califia's article worked in tandem with the other article in *Heresies* that dealt directly with the pressing sexual-political issues of the day, Paula Webster's "Pornography and Pleasure." Webster offered an articulate and well-balanced analysis of the antipornography movement. She began her argument by underscoring the ubiquity of the campaign, noting that "every feminist in the New York metropolitan area has heard of Women Against Pornography" and that it was "one of the best-organized and best-funded campaigns in movement history." Demonstrating how powerful the pornography issue had become, Webster declared that "political differences, both in theory and in practice, were set aside as pornography was assigned a privileged position in the discourse on women's oppression. . . . A vast sea of feminist solidarity swelled around the issue."[61]

Having squarely established the centrality of pornography, Webster described how difficult it was for those opposed to antipornography politics to claim any ground. "To move against the wave felt truly threatening . . . [and] . . . no dissenting movement developed. Criticism was kept to a minimum." Webster continued, "Yet, many women, under their breath, confided that something was missing from all this. . . . Dogmatism, moralizing, and censorial mystifying tended to dominate the antiporn campaign." What was missing, she pronounced, was a positive approach to sexuality, a women's movement that actually encouraged female sexual imagination and experimentation. The threat to sexual minorities was extreme. "I am convinced that the current anti-porn campaign holds significant dangers for feminists interested in developing an analysis of violence against women and extending an analysis of female sexuality," Webster wrote.[62] Instead, she urged women to use pornography to discover and explore sexual practices they might enjoy—including but not limited to SM. She challenged readers to focus on women's pleasure and imagined the creation of "a truly radical pornography that spoke to female desire as we are beginning to know it and we would like to see it acted out."[63]

Taken together, Califia and Webster's articles revealed dissent in the women's movement, and suggested that many feminists would come to reject the antiporn analysis and the movement itself. In fact, conflict surrounding the Barnard Conference and, later, the mid-1980s Dworkin-MacKinnon legislative campaigns against pornography contributed to the number of feminists who regarded antipornography theory with suspicion. Attacks on SM played a major role in the growing divide. Staunch defenders of SM as a feminist practice and sexual identity had long rejected antipornography politics. But now they were joined by increasing numbers of women who were unsure about SM as feminist per se, but who were turned off by the antipornography movement's increasingly dogmatic perspective on what many feminists perceived as a set of extremely complicated issues. These feminists had little tolerance for antiporn activists who defended their analysis as the sole legitimate feminist stance on SM.

Coming to Power

In response to this growing national conversation, in 1981 Samois published a full-length book, *Coming to Power*, which was a valuable resource book for women interested in exploring SM. The book defended SM against antifeminist charges and became an immediate center of controversy. The collective argued that as a result of attacks on SM, this form of sexuality was blamed for "practically every ill and inequity, large and small[that the] world has ever known, including rape, racism, classism, spouse abuse. . . ."[64] Practitioners were "being labeled anti-feminist, mentally ill or worse . . . we find ourselves, quite unexpectedly, on the 'other' side. We are being cast out, denied. We become heretics." Samois urged tolerance and acceptance and communication. "We must talk about what we do as much as who we do it with. . . . We must have precisely the same dialogues about the texture of our sexuality as we have been having about classism, racism, cultural identity, physical appearance and ability."[65] The diverse first-person narratives in the collection were clearly intended to stimulate conversation, to humanize the image of lesbian sadomasochists, and to educate the reader by confronting stereotypes about lesbian SM.

On the heels of the publication of *Coming to Power*, a group of New

York SM women organized in October 1981, and called themselves Lesbians into SM (later Lesbian Sex Mafia and LSM) This women-only support group was created by Jo Arnone and Dorothy Allison for "anyone actively involved in any aspect of 'politically incorrect sex' as well as those who have dreams but no actual experience to their credit." In its first month of existence, LSM held an educational work-shop called "Esoteric Expertise and Safety" and hosted a discussion with Pat Califia and Gayle Rubin titled "Sex Politics and Feminism." Women SM activists were now organizing and promoting their beliefs in ways similar to those modeled by the antipornography movement. West Coast activists like Califia and Rubin actively supported the cre-ation of the East Coast LSM organization, just as WAVPM had lent expertise and personnel to WAP.[66] With LSM's inception, the nascent women's SM movement became a national force.

As the women's SM community expanded, the feminist discussion regarding lesbian sadomasochism continued to intensify and become even more complex. In October 1981, the black feminist Alice Walker published "A Letter of The Times" in *Ms.* magazine. In it, Walker cri-tiqued the racialized politics of the lesbian SM movement by examin-ing an interracial master/slave relationship with the white woman as dominant and the black woman as her slave. Walker's assessment was grim. She argued that "the actual enslaved *condition* of literally mil-lions of our mothers [were] trivialized—because two ignorant women insisted on their right to publicly act out a 'fantasy' that still strikes terror in black women's hearts. And embarrassment and disgust, at least in the hearts of most of the white women in my class." Walker made it clear that for her the weight of history as it pertained to race outweighed individual desire for sexual fantasy because of its capac-ity to reinforce both historical and existing power differentials.[67] Yet Walker's analysis goes even further in explaining the problem with this particular version of sexual fantasy. "Many black women fear it is as slaves white women want them; no doubt many white women think some amount of servitude from black women is their due."[68] Walker thus challenged lesbian sadomasochists not because they re-created straightforward patriarchal abuses of power by men, but because they also threatened to re-create historically based power dif-ferentials between groups of *women.* This analysis provided a critique not only of SM but also of the state of U.S. racial politics in the 1970s.

As many women of color activists had done throughout the second wave, Walker demanded that feminists grapple with unequal power relationships within the movement, adding an important and incredibly significant subtlety to the debate. She did not speak for all women of color; in a landmark essay of the early 1980s, Amber Hollibaugh and Cherríe Moraga resisted the demonization of SM, with the Chicana lesbian activist Moraga expressing sympathy for a (presumably white) Samois member who was "really coping with power struggles in a tangible way with her lover."[69]

Conclusion: Sex War Rising

The issue of lesbian sadomasochism was foundational to the development of antipornography activity in the United States in the late 1970s and early 1980s. Feminist activists who wanted to identify a direct, causal relationship between pornography and violence settled on SM as an example of the physical and psychological harm that pornography exposure wrought, and they saw no redeeming value in the practice. In "A Report on the Sex Crisis," published in the March 1982 issue of *Ms.*, just prior to the Barnard Conference, Barbara Ehrenreich, Elizabeth Hess, and Gloria Jacobs explained that by the late 1970s, a new consensus had emerged among most women who considered themselves feminists that "*feminist* sexuality would be devoid of even a semblance of power transactions," a stance that left no room for SM and stimulated the "first cracks in the feminist consensus [which] appeared when women split over pornography." Indeed, the authors contended, it was the issue of lesbian sadomasochism that irrevocably broke the feminist sexual consensus, because women who desired and/or enjoyed SM could not condemn their own authentic sexuality as antiwoman. Whereas "most feminists still find pornography horrifying and sadomasochism, well, perverse," the authors admitted, "a sizable minority are glad to see some of the old shibboleths crumbling and new questions, new explorations opening up."[70]

One month after the publication of the article, the Barnard Conference shook the women's movement to its core. Ehrenreich, Hess, and Jacobs had tried to alert readers to what they saw as the coming "painful debates," yet reassured their readers that while "we do seem confused . . . we need to remind ourselves in times like these that we are the first movement in history . . . to address itself to sensual desire, to fantasy, to personal eroticism as *political issues*." So, they concluded, if "we find ourselves now where angels fear to tread, it is because we have had the courage to make the 'personal' political."[71]

In the wake of Barnard, the issue of pornography spread to a wider national audience, reaching conservative religious groups and mainstream Americans who were now asked to consider the potential harms of sexually graphic imagery. As this essay reveals, the "pornography question" presented to Americans in the 1980s, via the Reagandriven Attorney General's Commission on Pornography (1986), and the MacKinnon-Dworkin legislative initiatives, was structured and defined by feminists' debates over lesbian SM and its relationship to women's sexuality.

NOTES

1. "Regional Forecast," *New York Times* April 24, 1982; Susan Brownmiller, *In Our Time: A Memoir of a Revolution* (New York: Dial Press, 1999), 315; tacie dejanikus, "charges of exclusion & mccarthyism at barnard conference," *off our backs,* June 1982, 5.
2. Carole S. Vance, "Conference Flyer," *Diary of a Conference on Sexuality,* 1982, Barnard Center for Research on Women Archive, Barnard College, New York.
3. Coalition for a Feminist Sexuality and Against Sadomasochism, "We Protest," flyer, 1982 Scholar and the Feminist Conference, Barnard Center for Research on Women Archive. In addition to being inflammatory, many of these descriptions were factually inaccurate, according to some critics.
4. Coalition for a Feminist Sexuality and Against Sadomasochism, "We Protest," 2.
5. Sadomasochism (often referred to as SM) is, for the purposes of this study, defined in the broadest of terms to mean receiving sexual pleasure from either giving (sadism) or receiving (masochism) physical pain, participating in power-based role play (such as dominance and submission), and/or bondage. While the term BDSM (bondage, discipline/domination, submission/sadism, masochism) is more frequently used to define these behaviors in modern parlance, these pleasures, desires, and behaviors were not delineated as such during the historical period covered in this study.
6. Rosalyn Baxandall and Linda Gordon, eds. *Dear Sisters: Dispatches from the Women's Liberation Movement* (New York: Basic Books, 2000); Lisa Duggan and Nan D. Hunter, *Sex Wars: Sexual Dissent and Political Culture* (New York: Routledge, 2006); Alice Echols, *Daring to Be Bad: Radical Feminism in America, 1967–1975* (Minneapolis: University of Minnesota Press, 1989); Ruth Rosen, *The World Split Open* (New York: Viking, 2000).
7. Here, I am specifically thinking of and particularly grateful to Carolyn Bronstein's *Battling Pornography: The American Feminist Anti-Pornography Movement, 1976–1986* (Cambridge: Cambridge University Press, 2011) for elucidating the particulars of the antiporn movement, adding significantly to our collective understanding of the specifics of that part of this important story. Similarly, I am thankful to Whitney Strub's *Perversion for Profit: The Politics of Pornography and the Rise of the New Right* (New York: Columbia University Press, 2011) for helping me understand the complicated relationship between these larger social forces and movements and

the marketplace. Carrie Pitzulo's *Bachelors and Bunnies: The Sexual Politics of Play-boy* (Chicago: University of Chicago Press, 2011) likewise challenges dominant narratives about the rise of the porn industry, particularly as it played out with *Playboy*, asking us all to reconsider our understanding of the possibilities for an underlying feminist agenda inside what is often seen as an antiwoman industry.

8. I should note here that by "feminists" I am referring to women who either explic-itly or implicitly (by association with a group or employment with a particular periodical) align themselves with feminism.

9. Echols, *Daring to Be Bad*, 174 and 182. See also Sheila Cronan, "Fuck Marriage Not Men," n.d., 1–8, Mary Orovan Papers, Schlesinger Library, Harvard University; and Sheila Michaels, "The Archetypal Woman," n.d., 1–4, Mary Orovan Papers, Schlesinger Library, Harvard University.

10. Anne Koedt, "The Myth of the Vaginal Orgasm," 1–5, Mary Orovan Papers, Schlesinger Library, Harvard University; Echols, *Daring to Be Bad*, 211; John D'Emilio and Estelle Freedman, *Intimate Matters* (Chicago: University of Chicago Press, 1997), 263; Germaine Greer, *The Female Eunuch* (New York: Bantam Books, 1970), 5; Baxandall and Gordon, *Dear Sisters*, 120 and 166.

11. Dana Densmore, "On Celibacy," *No More Fun and Games* 1 (1969): n.p., Schlesinger Library, Harvard University; Roxanne Dunbar, "'Sexual Liberation': More of the Same Thing," *No More Fun and Games* 3 (November 1969): 49, Schlesinger Library, Harvard University; Abby Rockefeller, "Sex: The Basis of Sexism," *No More Fun and Games* 6 (May 1973): 34, Schlesinger Library, Harvard University.

12. Roxanne Dunbar, "Sexual Liberation," 53; Cell 16 member Dana Densmore artic-ulated similar opinions; see also, Densmore, "On Masochism," *No More Fun and Games* 6 (May 1973): 100–113, Schlesinger Library, Harvard University.

13. Andrea Dworkin, *Woman Hating* (New York: E. P. Dutton, 1974), 55–63, 183.

14. Karla Jay, "The Spirit Is Feminist but the Flesh Is?" *Lesbian Tide*, October 1974.

15. Ti-Grace Atkinson, "Why I'm Against S/M Liberation," *Majority Report*, Septem-ber 1977, 17; "About TES," The Eulenspiegel Society website, http://tes.org.

16. Atkinson, "Why I'm Against SM," 17. That Atkinson does not reference lesbian SM is particularly interesting, given the fact that later in the Sex Wars, Atkinson's article is printed and reprinted as ammunition against lesbian SM. This same arti-cle was later widely reprinted in *Against Sadomasochism*.

17. Susan Brownmiller, *Against Our Will: Men, Women, and Rape* (Toronto: Bantam Books, 1975), 5.

18. For more on the critiques of Brownmiller, see Annelise Orleck, *Rethinking Ameri-can Women's Activism* (New York: Routledge, 2015), 124–25.

19. Brownmiller, *Against Our Will*, 292.

20. Barbara Ruth, "CATHEXIS (on the nature of S&M)," *Lesbian Tide* 6, no. 6 (May/June 1977): 10. This article was reprinted in the *Lesbian Tide* but the original was in *Hera* 1, no. 5 (December 1975).

21. Ruth, "CATHEXIS," 10.

22. Ibid.,, 10–11.

23. Barbara Lipscutz (aka Drivenwoman), "Coming Out on S&M," *Journal of Radical Therapy* 5 (Spring 1976): 8. In fact, when Barbara Lipscutz (later Ruth) originally sent her article to *Radical Therapy*, she was not out and therefore had asked the editors "to print it under the psyeudonym [sic] 'Drivenwoman,'" a request she quickly revoked after she had "come out" as a sadomasochist to her local commu-nity. Rosenjoy, "Sado-Masochism: The Theory and the Practice," *Gay Community News*, February 7, 1976, 10–16. This article is confusing in that while the byline

is attributed to Rosenjoy, the author seems to be transcribing a conversation between feminists regarding lesbian sadomasochism. Whether or not these feminists and their dialogue are real or creations of the author is unclear.

24. " 'Snuff' Shut Down by Protests, Stink Bombs, Brick," *Lesbian Tide*, May/June 1976. On the history of WAVAW protests against *Snuff*, see Bronstein, *Battling Pornography*, chapter 4.

25. Baxandall and Gordon, *Dear Sisters*, 171.

26. Julia London, "Boycotting Pornographic Record Covers," in Baxandall and Gordon, *Dear Sisters*, 171–72. The boycott of Warner Communications' record companies, although it took three years, was successful. See Bronstein, *Battling Pornography*, for the complete history of the boycott.

27. While I recognize that Califia would subsequently self-identify as male and change his name to Patrick, I use "Pat" as an incredibly significant and deeply historicized marker of authorial self-positioning at the time of the historical events discussed in this chapter. I have reached out to Califia to ask him for clarification on how he would like this shift to be represented, but have received no response, and so I have attempted to both honor his later life while respecting that at the time it was incredibly relevant that "Pat" identified strongly with being a "woman." Califia himself has noted, in republishing his older essays, that he "chose to leave the older, female gendered essays alone," adding, "I wouldn't give away the life I had being a wildwoman. I don't think it's possible (or desirable) to erase the years I spent in the leatherdyke community and the sensibilities I acquired there." Califia, *Speaking Sex to Power: The Politics of Queer Sex* (San Francisco: Cleis, 2002), xii.

28. Jeanne Cordova, ed., "Towards a Feminist Expression of Sado-Masochism," *Lesbian Tide*, November/December 1976.

29. Ibid., 15.

30. Ibid., 14 and 17.

31. Ibid.

32. Susan Helenius, "S&M: The Boundaries of Feminism," *Lesbian Tide*, March/April 1977. See also "Letters on S&M and Feminism," *Lesbian Tide*, January/February, 1977; and "Continued Controversy on S&M," *Lesbian Tide*, March/April 1977.

33. Helenius, "S&M: The Boundaries of Feminism," 8–9.

34. It seems significant that the group was formed shortly after the White Night riots in San Francisco in which gay and lesbian citizens took to the streets, protesting and destroying property in a display of anger over the leniency in the conviction and sentencing of Dan White, former city supervisor, who assassinated Mayor Moscone and the city's first openly gay city supervisor, Harvey Milk.

35. Pat Califia, "A Personal View of the History of the Lesbian S/M Community and Movement in San Francisco," in Samois, *Coming to Power* (Boston: Alyson Publications, 1987), 247–49. For even more information on Cardea, see pages 10–14 of Society of Janus' institutional history, available at www.hawkeegn.com/bdsm/janhis.pdf.

36. Califia, "Personal View," 252.

37. Samois, "Our Statement," *What Color Is Your Handkerchief: A Lesbian S/M Sexuality Reader*, inside cover, 1–3.

38. Lindsy Van Gelder, "When Women Confront Street Porn," *Ms.*, February 1980, 64.

39. Bronstein, *Battling Pornography*, 288.

40. Califia, "Personal View," 255–57.

41. Women Against Violence in Pornography and Media, "Post Conference Actions," *Newspage*, February 1979, 10; Samois, "Our Statement," 4.

42. Van Gelder, "When Women Confront Street Porn," 64–66.

43. brooke, "life, liberty, & the pursuit of porn," *off our backs* 9, no. 1 (January 1979): 5; brooke, "Feminist Conference: Porn Again," *off our backs* 9, no. 10 (November 1979): 24; Andrea Dworkin, "Speech Exhorts March," *off our backs* 9, no. 1 (January 1979): 4.

44. Gloria Steinem, "Erotica and Pornography: A Clear and Present Difference," *Ms.*, November 1978, 54. It should be noted that Steinem was not one of the avid antipornography activists, thus her stance indicates how mainstream the antiporn feminist position became over time.

45. brooke, "life, liberty, & the pursuit of porn," 5.

46. Andrea Dworkin, *Right-wing Women* (New York: Perigee, 1978), 58.

47. Steinem, "Erotica and Pornography," 54.

48. For examples, please see Robin Ruth Linden et al., eds., *Against Sadomasochism: A Radical Feminist Analysis* (East Palo Alto, CA: Frog in the Well, 1982); and Anonymous from Colchester, "Responses," *Lesbian Connection* 5, no. 3 (September 1981): 13–16.

49. Van Gelder, "When Women Confront Street Porn," 66–67.

50. "Philly Bookstore Defends Sale of Porn," *Advocate*, April 17, 1980, 9.

51. Pat Califia, "Among Us, Against Us—The New Puritans," *Advocate*, April 17, 1980, 14–18.

52. WAVPM, "Questions We Get Asked Most Often," *Newspage*, July 1980, 1–6; "Feminist Perspectives on Sadomasochism," flyer, "Lesbian S/M" file, Lesbian Herstory Archives, New York City (hereafter LHA).

53. "Feminist Perspectives on Sadomasochism," LHA; Linden et al., *Against Sadomasochism*.

54. Samois, "Samois Newsletter," June 1979–October 1980.

55. Califia, "Among Us, Against Us—The New Puritans"; for critiques, see Andrena Zawinski, "Lesbians and Pornography," *off our backs* 10, no. 7 (July 1980): 9; Alice Henry, "Managing Sex, Control, and Power," *off our backs* 10, no. 10 (November 1980): 16.

56. See reader letters contributed to *Lesbian Connection*, November 1979–September 1981; *Plexus*, August–November 1980.

57. Letters to Samois from *off our backs*, *Big Mama Rag*, and *Inciter*, "Samois" vertical file, LHA.

58. "NOW Supports Lesbian Issues, but Veers Right on Boy-Love, S&M," *Body Politic*, December 1980 / January 1981, 23; "NEWS FLASH: Lesbian and Gay Rights," *Heresies*, Spring 1981, 93.

59. "Editorial," "Publication Information Page," and "Sex Issue," *Heresies*, Spring 1981, 1, 97, table of contents.

60. Pat Califia, "Feminism and Sadomasochism," *Heresies*, Spring 1981, 30.

61. Paula Webster, "Pornography and Pleasure," *Heresies*, Spring 1981, 48–50.

62. Ibid.

63. Ibid., 51.

64. Katherine Davis, "Introduction: What We Fear We Try to Keep Contained," in Samois, *Coming to Power* (Boston: Alyson Publications, 1982), 8.

65. Ibid, 7–14.

66. LSM, "Lesbian S/M," flyer, Fall 1981, "Lesbian S/M Support Group" vertical file, LHA.

67. Alice Walker, "A Letter of the Times," *Ms.*, October 1981, 63–64.

68. Ibid.

69. Cherríe Moraga and Amber Hollibaugh, "What We're Rollin' around in Bed With," (1983), in Hollibaugh, *My Dangerous Desires: A Queer Girl Dreaming Her Way Home* (Durham, NC: Duke University Press, 2000), 82.

70. Barbara Ehrenreich, Elizabeth Hess, and Gloria Jacobs, "A Report on the Sex Crisis," *Ms.*, March 1982, 61–68.

71. Ibid.

CHAPTER 11

Suppressing the Revolt of the Perverts

Gay Activist Filmmaking and the Child Pornography Panic of the Late 1970s

GREG YOUMANS

N 1977, TWO COMPONENTS of contemporary U.S. culture and politics appeared on the national stage and captured mass media attention: the gay rights movement and the moral panic around child sexual endangerment. They were, and remain, intimately entwined, together demarcating the legal and cultural boundaries of sexual citizenship. At the center of the gay rights movement is the "positive image" of the upstanding gay citizen, no different from heterosexual peers except for a sexual desire that is safely confined to consensual acts within the privacy of the bedroom (and, more recently, the institution of marriage). By contrast, at the center of the moral panic around child sexual endangerment is the "negative image" of the gay pedophile, a shadowy lurker whose perverse desire and predilection for child pornography threaten the normative sexual development of young boys and endanger the heterosexual family.

The gay rights movement and the moral panic around child sexual endangerment became entangled in a historic 1977 battle over gay rights in Dade County, Florida. Organizers of the Save Our Children campaign, which was publicly affiliated with singer Anita Bryant and is recognized as the first formal opposition to the gay rights movement, rallied opposition to an antidiscrimination, pro–gay rights ordinance by painting gay teachers as pedophiles who sought to recruit innocent boys into a deviant lifestyle. Other antigay activists took up this tactic and used it to fuel copycat campaigns across the nation from 1977 to 1979. Scholarship on the gay rights struggles of the late 1970s has emphasized the rise of the Christian Right and its role in antigay activism but has downplayed the centrality of the moral panic around child sexual endangerment.[1] When scholarship does mention the panic, it is characterized either as a hysteria that antigay activists got caught up in or as a convenient red herring that they cynically exploited.[2] In both cases, the scholarship gives the impression that social conservatives in the late 1970s improperly conflated two distinct categories: pedophilia and homosexuality.

There are at least two significant drawbacks to this framing of the history. First, it naturalizes the distinction between intragenerational homosexuality (i.e., between people within the same age group) and intergenerational homosexuality (i.e., across age groups), thereby obscuring how this very distinction was constructed and enforced through the events of the late 1970s. Second, it suggests that gay activists, in contradistinction to social conservatives, confronted the late 1970s panic calmly and never strayed in terms of their own political agenda. In this chapter, however, I demonstrate that the moral panic around child sexual endangerment significantly reshaped gay activist goals and strategies. On the one hand, it positioned a particularly desexualized version of liberal rights activism as the mainstream of U.S. gay and lesbian politics, a precursor to the almost exclusive focus in recent years on the right to marry. On the other hand, it channeled queer radicals, i.e., those activists who were critical of gay liberalism, away from an earlier gay-liberationist stance and toward a less oppositional sexual-libertarian one.

In this chapter I deploy the critical framework of "moral panic" despite the limitations and perhaps even the dangers of the term. By applying "moral panic" to the late-1970s concern about child sexual endangerment, the aim is not to "debunk" that concern, in other words, to insist that because so many of the claims were hyperbolic that the problem itself was illusory. Child sexual abuse exists, and new dimensions of the problem arguably came to light in the late 1970s. Nevertheless, "moral panic" is a useful analytical framework, as opposed to more apparently neutral terms such as "the social construction of problems" or "the rhetoric of child-protectionism," because it foregrounds the primacy of emotion and the sidelining of reason that were evident in assessments and responses to child sexual abuse.[3] In the late 1970s, gay rights activists were suddenly confronted with an issue that challenged their own agenda and short-circuited any attempt at a direct, dispassionate, or rational response. Regardless of whether these activists had anything to contribute to addressing the real problem of child sexual abuse—and, certainly, much of gay-liberationist analysis was underdeveloped and overly romantic in its understanding of youth sexuality—it is clear that many gay activists entered the late 1970s with an understanding that intergenerational relationships were not, by definition, abusive. Indeed, this understanding would become foundational to the field of queer theory through its articulation in Gayle Rubin's path-setting 1984 essay, "Thinking Sex."[4] At the same time, the moral panic and the entrenchment of a rights-oriented mainstream within gay politics precipitated the loss, suppression, and tactical sidelining of this viewpoint. As importantly, the ability or willingness of gay activists to engage directly and candidly with the topic of youth homosexuality was also inhibited in the late 1970s. Activists were anxious to distinguish themselves from pedophiles and careful to ensure that their representations, especially films, did not contain material that could invite the label of child pornography, a category that enjoyed almost no quarter at the end of the otherwise porn-positive 1970s.

In 1977, child pornography established itself as a representational black hole: an absent center that was impossible to look at directly (through a combination of interdiction and real absence) yet paradoxically able to function as indexical evidence of a widespread corruption of youth. As a vacuum, it asserted a powerful pull on peripheral issues, including adult pornography, obscenity law, sexual education, law enforcement practices, and the rights of the accused, in addition to gay rights.[5] After tracing the history and politics of the panic, I will turn in the second half of the chapter to an analysis of the efforts of gay activist media makers to resist it, with particular attention to what was likely the most transgressive queer documentary of the era, Rosa von Praunheim's 1979 film *Army of Lovers, or Revolt of the Perverts*.

Praunheim's film offers a tour of sexually marginalized groups within the United States that includes a visit with self-proclaimed "boy-lovers" in Boston, and it makes a strong case for their legitimacy as sexual citizens despite police harassment and social opprobrium. At the same time, the film evinces great difficulty in representing this group: in contrast to the sexual frankness of other parts of the film (on sadomasochism, cruising, and pornography involving adult gay men), the section on intergenerational relationships is marked by circumlocutions on the audio track and lacunae in the visual track. The late-1970s panic initiated waves of ever more intensive legislation against child pornography over the next four decades; meanwhile, frank discussion and representation of these issues have become increasingly scarce within queer politics. A number of theorists have explored the difficulty of mustering opposition to pernicious political developments when they are presented as being in the best interests of children.[6] In this chapter I explore the historical roots of that political and conceptual impasse.

The Entangled Origins of the Gay Rights Movement and the Moral Panic around Child Sexual Endangerment

The late-1970s entrenchment of gay rights organizing signaled the end of the liberationist period of the late 1960s and early 1970s, when groups such as the Gay Liberation Front, Radicalesbians, and Third World Gay Liberation had pursued a more radical and transformative activism often informed by Marxist analysis. At the same time, rights organizing has had an unbroken history within U.S. gay activism since the 1950s, when it was a central component of the pioneering work of the Mattachine Society and the Daughters of Bilitis, groups that took much of their inspiration, analysis, and tactics from the African American civil rights movement.[7]

During the first half of the 1970s, much gay rights activism occurred behind the scenes and without much fanfare. Fred Fejes points out that by January 1977, more than thirty-five cities, counties, and states had laws and policies protecting lesbians and gay men from discrimination, many of which were passed into law as logical and noncontroversial extensions of the federal Civil Rights Act of 1964 that barred discrimination on the basis of "race, color, religion, sex, or national origin." A similar scenario was unfolding when the Dade County Metro Commission heard the proposed amendment to its own civil rights law in December 1976 and voted unanimously to bring it to a second and final vote on January 18, 1977.[8] Historian Gillian Frank explains that this particular ordinance was "groundbreaking not in its passage but rather in the massive resistance it engendered from religious groups and conservatives."[9] These actors came together to fight the ordinance under the banner of the Save Our Children campaign. After the county commissioners voted the ordinance into law that January, the group gathered almost sixty thousand signatures, six times the required amount, to bring the ordinance to referendum. This would allow the voters to decide the matter for themselves and offered the possibility of repeal.

From the middle of March 1977 until the June 7 vote, Save Our Children waged an intensive campaign to build opposition to the ordinance. In public appearances, direct mailings, and newspaper ads, they evoked a threat to children and schools. Because the law would make it illegal to discriminate against gay teachers, they argued that parents would not be able to prevent children from encountering openly gay role models and pro-gay teachings. They claimed that the law thus violated the "civil rights of parents" to oversee the moral education of their children. This relatively polite argument was paired with a more sinister one: spokesperson Anita Bryant famously said, "homosexuals cannot reproduce—they must recruit." This language of "recruiting" encompassed everything from role modeling and mentoring to sexual seduction and molestation. Many of the group's mailings and flyers featured collages of newspaper articles about same-sex child sexual abuse, suggesting that the ordinance was an open invitation for predatory gay pedophiles to flood Florida schools.[10] Bryant was a national celebrity: a former beauty queen, popular singer, and the advertising spokesperson for Florida orange juice. As a result, news media far beyond Dade County covered the story.[11]

The 1977 ordinance campaign signaled the arrival of the Christian Right as a major force in U.S. politics. It became a central player in the "New Right" coalition that would support the 1980 presidential election of Ronald Reagan. The New Right foregrounded what it termed "family values" issues, including abortion, pornography, homosexuality, and feminism, rather than—or, as many commentators have argued, as a screen for—the discredited "Old Right" agenda of racial segregation, as well as the Reaganite, procorporate agenda of economic deregulation and privatization.[12] The Christian Right's ability to set the U.S. cultural and political agenda in the late 1970s spurred what Fejes characterizes as "the first major national debate about gay rights."[13] This high-stakes battle against a newly organized opponent in turn provoked unprecedented unity and collaboration among U.S. gay and lesbian activists, who formed a national network to send people, money, and tactical know-how to Miami. After Save Our Children succeeded in repealing the Dade County ordinance in June, this national network shifted its support to other states and municipalities gripped by copycat antigay campaigns over the next two years.[14] The idea of a unified national gay and lesbian movement focused primarily on rights activism took shape for the first time at this moment in the late 1970s.

Save Our Children's campaign was apparently inspired by the activism of law-enforcement personnel. Bryant told an interviewer that she first learned of the homosexual threat to children when "a local police sergeant gave a presentation in our church basement with slides and all about child pornography and it shocked our whole congregation."[15] In 1977, Bryant stood alongside a number of law-enforcement officials, politicians, and social workers who publicized the dangers that children faced from child pornographers, pedophile rings, and sex traffickers. Their actions prompted congressional hearings on the subject to determine the shape and scope of the problem and whether new legislation was needed.[16] The hearings resulted in the Protection of Children Against Sexual Exploitation Act of 1977, which made it a crime to produce or distribute obscene visual depictions of persons under sixteen years of age for interstate or foreign commerce.[17]

However reasonable this law may have appeared, the characterizations of the problem motivating its passage had all the hallmarks of a moral panic. The term "moral panic" refers to moments when public imagination suddenly seizes on a "folk devil," a figure or group perceived to pose an imminent threat to the social order.[18] In his prepared statement to the House Subcommittee on Crime, Robert Leonard, the president-elect of the National Association of District Attorneys, described a sudden pandemic of child abuse: "We're here today to address a problem that was virtually unrecognized as recently as six or eight months ago."[19] According to cultural historian Philip Jenkins, the term "child abuse" "acquired its modern implication of sexual exploitation" in 1977. Whereas earlier "child abuse" had conjured up images of physical harm and neglect, it now came to denote sexual violation that led to irreparable psychological damage.[20] The sudden awareness of and interest in the problem of child sexual abuse were coupled with a skewed and inflated characterization of its scope. Witnesses before Congress insisted that 1.2 million children were involved in an underground multimillion-dollar child pornography and prostitution industry, but they offered little evidence. These initial claims escalated as they were taken up and repeated by journalists and other advocates.[21] Sensational examples of worst-case scenarios, sometimes actual and sometimes not, circulated widely.[22] Moreover, the child sexual endangerment panic of the late 1970s focused inor-

dinately on "stranger danger," threats from pedophiles lurking outside the home, despite the far greater prevalence of child sexual abuse
perpetrated by family members and others known to the victim.
Particularly in an era when gay families were less visible, this distinction between stranger danger and familial abuse mapped tidily onto
the distinction between homosexuality and heterosexuality and is an
indication of the homophobia that fueled the panic.

Indeed, the specter of homosexual pedophilia haunted the congressional hearings in 1977. Witnesses painted a picture of vast networks
of wealthy homosexual boy-lovers funding a trade in prostitutes
and pornography. Child-welfare advocate and psychiatrist Judianne
Densen-Gerber presented the committee with statistics on child prostitution derived from Robin Lloyd's *For Money or Love: Boy Prostitution
in America,* a 1976 book that had helped spur the panic by claiming
that some 300,000 boys were being victimized. Leonard made it clear
that, for him, one of the most dire consequences that sexual abuse
could produce in a (male) child was "a reversal of his heterosexual
identification." However small the proportion of homosexuals within
the general population, the witnesses seemed certain that they were
overrepresented among pedophiles.[23]

Six of the ten sessions of the congressional hearings, which were
heavily reported and partially televised, occurred less than two weeks
before the June 7 vote in Dade County. In the six months leading up to
the vote, the national media lent credibility to the Save Our Children
cause by publishing and broadcasting an unprecedented number of
stories on child pornography, prostitution, and sexual abuse. *Time*
magazine published an exposé titled "Child's Garden of Perversity"
on April 4. *The Chicago Tribune* ran a major multipart series from May
15 through May 18.[24] NBC aired *Alexander: The Other Side of Dawn,* a
made-for-television movie about a teenage hustler and the adult gay
men who exploit him, on May 16. That same day, a reviewer in the
New York Times connected the movie to a segment on "Kiddie Porn"
that had aired on CBS's *60 Minutes* the night before.[25] The relationship
between media coverage of child sexual abuse and antigay organizing
was especially close in Miami, where, between January and June 1977,
local papers reprinted many articles published elsewhere. In a sense,
the Miami papers scoured the nation's headlines on behalf of Save
Our Children, making it easier for the group to pull together the collages that it then published in the local papers as full-page advertisements urging repeal of the gay rights ordinance.[26] These overlaps sug-

gest that antigay organizing and the moral panic around child sexual endangerment were not distinct developments: the journalists and congressional witnesses of the era, with their statistically unfounded overemphasis on stranger danger and same-sex child sexual abuse, were actors in antigay organizing, just as Anita Bryant and the other organizers of Save Our Children were among the main instigators and propagators of the panic.

The Representational Black Hole of Child Pornography

Child pornography was central to the late 1970s panic around the sexual exploitation of children. Although Congress heard testimony in 1977 on a range of related issues, including child sexual abuse, intergenerational sex, and child prostitution, the resulting federal legislation pertained only to the production and distribution of child pornography. Likewise, in two important articles published in 1980 in the gay magazine the *Advocate*, author and SM activist Pat Califia framed the interconnected events and issues as "The Great Kiddy-Porn Panic of '77."[27]

The primacy of child pornography to the panic of 1977 can be explained in several ways. First, child pornography had synecdochic value: child-protection crusaders understood it as being bound up with all aspects of the broader problem. By this logic, child pornography was an indexical record of child sexual abuse, an indicator of intergenerational desire, and an instance of commercial exploitation of child sexuality. Next, laws were already in place to prevent and/ or criminalize child sexual abuse, intergenerational sex, and child prostitution, but no federal law yet existed that specifically targeted child pornography. Finally, the existence of commercially produced and distributed child pornography in the United States was, by most accounts, a new development in the 1970s, one that arose in tandem with, though to a significantly lesser extent than, the commercial production and consumption of adult pornography, both gay and straight.

Child pornography statistics are notoriously unreliable. Densen-Gerber presented Congress with a trunk filled with child pornography at the start of her testimony and proceeded to brandish magazines and read salacious titles aloud. She testified that she had counted "264 different magazines produced each month" containing child pornography.[28] In the late 1980s, attorney and scholar Lawrence Stanley sought to debunk the panic and conducted a content analysis of commercially available child pornography-related publications in the United States and Europe from the late 1960s to the mid-1970s. He found approximately 1065 issues (not monthly magazines) that contained at least one depiction of minors (under the age of sixteen) engaged in sexual activity or presenting lewd or lascivious exhibition of the genitals.[29] Despite the discrepancies between these two sets of findings, together they indicate that child pornography circulated commercially and aboveground in the 1970s to a degree that is unimaginable today.

Notwithstanding the trunk at her side, Densen-Gerber told Congress that since the beginning of 1977, when she had first started giving press conferences and picketing businesses to raise concern about child pornography, "much of 'kid porno' ha[d] disappeared from the Nation's adult book stores." Stanley's analysis from 1989 supports this point: he claimed that the "relatively insignificant" market of the 1970s had dried up by the 1980s, though some child pornography continued to be made in small quantities on a noncommercial basis.[30] Unlike Stanley, Densen-Gerber insisted that child pornography had not dried up but had gone underground, where it became all the more sinister and dangerous.

One of the most enduring results of the late 1970s panic has been the steady stream of child pornography legislation that has been produced since that time, legislation that is increasingly expansive and punitive. In the 1982 *Ferber* decision, the U.S. Supreme Court decoupled "child pornography" from "obscenity," thereby expanding the definition of the former and removing it from First Amendment protections. Justice Byron White explained that a work "need not be 'patently offensive' in order to have required the sexual exploitation of a child."[31] In 1984, federal lawmakers updated the Child Protection Act to follow suit and raised the age of majority for participation in pornography from sixteen to eighteen. The act also made possession of child pornography a crime, whereas before the law had been restricted to production and distribution.[32] In subsequent cases, judges found nudity alone to be sufficient grounds for prosecution, in the absence of sexual activity or even "lewd exhibition of the genitals." In response to the rise of the porn-saturated internet and new computer-imaging technologies in the 1990s, lawmakers proposed legislation that would outlaw not only photography-based child pornography but also digitally created images of what *appear to be* minors engaging in sexual acts. Many of these laws were struck down through court challenge, but the 2003 PROTECT Act (the Prosecutorial Remedies and Other Tools to End the Exploitation of Children Today Act) stuck: it makes virtual child pornography prosecutable and has resulted in the conviction, among others, of a collector of Japanese manga featuring drawings of clearly fictitious children.[33]

In his book *Perversion for Profit: The Politics of Pornography and the Rise of the New Right,* Whitney Strub traces the history of child pornography laws, convictions, and case precedents from the late 1970s to 2009, presenting it as a stair-step dismantling of the original insistence on a connection between child pornography and the actual abuse of children.[34] There has always been a tension in legal definitions of pornography between the object and the beholder, between such qualifiers as "lewd depiction of the genitals" on one hand and "intended for prurient use" on the other. Considering that the scope of prosecution now encompasses the private consumption of clearly fictive, nondocumentary drawings, child pornography law seems to be more concerned with stamping out deviant desire than it is with ending actual child sexual abuse. In a 2011 article, legal scholar Carissa Byrne Hessick explores the now-frequent phenomenon of sentences for the mere possession of child pornography exceeding sentences meted out for the actual sexual abuse of children. Hessick attributes this odd state of affairs "not to conscious legislative design, but rather to the piling on of various sentencing enhancements"; for instance, many states now multiply sentences by the number of images an offender possesses.[35] At the same time, it is important to keep in mind that the legal and cultural disproportionality between child pornography and child sexual abuse is rooted in the heteronormativity that shaped the panic from the beginning: the conceptual distinction between these crimes maps onto the distinction between stranger danger and familial abuse, which maps in turn, as already pointed out, onto the distinction between homosexuality and heterosexuality. In this way, the child pornography panic is an obfuscation and a distraction from the prevalence of sexual abuse within the heterosexual family.

Cinema and Moral Panic

The moral panic around child sexual endangerment gained strength as the object at its center, child pornography, disappeared from public view. By the end of 1977, child pornography had established itself as a black hole of representation at the national level—Densen-Gerber's trunk had closed—and became capable of pulling other issues, including gay rights, across its event horizon. As a result, a number of miniature black holes began to appear in gay-produced media of the time, as filmmakers endeavored to produce frank depictions of youth homosexuality and intergenerational relationships but found that they could not represent them directly.

Jon Davies offers a pertinent discussion of "black holes of representation" in an article about the wave of independent narrative features in the mid-2000s that deal with pedophilia, such as *The Heart Is Deceitful above All Things* (dir. Asia Argento, 2004), *Mysterious Skin* (dir. Gregg Araki, 2004), and *The Woodsman* (dir. Nicole Kassell, 2004).[36] These films circle visually around that which cannot be represented, namely the scene of an adult-child sexual encounter, and draw much of their narrative power from the magnetic pull of that absent center. Often, story lines trace the effort of a character to recollect and then heal from a repressed scene of trauma. This framework of repressed memory became entrenched in the 1980s, particularly through the work of psychiatrist Judith Herman.[37] It now maps tidily onto the black hole of representation originally created by the criminalization of child pornography: in other words, that which legally cannot be shown has become that which psychologically cannot be handled. However, this overdetermination was not yet established in the late 1970s, when filmmakers (both activist and mainstream) navigated the nascent panic.

Thomas Waugh and Jason Garrison offer a thorough history of narrative feature films about intergenerational relationships between men and boys in their study of the 1974 Canadian film *Montreal Main* (dir. Frank Vitale).[38] This particular film is an artifact of a pre-panic era, or at least of a liminal phase before the panic's full onset: characters in the film respond with concern to a budding unorthodox relationship between a twelve-year-old boy and a twenty-five-year-old man, but instead of imposing frameworks of criminalization, abuse, and trauma onto the relationship they (including the boy's mother) try to investigate it carefully through respectful discussions with both parties. Waugh and Garrison's roster of narrative films is international in scope, and though it includes a number of titles, many from continental Europe, going back to the early 1970s, it features very few U.S. titles from before the mid-1990s. When U.S. filmmakers broached the topic in earlier films, they tended to do so carefully and soberly, and more frequently through documentary than narrative fiction.[39]

Even the most measured gay-liberal documentary of the late 1970s,

Word Is Out: Stories of Some of Our Lives (dir. Mariposa Film Group, 1977), includes discussion of the topic of intergenerational sex. The two-hour film, which had a national PBS broadcast in 1978 and played a major role as an activist tool in the gay rights battles of the era, is comprised of talking-head interviews with a multigenerational cast of about twenty-five lesbians and gay men. Because a six-person collective (three men and three women) made the film and decided many things by informal committee, it is often difficult to determine why particular casting and editing choices were made.[40] However, it is evident that the film project became more circumspect in its representation of both intergenerational sex and youth sexuality across its four-year production history. Producer Peter Adair's original proposal for the film, dated 1974, included a projected scene (fictional but meant to stand in for what the documentary might include) in which a gym teacher reflects on an incident fifteen years earlier when he caught two high school students engaging in sexual activity in the showers.[41] One of the boys, who now identifies as gay (the other, we are told, is straight), is also interviewed, and his statement that "the whole thing was really a nightmare for us" clearly points the finger not at adolescent sexual experimentation but at the ignorance and shamemongering of adult authority figures. The filmmakers also preinterviewed more than a hundred people on videotape before choosing their final cast. Adair conducted one of these interviews with a young man, Dominic Ybarro, who was likely seventeen or eighteen years old at the time and who spoke positively about sexual encounters across the age of consent beginning with his first experience when he was "thirteen or fourteen": "But I wasn't molested or raped or anything, I knew what was going on, I wanted to experience it, I wanted to have sex with a male." When the other collective members reviewed the tape, they recognized that Ybarro was "probably pretty special" in his attitude and experience, but there is no indication in their notes that they felt the subject matter was unacceptable or taboo or should not be included in the film.[42]

Somewhere along the way, the filmmakers became more careful. In the release version of the film, the younger cohort of interviewees (all of them eighteen to thirty-five years old, none younger) is remarkably coy on the topic of sex, even about sexual activity with people their own age. By contrast, the older generation (thirty-five and over) reminisces frankly about sexual experiences, including Rick Stokes, George Mendenhall, and Mark Pinney, who all seem to have had positive sexual encounters across the age of consent when they were minors. By restricting such tales to older people, the film relegates the behavior to the pre-Stonewall past. Only Mendenhall makes a statement that clearly engages with the rhetoric of the Save Our Children campaign, which was ramping up in the film's final year of production. He recalls that when he was a young teenager he tried, unsuccessfully, to cruise older men: "It's very amusing to me where you consider that an adult male is being accused of molesting a person that age when he has sex with him, when actually, at that age, fourteen, fifteen, I was the aggressor, definitely the aggressor." Mendenhall could not understand why none of the men responded, but later on someone explained to him that they were afraid of the law, "which was very restrictive, and the laws say that children don't have sex, you know, children don't have sex lives, and that if they do they are being forced into sex with adults which is a bunch of baloney."[43] It is remarkable that a gay-liberal film included such a statement; it would be hard to imagine one doing so today. At the same time, the overall design of *Word Is Out*, especially its desexualized presentation of gay young people, indicates how carefully the filmmakers were negotiating the moral panic around child sexual endangerment.[44]

Army of Lovers and the Limits of Sexual Libertarianism

Rosa von Praunheim's 1979 documentary *Army of Lovers, or Revolt of the Perverts* is in many respects a work of counteractivism to the gay-liberal approach exemplified by *Word Is Out*. Praunheim's film foregrounds sexual imagery, refuses to trade in "positive images," and never presents a fantasy of a socially and ideologically unified gay and lesbian movement. The West German filmmaker established himself as an enfant terrible of queer cinema with his 1971 film *Nicht der Homosexuelle ist pervers, sondern die Situation in der er lebt (It Is Not the Homosexual Who Is Perverse but the Society in Which He Lives)*, a camp Marxist manifesto that indicted gay men for egotism, self-hatred, and the aping of bourgeois conventions. When Praunheim toured this film to New York City in 1971, he became profoundly interested in U.S. gay politics, at a time when the gay-liberationist spirit of the late 1960s still filled the air. Upon returning a few years later, in 1974 and 1975, he was saddened to find the situation markedly changed: "There was no longer any trace of the revolutionary spirit that had made such a promising start."[45] But then, when the San Francisco Art Institute invited him to be a visiting filmmaker in 1977, he was heartened to see gay people's spirited response to the Save Our Children campaign, including the dramatic spike in attendance at the city's Gay Freedom Day Parade that summer. For Praunheim, "Anita Bryant [was] the best thing that ever happened to the gay movement." Unlike many other lesbians and gay men of the time, he did not believe Bryant was a nut whose extreme rhetoric and fundamentalism would make gays and lesbians look reasonable and respectable by contrast. Instead, he believed she was expressing the actual sentiment of middle-class, straight liberals, and this realization would provoke gay people to "stand up and see that it's not enough to adapt to and integrate into society as a gay person because we will always be vulnerable, even if we get to be rich capitalist pigs."[46] During this period, Praunheim conceived of a documentary project on U.S. gay activism under the working title "From Stonewall to Anita."[47] *Army of Lovers* premiered two years later, in March 1979.

The feature-length documentary begins with a quick, rough survey of twentieth-century gay political history and then turns in its second half to an ethnographic tour of different queer subcultures. It introduces such denizens of the margins as sadomasochistic porn star and filmmaker Fred Halsted, hustler and writer John Rechy, and even Los Angeles's leading gay Nazi. Praunheim gets in front of the camera to engage in sexual foreplay with Halsted in the bushes on the side of a road in a setting reminiscent of the pastoral first sequence of Halsted's 1972 film *LA Plays Itself*. *Army of Lovers* also includes footage of an innovative lesson from Praunheim's class at the art institute, for which he invited "Glenn, a model [he] had seen in a porno movie," to have sex with him as his students circled around them and filmed the encounter. The lesson reflects Praunheim's belief that gay liberation required a wholesale transformation of sexual mores, which he insisted required an honest, open look at queer sexual practices and subcultures.

But nothing in the film is as provocative as its nonstigmatizing presentation of "man-boy love." In a sequence toward the end of the film, Praunheim interviews boy-lover and activist Tom Reeves as well as one of the defendants in a notorious "pedophile sex ring" controversy that erupted in Revere, Massachusetts, outside of Boston, in 1977. More than any other part of *Army of Lovers*, this sequence on intergenerational sex seemed to risk playing into the hands of antigay activists. It is also arguably the most restrained section of the film. The visuals are remarkably tame after an hour and a half's insistence on the political importance and liberatory potential of pornography. As with *Word Is Out*, *Army of Lovers* largely restricts its engagement with the issues of youth homosexuality and intergenerational relationships to spoken analysis on the voiceover track. Nowhere is the moral panic's power to circumscribe and censor queer representations of the sexual margins more apparent than in this ostensibly radical film's faltering effort to engage these topics candidly and coherently.

The political viewpoint of *Army of Lovers* can best be characterized as *sexual libertarianism,* a position caught between the gay-liberationist politics of a decade earlier and the gay-liberal politics dominant in the late 1970s. Like gay liberals, sexual libertarians were primarily concerned with rights; the difference was that sexual libertarians made the case that marginalized people have the right to citizenship not because of their ability to practice self-restraint or good behavior, but because the government itself does not (or should not) have the right to encroach on anyone's personal freedom except in cases where a person's actions infringe on the health or freedom of others. Regarding the issue of intergenerational sex, sexual libertarians were less anxious than gay liberals to insist on a categorical distinction between homosexuality and pedophilia. They moved instead in the direction of a more classically gay-liberationist position, which insisted that cross-generational desire is a natural part of the sexuality of all people and advocated its decriminalization as part of a larger project of creating a less oppressed, oppressive, and hypocritical society. But alongside this gay-liberationist frame of analysis, sexual libertarians also deployed the language and tactics of civil rights organizing, insisting that there were distinct sexual minorities defined by their sexual practices, including a "sexual fringe" of boy-lovers, sadomasochists, fetishists, and so forth, and that these minorities, no matter how socially stigmatized, were entitled to basic rights (freedoms from discrimination, from invasions of privacy, and from restrictions on speech and sexual expression) because their practices were consensual and of no harm to anyone else.[48] Praunheim's film is an example of the displacement of a gay-liberationist position by a more centrist sexual-libertarian one in the late 1970s. Because the latter position was less ideologically distinct from gay liberalism, it had more trouble articulating a strong political opposition to it.

The film's discussion of intergenerational sex is nested within a longer sequence about age and homosexuality. The sequence begins with a segment on the G40+ Club, a support group for gay men over forty, many of whom express dissatisfaction with the youthful orientation of gay-male culture. The members are shown seated around the perimeter of a barren white room in what is presumably a community center. This is followed by a segment on a group called Coming Out, whose meeting unfolds in a similarly sterile space. A teenager named Ann explains that the group is designed to get young gay people off the street and into a space where there's not "too many old people" and where they can socialize with peers. After Ann's statement, the camera moves to the other end of the couch to focus, somewhat unrelentingly, on a boy named Paul. On the audio track, which is not synched to the image, Paul says that he first knew he had romantic and physical feelings for men—"in fact, I rephrase that: for males"—when he was eleven years old and had an intense friendship with another boy at summer camp; however, he grew up in a strict and sexually repressive family, so he did not act on such feelings until he was older. He says he decided he was gay at age fifteen. As Paul says all of this, the image track presents him fidgeting, smiling shyly, laughing, and speaking (inaudibly) to the rest of the group off-camera. He seems uncomfortable as he tries to return the camera's gaze, breaks off, and then tries again. From one perspective, Praunheim seems to be bringing predatory adult desire into what has been presented as a safe space for queer teens. From another, it is only the moral panic that would lead anyone to view the extended shot of Paul with discomfort or suspicion. A second statement from Ann provides a sound bridge to the segment of the film on boy-lover and activist Tom Reeves. Ann says that she mainly hangs out with gay men, and that she wishes she had the company of an older woman sometimes: "I wish somebody sat down with me and told me what was the game of being gay." The edit implies that Reeves and other boy-lovers provide this kind of mentorship to gay boys.

As the new segment begins, the American-voiced commentator of the film, Mike Shephard, explains that Reeves teaches contemporary politics at a predominantly black college in Boston and came out publicly as a boy-lover in February 1978. Shephard's commentary is ideologically aligned with Reeves, insisting that he and his fellow boy-lover activists "fight with openness and great courage since contention over the human rights of young people is the hottest gay issue in America today." For much of the segment, Reeves is shown driving through Boston in a banal shot taken from the passenger seat of the car. Meanwhile, on the audio track, Reeves presents an argument for intergenerational relationships that is strongly liberationist in flavor. He insists that man-boy love is a challenge to the nuclear family and mandatory heterosexuality, and he boldly courts the Save Our Children campaign's infamous rationale that homosexuals cannot reproduce, so they must recruit:

> Well yeah, I think the gay movement has said that we don't recruit children and that we're not interested in adolescents. Well I'm interested in recruiting teenagers and I'm interested in recruiting every gay teenager that's out there. I want him to know he's gay. I want him to be proud of it as soon as possible, as early as possible. I think if a teenager can know and be aware of his sexuality when he's thirteen, his whole life fits better for him than if he has to painfully struggle and find out when he's in his twenties. Also I'm very happy to say that I recruit people away from the middle-class, uptight violent family. That doesn't mean that a boy would necessarily be exclusively homosexual, but that he simply wouldn't want to reproduce exactly the robot kind of family that he grew up in and was unhappy in. I'd like to see everybody rebel against that. I'd like to see that disappear.[49]

Here Reeves expresses the liberationist idea that adolescent sexuality, once unleashed, will topple the heterosexual family. At the same time, this classically liberationist position is marred by internal contradictions that reflect the transformations of the late 1970s.

The main contradiction is that Reeves insists on a liberationist framing of boys' sexuality while insisting on a libertarian framing of the sexuality of adult boy-lovers. Before Reeves's statement, Shephard explains, "Tom and his family of young friends and lovers live among the working class, where boy-love is more accepted than by the repressive middle class." This statement is aligned with Reeves's own ideas, as expressed in the transcript of his full film interview included in the accompanying book to *Army of Lovers*. Here and elsewhere Reeves presents the working-class, Italian-American neighborhoods of Baltimore and Boston as places where boy-love is widely practiced and nonstigmatized.[50] For Reeves, working-class boys are a precivilized force that can liberate the overcivilized man from his behavioral and emotional shackles. This romantic conception of the liberatory potential of the sexuality of nonbourgeois young people was hardly new in the late 1970s: much of earlier gay-liberationist analysis harnessed Freudian ideas of the inherent polymorphous perversity of youth sexuality. However, liberationists argued that this polymorphous perversity was repressed but still existent in everyone, including ruling-class adults, and that it could be unleashed for the liberation and betterment of all.[51] This other half of the liberationist equation is hard to find in Reeves's analysis. Instead, the liberationist vision of working-class youth is awkwardly glued to a libertarian analysis of adult sexuality that was more viable to the struggle for rights. Reeves and other activist boy-lovers argued that adults were essentially fixed in their sexuality, that boy-lovers in particular constituted an unchangeable identity and a bounded sexual community, and, as such, that they were deserving of the same rights and protections as the parallel and separate class of adult-desiring homosexuals.[52]

This application of a civil-rights model of organizing to the issue of man-boy love was almost entirely a product of the late-1970s moral panic and the gay-liberal turn. District attorney Robert Leonard urged fellow district attorneys in the spring of 1977 to rid their respective communities of child molesters and child pornography. Garrett Byrne, the district attorney for Massachusetts' Suffolk County, which is comprised of Boston and three smaller towns, including Revere, heard the message. He was facing reelection in 1978 and saw the merit in Leonard's crusade. In December 1977, Byrne indicted twenty-four men on over one hundred felony counts: rape and abuse of a child under sixteen, sodomy, unnatural acts, open and gross lewdness, and indecent assault. The district attorney's office told the press that they had uncovered a "sex ring" involving the exploitation of boys ranging from eight to thirteen years old who had been lured to prostitution, pornography, and molestation with the temptation of games, drugs, and money. (It later came to light that in all but one of the indictments the boys were thirteen to fifteen years old.) The day after the arrests, the names and addresses of fifteen of the men appeared on the front page of the *Boston Herald–American*.[53]

A group of gay men, including Reeves, many of them on the collective of the Boston anarchist gay men's publication *Fag Rag*, organized to contest the district attorney's actions and aid the accused men. They formed the Boston/Boise Committee (B/BC), whose title connected the events around Boston to a similar panic over intergenerational gay male sex in Boise in the 1950s. The B/BC managed to convince all but one of the Revere defendants to demand an open trial, which did much to defuse the shame and secrecy that fuels a panic. The B/BC also set up a legal subcommittee to assist men accused of non-forcible sex with a minor. This committee sponsored the December 2, 1978, meeting that gave rise to the North American Man Boy Love Association (NAMBLA), the contemporary advocacy group for adult-youth relationships. Through the founding of this group, boy-lovers publicly demanded rights for themselves (as well as for youth, though more complicatedly so) through a civil rights framework.[54]

In the final segment of the film's extended sequence on homosexuality and age, one of the Revere defendants is filmed from behind as he walks along the waterfront. On the audio track, he worries what the future holds for him after his arrest on December 8, 1977, on the charge of "child rape" of a boy who he says was fourteen or fifteen years old at the time. "I can get a life term . . . depending on the whim of the judge. The minimum is five years. Five years for making what? For making love?" The man says that he himself first had sex with a man when he was thirteen. "I didn't grow up to be a monster. I grew up to be a champion." As the man is heard speaking, the visual track shows him talking to various teenage boys along his path. The camera lingers on the face, chest, and stomach of one teenager who takes a break from sunning himself to chat with the man. A few cutaway shots show other boys lying in the sun, horsing around, and posing for the camera.

Although this mise-en-scène is reminiscent of the pastoral outdoor settings that frame many of the film's other sequences about male sexuality, the visual approach is incongruous in virtually all other respects. In sequences focused on desire between adult men, the film presents kissing, touching, and sex on camera. Likewise, though the Boston scenes give a vague sense that sexually precocious and potentially available teenagers circulate around the boy-lovers, no apparent intergenerational couples, either fleeting or long-term, are shown. There are a number of possible reasons for this reticence: the criminalization of child pornography, the criminalization of intergenerational sex, the lack of real-world examples of such relationships for Praunheim to film, or his assessment of how best to shape the film's argument so as to reach potentially sympathetic viewers. It points as well, though, to the difficulty he had in bringing a liberationist framework to bear on the topics of youth homosexuality and intergenerational sex. In this extended sequence, the liberationist spirit evacuates the image track and takes refuge in the audio track, where it is restricted to manifesto-like statements by Reeves, the Revere defendant, and the film's narrator. In the images themselves there is neither an enveloping polymorphous perversity nor a pornotopian liberation through sex.[55]

Not surprisingly, *Army of Lovers* had a very different exhibition history than *Word Is Out*. The film's exposure was limited largely to urban gay audiences and the film literati who saw it at such high-culture venues as the Los Angeles Film Forum and the New York Museum of Modern Art. Even the gay activist viewers who criticized *Word Is Out* for soft-pedaling sex and politics did not necessarily praise Praunheim's more "radical" film. Many noted the film's idiosyncratic choices of content (e.g., the gay Nazi) and lack of a coherent ideological through line. Film scholar Richard Dyer argued that "a proliferation of instances does not amount to an analysis of the social situation of gay people" and criticized the film for its incoherent meshing of a freewheeling "libertarianism" with a dogmatic "vanguardism."[56] The muddled political stance of *Army of Lovers* reflects its historical moment in the late 1970s, when queer activists on the left were struggling to find their footing in the face of both a consolidating gay liberalism and a wider U.S. cultural and political shift to the right. In the same way, the reticence of the film's image track demonstrates that the moral panic around child sexual endangerment stripped these activists of any visual means of addressing or combating the panic that could not itself be construed as child pornography.

Not only has this predicament endured, it has gotten worse. As the mainstream media continues to generate and perpetuate child pornography scandals around such spurious targets as teenagers sexting each other and pencil-drawn American Apparel ads, gay rights activism has moved from its earlier emphasis on a broad spectrum of anti-discrimination protections for individuals to the much more narrow focus on "marriage equality." Just as in this chapter I have investigated the role of the moral panic around child sexual endangerment in pulling gay and lesbian politics away from radicalism and toward liberalism in the late 1970s, it behooves us to consider the part played by the ongoing panic in the recent emphasis on marriage, a cause that is intimately bound up with a politics of respectability, including the anxious need to demonstrate that monogamous, privatized, state-sanctioned gay couples can and do produce healthy (i.e., nonabused and nonperverted) children.[57] Considering these developments, it is unlikely that frank discussions of intergenerational relationships or an honest recognition of the sexuality of queer youth will become the norm within gay activist media anytime soon.

NOTES

1. See, for instance, Dudley Clendinen and Adam Nagourney, *Out for Good: The Struggle to Build a Gay Rights Movement in America* (New York: Simon & Schuster, 1999); Tina Fetner, *How the Religious Right Shaped Lesbian and Gay Activism* (Minneapolis: University of Minnesota Press, 2008); and Fred Fejes, *Gay Rights and Moral Panic: The Origins of America's Debate on Homosexuality* (New York: Palgrave Macmillan, 2008). Fejes's book is the most surprising in this regard considering its title. The book discusses the "concern over child pornography" (90–92) but does not deploy the term "moral panic" in relation to it; Fejes reserves the term instead to characterize the social anxiety over homosexuality during the era (19).

2. Patrick McCreery's work, however, stands apart for its nuanced discussion of the connection between the Save Our Children campaign and the moral panic around child sexual endangerment. See McCreery, "Miami Vice: Anita Bryant, Gay Rights, and Child Protectionism" (PhD diss., New York University, 2009); as well as McCreery, "Save Our Children / Let Us Marry: Gay Activists Appropriate the Rhetoric of Child Protectionism," *Radical History Review* 100 (2008): 186–207.

3. As examples, Joel Best uses the framework of "social construction of problems" in *Threatened Children: Rhetoric and Concern about Child-Victims* (Chicago: University of Chicago Press, 1990); and Patrick McCreery uses the framework of "the rhetoric of child-protectionism" in "Miami Vice" and "Save Our Children / Let Us Marry."

4. Gayle Rubin, "Thinking Sex: Notes for a Radical Theory of the Politics of Sexuality," in *Pleasure and Danger: Exploring Female Sexuality,* ed. Carole Vance (Boston: Routledge, 1984), 267–319. The essay was revised and expanded as the first chapter of the seminal queer-theory anthology *The Lesbian and Gay Studies Reader,* ed. Henry Abelove, Michèle Barale, and David Halperin (New York: Routledge, 1993), 3–44.

5. For work connecting the panic over child pornography and the larger moral panic around child sexual endangerment to these other issues, see Philip Jenkins, *Moral Panic: Changing Concepts of the Child Molester in Modern America* (New Haven: Yale University Press, 1998); Roger N. Lancaster, *Sex Panic and the Punitive State* (Berkeley: University of California Press, 2011); Chrysanthi S. Leon, *Sex Fiends, Perverts, and Pedophiles: Understanding Sex Crime Policy in America* (New York: New York University Press, 2011); Judith Levine, *Harmful to Minors: The Perils of Protecting Children from Sex* (Minneapolis: University of Minnesota Press, 2002); and Whitney Strub, *Perversion for Profit: The Politics of Pornography and the Rise of the New Right* (New York: Columbia University Press, 2011).

6. Lee Edelman, *No Future: Queer Theory and the Death Drive* (Durham, NC: Duke University Press, 2004); Lauren Berlant, *The Queen of America Goes to Washington City: Essays on Sex and Citizenship* (Durham, NC: Duke University Press, 1997).

7. For overviews of the history of U.S. gay activism from the 1950s through the 1970s, see John D'Emilio, *Sexual Politics, Sexual Communities: The Making of a Homosexual*

Minority in the United States, 1940–1970 (Chicago: University of Chicago Press, 1983); Clendinen and Nagourney, *Out for Good*; and Marc Stein, *Rethinking the Gay and Lesbian Movement* (New York: Routledge, 2012).

8. Fejes, *Gay Rights and Moral Panic*, 1–9, 53–83.

9. Gillian Frank, " 'The Civil Rights of Parents': Race and Conservative Politics in Anita Bryant's Campaign against Gay Rights in 1970s Florida," *Journal of the History of Sexuality* 22, no. 1 (January 2013): 126–60; quote at 141.

10. For the history of the 1977 battle over gay rights in Dade County, Florida, see Fejes, *Gay Rights and Moral Panic*; Frank, "Civil Rights of Parents"; and McCreery, "Miami Vice."

11. On Bryant, see Fejes, *Gay Rights and Moral Panic*, 78–79; Mark D. Jordan, *Recruiting Young Love: How Christians Talk about Homosexuality* (Chicago: University of Chicago Press, 2011), 129–49; and *Anita Bryant: The Woman Behind the Controversy*, special edition magazine (New York: Ideal Publishing Corporation, October 1978), a copy of which is housed in the Division of Rare and Manuscript Collections, Cornell University Library, Ithaca, NY.

12. Sara Diamond, *Roads to Dominion: Right-Wing Movements and Political Power in the United States* (New York: Guilford Press, 1995), 109–202. See also Frank, "Civil Rights of Parents," which connects the 1977 battle over gay rights in Dade County to recent and concurrent battles over the ratification of the Equal Rights Amendment and mandatory busing to desegregate schools. Frank demonstrates that child protectionism, including anxieties about the sexual endangerment of children, shaped all three issues.

13. Fejes, *Gay Rights and Moral Panic*, 4.

14. On the nationalization of the gay rights movement in the late 1970s, see Fejes, *Gay Rights and Moral Panic*, as well as Clendinen and Nagourney, *Out for Good*, 269–440.

15. Ken Kelley, "Playboy Interview: Anita Bryant," *Playboy*, May 1978, 74, 250, reprinted in *The Playboy Interview*, ed. G. Barry Golson (New York: Playboy Press, 1981), 550–77, quote at 553.

16. There were three sets of Congressional hearings held in 1977 on the topic of child sexual abuse and endangerment: "Sexual Exploitation of Children," Hearings before the Subcommittee on Crime of the Committee on the Judiciary, House of Representatives, 95th Cong., 1st Sess., held in Washington, DC, on May 23, May 25, June 10, and September 20, 1977; "Sexual Exploitation of Children," Hearings before the Subcommittee on Select Education of the Committee on Education and Labor, House of Representatives, 95th Cong., 1st Sess., held in Los Angeles on May 27 and 28, in New York City on May 31, and in Washington, DC, on June 10, 1977; and "Protection of Children Against Sexual Exploitation," Hearings before the Subcommittee to Investigate Juvenile Delinquency of the Committee on the Judiciary, U.S. Senate, 95th Cong., 1st Sess., held in Chicago on May 27 and in Washington, DC, on June 16, 1977. In sum, Congress's first investigation of the sexual exploitation of children involved hearings by one Senate and two House subcommittees across four cities and ten sessions.

17. Because anything "obscene" is already criminal, the law in its initial form was largely redundant, an example of the overkill characteristic of a moral panic. For analyses of the 1977 federal law, see David Shouvlin, "Preventing the Sexual Exploitation of Children: A Model Act," *Wake Forest Law Review* 17 (1981): 535–60; Lawrence Stanley, "The Child Porn Myth," *Cardozo Arts & Entertainment* 7 (1989): 295–358; and Annemarie J. Mazzone, "United States v. Knox: Protecting Children

from Sexual Exploitation through the Federal Child Pornography Laws," *Fordham Intellectual Property, Media, and Entertainment Law Journal* 5, no. 1 (1994): 167–234. These three legal scholars approach the law from varying ideological perspectives and with differing degrees of faith in the statistics and claims of the 1977 Congressional witnesses. The "interstate or foreign commerce" provision of the 1977 law is what defined the offence as a matter of federal rather than state law. Most of the state laws targeting child pornography developed along a parallel timeline to the federal law, though many of them are more punitive. On the varying sentencing provisions of the state laws, see Carissa Byrne Hessick, "Disentangling Child Pornography from Child Sex," *Washington University Law Review* 88, no. 4 (2011): 853–902.

18. The term "folk devil" comes from Stanley Cohen's pioneering book in the field, *Folk Devils and Moral Panics: The Creation of the Mods and Rockers,* 3rd ed. (1972; repr., London: Routledge, 2002).

19. *Sexual Exploitation of Children: Hearings before the Subcommittee on Crime of the Committee on the Judiciary, House of Representatives* (Washington, DC: GPO, 1977), 74.

20. Philip Jenkins, *Decade of Nightmares: The End of the Sixties and the Making of Eighties America* (New York: Oxford University Press, 2006), 13; see also the chapter "The Politics of Children: 1977," 108–33. Los Angeles police inspector Lloyd Martin referred to the sexual exploitation of children as "worse than homicide" in his testimony before Congress: "To me, a crime against a child has no equal. It's worse than a homicide. A homicide is terrible, but it's over with very shortly. The victim of sexual exploitation has to live the rest of his or her life with those memories of what pornography and sexual deviation brings [sic] upon them"; *Sexual Exploitation of Children: Hearings before the Subcommittee on Crime,* 62–63.

21. See *Sexual Exploitation of Children: Hearings before the Subcommittee on Crime* for Judianne Densen-Gerber's estimate that 1.2 million minors were victims of sexual exploitation in the United States (40). This was soon followed by her statement that it may be "in the neighborhood of 2 million" (46). Multiple witnesses testified before Congress to a "multimillion-dollar" industry of child pornography and prostitution, e.g., Lloyd Martin (61); Robert Leonard (74); and Kenneth Wooden (203). Densen-Gerber gave a series of press conferences throughout 1977 to raise awareness of the problem of child pornography at which she reportedly claimed that there was a $1 billion annual traffic in child pornography: "Group Protests Child Use in Pornographic Material," *New York Times,* February 15, 1977. A few years later, feminist child-welfare advocate Florence Rush stated that child pornography was a $2.4 billion industry without providing a source or offering other evidence to support the claim; Florence Rush, *The Best Kept Secret: Sexual Abuse of Children* (Englewood Cliffs, NJ: Prentice-Hall, 1980), 163. For more on the spurious statistical claims that fueled the panic, see Jenkins, *Moral Panic,* 146–48.

22. Sociologist Joel Best refers to these as "atrocity tales" in *Threatened Children,* 28–29. As an example, in his testimony before the House committee, Los Angeles police inspector Lloyd Martin told a perhaps apocryphal story of a seasoned eight-year-old boy prostitute who cruised Venice Beach looking for older men to sell sex to for ten dollars; *Sexual Exploitation of Children: Hearings before the Subcommittee on Crime,* 61.

23. *Sexual Exploitation of Children: Hearings before the Subcommittee on Crime,* 40 (Densen-Gerber), 76 (Leonard); see also the statement and testimony of Los Angeles police detective Lloyd Martin (57–73). Robin Lloyd testified before the House Subcommittee on Select Education in Los Angeles on May 27, 1977; *Sexual Exploitation of*

Children: Hearings before the Subcommittee on Select Education of the Committee on Education and Labor, House of Representatives (Washington, DC: GPO, 1977), 112–21. See Jenkins, *Moral Panic*, 121–25, for more on the antihomosexual sentiment on display throughout the 1977 Congressional hearings. A number of feminist activists also raised the alarm about the sexual exploitation of children in the late 1970s, among them Florence Rush and Gloria Steinem. They were often insistent that child sexual abuse and child pornography more frequently affected girls than boys. However, none of these avowed feminists testified before Congress, nor were their publications entered into the Congressional record. This would change a few years later when antipornography feminists played a significant role in the 1984 Meese Commission hearings. See Gloria Steinem, "Is Child Pornography . . . about Sex?" *Ms.*, August 1977, cover story, 43–44; Florence Rush, "Child Pornography," in *Take Back the Night: Women on Pornography*, ed. Laura Lederer (New York: William Morrow, 1980), 71–81; and Rush, *Best Kept Secret*.

24. "Child's Garden of Perversity," *Time*, April 4, 1977, 55–56. The *Chicago Tribune* series, reported by George Bliss and Michael Sneed, is reprinted in the appendix of *Protection of Children Against Sexual Exploitation: Hearings before the Subcommittee to Investigate Juvenile Delinquency of the Committee on the Judiciary, U.S. Senate* (Washington, DC: GPO, 1978), 130–50. (The *Tribune* reporters also testified before both the House and the Senate.) See also John Hurst, "Children—A Big Profit Item for the Smut Producers," *Los Angeles Times*, May 26, 1977.

25. John J. O'Connor, "TV: 'Alexander,' Effective Story of Male Hustler," *New York Times*, May 16, 1977. The transcript of the *60 Minutes* "Kiddie Porn" story is included in the appendix of *Protection of Children Against Sexual Exploitation*, 123–30. Mike Wallace reports at one point in the program, "Boys are more in demand for child pornography than girls, which, says Sergeant [Lloyd] Martin, is one reason Los Angeles is such a center for the industry. There are so many boys there hungry, alone, and available" (126).

26. Frank, "Civil Rights of Parents," 146.

27. Pat Califia, "The Age of Consent: The Great Kiddy-Porn Panic of '77" and "The Aftermath of the Great Kiddy-Porn Panic of '77," reprinted in *Public Sex: The Culture of Radical Sex*, 1st ed. (San Francisco: Cleis Press, 1994). Califia removed these two articles from the second edition of the book.

28. *Sexual Exploitation of Children: Hearings before the Subcommittee on Crime*, 42–43; Robin Lloyd, *For Money or Love: Boy Prostitution in America* (New York: Ballantine Books, 1976).

29. Stanley, "Child Porn Myth," 307–11. See also Lawrence Stanley, "The Hysteria over Child Pornography and Paedophilia," in *Dares to Speak: Historical and Contemporary Perspectives on Boy-Love*, ed. Joseph Geraci (London: Gay Men's Press, 1997), 179–206, in which he offers a similar count and content analysis though this time spanning from the late 1960s to 1982.

30. *Sexual Exploitation of Children: Hearings before the Subcommittee on Crime*, 42; Stanley, "Child Porn Myth," 310–11. Kenneth Wooden, who was the director of the National Coalition of Children's Justice and a producer of the *60 Minutes* segment "Kiddie Porn," countered Densen-Gerber's claim in his own testimony before Congress on September 20, 1977 (four months after Densen-Gerber had testified), insisting, "Child porn has not slowed to a trickle." *Sexual Exploitation of Children: Hearings before the Subcommittee on Crime*, 204.

31. White cited in Strub, *Perversion for Profit*, 196–97.

32. The 1984 amendments to the 1977 law are traced in Stanley, "Child Porn Myth,"

302–3; and Mazzone, "United States v. Knox," 179–86. Other amendments included the striking of the "commercial" provision and the raising of maximum fines.

33. For more on this issue, see Chuck Kleinhans, "Virtual Child Porn: The Law and the Semiotics of the Image," in *More Dirty Looks: Gender, Pornography, and Power*, ed. Pamela Church Gibson (London: BFI Publishing, 2004), 71–84.

34. Strub, *Perversion for Profit*, 256–97.

35. Hessick, "Disentangling Child Pornography," 861. In the article, Hessick investigates and challenges the arguments used by lawmakers to justify such harsh sentencing, for instance, the argument that these are preventative laws because possessors of child pornography are likely to engage eventually in child sexual abuse, so that by catching, punishing, and curbing the former, the law can help to prevent the latter. See Mazzone, "United States v. Knox," for a related discussion; unlike Hessick, Mazzone is supportive of these arguments from lawmakers and the expanded laws.

36. Jon Davies, "Imagining Intergenerationality: Representation and Rhetoric in the Pedophile Movie," *GLQ* 13, no. 2–3 (2007): 369–85.

37. Judith Lewis Herman, *Father-Daughter Incest* (Cambridge: Harvard University Press, 1981).

38. Thomas Waugh and Jason Garrison, *Montreal Main: A Queer Film Classic* (Vancouver, BC: Arsenal Pulp Press, 2010).

39. Arthur Bressan is a notable exception. For a discussion of his 1983 narrative feature *Abuse*, see Waugh and Garrison, *Montreal Main*, 217.

40. The Mariposa Film Group was comprised of Peter Adair, Nancy Adair, Andrew Brown, Rob Epstein, Lucy Massie Phenix, and Veronica Selver.

41. Peter Adair, "Coming Out: A Proposal for a Gay Film," in Peter Adair Papers (GLC 70), box 33, folder 26, James C. Hormel Gay and Lesbian Center, San Francisco Public Library, 5–6.

42. A viewing copy of the video preinterview with Ybarro, which was likely conducted in October 1975, is included in the Peter Adair Papers (GLC 70), box 64, James C. Hormel Gay and Lesbian Center, San Francisco Public Library. The videotape transcript and screening notes are in box 42, folder 76.

43. Mendenhall would have been fourteen in 1944, so he is recollecting an earlier, midcentury panic. See George Chauncey, "The Post-War Sex Crime Panic," in William Graebner, ed., *True Stories from the American Past* (New York: McGraw-Hill, 1993), 160–78; Estelle Freedman, "Uncontrolled Desires: The Response to the Sexual Psychopath, 1920–1960," *Feminism, Sexuality, and Politics* (Chapel Hill: University of North Carolina Press, 2006), 121–39; and Jenkins, *Moral Panic*, 49–93. Mendenhall's interview for the film was likely conducted in early 1976, which is a bit surprising, as his statements seem tailored to the context of Anita Bryant and John Briggs. This prescience likely resulted from Mendenhall's work as an activist journalist. Among other topics, he had written a number of pieces about the policing and treatment of sex offenders for publications such as the *Advocate* in the mid-1970s.

44. For a much fuller discussion of the film than is provided here, see Greg Youmans, *Word Is Out: A Queer Film Classic* (Vancouver, BC: Arsenal Pulp Press, 2011).

45. Rosa von Praunheim, *Army of Lovers* (London: Gay Men's Press, 1980), 13.

46. Ibid., 117.

47. Keith Kelly, "The Sexual Politics of Rosa Von Praunheim," *Millennium Film Journal* 3 (1979): 115–18; quote at 115.

48. The term "sexual fringe" is taken from Gayle Rubin, "Sexual Politics, the New

Right, and the Sexual Fringe," in *The Age Taboo: Gay Male Sexuality, Power, and Consent*, ed. Daniel Tsang (Boston: Alyson Publications, 1981), which is an example of the sexual libertarian position described here. See also Rubin, "Thinking Sex"; Califia, "Age of Consent" and "Great Kiddy-Porn Panic of '77"; and other contributions to Tsang, *Age Taboo*. While the distinction between "gay liberationism" and "gay liberalism" is common among historians of U.S. gay political history (see, for instance, Stein, *Rethinking the Gay and Lesbian Movement*, 84–85), the distinction I am making between "gay liberalism" and "sexual libertarianism" is not established, though "libertarianism" does appear in writings from the era used similarly to how I am using it. I make this distinction in order to compare two significant gay political tendencies of the late 1970s, both of which were concerned with rights and were distinct from the gay liberationism of a decade earlier.

49. A fuller transcript of Reeves's interview is included in Praunheim's accompanying book to the film, *Army of Lovers*, 163–75, with this particular passage on 170. The passage was apparently edited down for the film. Reeves also ends the passage in the book by differentiating the idea of recruiting that he has just presented from the one circulated by Bryant: "So it is a lie. We do not want to recruit in that sense."

50. Ibid. See also Tom Reeves, "Loving Boys," in Tsang, *Age Taboo*, 25–37.

51. Herbert Marcuse gave the Freudian idea of "polymorphous perversity" a Marxist spin and applied it to a systemic critique of U.S. society in his 1955 book *Eros and Civilization: A Philosophical Inquiry into Freud* (Boston: Beacon Press, 1955). Marcuse's ideas were in turn influential to gay liberationist thought in the late 1960s and early 1970s. See, for instance, Dennis Altman, *Homosexual: Oppression and Liberation* (New York: Avon Books, 1971).

52. See Tsang, *Age Taboo* for arguments in this vein by Reeves and others.

53. John Mitzel, *The Boston Sex Scandal* (Boston: Glad Day Books, 1980).

54. Ibid., 48–52. For an account of this meeting, see Daniel Tsang, "Men and Boys: The Boston Conference," in Tsang, *Age Taboo*, 38–43. NAMBLA, like the B/BC before it, was from the beginning a group that included boys as well as boy-lovers, though always more of the latter than the former.

55. On "pornotopia," see Steven Marcus, *The Other Victorians: A Study of Sexuality and Pornography in Mid-Nineteenth Century England* (New York: Basic Books, 1964).

56. Richard Dyer, *Now You See It: Studies on Lesbian and Gay Film* (London: Routledge, 1990), 222.

57. See McCreery, "Save Our Children / Let Us Marry," for an argument in this vein.

IV

PRESERVING PORNOGRAPHY

History, Memory, Legacy

CHAPTER 12

Bridging the Gap

Adult Video News *and the* "Long 1970s"

PETER ALILUNAS

Accessibility leads to acceptability.
— *Steven Hirsch, cofounder of Vivid Video, 2004*

EEP IN AN ESSAY from November 1971, film scholar Joseph Slade buried a crucial detail in the history of pornography. Relating his experiences visiting the grimy porn theaters off of New York City's Times Square, Slade noted the limited screening of poor quality "homemade videotapes."[1] Coming almost four years before videotape was widely available to the average consumer, and temporally on the cusp of what has since come to be known as the "Golden Age" of celluloid adult film, Slade's brief mention raised tantalizing questions. As films such as *Boys in the Sand* (dir. Wakefield Poole, 1971), *Deep Throat* (dir. Gerard Damiano, 1972), and *Behind the Green Door* (dir. Jim and Artie Mitchell, 1972) were set to unspool in theaters, ushering in a brief period of widespread public awareness of pornography (and a modicum of fleeting acceptance), Slade's observation raises important questions.[2] What were these videotapes? Were they available for sale to a variety of theaters, or made exclusively for single locations? What was the content? In short: *What was Slade watching?*

This early appearance of video stands as both anomaly and portent: adult theaters would still sell upward of 100 million tickets per year as late as 1983, yet by 1987 the number of annual adult video rentals exceeded 100 million.[3] Video technologies transformed the adult film industry, permanently shifting consumption away from the shared public space of the theater to the private sphere of the home.[4] In this essay I explore the complex social and technological changes that accompanied the transition to video, paying special attention to the new communication channels and modes of address among producers, distributors, retailers, and consumers.

The most important industry-to-consumer publication in this period was *Adult Video News* (*AVN*), a newsletter created by Paul Fishbein, Irv Slifkin, and Barry Rosenblatt in Drexel Hill, Pennsylvania, in 1982. Still published today, the magazine has changed its format to target adult video retailers and industry professionals, and has an average monthly circulation of roughly forty thousand. Each issue features up to five hundred adult video reviews, which appear alongside copious amounts of industry advertising, which comprises the magazine's primary content. Parent company AVN Media Network also sponsors trade shows, maintains various online platforms, and has, since 1984, hosted the well-known AVN Awards, which are often described as the "Oscars" for the adult film industry.[5]

At the time of its founding, however, *AVN* played a significant role in bridging the gap between the Golden Age of the 1970s and the shot-on-video era of the late 1980s by implementing a set of strategies aimed at legitimizing the adult entertainment industry and expanding its customer base.[6] Rather than separating celluloid and video into two distinct eras based on exhibition technologies, I propose that the in-between period during which this transition occurred might better be understood as the "long 1970s." This paradigm acknowledges the lasting influence that the Golden Age had on the industry and those struggling to establish a successful and stable video component of the business. As the example with Slade watching a videotape in a public theater illustrates, there was no one definable moment that marked when the industry began or completed the transition; instead, many small steps eventually added up to dramatic and permanent change.

As one of those steps, *AVN* built unprecedented relationships between the industry and consumers, effectively providing a way for these parties to communicate with each other. *AVN* allowed industry insiders to offer consumers advice, encouragement, and reassurance during a contentious and often confusing period. In his historical work on home video rental and the VCR, Joshua Greenberg foregrounded the critical process of "mediation," which he described as occurring "in the less-explored spaces *between* the media corporations, technology manufacturers, and lawmakers who are the traditional protagonists of the VCR's history."[7] *AVN* performed a similar function for the adult film industry, emphasizing the continued presence of "quality" filmmaking practices familiar from the Golden Age in the new video releases. This practice both alleviated consumer doubt and guided the industry smoothly away from its reliance on one technology and into another, all while working toward greater cultural respectability.

Given the myriad legal, cultural, and technological problems facing the industry in the "long 1970s," *AVN*'s creation and subsequent success was groundbreaking, and remains crucial to a broad understanding of the history of pornography, particularly during its home video era. Beginning with the first issue, the magazine deliberately offered what had not previously existed for adult film: a dual space to report on and market the industry in the ways *Variety* and the *Hollywood Reporter* did for mainstream cinema. Ultimately, *AVN* signified the transition of the adult film industry to both a new mode of exhibition and a modern and efficient example of corporate capitalism.

The Founding of *AVN*

Fishbein and Slifkin were well positioned to recognize the early market for a publication dedicated to adult video. Beginning in 1980, while undergraduate students at Temple University in Philadelphia, the two worked for Movies Unlimited, one of the earliest and largest video rental stores in the United States. They witnessed the explosive growth and profitability generated by the new medium.[8] After the introductions of the Sony Betamax videotape player system in May 1975 (fig. 12.1) and rival VHS system (a JVC product, though it would be licensed to a large variety of manufacturers) shortly after, home video was available to consumers, although the machines were, at least at first, inordinately expensive, running upward of $1,500.[9] Indeed, by 1978, Americans had purchased fewer than 175,000 VCRs, but after a steep drop in price due to competition between the two systems, the sales figures exploded. Four million VCRs were sold in the United States by 1982, rising to twenty-six million by 1985, soon thereafter becoming ubiquitous across the country.[10] Adult film's share of the initial content market for the new machines was substantial, accounting in some estimates for at least half of all videotapes available to consumers.[11] Adult film industry veteran David Friedman noted in 1980 that of the roughly six hundred adult films made in the latter half of the 1970s, nearly all were available on video, evidencing the quick

FIGURE 12.1. In 1975, Sony launched the Betamax domestic videocassette recorder in Japan. Like VHS, it offered around three hours of recording time, with fully automated recording. The Betamax system used half-inch tape cassettes. Getty Images: Science and Society Picture Library.

embrace by the industry of the new format even before a substantial customer base existed for the material.[12] The national growth of video rental stores in this period followed a similar pattern, climbing from 4,000 in 1978 to 10,000 in 1983 and 22,000 in 1985. Estimates suggest that single-store operators owned and managed 90 percent of these prior to the emergence of chains such as Blockbuster and Hollywood Video.[13] Like speculators sensing an impending gold rush, Fishbein and Slifkin saw untapped markets of retailers and consumers seeking reliable information about adult video.

They also had the publishing experience to support the conceptualization of *AVN*. As a teenager, Fishbein created *Universal Wrestling* with classmate Stuart Franks, a fan magazine that they sold to subscribers for $10 per year.[14] While at Temple, Fishbein and Slifkin majored in journalism and founded *In Print,* a magazine aimed at college students that eventually reached a circulation high of thirty thousand and won a Hearst Foundation journalism award.[15] The two self-confessed "film buffs" also wrote a home video column for the *Philadelphia Bulletin,* and briefly considered professional work as syndicated newspaper columnists. Instead, in 1982, they created *Adult Video News,* on a shoestring budget of $900. Fishbein and Slifkin each contributed $300 to get the publication going, and they recruited their friend, graphic design student Barry Rosenblatt, to join their effort.

Rosenblatt contributed $300 as well. They wrote the content for the first issue, drummed up classified ads from a few adult entertainment mail order companies, and boldly declared themselves "experts" on the basis of their rental clerk experience. Reflecting on those early years, executive editor Gene Ross described the original idea as a desire to "publish a magazine that would be a classy, intelligent, and informative critique of the goings-on in the adult film, and the soon-to-come-on-like-gangbusters, shot-on-video industry."[16]

Given the powerful (and profitable) contemporary status of the company, as well as the explosive growth of adult video, it may seem self-evident that the success of the venture was a foregone conclusion. At the time, however, the concept was risky and groundbreaking, particularly since celluloid still reigned in terms of adult industry practice and audience preference. Released in February 1983, the first issue of *AVN* was a two-color, eight-page newsletter, with a cover price of two dollars and twenty confirmed subscribers.[17] The first issue offered seven video reviews, industry news, and an interview with actress Veronica Hart. Of the titles reviewed, only one, *Valley Vixens* (dir. Bobby Hollander, 1983) was shot on video; the other six were theatrical releases transferred to tape, the standard practice at the time. Fishbein and Slifkin continued to work at Movies Unlimited while running their small business out of a nearby post office box, but the venture quickly began to grow.[18] The growth stemmed in part from critical editorial and aesthetic decisions that Fishbein, Slifkin, and Rosenblatt made, decisions that would set the magazine apart from traditional adult magazines, whose pages had long provided the primary space available for adult film marketing.

Adult Magazines and "Sampling"

By 1980, more than 200 hardcore and 165 softcore magazines offered nudity and sex as their primary content.[19] The most well-known among these, *Playboy, Hustler,* and *Penthouse,* offered reviews to some degree, but did not cover the adult film industry in detail.[20] Other magazines, such as *Adam Film World, Cinema-X,* and *Video-X,* focused on the industry—but did so squarely within what I call the "sampling" model. In these magazines' pages, the adult film industry offered samples of its content in the form of synopses, interviews, "on the set" stories, industry gossip, and loose reviews that served more as publicity than criticism. Most predominant, however, were pictorials of nude performers (either film stills or photographs taken in separate photo shoots), accompanied by "narratives," often in the form of anecdotes, quotes, or simple stories told in pictures, long a familiar and foundational element in adult magazines.[21]

As the industry began transitioning to videotape in the late 1970s, these magazines continued to present samples from theatrical releases as their primary content, but they also made tentative efforts to examine the new technology. For example, the July 1980 issue of *Adam Film World* teased "Latest X-Raters on Videotape" on its cover but devoted little space inside to the topic beyond a short list of available titles. Instead, the issue primarily features a collection of stills from adult films then in theatrical release alongside mainstream book and film reviews, as well as Hollywood news related to sex—all the elements it had long used to emulate *Playboy*. In fact, Knight Publications had created *Adam* in 1957 to rival *Playboy*, and spun off *Adam Film Quarterly* in 1966 to cover sexploitation films (low-budget films of the 1960s that featured nonexplicit sexual situations and nudity). In 1969, the magazine was renamed *Adam Film World* and issued monthly, gradually shifting toward sampling as its primary content.

The February 1980 *Cinema-X*, that publication's second issue, avoided mainstream content entirely in favor of extensive sampling. The issue contained interviews with Golden Age director Chuck Vincent and performer Annette Haven; a "Questions from Readers" feature with answers from performer Leslie Bovee; a "Rising Stars" section introducing acting newcomers Scarlett Kennedy, Sue Leighton, and Susanne Nero; a fan club section linking readers with performers; and a gossip column. All of this content linked *Cinema-X* to celluloid films then in theatrical release.[22] The magazine acted as a mediator between the industry and a curious public—but depended on the samples that made up the bulk of its content to drive sales. For example, Bovee not only served as the fan mail correspondent in that issue but also appeared on the cover, in an interview, as the centerfold, and in a two-page mail order advertisement for her films (on 8 mm format). This illustrates how *Cinema-X* partnered with the industry to serve as a marketing platform, sampling its products for readers in a mix that served as both entertainment and purchasing guide.

Video X magazine, in its inaugural March 1980 issue, focused entirely on video rather than theatrical releases but maintained familiar publishing strategies. In its opening pages, the magazine made its sampling intentions clear: "Save money by previewing extensive pictorials from no less than 15 major adult video features each month." Readers could purchase the tapes "directly from our mail-order department, which just happens to boast the world's largest selection of adult video titles at all times."[23] Orders went to Vydio Philms of Surfside, Florida, one of the largest early adult video distributors and a clearinghouse for major production companies of the era: Video Classics, Quality X Video Cassette Company, Cinema-X, Leisure Time Booking, Gail Palmer's Pleasure Productions, and Wonderful World of Video. Thus, *Video X* was more than just an entertainment and marketing platform for adult video producers, it was also a *literal* catalog for consumers.

This was the publishing environment into which Fishbein, Slifkin, and Rosenblatt introduced *AVN*, a landscape defined by sampling. As Andrew Ross notes, "Increasingly, the porn magazines [were] tailored to function as trailers, previews, fanzines, and supporting literature for the main attraction of the videos and their stars."[24] However, the industry still lacked a publication that talked critically *about* the content and its production values rather than merely offering tidbits and teasers as entertainment. While *AVN* would continue the tradition of serving as a marketing and public relations arm for the industry, it radically altered the presentation methods, and, in the process, veered away entirely from sampling.

Selling XXX without the Sex

The changes Fishbein, Slifkin, and Rosenblatt envisioned were evident in *AVN*'s initial masthead, which read, "A Monthly Newsletter for Today's Sophisticated X-Rated Viewer." This descriptor offered a clear image of the credibility, expertise, and sincerity carefully constructed by the editors, and also an indication of the type of audience member they were hoping to *avoid*. The editors wanted to build reader trust in the magazine's proclaimed expertise and coverage *of* the industry, rather than providing entertainment content *from* the industry, a deliberately crafted strategy intended to position the publication as something respectable, an industry trait that would be crucial to further economic development. Emphasizing the technical aspects, narrative sophistication, and craft of adult video—and pursuing the consumer who appreciated fine aesthetics—was foundational to this process.

Even more important was the editors' decision to eliminate all nudity and explicit language from the magazine, a startling and unprecedented strategy that emphasized their desire to discuss, rather than present, pornography. They crafted an accessible, knowledgeable tone targeted at serious consumers seeking reliable information on the products that had migrated from public to private spaces. The primary goal was to normalize home consumption of adult video, and to link this practice to traditional retail contexts, namely local video stores. This initial vision was captured in an essay co-authored by Fishbein and Slifkin in the second issue, titled " 'I Want One With a Story!' " Its introduction exemplified the magazine's early tone and overall purpose:

> The young couple had been married merely a month, and already they needed a spice added to their sex lives. They walked into their local video shop and headed right for the adult films. Leslie, a blonde vixen who really hadn't even seen an X-rated film ("I saw part of *Emmanuelle* once at the drive-in!") looked sheepishly at the salesman, lowered her head, and let herself be dragged into that section of the shop. Max, her husband, had seen some adult films. He knew that there had to be films sexy enough to turn his new wife on. The salesman trotted into the X-rated area and chirped, "May I help you?" Leslie was quick to answer, "I want one with a story!" The salesman had heard that request before. He even had a list of the adult films that had plots interesting enough to keep both the novice and the experienced viewer hot and happy.[25]

Here, the mediation role sought by *AVN* is clear, particularly in its inclusion of the perspectives of both retailer *and* consumer within a single narrative. The essay also exemplifies the hopeful attitude *AVN* held for the possibility that home video might improve the negative cultural stereotypes surrounding pornography in the "long 1970s." Crucially, the depiction of a married, heterosexual couple seeking adult video advice functioned to deflate the long-standing mythology that adult films were the province of perverted single men (colloquially known as "raincoaters" during the theatrical era). The clerk is painted as a cheerful and well-trained professional, ready to advise customers without judgment. Finally, the encounter occurs at a neighborhood video store rather than an adult bookstore—a clear suggestion of the locus of the new market and a reassurance to anxious consumers that such transactions were commonplace, and were carried out using familiar customer service terms. The takeaway was both psychological and economic: renting adult videos, with the assistance of professional retailers, could be easy, effortless, enjoyable, and available everywhere. That it was a heterosexual couple also adds an additional layer of patriarchal, heteronormative security for those store-owners anxious about who might be renting their inventories.

The most important detail in this introduction, however, is the one signaled in its title: the story. In the endless quest to attain legitimacy and respectability (both legally and culturally) for pornography, many of the industry's proponents have long sought ways to make it mean "something more" than simply a tool for sexual pleasure.[26] Narrative frequently performs this function, granting pornography a level of intellectual sophistication; after all, a story means there is "something more" than simply depictions of sexual acts. Such tactics, at their most extreme, typically mean a distancing from the term "pornography" itself, most commonly by reinscribing the material as "erotica." That term emerged in 1853, only a few years after "pornography," and then gained popularity in the 1950s and 1960s to confer a level of respectability not granted to pornography. The label "erotica" was reserved for "quality" materials that dealt with sex but also included narrative as a core component.[27] Put bluntly: the inclusion of "something more" makes pleasure "safe." Yet these tendencies also carry with them deeply essentialized views that reify and solidify deeply regressive, stereotyped views of gender, as well as inevitably creating binaries of "normal" and "abnormal" sexual behavior.[28]

As Ross describes, erotica typically deals in "representational codes of romantic love, with an emphasis on traditionally 'feminine' qualities like tenderness, softness, wholeness, sentiment, sensuality, and passion."[29] This is in contrast to pornography's strict emphasis on bodily pleasure. Art, in order to be art in such reasoning, cannot simply arouse, which is why the moment in the *AVN* introduction when Leslie asks for "one with a story" stands out in such stark relief. The magazine's editors, in their quest to encourage the industry to seek legitimacy, played directly into the gendered stereotype that female viewers would not respond to images of sexual acts without the context of a romantic story. Rather than presenting a novice female consumer who was as sexually avid as her husband, *AVN* discursively participated in and re-created gender stereotypes in its efforts to seek legitimacy for the industry.[30]

If respectability occupied *AVN*'s editors during its foundational period, a second critical topic was the anxiety surrounding the visual quality of videotape. Audiences accustomed to celluloid projection on massive screens were now watching adult films transferred to magnetic tape and played on television screens, or viewing productions shot directly on videotape. Reactions were not always positive. For example, critic and historian Jim Holliday described shot-on-video (which he called "shit-on-video") productions in 1986 as "critically and creatively impoverished," and only reluctantly included them in his otherwise comprehensive guide to adult film.[31] For Holliday, such releases were little more than collections of sex scenes misleadingly advertised as features—a sentiment shared by both industry members and consumers during the early years of adult video.

Reader correspondence from March 1985 demonstrates how the magazine's editors dealt with such skepticism. One reader wrote to *AVN* to ask why manufacturers often refused to identify video or celluloid production on the box. "The people where I shop have absolutely no idea what's going on and I'm getting sick and tired of going home and finding these lousy quality videos when I was expecting a movie."[32] If that letter illustrates why the industry needed a mediator like *AVN*, another offers evidence of how such mediation worked: "I am opening a new store in my town, and I must say that my subscription to *Adult Video News* has been very helpful in stocking the store. When it opens next month, I feel it will have the best adult section in the area."[33] From the *AVN* perspective, the second letter was the answer to the first: the well-stocked neighborhood store with knowledgeable management was the way to ensure the high quality familiar from the Golden Age, delivered via new technology and retail practices.

In addition to reviews and industry news and interviews, *AVN* ran numerous lengthy articles about the new medium, probing the implications of the transition to video production methods. Veteran Golden Age directors such as Chuck Vincent, Cecil Howard, Anthony Spinelli, and Henri Pachard gave lengthy interviews to *AVN* that focused on shifts within the industry. The *AVN* editors also offered opinions, frequently criticizing producers who flooded the market with fancy (and often misleading) box covers filled with hastily produced and aesthetically impoverished shot-on-video content.[34] *AVN* regularly reviewed theatrical releases, and consistently separated shot-on-film (and then transferred to video) from shot-on-video reviews through the 1980s, presumably to the delight of the letter writer who had complained about the need for differentiation. Across both formats, however, *AVN* encouraged consumers to seek out high-quality productions, using standards familiar from the Golden Age. Regardless of the medium, the magazine invariably defined "quality" as strong, well-written, and creative scripts; characters engaged in complex situations; and technically proficient auteurs emphasizing sophisticated and thoughtful visual presentation.

In its early issues, *AVN* connected producers who made the content; retailers, who were instructed to maintain a professional, informative demeanor; and consumers, who were encouraged to seek out quality rentals. This communicative function, along with the deliberate, calculated decision to eliminate sampling—and the overall avoidance of nudity and explicit language—set *AVN* apart. By joining the industry, retailers, and consumers in a web of dedication to the characteristics of the Golden Age, the magazine attempted to foster in all three a sense of respectability regarding pornography. While *AVN* was conceived as a newsletter for consumers, it did not take long for the industry to realize the potential of the publication to assume a much different role. It was the combination of its core functions—mediation of the distribution chain and platform for the industry—that moved *AVN* within a few issues from a small newsletter originally intended for the average consumer to the leading trade journal in the world of adult film.

Transition to Trade Journal

A brief news item in the March 1983 issue foreshadowed *AVN*'s gradual transformation. Video-X-Pix, a leading adult video distributor, announced that it would release *The Erotic World of Angel Cash* (dir. Don Walters, 1982) for $39.95, well below the typical $60 to $100 price per videotape common at the time.[35] The production company was following the lead of Paramount Pictures, which had lowered prices on *Star Trek II* (dir. Nicholas Meyer, 1982) to "sell through" directly to customers at affordable rates. Three issues later, Video-X-Pix placed an ad for *Angel Cash*, prominently displaying the reduced price (fig. 12.2).[36] This pair of events indicated *AVN*'s capability to mediate between buyers and sellers of adult film *without samples*, both covering the day-to-day operations of the industry and providing a marketing platform. Similar advertising followed, as other companies took note of Video-X-Pix's strategy. By the fifth issue, distributors had seized the opportunity to market their products, and by late summer 1983, ads occupied as much space as the content, a ratio now standard in the magazine.

FIGURE 12.2. Video-X-Pix leads the way in lower-cost video pricing to "sell through" with *The Erotic World of Angel Cash* (*Adult Video News*, 1985, 5).

The editors of *AVN* quickly discovered an unintended but obvious audience: retailers, not consumers, found the most use in the magazine. Rather than the *couple* in the "I Want One with a Story!" essay, it was the *retail clerk* who emerged as the most important beneficiary of *AVN's* content. This represented a shift from the initial address crafted in the magazine, which seemed to be directed to the home viewer rather than retailer. Indeed, early interviews presented questions to industry members from a "fan's perspective," and reviews emphasized the entertainment value for the home spectator. However, *AVN* soon crafted its content to appeal to retailers seeking reliable ordering advice to satisfy the customers who were frequenting video stores for adult titles. Many of the early retailers were unfamiliar with pornography and anxious about including it in their inventories, thus *AVN* was an ideal partner, particularly in its insistence on marketing pornography in a respectable, sophisticated manner.

Targeting retailers marked the key turning point for *AVN* in its move toward full-time industry mediation. Circulation figures reflected this change. Subscriptions increased in the second year to nine thousand, with four thousand copies sent free of charge to stores—illustrating *AVN's* growing presence in rental locations, as well as a clear indication that advertising had become the primary source of revenue.[37] Content changed as well, including a new feature called "Newsline" in May 1984 that offered information intended for retailers, such as the legal challenges involved with renting and selling pornography. This frank discussion made *AVN* a critical source on a topic that grew in importance as retailers across the country faced obscenity charges.[38]

Indeed, *AVN* offered one of the few supportive spaces for retailers seeking reassurance and advice following the 1986 Attorney General's Commission on Pornography.[39] Concluding that pornography was harmful to society and individuals, the commission's *Final Report* offered ninety-two specific recommendations, all designed to stifle or prevent pornography from reaching the market, and condemning those who derived pleasure from it as dangerous and perverted.[40] *AVN* responded with frequent editorials and essays examining these charges, reassuring retailers that rape, child pornography, bestiality, and extreme violence were not condoned by the adult film industry, nor were those elements present in the titles that could make up a respectable inventory.[41] The message was consistent, clear, and strategic: if the industry continued to maintain professional practices in the production, distribution, and retail processes, consumers and cultural legitimacy would follow.

Industry economics became *AVN*'s primary focus by the mid-1980s. Sales and rental data debuted in the magazine in June 1984, as did editorials covering a wide range of industrial, political, and economic issues pertaining to retailers. Distributors willing to sell complete video collections to retailers started running full-page ads in September 1984. Guides to star performers and essential titles also became fixtures, designed to assist retailers in purchasing initial stock or invigorating stale inventories. The advertising, too, rhetorically changed. In the January 1985 issue, VCA Pictures placed an ad aimed at retailers suggesting that the company's titles were "guaranteed to bring you explosive profits," a significant discursive change from *AVN*'s early issues that emphasized entertainment value for individual viewers.[42]

The timeline of these changes paralleled the explosive growth of VCR sales, as well as the steady closure of adult theaters across the country. When asked in 1984 about video's impact, Al Goldstein, publisher of *Screw* magazine, replied that if he owned an adult theater he would tear it down and build a parking lot—a prescient idea that theater owners would have been wise to follow.[43] As the theaters faded from the landscape, local video rental stores become primary outlets for pornography. Adult magazines, too, lost customer share to the new technology. In November 1986, *Playboy* cut its advertising rates by 17 percent after a tumble in subscriptions, and, by that point, *Hustler* had lost more than half its readership.[44] But consumers were not losing interest in pornography; rather, they were flocking to video.

As *AVN* grew, major shifts also took place on the editorial side. Slifkin departed, amicably and without compensation, after the first year. Rosenblatt lasted longer but used legal means to negotiate his exit. Fishbein brought in a silent partner: former classmate (and *Universal Wrestling* cocreator) Stuart Franks, whose Printers Trade shop in Philadelphia had long produced *AVN*'s copies.[45] In February 1985, *AVN* moved to full-color, glossy publication, and a month later the publishers unveiled *Confidential*, a second publication aimed squarely at retailers seeking marketing and legal advice. Over the next ten years, Fishbein introduced several other consumer and industry-directed publications, but none was as successful as *AVN*. *AVN* was unique in its core strategy to bridge the gap between producers, retailers, and consumers through the "long 1970s" and into the video era. That strategy continued to pay dividends in the 1990s as circulation, advertising revenues, and page counts all increased. The primary message—garner cultural legitimacy by encouraging narrative and aesthetic quality—remained intact (fig. 12.3).

Impact on the Industry

Just as *AVN* had solidified its purpose and structure, the adult film industry, too, settled into its transition, finally moving out of the "long 1970s" and into a new era that embraced shot-on-video production. While it may seem tempting to see the long-term move from celluloid to video as the inverse of the "quality" embodied by the Golden Age theatrical releases and championed by *AVN*, there can be little doubt that narrative and aesthetic attention to detail maintained its hold on the industry, albeit in new ways. Underground experimentation clearly began as soon as video was available (as evidenced by the tapes seen by Slade in Times Square), and formal production companies such as Love TV and Scorpio Video began shooting directly on video as early as 1978, bypassing theatrical exhibition entirely in favor of the home market.[46] Veteran outfits were slower to make the

P 38

ATTENTION: VIDEO RETAILERS DISTRIBUTORS MANUFACTURERS . . .

COMING NEXT MONTH
"A NEW ADULT VIDEO NEWS PUBLICATION"
We present the debut of . . .

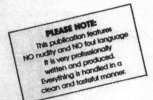

PLEASE NOTE:
This publication features
NO nudity and NO foul language
It is very professionally
written and produced.
Everything is handled in a
clean and tasteful manner.

THE COMPLETE GUIDE TO
ADULT VIDEO PRODUCTS FOR
RETAILERS, DISTRIBUTORS
AND MANUFACTURERS.

IT'S ESSENTIAL FOR EVERY VIDEO STORE OWNER!
EACH MONTH WE WILL PRESENT:

* RECOMMENDED BUYS - WHAT SELLS AND WHICH TAPES TO AVOID
* MARKETING FEATURES - HOW TO SELL YOUR TAPES, P.O.P. - PROMTIOAL IDEAS, ETC.
* INTERVIEWS - WITH TOP EXECUTIVES IN THE ADULT INDUSTRY
* LEGAL ISSUES - LOCAL, STATE AND FEDERAL LAWS THAT EFFECT YOU. SPECIAL INTEREST IN 1st AMMENDMENT ISSUES
* V.S.D.A. REPORT - STRAIGHT SCOOP FROM THE VIDEO SOFTWARE DEALERS ASSOC., CONCERNING SELLING & RENTING OF VIDEO TAPES.
* NEWS AND INFORMATION - WE COVER THE INDUSTRY - NEW TITLES - NEW COMPANIES - PROMOTIONS - PRICE REDUCTIONS, ETC.
* CONSUMER FEEDBACK - FROM AMONG OVER 13,000 READERS OF **ADULT VIDEO NEWS** - BESIDES, THE CONSUMER SHOULD HAVE "THE FINAL SAY"
* TOP 20 CHART - A COMPREHENSIVE BEST SELLING AND RENTING TAPE LIST - TO SHOW YOU WHICH TAPES ARE HOT!

PLUS - **Adult Video News Confidential** BUYER'S GUIDE - where to reach people in the adult industry.

FIGURE 12.3. Fishbein, Slifkin, and Rosenblatt announce their new publication, *Adult Video News*, 1983.

move. For example, Russ Hampshire's VCA, among the largest and most successful theatrical producers, had long transferred its celluloid inventory to videotape but did not create Wet Video, a subsidiary designed solely to market shot-on-video adult content, until the mid-1980s.[47] Most major producers and distributors followed suit, making video the only production method, and eliminating the need for differentiation.

Many of the old guard directors eventually made the move to video, despite their initial hesitations. Henri Pachard, working for Essex Video, made the technological shift in 1984 with *Hot Licks*, *Give It to Me*, and *Long Hard Nights*. Producer and director Harold Lime, known for such celluloid films as *The Ecstasy Girls* (1979), *Amanda By Night* (1981), and *Society Affairs* (1982), produced the low-budget *Undressed Rehearsal* on video in 1984 with director Jack Remy. The editors of *Erotic X-Film Guide* made note of the impact: "The fact that former giants of the industry like Harold Lime have slipped off into the video market is an indication that the X-rated market is undergoing a profound change, and that video is slowly driving the theatrical fuck film into second-class status."[48] Veteran Cecil Howard made the epic four-part *The Last X-Rated Movie* (1990) on video, a production that won multiple awards and was later called "the best multi-part adult series ever shot on video."[49] "Amateur" adult video also boomed, aided by the introduction of affordable and easy-to-use camcorders. That genre became commercialized in 1982 when a group of San Diego swingers began trading their personal videotapes and then, sensing a market for such material, turned it into a successful business with Homegrown Video in 1982, a company that still thrives today.[50]

Yet it was a new group of filmmakers who took full advantage of video technology to create stylized entertainment in ways that *AVN* could never have predicted. Candida Royalle, a former Golden Age performer, founded Femme Productions to create adult videos for female viewers. She capitalized on the privacy of the medium to reach an underserved demographic, and, as Carolyn Bronstein shows in this volume, one that male pornographers had utterly failed to understand or entice. Royalle's first production, *Femme* (1984), presented a series of music video vignettes without dialogue, creatively using video technology as a deliberate aesthetic choice rather than a limitation.[51] Similarly, the Dark Brothers, producer Walter Gernert and director Gregg Brown, made a series of critically acclaimed shot-on-video features in 1985, including *Let Me Tell Ya 'Bout White Chicks*, *Black Throat*, *White Bun Busters*, and *Between the Cheeks*, all of which critics heralded as promising examples of the new technology, given the rapid cutting, visual style, and sense of humor.[52]

Gernert and Brown also produced the groundbreaking *New Wave Hookers* in 1985, a film that signaled important changes ahead, despite its production on celluloid. With its ultracontemporary soundtrack, tongue-in-cheek narrative, and stylized, minimalist presentation,

New Wave Hookers made use of aesthetics familiar to MTV viewers.[53] It featured Ginger Lynn, who might be considered the first video porn star.[54] *AVN* marked that status with Lynn's appearance on the magazine's February 1985 cover (the first in color), and by naming her Best New Starlet at the second AVN Awards in 1985 and Best Actress in 1986. Most important, though, was Lynn's exclusive contract with Vivid Video, a major player in the new market and the first video-based company to find widespread public success—which it achieved primarily through a rigorous set of marketing strategies designed to appeal to the widest possible audience, putting into practice the strategies advocated by *AVN*.[55]

Whereas *New Wave Hookers* still presented its stylized aesthetics within a concrete story structure, many adult filmmakers all but abandoned narrative entirely by the end of the 1980s, preferring instead to take full advantage of video's capabilities to offer something radically different. The genre *AVN* would later call "Gonzo" emerged in 1989 when John Stagliano, Jamie Gillis, and Ed Powers released *Buttman, On the Prowl*, and *Bus Stop Tales*, respectively, creating a radically new style.[56] Jay Kent Lorenz defined the genre as "an adult video that *appears* documentary in nature, that features a male narrator-cum-host who usually doubles as the videographer and is often involved in the video's sexual activity."[57] The resulting films offered little narrative beyond sexual activity, usually from the perspective of the male character involved in the action, and with extremely minimal settings, props, locations, lighting, and crew. These films creatively incorporated the economic and technological characteristics of video production and reception to turn them into an aesthetic practice, illustrating what David James calls the "internalization" of the conditions of production.[58] If the theatrical mode of production and reception encouraged classical Hollywood models, with sophisticated narratives and character development played out on large screens that could accommodate a variety of camera angles and distances, the Gonzo genre swept all that aside to present more intimate and immediate depictions of sexual pleasure designed for television screens and close spectatorial proximities.[59]

Furthermore, the VCR (and its remote control) enabled the home viewer to control the exhibition experience. As Hilderbrand describes, this often meant "scanning past boring bits," or repeating sections holding particular appeal.[60] In many cases, and certainly in the popular cultural imagination, that meant skipping through the narrative to get directly to the sexual activity desired by the viewer, letting spectators serve as editors of their own programming. As Peter Lehman has argued, this means that the traditional conception of "quality" narratives might be inadequate for understanding the greater function of home video pornography, and that the fragmented "loop" system familiar from earlier eras might be the ideal narrative means for the conveyance of mediated sexual pleasure. "Porn may never have been suited fully to the feature format," he observed.[61] The editors of *AVN* may not have agreed in the early years, but the growth of the magazine peaked after the new aesthetics of home video found overwhelming financial and popular success, finally wiping away the "long 1970s" and initiating a new era for pornography.

In its early years, *AVN* could not have predicted the immense success and impact of the Gonzo genre, nor the subsequent massive technological shifts with DVD and streaming video online that followed. Indeed, in mid-1986, the editors of *AVN* were still invested in the type of filmmaking that characterized the Golden Age. "The days of overwhelming garbage are vanishing," wrote Mark Kernes, "competition is fierce and quality will win out."[62] This belief, that a very specific type of quality would keep the industry profitable but increasingly culturally acceptable, is precisely why *AVN* can be understood as historically crucial during the "long 1970s." The magazine's desire for complex narratives, replete with developed characters and sophisticated cinematic techniques, was based in a deeper desire for the crossover of adult film from pornography to art, which, proponents hoped, would finally deliver full measures of cultural respectability and legitimacy.[63] This foundational insistence was most clearly evident in the omnipresence in *AVN* of "sophistication" as the most desirable goal—in its own pages, in its encouragement of consumers' tastes, in retail strategies, and on industrial production practices. Yet, as I have shown, "sophistication" often carries unintended and highly gendered discourses.

In the end, no other publication tracked the growth, provided the expertise, or did more to champion the legitimacy of pornography during the "long 1970s" as video replaced celluloid, than *AVN*. Nor, importantly, did any other magazine so successfully create and shape its own status within the new industry. *AVN* eventually became the "voice" of adult video, even if, as some have argued, the fundamental nature of its purpose as a marketing platform eventually resulted in a reliance on advertising that eliminated objectivity.[64] Indeed, as the magazine's success grew, it became increasingly difficult to differentiate it from the industry it had long covered. By 1991, Fishbein had moved *AVN*'s offices from Philadelphia to Chatsworth, California, squarely in the heart of the adult film industry's territory and a spatial illustration of the partnership that had formed. Fishbein sold the company in 2010, slowly easing into a consultant's role and finally leaving in March 2012.[65]

Looking back at *AVN*'s early growth in February 1986, Fishbein and Rosenblatt diminished their own economic goals in favor of the political side of their creation. "The adult video industry, constantly under fire and always scorned, needed to be legitimized," they said.[66] Given the rising pressure from the Attorney General's Commission, antipornography feminists, and cultural conservatives as the 1980s progressed, that need became increasingly pressing—and made the magazine highly profitable.[67] While it remains true that the adult film industry was increasingly legitimized through *AVN*'s efforts, the most visible measure of that legitimacy has been its dramatic economic growth. What *AVN* knew from the beginning has been made clear in the years since: financial success goes a long way toward creating cultural respectability. In a telling moment, at the 2004 AVN Awards, *Hustler* magazine publisher Larry Flynt thanked Fishbein for "lifting this industry out of the gutter," a perfect encapsulation of the way the magazine labored to reconfigure the discourses around pornography and, in the process, helped ensure its continued economic survival through the transition out of the "long 1970s" and into the era of home video.[68] Indeed, it was *AVN*'s encouragement of the industry's *other* great transition—from the long-forgotten homemade videotapes Slade watched in Times Square to modern, efficient corporate enterprise—that might be the magazine's most lasting legacy.

NOTES

My thanks to the librarians and archivists at the Kinsey Institute at the University of Indiana at Bloomington for their assistance with this research. *Epigraph:* Clint O'Connor, "Cleveland's X-Rated Connection," *The Plain Dealer*, January 4, 2004.

1. Joseph Slade, "Pornographic Theaters Off Times Square," in *Transaction*, November / December 1971. Reprinted in *The Pornography Controversy: Changing Moral Standards in American Life*, ed. Ray C. Rist (New Brunswick, NJ: Transaction Books, 1975), 123.

2. Adult films not only found success in the mid-1970s at the box office, they also

received a level of unprecedented critical attention. For example, *The Devil in Miss Jones* (dir. Gerard Damiano) ranked seventh in total box office gross (not just adult) in 1973, received glowing praise from a variety of mainstream critics, and was even hailed by Addison Verrill of *Variety* as "approaching an art form." The apotheosis of this public awareness occurred with Ralph Blumenthal's 1973 *New York Times* essay, in which he coined the term "porno chic," calling *Deep Throat* "a premier topic of cocktail-party and dinner-table conversation in Manhattan drawing rooms, Long Island beach cottages, and ski country A-frames." Addison Verrill, "*The Devil in Miss Jones*," *Variety*, February 21, 1973, 18, 24; Ralph Blumenthal, "Porno Chic: 'Hard-Core' Grows Fashionable—and Very Profitable," *New York Times Magazine*, January 21, 1973, 272. For more on the role of critics during the Golden Age, see Raymond J. Harberski Jr., "Critics and the Sex Scene," in *Sex Scene*, ed. Eric Schaefer (Durham, NC: Duke University Press, 2014), 383–406. For more on the prehistory of the Golden Age, see Kevin Heffernan, "Prurient (Dis) Interest: The American Release and Reception of *I Am Curious (Yellow)*," in Schaefer, *Sex Scene*, 105–25; Jeffrey Escoffier, "Beefcake to Hardcore: Gay Pornography and the Sexual Revolution," in Harberski, *Sex Scene*, 319–50.

3. Chuck Kleinhans, "The Change from Film to Video Pornography: Implications for Analysis," in *Pornography: Film and Culture*, ed. Peter Lehman (New Brunswick, NJ: Rutgers University Press, 2006), 156–57.

4. As Eric Schaefer has shown, home viewing of adult films preceded video by decades, in the form of a thriving 8 mm market. See "Plain Brown Wrapper: Adult Films for the Home Market, 1930–1969," in *Looking Past the Screen*, ed. Jon Lewis and Eric Smoodin (Durham, NC: Duke University Press, 2007): 201–26.

5. For more on the AVN Media Network and its current publications and ventures, see avn.com and avnmedianetwork.com. For more on the AVN Awards, see "1st AVN Awards Announced," *Adult Video News*, February/March 1984, 1.

6. VCA Pictures and Caballero (the two largest production houses at the time) began shooting primarily on videotape rather than celluloid in 1986, all but finalizing the process for the industry as a whole. Lawrence Cohn, "Pornmakers Surface in the Mainstream," *Variety*, March 9, 1988, 3, 26.

7. Joshua M. Greenberg, *From Betamax to Blockbuster: Video Stores and the Invention of Movies on Video* (Cambridge: MIT Press, 2008), 6.

8. "King Smut," phillymag.com, November 2004, www.phillymag.com.

9. For more on home video history, see Frederick Wasser, *Veni, Vidi, Video: The Hollywood Empire and the VCR* (Austin: University of Texas Press, 2002); James Lardner, *Fast Forward: Hollywood, the Japanese, and the Onslaught of the VCR* (New York: Norton, 1987).

10. Paul Cahill, "The United States and Canada," in *Video World-Wide: An International Study*, ed. Manuel Alvarado (Paris: UNESCO, 1988), 127–28.

11. Jonathan Coopersmith, "Pornography, Videotape, and the Internet," *IEEE Technology and Society Magazine*, Spring 2000, 27.

12. Howard Polskin, "Pornography Unleashed," *Panorama*, July 1980, 35.

13. Cahill, "United States and Canada," 132.

14. Anthony Layser, "Porn Supremacy," philadelphiaweekly.com, January 9, 2008.

15. "King Smut."

16. Gene Ross, "Adult Video News: The First Five Years," *Adult Video News*, February 1988, 46.

17. Clyde DeWitt, "Adult Video Newsmaker," *AVN* 28, no. 3 (March 2012): 38–39.

18. DeWitt, "Legalese."

19. Henry Schipper, "Filthy Lucre: A Tour of America's Most Profitable Frontier," *Mother Jones*, April 1980, 32.

20. For more on *Playboy*, see Elizabeth Fraterrigo, *Playboy and the Making of the Good Life in Modern America* (New York: Oxford University Press, 2011); Russell Miller, *Bunny: The Real Story of Playboy* (New York: Henry Holt & Co., 1985).

21. For a firsthand account of working for adult magazines of the video era, see Robert Rosen, *Beaver Street: A History of Modern Pornography* (London: Headpress, 2010).

22. "Rising Stars," *Cinema-X*, February 1980, 69.

23. "The Source!," *Video X*, March 1980, 5.

24. Andrew Ross, "The Popularity of Pornography," in *No Respect: Intellectuals and Popular Culture* (New York: Routledge, 1989), 173.

25. Paul Fishbein and I. L. Slifkin, " 'I Want One with a Story!,' " *Adult Video News*, March 1983, 5.

26. This desire for "something more" is firmly echoed in obscenity law, which divides legal pornography from illegal obscenity, in part, by the application of the vague notion of "prurience," or an inordinate interest in sex. Nearly the entire history of pornography regulation hinges on this tension, and legal defenses of pornography have invariably rested heavily on the possibility of *other* values such as artistic, intellectual, or political merit—leaving the possibility of sexual pleasure, in itself, as far too dangerous to be considered worthwhile. For more on the complex and lengthy history of pornography regulation, see Whitney Strub, *Obscenity Rules: Roth v. United States and the Long Struggle over Sexual Expression* (Lawrence: University of Kansas Press, 2013); Walter Kendrick, *The Secret Museum: Pornography in Modern Culture* (Berkeley: University of California Press, 1987); Thomas C. Mackey, *Pornography on Trial: A Handbook with Cases, Laws, and Documents* (Santa Barbara, CA: ABC-CLIO, 2002).

27. Kendrick, *Secret Museum*, 244.

28. Gayle Rubin theorizes this "good/bad" dichotomy, and outlines the notion of what she terms the "charmed circle" of sexual behaviors within culture. She writes, "Sexuality that is 'good,' 'normal,' and 'natural' should ideally be heterosexual, marital, monogamous, reproductive, and non-commercial. It should be coupled, relational, within the same generation, and occur at home. It should not involve pornography, fetish objects, sex toys of any sort, or roles other than male or female. Any sex that violates these rules is 'bad,' 'abnormal,' or 'unnatural.' " Pornography, in its depictions and on-set performances, flagrantly and deliberately violates these rules, marking it as an extreme example of what Rubin calls the "outer limits" of sexuality. Gayle Rubin, "Thinking Sex: Notes for a Radical Theory of the Politics of Sexuality," in *Pleasure and Danger: Exploring Female Sexuality*, ed. Carole S. Vance (New York: Routledge, 1984), 280–81.

29. Ross, "Popularity of Pornography," 185.

30. Pornography has frequently replicated, rather than liberated, the construction of binaries and boundaries around gender and sexual behavior. On this point, see Linda Williams, *Hard Core: Power, Pleasure, and the "Frenzy of the Visible"* (Berkeley: University of California Press, 1989), 22.

31. Jim Holliday, *Only the Best* (Van Nuys, CA: Cal Vista Direct Ltd., 1986), 187.

32. R. Smith, "Bad Boxes," *Adult Video News*, March 1985, 3.

33. Jack Bailey, "Store Help," *Adult Video News*, March 1985, 3.

34. Mark Kernes, "Shot-on-Video: The Future Is Now," *Adult Video News*, June 1986, 16. The poster boy for such practices was Mark Carriere. Uninterested in artistry

or narrative, and seeking as much financial return on investment as possible, Carriere and his partners in Video Exclusives began cranking out "one day wonders" in 1983 from their Los Angeles warehouse, flooding stores with their tapes and causing a price spiral across the market. By the mid-1980s, distributors were selling tapes to retailers for as little as $2 each, creating a bargain effect that extended beyond price into the "value" of the industry itself that *AVN* stridently worked to counter. "Demand Is Strong, but Police Crackdowns and a Saturated Market Spell Trouble for One of L.A.'s Biggest Businesses," *Los Angeles Times*, February 17, 1991.

35. "*Angel Cash* to Retail for $39.95," *Adult Video News*, March 1983, 6.

36. *The Erotic World of Angel Cash* advertisement, *Adult Video News*, July 1983, 5.

37. Paul Fishbein, "Editorial for Our Readers," *Adult Video News*, March 1984, 4.

38. John H. Weston, "It's the Law? Obscenity Laws and the Effects on Video Retailers," *Adult Video News Confidential*, September 1987, 12.

39. Attorney General's Commission on Pornography, *Final Report* (Washington. DC: U.S. Government Printing Office, 1986); Robert Pear, "Panel Calls on Citizens to Wage National Assault on Pornography," *New York Times*, July 10, 1986.

40. For two of the best critical responses to the *Final Report*, see Philip Nobile and Eric Nadler, *The United States of America vs. Sex: How the Meese Commission Lied about Pornography* (New York: Minotaur Press, 1986); and Carole S. Vance, "Negotiating Sex and Gender in the Attorney General's Commission on Pornography," in *Uncertain Terms: Negotiating Gender in American Culture*, ed. Faye Ginsberg and Anna Lowenhaupt Tsing (Boston: Beacon Press, 1990).

41. Jim Holliday, "Truths, Misconceptions, and Observations," *Adult Video News*, October 1986, 4, 50.

42. VCA Pictures advertisement, *Adult Video News*, January 1985, 5.

43. Ben Pesta, "X Rated Video: Will It Make Adult Theaters and Men's Magazines Obsolete?," *Hustler*, October 1984, 52.

44. Nicholas D. Kristof, "X-Rated Industry in a Slump," *New York Times*, October 5, 1986.

45. "King Smut."

46. For a firsthand account of this early period of shot-on-video production, see David Jennings, *Skinflicks: The Inside Story of the X-Rated Video Industry* (Bloomington, IN: 1st Books, 2000). For a more detailed account of the industrial transition to shot-on-video production, see Peter Alilunas, *Smutty Little Movies: The Creation and Regulation of Adult Video* (Berkeley: University of California Press, 2016). When I asked Slade directly about the material that he had seen more than forty years earlier in Times Square, he speculated that the tapes were probably Sony U-Matic transfers of catalogue titles or quickie productions made locally for sale directly to the theaters. Joseph Slade, e-mail to author, March 15, 2013.

47. John Paone, "Interview: Russ Hampshire of VCA Pictures," *Adult Video News Confidential*, February 1987, 14, 24.

48. "Undressed Rehearsal," *Erotic X-Film Guide*, June 1985, 39.

49. "Hotmovies Honors Cecil Howard's B'day with 'Last X-Rated Movie,'" avn.com, February 23, 2012.

50. Rodger Jacobs, "Homegrown Video," Xbiz.com, January 3, 2006.

51. For a more complete history and analysis of Femme Productions, see Williams, *Hard Core*, 246–64. Royalle, who died as this essay was being completed, was a feminist pioneer in the adult industry. Femme inspired many other women to form their own production companies, and also opened new feminist dialogues

about pornography that were not fixated on its eradication. She authored *How to Tell a Naked Man What to Do: Sex Advice from a Woman Who Knows* (New York: Fireside, 2004) and "What's a Nice Girl Like You . . ." in *The Feminist Porn Book*, ed. Tristan Taormino et al. (New York: Feminist Press, 2012): 58–70, among other pieces.

52. For example, the editors of *Adam Film World*, in their 1987 *Directory of Adult Films*, described *Black Throat* as "a speedball—fast, sunny, and filthy in the best Dark Bros. tradition," and "beautifully shot on video." "Review: *Black Throat*," *Adam Film World Guide: 1987 Directory of Adult Films* (*Adam Film World* 3, no. 5): 45.

53. Holliday, *Only the Best*, 190–91. The Plugz, founded in 1978 and among the first wave of LA punk bands (as well as one of the first Latino punk bands in the United States), appeared on the soundtrack, and won the Adult Film Association of America award for Best Song for "Electrify Me." The band also featured prominently on the soundtrack for Alex Cox's *Repo Man* (1984).

54. The film also starred Traci Lords—who might, under different circumstances, have been considered the first video star. She appeared in 106 films, and was a frequent *AVN* cover subject and the talk of the industry. However, in May 1986, authorities discovered she was underage during production of the films. An overnight purging of her (very popular) titles took place around the country, many of her scenes were reshot with other actresses (as was the case with her scenes in *New Wave Hookers*), and the industry quickly disassociated itself from her. Only one film, *Traci, I Love You* (dir. Jean Charles, 1987), made after her eighteenth birthday, is legally available in the United States. For more, see John Paone, "The Traci Lords Saga: Still Not Many Answers," *Adult Video News*, September 1986, 18, 20, 51.

55. For more on Vivid Video, see Ralph Frammolino and P. J. Huffstutter, "The Actress, The Producer, and Their Porn Revolution," *Los Angeles Times Magazine*, January 6, 2002, 10; Jared Rutter, "The Man Who Changed Adult," *Adult Video News*, September 2009, 76–80, 84, 86, 90, 92, 113.

56. The term "gonzo" comes from Hunter S. Thompson's writing style, most famously displayed in his 1971 novel *Fear and Loathing in Las Vegas*, which utilizes a first-person, exaggerated combination of journalism and fiction, in effect a heightened "documentary" style seeking some inner "truth" rather than merely reality. Gene Ross, a longtime editor at *AVN*, suggested "gonzo" as a way to describe the loose first-person storytelling in the genre that simultaneously broke the fourth wall and presented a quasifictional story. Rich Moreland, "Recognition of the Cameraman," 3hattergrindhouse.com, March 22, 2012.

57. Emphasis in original. Jay Kent Lorenz, "Going Gonzo!: The American Flaneur, the Eastern European on/Scene, and the Pleasures of Implausibility," in *Porn 101: Eroticism, Pornography, and the First Amendment*, ed. James Elias, Veronica Diehl Elias, Vern L. Bullough, Gwen Brewer, Jeffrey J. Douglas, and Will Jarvis (New York: Prometheus Books, 1999), 352–58.

58. David James, *Allegories of Cinema* (Princeton: Princeton University Press, 1989), 12.

59. The "classical Hollywood system" of film production is described in David Bordwell, Janet Staiger, and Kristin Thompson, *The Classical Hollywood Cinema: Film Style and Mode of Production to 1960* (New York: Columbia University Press, 1985). Williams examines the generic characteristics and specifics of adult film in *Hard Core*.

60. Lucas Hilderbrand, *Inherent Vice: Bootleg Histories of Videotape and Copyright* (Durham, NC: Duke University Press, 2009), 8.

61. Peter Lehman, "Revelations about Pornography," in *Pornography: Film and Culture*, ed. Peter Lehman (Piscataway, NJ: Rutgers University Press, 2006), 92.

62. Mark Kernes, "Shot on Video: The Future Is Now," *Adult Video News*, June 1986, 16.

63. Traditional narratives and filmmaking practices did not disappear from the adult film industry after the advent of the gonzo genre, nor did *AVN* stop praising them. *Uninhibited* (dir. Buck Adams, 1995) initiated an escalation of adult feature film-making in terms of budget and score never before seen, even at the height of the Golden Age. Wicked Pictures followed with *Conquest* (1997), and *Flashpoint* (1998), both directed by Brand Armstrong and featuring Jenna Jameson, Lynn's succes-sor in adult film superstardom. The trend continued with Stagliano's epic four-hour *Fashionistas* in 2002, while *Pirates* (dir. Joone, 2005) and *Pirates II: Stagnetti's Revenge* (dir. Joone, 2008) took adult filmmaking to new budgetary and special effects territory, a trend showing no signs of abatement. Hustler Video's *This Ain't Avatar XXX* (2010), directed by Axel Braun and serving as a hardcore parody of James Cameron's record-breaking film (and like that film produced in 3-D), was reported to be the highest-budgeted adult film ever, and remains indicative of the "parody" genre that has all but taken over the industry in more recent years.

64. "King Smut."

65. Well before his retirement from *AVN*, Fishbein had already parlayed his expertise into new ventures. For example, in the early 2000s, he opened the eight-store Ex-citement Video adult chain in the Philadelphia area. In spring 2013, he and former *AVN* CEO Darren Roberts founded X3Sixty Network to provide original television programming related to adult industry news to cable systems in North America and Eastern Europe. "King Smut"; DeWitt, "Legalese"; "Paul Fishbein Announces Full-Time Departure from AVN," xxxwasteland.com, June 1, 2011; "New Television Network Launched to Provide Consumer News, Entertainment, Documentaries & Talk Shows about the Adult Industry," prweb.com, March 20, 2013.

66. Paul Fishbein and Barry R. Rosenblatt, "Editorial to Our Readers," *Adult Video News*, February 1986, 3.

67. For thorough histories of the antipornography feminist and conservative move-ments, see Carolyn Bronstein, *Battling Pornography: The American Feminist Anti-Pornography Movement, 1976–1986* (New York: Cambridge University Press, 2011); and Whitney Strub, *Perversion for Profit: The Politics of Pornography and the Rise of the New Right* (New York: Columbia University Press, 2011).

68. "King Smut."

CHAPTER 13

Historical Fantasies

1970s Gay Male Pornography in the Archives

LUCAS HILDERBRAND

I
N 2008 THE LOS Angeles gay and lesbian film festival, Outfest, presented a thirty-fifth anniversary screening of *Nights in Black Leather* (1973), the pornographic feature that, as the festival phrased it, "thrust" the 1970s gay porn actor Peter Berlin into stardom.[1] The film print had been privately restored for a commemorative DVD release and then donated to the Outfest Legacy collection at the UCLA film archive, the nation's largest repository for queer cinema classics. The event prompts scholarly reflection on historical gay male pornography as the heritage of gay male culture itself, and this particular film stands out as a formally remarkable classic of the genre, though not necessarily representative of it. In the 1970s, the project of reclaiming gay histories began in the wake of Stonewall and the burgeoning gay rights movement. Now the gay 1970s itself is historical and in need of documentation and interpretation, with the early "classics" serving as key sources to make sense of this cultural moment. Peter Berlin's *Nights in Black Leather* now appears in multiple iterations in various archives: as a restored film print, as various home formats donated by individual collectors, and via advertising, reviews, articles, pictorials, and other discourses in the gay press.

Looking back on gay print culture and cinema, I have come to recognize that pornography constitutes much of if not *the* dominant content of gay visual culture of the 1970s, and arguably beyond. Pornography was the *mainstream* of gay popular culture at one time, and it has arguably remained its most prolific form. What is so important about gay pornography is not its obscurity or illicitness, but rather its historical *abundance.* Although the early 1970s "porno chic" era of straight porn (exemplified by such prominent films as *Deep Throat* and *The Devil in Miss Jones*) holds a prominent place in the popular memory of the sexual revolution, gay pornography was even more centrally part of the emergence—nay, explosion—of gay male public culture and media in the immediate postliberation moment. As I suggest below, adult cinema and pornographic print culture were foundational to gay culture and sensibility during this formative period.

From the start, "gay" or "male" cinema was adult cinema, such as the 1960s queer underground cinema of auteurs Kenneth Anger, Jack Smith, and Andy Warhol and the early softcore "male film festivals" promoted by Pat Rocco.[2] Early 1970s hardcore gay films by Wakefield Poole, Fred Halsted, Jerry Douglas, Joe Gage, and Peter Berlin were immediately canonized as instant classics (in contrast to films by once prominent auteurs such as J. Brian and Gorton Hall, which seem to be less remembered today); they achieved a subcultural textual prominence in their own moment that no longer seems possible for gay pornography today, when nonerotic representations of gay male life circulate and achieve comparatively more mainstream attention— even if more pornographic images, including amateur autoerotic ones that circulate online and via messaging apps, are produced now than before. These specific films remain touchstones of our cultural fantasies of the 1970s. As I will suggest, these are only the most prominent and best remembered among dozens of other films, not to mention the flurry of print media featuring nudity and frank discussions of sexual practices.[3]

Pornography exists now in historical archives as a queer kind of evidence, for it gives representation to erotic fantasies rather than explicitly documenting the events or facts of the past. But as the most pervasive visual materials of this past, vintage porn also surely shapes how we might now see the early 1970s. In the decade following gay liberation, film pornography, unlike print pornography, would primarily have been consumed in *public* in theaters and thus promised at least proximity to and often the actuality of physical contact between men. Gay pornography, then, embodies a series of contradictions: reflective yet fantastical, explicit yet mainstream, commercial yet public, social yet private, and, like so many forms of popular culture, ubiquitous yet ephemeral. In addition to discussing the formative gay pornography of the 1970s period, I reflect on archival encounters with this pornographic past, both print and filmic, and the challenges inherent in studying material that was not generally considered worthy of preservation at the time of its production. The chapter includes a particular focus on the 1970s films of Peter Berlin, a photographer, filmmaker, international celebrity, and gay sex symbol. Although I am often skeptical of allegorical textual analysis as a stand-in for historiography, these films' position as "legacy" texts suggests their privileged historical importance, and their narrative forms arguably reflect and counter recurrent themes and issues in gay male pornography in insightful ways.

Archive Fever and Other STDs

In the time since I attended Outfest's screening of *Nights in Black Leather*, I have traveled to a number of gay archives and special collections related to human sexuality across the country. Their holdings reveal that the gay media from the 1970s was both richer and more pervasive than we are likely to realize now. Regardless of whether such archives have become fully institutionalized or operate as ad hoc volunteer repositories, I have repeatedly come to recognize that much of what constitutes their holdings is pornography—much of it print, some of it photographic, more than desired on VHS now that the format has fallen out of favor, and a minority of it on film. Archivists are frequently bemused by these titillating collections, yet uncertain how to manage them in their excessive materiality. Such holdings often create an ambivalent affect of custodianship for the archivists, who may blush or boast, depending on the visitor. Indeed, film archives generally are often home to porn collections that are the institutions' "dirty little secrets."[4] In fact, encountering the erotic is nearly unavoidable, even if you are actually looking for something else.

Although it may be obvious, it merits reiterating that most special collections related to gay male cultures were not institutionally founded but rather started as *personal* collections. These personal collections were either donated to preexisting institutions such as the ONE National Gay and Lesbian Archives for stewardship and public research access or became so large as to have become their own, often idiosyncratic, institutions. The provenance of this material is typically individual male collectors who have donated or bequeathed their porn stashes; such personal collections reflect the specific erotic proclivities of their original owners, but we know relatively little about the meanings these materials might have generated for their original consumers, particularly for material donated anonymously. Although much of this homoerotic material was both made and donated anonymously, I surmise that most producers and collectors were white males, given both who likely would have had access to create or consume pornography and the predominance of white bodies in the images. Men of color appear comparatively rarely in early or liberation-era gay pornography, and often in racially fetishizing ways when they do. This reflected structural racisms that too often failed to imagine the possibility of men of color as gay, too, or to recognize them as part of the audience, and thereby reinforced the normalizing and privileging of whiteness in gay male culture, media representations, and conventions of desirability. Media and archival elisions challenge reconstructing queer-of-color pasts and perhaps necessitate even more historiographic inventiveness.[5]

Gay collecting practices perhaps bordered on hoarding, but such collectors saw the value in gay and erotic ephemera and possibly also imagined the material's future value. In no way do I mean to pathologize or demean such amateur preservationists, but rather simply signal that there seems to be a very personal compulsion to collect and record among these men, one that I imagine was formed in reaction to a perceived absence of contemporaneous gay historiography and archiving. Such projects are impassioned missions to preserve, though are often conducted according to a singular personal logic and with a—perhaps paranoid, perhaps historically provoked—suspicion of established institutions and universities. For researchers now, what stands out will surely also be that which surprises or elicits an aroused response, intellectual or otherwise. These materials' original gay collectors had preservation fantasies, and these documents now provide an index of desire.

Pornography held a particular significance in the twentieth-century histories of gay male experience. Prior critics and scholars, such as Michael Bronski and Thomas Waugh, among others, have already explicitly asserted the status of gay male pornography as a form of cultural heritage.[6] As Tim Dean has written, "porn is itself an archive—of sex, of fantasy, of desire, of bodies and their actions, and of pleasure."[7] If homosexuality was understood primarily in terms of erotic object choice rather than a broader culture, nude images of men and narratives of same-sex seduction gave representation to homosexual acts and fantasies. Until recently, mainstream media has only rarely—and even then, rarely affirmatively—given representation to same-sex male desire, so that pornography was one of the few places to find *any* acknowledgment of gay male life.

In an influential 1996 essay, the late performance studies scholar José Esteban Muñoz made a claim for "ephemera as evidence," pointing to the conditions of queer experience as often only lingering in traces and residues rather than official documentation. He wrote, "While seriously engaged in establishing an archive of queerness, it simultaneously disrupts the very notion of officially subsidized and substantiated institutions."[8] Muñoz's essay was published the same year as Waugh's *Hard to Imagine,* the foundational account of the history of male homoerotic images, and the English translation of Jacques Derrida's *Archive Fever: A Freudian Impression,* which generated a body of theoretical discourse about "the archive."[9] Since the mid-1990s, gay pornography has become semirespectable as a site of research, and gay archives themselves have become increasingly institutionalized and prominent. So the very conditions of researching this history of gay male desire have changed, but I remain compelled to think through the porn collections that tread the line between mass media, personal collections, and (now) public records. Furthermore, the very type of documentation pornography offers is a lens less onto social histories of oppression and political organizing than onto past expressions of sexual desire. Drawing from Raymond Williams's formulation of "structures of feeling," through which Marxist historical materialism and affect intersect, Muñoz wrote, "Art [one might substitute "pornography" here] conveys, translates, and engenders structures of feelings—tropes of emotion and lived experience that are indeed material without necessarily being 'solid.' "[10] Muñoz's essay prefigured queer theory's parallel interests in temporality ("ephemera") and in archives ("evidence").[11] Thinking about porn in archives necessitates both engaging with the material holdings of institutions themselves and the more elusive erotic meanings the films and publications exhibit.

"The archive" has been a recurrent subject for more than a decade of queer theory in ways that have both expanded our conception of what counter-forms archives might take and at times undervalued actual brick-and-mortar collections. In foundational queries that extend the logic of Muñoz's investigation of the elusive histories of sexuality, Ann Cvetkovich has sought to think through affective histories of queerness as embodied in material traces, while Judith Halberstam has proposed a shift away from the sanctioned holdings of official repositories toward more popular texts and subcultural sites.[12] Returning to archives proper, Anjali Arondekar has surveyed histories of sexuality that draw from colonial archival material and has demonstrated how to search for something—such as same-sex activity—that was known to be prevalent yet often appears only in the fissures of official documentation.[13] More recently, Sara Edenheim has suggested that it was precisely deviants such as queers who have been most thoroughly recorded by the state; in her critique of queer scholars who have dabbled in archive theory, she has signaled gaps in the conceptual frameworks of literary scholars who are the driving force of queer theory and historians who actually engage special collections but who have largely not contributed to these discussions.[14] Describing what has often become my own experience of the archive, Simon Ofield suggests a research method akin to queer sexual seeking: "For me, one attraction of cruising as an approach to research is that you can never be quite sure if you will find what you are looking for, or if you will come across something you never knew you wanted, or even knew existed. In this way, cruising is a productive rather than reductive process, and has an in-built potential for diversion, irregular connections and disorderly encounters."[15]

Outside the framework of queer studies, Carolyn Steedman has offered one of the most cogent reflections on Derrida's *Archive Fever* and his intellectual legacy on the subject—as well as an engagement in actual archives. Steedman writes, "It is a common desire—it has been so since at least the end of the nineteenth century—to use the Archive as metaphor or analogy, when memory is discussed. But the problem in using Derrida discussing Freud in order to discuss Archives, is that an Archive is not very much like human memory, and it is not at all like the unconscious mind."[16] Steedman, however, does not divorce the archive from desire. "The archive is . . . to do with longing and appropriation. It is to do with wanting things that are put together, collected, collated, named in lists and indices; a place where a whole world, a social order, may be imagined."[17]

This gloss on the theoretical discourses on archives raises a question: Why do the terms "desire," "attraction," "fantasy," and "imagination" recur so often in theories of the archive? The archive, like the pornography that now fills it, suggests a fundamental fantasy vision of the world in which every desire—documentary, historiographic, intellectual, or sexual—can be satisfied.[18]

Cruising the Movies

The 1970s saw a cinematic wave of gay-oriented feature films that, in effect, brought the strategies of 1960s pulp novels into the cinema,[19] and a key film in this transition from paperback racks to cinema screens was the 1970 film adaptation (directed by Andrew Herbert) of Richard Amory's hugely popular—and, in retrospect, surprisingly lovely and erotic—1966 pastoral novel *Song of the Loon*. The film version was both prominently advertised and repeatedly referenced in Patricia Nell Warren's 1974 celebrated gay novel *The Front Runner*.[20] Signaling that the film adaptation fell short of the novel's eroticism (and, to my mind, every other element of the novel as well), however, the 1972 film *Reflections of an Indian Boy* was marketed as "sexually everything 'Song of the Loon' should have been and now is!"[21] Both films had actually been produced by Monroe Beehler, who founded the important early gay film company Jaguar Films. With the release of the high-profile adaptation of Mart Crowley's hit play *Boys in the Band* (directed by William Friedkin) as well, the year 1970 marked a moment when commercial feature films were made for a recognized gay male market.[22] *Boys in the Band,* in turn, would soon become the obvious intertextual reference for the playful title of Wakefield Poole's seminal gay porn feature *Boys in the Sand* (1971). Confirming that gay cinema should be an explicit cinema at this moment, *Boys in the Sand* was embraced far more enthusiastically by gay audiences as more reflective of liberationist values than the seemingly "dated" *Boys in the Band*. Nonetheless, that many of the initial wave of homoerotic adult films were marketed as "male" rather than "gay" indicates that they promised male flesh on screen and homosocial crowds in the audience but not necessarily overtly gay identities among characters or progressive ideologies in their content; furthermore, they precluded any gesture toward solidarity with lesbians.

A 1973 feature article on gay pornography in the Canadian film magazine *Take One* suggested that adult gay cinema was generally dismissed, even by gay liberationists; it did, though, reserve an already canonical status for directors Poole and Halsted.[23] Writing in retrospect, film scholar Jack Stevenson has suggested that commercial gay adult cinema quickly became formulaic: "By the mid-70s, commercial gay porn feature filmmaking was out of the closet, but there was nowhere for it to go—it came up against the same genre limitations that doomed creative development in all forms of hardcore pornography."[24] In the 1980s, hardcore moving-image pornography transitioned from a primarily theatrical and public medium to a home video and domestic one, which made pornography more collectable than ever (though small-gauge film versions had long been available)—and thus fodder for future archives.[25]

While in archives paging through back issues of the *Advocate*, the most prominent and longest-running national gay newsmagazine in the United States, I noticed that during the early 1970s, issue after issue had ads and reviews for gay adult feature films—not just for the most famed titles, such as *Boys in the Sand* and *LA Plays Itself* (Fred Halsted, 1972), but also dozens I'd never heard of. Some of these films were regularly reexhibited theatrically and released in a series of home viewing formats; some of them are now marketed as nostalgia erotica, at times labeled "precondom classics" that create a fantasy that is not only sexual but also historical. Indeed, the framing of "precondom classics" does not merely create an anachronistic conception of barebacking before AIDS but furthermore points to the larger queer archival crisis: not only has so little of queer history been overt and documented, but soon after there *could be* a critical mass of queer public life and popular culture, the AIDS epidemic that began in the 1980s wiped out almost a generation of gay male lives and memories.

Only the most canonized of the early gay adult films remain in circulation, primarily via gay adult video retailer TLA or the website Bijouworld.com. Yet, in 1973 alone, as covered in the *Advocate*, at least forty-six gay adult feature films were released, and a now little-referenced film titled *The Experiment* claimed to have been the "most popular" gay film of the year in its ads.[26] In some cases, films were advertised for months on end, or with multiple full-page ads in the same issue, demonstrating the visibility of pornography to gay readers at this time. The *Advocate* featured reviews of the various gay adult film releases, giving evidence that the films were taken seriously enough to prompt critical discourse. During this time, there was also a phenomenon of gay adult film advertisements with extensive quotations from reviews, thus asserting their quality and, possibly, cultural legitimacy, even if they lacked the production values or naturalistic acting of studio films.[27] In early 1974, the *Advocate* film critic offered a year-end "ten best" list of gay films from 1973, along with a list of the worst, suggesting a critical mass; in this annual recap, *all* of these were pornographic films, rather than Hollywood or art house features with gay themes—which further suggests that the *only* films the critic considered to embody gay perspectives and audience address were these independent adult films.[28] Between the late 1960s and mid-1970s, frank discourses about sexual practices were *inseparable* from any other discussions of gay politics and lifestyles, as reflected in the ways that nudity and eroticism permeated the gay press and gay cinema of the time.

I suggest that it was in *retrospect* that these early 1970s films have come to be understood and categorized primarily as "pornographic" rather than as "gay." Yet by 1973, such films were also already being framed in historicist terms with the release of Tom DiSimone's *Erotikus: A History of the Gay Movie;* this gay erotic complication film, narrated by Halsted, functioned as a gay version of Alex de Renzy's *A History of the Blue Movie* (1970). De Renzy's stag-film anthology boasted a loose historicizing framework that gave the "documentary" a "redeeming social value" in order to legitimize itself against claims of obscenity. Such legal strategies surely informed *Erotikus* as well, but it also signaled a new drive to recover and legitimize gay history itself by searching for a longer history of cinematic homosexuality—a history comprised of representations of same-sex erotic acts.

Circa 1974, the *Advocate* critic still framed these films as "gay" rather than "pornographic," which suggests that films made to target gay audiences were presumed to be explicit. But soon separations would appear, for instance when the *Advocate* began to consolidate all of its sex-related content and advertisements into the new "Trader Dick's" pullout section, which remained literally and metaphorically at the center of each issue. In the decades since, it has become difficult to imagine or remember erotic content as fully integrated and, indeed, central—as opposed to shamefully sequestered to the back pages—in gay news and lifestyle periodicals.

Nonetheless, browsing the *Advocate* counters notions of a paucity of gay cinema—or of its invisibility to the gay community—that has become a dominant historical narrative, particularly since survey accounts from Vito Russo's *The Celluloid Closet* onward have tended to elide erotic cinema—gay cinema's most pervasive form. In contrast, Parker Tyler's earlier *Screening the Sexes: Homosexuality in the Movies,* published in 1972 just as these films were emerging, *did* incorporate adult films into its genealogy.[29] The important point here is that there actually *was* a pervasive gay cinema at this time, and that it was largely understood as sex cinema. Less explicit—if more didactic—liberationist documentaries and more conventional narrative features would come later.

At the forefront of this gay cinematic abundance, the short-lived company Jaguar Films appeared as the company that advertised and branded its films most aggressively during the early golden age of gay hardcore, promoting its films with expensive full-page ads or two-page-spread campaigns. This company was founded by the afore-mentioned Monroe Beehler, who had been a projectionist and later programmer at the Park Theater in Los Angeles. He innovated pre-senting all-male films at the Park, often enlisting Pat Rocco to make films to screen. He became a major figure in adult film exhibition and distribution, first by working with Shan Sayles as vice president of Continental Theatres, a circuit of numerous straight adult theaters. Beehler founded Jaguar films as a production and distribution com-pany, which began releasing films with *Come of Age* in October 1971. Through his exhibition connections, he established relationships with a stable circuit of theaters across the country for his films; thus, he changed what had previously been a project-by-project artisanal production model for gay cinema into a fully structured industry. Jaguar specialized in gay adult features with storylines, ranging from exploitation films to sentimental fare that aspired to more middlebrow tastes—though they reflected the often peculiarly sex-negative values that marked much of 1960s (predominantly straight) sexploitation cin-ema. Beehler also purchased his own theater, a six-hundred-seat 1920s cinema with a massive screen called the Century Theater located on Hollywood Boulevard.

The debut feature at the Century was the Peter Berlin film *Nights in Black Leather,* which had been produced independently but was dis-tributed by Jaguar. Claiming to have upped the "quality" of "male cin-ema" and adopting the language of gay pride, the company nonetheless explicitly claimed *Nights in Black Leather* as part of its branded roster of titles in a two page center-spread advertisement promoting the film alongside its films *The Light from the Second Story Window, Greek Lightning, A Ghost of a Chance,* and *Sojourn.*[30] The company ceased production in 1974 with *Zoomerang* (released 1975), though it continued to rerelease films or distribute films such as *Grease Monkeys* (1978) in conjunction with the opening of the San Francisco Century Theater. That few of Jaguar's films may be remembered reflects that many featured rudi-mentary narratives and stiff acting, two impediments that would be minimized as porn features increasingly became just back-to-back sex scenes. The latter-day obscurity of these films may also be attributed in part to the fact that Beehler was reluctant to release Jaguar's films on

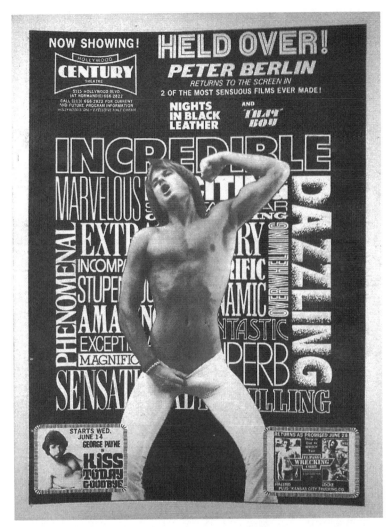

FIGURE 13.1. A full-page advertisement for a return double-bill of Peter Berlin films at the Century Theater in Los Angeles. From the *Advocate*, June 28, 1978. Courtesy of the ONE National Gay and Lesbian Archives at the University of Southern California Libraries.

home video after experiences with piracy, and most of his titles received only a belated and short-lived release on VHS in the mid-1990s.[31] Peter Berlin's films would have much more prominent afterlives than most Jaguar releases; both *Nights in Black Leather* and *That Boy* (1974) had a well-publicized return engagement as a double bill at the Century in 1978 and would be released repeatedly on home video (fig. 13.1).

That Star

Peter Burian, as Berlin was known at the time, was featured on the cover of the *Advocate,* and two full pages of editorial content focused on *Nights in Black Leather* and an interview with its star in May 1973. The film's openings in San Francisco and Chicago were promoted with a full-page ad in June, and its New York release with a comparably splashy ad in July; the film's eventual Los Angeles theatrical engagement would be promoted with a two-page center spread in December. Thus, *Nights in Black Leather*'s promotional campaign extended across seven months in the largest national gay publication. Although Berlin was already known as something of a character about town in San Francisco, the films and his self-portrait photography made him legendary. In the documentary *That Man: Peter Berlin* (Jim Tushinski, 2005), the star credits this ad campaign with building up both his star image and major audience anticipation for the film. Berlin would end up making only two feature films, directing his follow-up *That Boy* by himself. Five years later, both films were revived for a well-publicized return engagement. Although Berlin was and remains in many ways an oddity, he was absolutely in the mainstream of gay male visual culture.

In the in-depth review of *Nights in Black Leather* in the *Advocate,* Harold Fairbanks comments that the film "defies all the progressive steps taken by gay films in the past year"—in that "its story is wispy to the point of non-existence." He informs the audience that the film's director (Richard Abel, working under the pseudonym Ignatio Rutowski) had a background in still photography and lit the film as if for that medium. The reviewer concludes that *Nights in Black Leather* is "a superficial movie. The surfaces are visually glossy, beautiful, ornate, and it's all designed to divert attention from the emptiness underneath."[32] Yet the review is, on balance, a rave. In an interview accompanying the review, the writer comments, "To those who've tried getting to know [Peter] and have failed, he is attractive, narcissistic, self-centered, arrogant, imperious, aloof, distant, and a few even more pungent adjectives, depending on whom we're talking to and the degree of envy or rejection they feel." For good measure, a separate paragraph explains, in its entirety, "Peter Burian is a Capricorn."[33] In contrast to contemporaneous gay porn star Casey Donovan's affable hunk-next-door appeal, Berlin's Germanness marked him as "exotic" and even more unknowable despite his blond locks and white skin.

In *Nights in Black Leather,* Berlin appears as an unusually narcissistic and exhibitionistic star and seems almost uninterested in sex with *other* men. The film has a cursory framing narrative about Peter's visit to California, though the actor had been living in the United States for some time, already residing in San Francisco rather than just arriving as a tourist. The film is narrated as a series of flashbacks as Berlin writes a letter to a friend back home in Germany, yet Peter shows little interiority. Everything about him—in the film—is about surfaces and appearances. Thus, he offers little insight into the thinking and the attitudes of the 1970s, just the look of the era—and even on this front, Peter was exceptional rather than representative. Nor does Berlin become transformed as a character over the course of the narrative, as others would in a number of contemporaneous gay films; rather, he remains almost unaffected by his encounters.

The film presents fundamentally different registers for exterior shots that situate the act of gay cruising—looking in public places for a casual sex partner—within the historical actuality of the streets of San Francisco or Santa Monica, and for the interior spaces of staged sexual encounters that are wholly fantastical. The film includes repeated images of Berlin on the streets of San Francisco, parading his package, occasionally shot in close-ups at crotch level as Berlin saunters in public. Thus the film manages to simultaneously achieve a combination of on-the-street *cinéma vérité* realism and fetishistic objectification. Against porn conventions but perhaps reflecting the realities of cruising practices, Berlin frequently rejects the men who desire him and mostly seems to be cruising himself. In addition, midway through the film, he attends a party with drag queens and hippies; he describes the scene as a "bore," and the set-up never develops into the orgy that would be typical of a porn film party scene. Instead, this, like other scenes in Berlin's films, presents his refusal to hook up. The climactic and most rapidly edited sex scene in the film (and the only one with an accompanying musical score), presents a three-way to which Peter nearly seems incidental. Even more pointedly, the two standard sex scenes are the least interesting in the film.

Peter's most expressive sexual performance occurs during an extended real-time phone sex scene that never cuts away to the man on the other end of the line. This technique allows Peter's body to remain in focus and unsullied by another man's presence or touch. Instead, we get an extended sequence of Peter pleasuring himself with a disembodied—and acoustically mismatched—voice talking dirty

FIGURE 13.2. Peter Berlin performs phone sex in *Nights in Black Leather* (Peter Berlin, 1973). DVD frame enlargement.

(fig. 13.2). As the sequence climaxes, however, repeated ruptures in continuity bring us farther and farther from the realism of the film's frequent on-location street sequences. Although set entirely in Peter's living room, the scene, obviously shot with a single camera, inevitably reveals that it was filmed out of sequence. These discrepancies of historical verisimilitude and erotic fantasies are accentuated by the editing. During the phone sex sequence, each time the film cuts to a different angle or goes in for a close-up, the continuity is broken, as it cuts from a white wall to a black background and from flat bright illumination to backlighting that shines against Peter's Vaseline-covered torso to allow maximum visibility for his cum shot.[34] The shifts in background, lighting, contrast, and glisten rupture any cohesive illusion of realism, and the film's celluloid restoration further makes the image look too pristine, which, in representing Peter's too-perfect body, creates a kind of aestheticized distantiation. The sound mix, too, departs from aural fidelity as the voice on the phone remains at the same volume in the sound mix, though Peter obviously cannot hear the voice by the time he's masturbating with the receiver held down to his cock. Peter's flat affect when he thanks the anonymous caller and hangs up further gives a feeling of disconnection, as does his voice-over as he belittles the exchange as a "pleasant diversion." Peter's body is presented as a product for consumption yet always remains just out of reach. As a piece of gay history, it was always already seemingly at a remove.

If *Nights in Black Leather* introduced Peter Berlin, his follow-up film *That Boy* presents an even more totalizing work of self-invention, as it not only starred but was also written and directed by Berlin himself. Almost as a commentary on the prior film's reception, *That Boy* presents a narrative comprised of a series of fantasies as various men gaze at Berlin and project fantasy encounters onto him that *never actually happen* in the film's diegesis. Peter can be looked at but never actually touched, not by the men on the street in the film, not by his audience in the 1970s, nor by historical fetishists today. Peter presents himself as a fantasy image. Yet, extraordinarily, his character in the film desires only one man: a young blind boy, the only person in the film who cannot see his beauty. Peter speculates in voice-over about the blind boy; fascinated, he likes being part of the boy's sexual imagination and memory: "What dreams, what memories?" Berlin ponders. "He will never know me, except in his imagination." Peter shows more tenderness and humanity in this film, but still Peter wants only to be looked at and refuses to reciprocate. During an early exchange, filmed on the street, a man hails him, "Hey man, can't you do anything else with your cock besides show it off? . . . Let's go fuck." Peter flatly responds, "I don't want to."

That Boy seems almost self-aware of its own structural mediation of gay male desire and sex. The film is not a free-floating fantasy but a particular expression of a series of envisioned and narrated sexual scenarios—scenes that are unusually complex in their articulation because they are at once "authored" by Berlin but presented as originating from a number of different characters' points of view (including Berlin's character). In addition to the nonfixity of narrational point of view, the film's soundtrack is entirely postsynched—in other words, constructed and juxtaposed later than the image, thus pointing to a separation of the temporalities and perspectives of image and sound. (Shooting film footage silently and postsynching sound was commonplace in low-budget erotic filmmaking until the transition to video production.) This is most vividly staged during a sequence when Peter plays model for a photographer who longs for him; Peter's "to-be-looked-at-ness" (to anticipate a famous phrase from feminist film

FIGURE 13.3. Peter Berlin performs a playfully self-reflexive striptease in *That Boy* (Peter Berlin, 1974). DVD frame enlargement.

theory[35]) is foregrounded in the act of posing and having his image captured—and later making love to his own image in a mirror and amid photos of himself—and is thus reflexively presented. But even beyond the mise en abyme of images of Peter, he playfully taunts the photographer in the film and the audience of the film by stripteasing a preposterous number of garments before his flesh become fully into view: white drawstring pants, leather shorts, white euro trunks, another leather jock strap with snaps, white bikini briefs, a black netted G-string, and a cock ring. Even once he's nude, after a cut, the photographer can touch Peter only after his cock has been encased in a leather sheath. The film presents the fundamental inability to know or make contact with Peter; one can look but can enjoy only his *image* (fig. 13.3). Is this not like the condition of historiography, in which one might look upon and touch documents but can only *imagine* the past? One's way of knowing the past is largely through projection upon the stuff we collect to make sense of history.[36]

Peter Berlin stands as a peculiar synecdoche for the period: Can a star who seems to reflect nothing but himself reflect a larger cultural

Not every body has the gut(s) to wear a T-Shirt...

to **THE ENDUP T-SHIRT CONTEST**, 9 p.m. Tuesday, May 31st . . .
but everybody's invited to join in the fun! Wear a printed T-Shirt and you may win a $50 gift certificate
from **THE ALL-AMERICAN BOY** on Castro Street, plus other prizes. and don't forget our Concert
Hour every other Sunday and the Jockey Shorts Contest the first Sunday each month! All at . . .

THE ENDUP, a dance bar
at the corner of
6th and Harrison
in San Francisco

BAY AREA REPORTER MAY 26, 1977 PAGE 29

FIGURE 13.4. An ad for the San Francisco gay bar The Endup featuring such 1970s gay icons as Olympian Bruce (now Caitlyn) Jenner, openly gay retired NFL player David Kopay, physique model and Warhol film star Joe Dallesandro, porn star Casey Donovan, bodybuilder Arnold Schwarzenegger, and Peter Berlin. Published in the *Bay Area Reporter*, May 26, 1977. Courtesy of the ONE National Gay and Lesbian Archives at the University of Southern California Libraries.

moment? Does his antisocial exhibitionism counter any potential to read these films as evidence of a community history? Was he even of his time to begin with? Curiously, *That Boy* begins with an evocation of classicism: Peter's marble-hard body appears in a verdant field in Golden Gate Park with the strains of Johann Pachelbel's Canon in D Major on the soundtrack. The film both documents San Francisco's queer counterculture at the moment, with members of the Cockettes in cameos, and makes references to historical gay male iconography, such as sailors, physique models, and Greco-Roman style nude statuary. Thus, Berlin's self-portraiture elevates his own body and his image to the status of relic or icon of gay male history. In his own film, he imagines himself already part of the vernacular gay genealogy. Or, alternatively, Berlin treats his own body as a work of art, and we might understand his practice less as pornography than as self-portraiture. But Berlin's films also anticipate a transition in gay male pornography from an emphasis on representing how sex *feels* to a preoccupation to how it should *look,* as suggested by Daniel Harris.[37] But Berlin's status as iconic of 1970s gay male culture was further evidenced in a 1977 ad for the San Francisco gay bar The Endup, which featured a caricature of Berlin among such figures as physique model and Warhol film star Joe Dallesandro, fellow porn star Casey Donovan, and bodybuilder Arnold Schwarzenegger (fig. 13.4).

ONE OF THE SIGNATURE TRAITS of early gay hardcore from the 1970s is the structure of prolonged scenes of male-male cruising—though in Berlin's films cruising less often leads to connection than in most others. As director Wakefield Poole told the *Advocate* at the time, cruising is "three-quarters of gay life."[38] That search might now describe the desire for finding traces of the gay past. This sense of search and projection pervades the 1970s gay erotic films. I have been struck by the possibility for experimentation in their form and even more so that their recurring narrative conceits are structured as memories, daydreams, period pieces, and drug-altered consciousness. From the daydreams of *Boys in the Sand* to the nonlinear structure of *LA Plays It-self* to the surrealism of *Bijou* (Wakefield Poole, 1972) to the flashbacks of *Nights in Black Leather* to the multiperspectival narrative fantasies in *That Boy,* such early feature-length gay films repeatedly and explicitly foreground nostalgia and fantasy, not realism or diegetic "actuality," as their primary narrative logics. Such recurrent strategies both suggest continuities with avant-garde queer cinema of the previous decade (such as the films of Kenneth Anger, Jack Smith, Steven Arnold, and even Pat Rocco) and the search for ways to express a specifically gay consciousness and history before formulaic conventions had been established.[39] By returning to the archives, we might recognize that gay cinema and pornography were more pervasive than we might have realized, yet such texts themselves offer curious documentation through images and narratives that were always already elusive in their fantasies of projection and retrospection, that always already refused to be fixed in the reality of their own time or place.

Despite its indexical form, what pornography presents us with are feelings and fantasies more than facts. At stake for me are methods of historiography and of strategies for making sense of the past: what I've learned—and what has driven this query—is that archives are in fact full to bursting with pornography, such that what was sometimes obscene, crassly commercial, and assumed to be disposable in its own time has instead proven to be cared for, collected, and cataloged. The sheer surplus of gay pornography now in archives, like much of its narrative and visual content, suggests a historical moment in which sex and the search for sex publicly permeated all forms of gay male experience and representations.

NOTES

Thank you to the organizers, co-panelists, and audiences at the Cultural Studies Association Conference (University of California, San Diego), at the University of California, Davis, and at the Sex, Media, Reception: New Approaches conference (University of Michigan); to Rostom Mesli, Elena Gorfinkel, and Joe Rubin; and to my editors Carolyn Bronstein and Whitney Strub for feedback on various iterations of this essay.

1. Outfest 2008 screening, July 13, 2008, Redcat Theater in Los Angeles. Fred Halsted's *LA Plays Itself* would be featured on its thirtieth anniversary *Outfest* (2012).

2. For important histories of early gay cinema, see Kenneth Turan and Stephen F. Zito, *Sinema: American Pornographic Films and the People Who Make Them* (New York: Praeger, 1974); Paul Siebenand, *The Beginnings of Gay Cinema in Los Angeles: The Industry and the Audience* (PhD diss., University of Southern California, 1975); Richard Dyer, *Now You See It: Studies in Lesbian and Gay Film* (New York: Routledge, 1990); Thomas Waugh, "A Heritage of Pornography," *Body Politic* (January/February 1983): 29–33; Thomas Waugh, *Hard to Imagine: Gay Male Eroticism in Photography and Film from Their Beginnings to Stonewall* (New York: Columbia University Press, 1996); Juan A. Suarez, *Bike Boys, Drag Queens, and Superstars* (Bloomington: Indiana University Press, 1996); Jack Stevenson, "From the Bijou to the Bedroom: A Secret History of Gay Sex Cinema," *Film Quarterly* 51, no. 1 (Autumn 1997): 24–31; Janet Staiger, "Finding Community in the Early 1960s: Underground Cinema and Sexual Politics," in *Swinging Single: Representing Sexuality in the 1960s*, ed. Hilary Radner and Moya Luckett (Minneapolis: University of Minnesota Press, 1999), 39–76; José B. Capino, "Seminal Fantasies: Wakefield Poole, Pornography, Independent Cinema and the Avant-Garde," in *Contemporary American Independent Film: From the Margins to the Mainstream*, ed. Chris Holmlund and Justin Wyatt (New York: Routledge, 2005); José B. Capino, "Homologies of Space: Text and Spectatorship in All-Male Theaters," *Cinema Journal* 45, no. 1 (Autumn 2005): 50–65; Jeffrey Escoffier, *Bigger Than Life: The History of Gay Porn Cinema from Beefcake to Hardcore* (Philadelphia: Running Press, 2009); Jeffrey Escoffier, "Beefcake to Hardcore: Gay Pornography and the Sexual Revolution," in *Sex Scene: Media and the Sexual Revolution*, ed. Eric Schaefer (Durham, NC: Duke University Press, 2014), 319–47; William E. Jones, *Halsted Plays Himself* (New York: Semiotext[e], 2011); and Whitney Strub, "Mondo Rocco: Mapping Gay Los Angeles Sexual Geography in the Late-1960s Films of Pat Rocco," *Radical History Review* 113 (Spring 2012): 13–34. The seminal study of straight film pornography remains Linda Williams, *Hard Core: Power, Pleasure, and the "Frenzy of the Visible,"* 2nd ed.

(Berkeley: University of California Press, 1999), originally published 1989; for a foundational account of pornography in archives, see Walter Kendrick, *The Secret Museum: Pornography in Modern Culture* (Berkeley: University of California Press, 1996), originally published 1987.

3. On the liberation-era rise of explicit male images in the gay press, see Marc Stein, *City of Brotherly and Sister Loves: Lesbian and Gay Philadelphia, 1945–72* (Philadelphia: Temple University Press, 2004), 231–40; and Lucas Hilderbrand, "A Suitcase Full of Vaseline, or Travels in the 1970s Gay World," *Journal of the History of Sexuality* 22, no. 3 (September 2013): 373–402.

4. Eric Schaefer, "Dirty Little Secrets: Scholars, Archivists, and Dirty Movies," *Moving Image* 5 no. 2 (Fall 2005): 79–105.

5. Artist Glenn Ligon's work *A Feast of Scraps* (1994–98) addresses his own experience of *not* encountering erotic images of African American men that might have validated his own desires and self-perception of desirability. Recent work in porn studies has also importantly if belatedly expanded our analytical lenses for understanding racialization in explicit media; see Nguyen Tan Hoang, *A View from the Bottom: Asian American Masculinity and Sexual Representation* (Durham, NC: Duke University Press, 2014); Jennifer C. Nash, *The Black Body in Ecstasy: Reading Race, Reading Pornography* (Durham, NC: Duke University Press, 2014); Mireille Miller-Young, *A Taste for Brown Sugar: Black Women in Pornography* (Durham, NC: Duke University Press, 2014); and Juana Maria Rodriguez, *Sexual Futures, Queer Gestures, and Other Latina Longings* (New York: NYU Press, 2014). Whitney Strub examines the various questions that arise from anonymous porn collections in archives in his essay "Indexing Desire: The Gay Male Pornographic Video Collection as Affective Archive," in *Out of the Closet, Into the Archives: Researching Sexual Histories*, ed. Amy Stone and Jaime Cantrell (Albany: SUNY Press, 2015), 125–47.

6. Michael Bronski, *Culture Clash: The Making of Gay Sensibility* (Boston: South End Press, 1984); and Waugh, "A Heritage of Pornography" and *Hard to Imagine*.

7. Tim Dean, "Introduction: Pornography, Technology, Archive," in *Porn Archives*, ed. Tim Dean, Steven Ruszczycky, and David Squires (Durham, NC: Duke University Press, 2014), 9.

8. José Esteban Muñoz, "Ephemera as Evidence: Introductory Notes to Queer Acts," *Women and Performance* 8, no. 2 (1996): 6.

9. Jacques Derrida, *Archive Fever: A Freudian Impression*, trans. Eric Prenowitz (Chicago: University of Chicago Press, 1996). Although I do not buy into Freud's particular interpretation on the matter of collecting, it might be remiss, in an essay on gay archives, not to mention that he saw the practice as related to anal eroticism.

10. Muñoz, "Ephemera as Evidence," 10.

11. Valerie Rohy's essay "Ahistorical" may be the richest consideration of the structural tensions in queer historiography and conceptions of queer temporality or anachronism. See Rohy, "Ahistorical," *GLQ* 12, no. 1 (2006): 61–83.

12. Ann Cvetkovich, *An Archive of Feelings: Trauma, Sexuality, and Lesbian Public Feelings* (Durham, NC: Duke University Press, 2003); and Judith Halberstam, *In a Queer Time and Place: Transgender Bodies, Subcultural Lives* (New York: NYU Press, 2005). See also Michael Camille and Adrian Rifkin, eds., "Other Objects of Desire: Collectors and Collecting Queerly," special issue, *Art History* 24, no. 2 (2001).

13. Anjali Arondekar, "Without a Trace: Sexuality and the Colonial Archive," *Journal of the History of Sexuality* 14, no. 1 (2006); and Anjali Arondekar, *For the Record: On Sexuality and the Colonial Archive in India* (Durham, NC: Duke University Press, 2009).

14. Sara Edenheim, "Lost and Never Found: The Queer Archive of Feelings and Its Historical Propriety," *differences* 24, no. 3 (2014): 36–62.

15. Simon Ofield, "Cruising the Archive," *Journal of Visual Culture* 4, no. 3 (2005): 357. In 2011, the ONE: National Gay & Lesbian Gay Archives in Los Angeles produced an exhibition and catalogue based on its art holding advancing the same logic, under the title *Cruising the Archive*. David Frantz and Mia Locks, eds., *Cruising the Archive: Queer Art and Culture in Los Angeles, 1945–1980* (Los Angeles: ONE National Gay and Lesbian Archives, 2011).

16. Carolyn Steedman, *Dust: The Archive and Cultural History*, New Brunswick, NJ: Rutgers University Press, 2002), 68.

17. Ibid., 81.

18. I have continued to examine pornography in gay archives in two additional projects: Lucas Hilderbrand, "The Uncut Version: The Mattachine Society's Pornographic Epilogue," *Sexualities* 19, no. 4 (June 2016): 449–64, and the co-curated exhibition and co-edited catalogue, David Evans Frantz, Lucas Hilderbrand, and Kayleigh Perkov, *Cock, Paper, Scissors* (Los Angeles: ONE Archives, 2016).

19. Editors Drewey Wayne Gunn and Jaime Harker's important recent anthology *1960s Gay Pulp Fiction: The Misplaced Heritage* (Amherst: University of Massachusetts Press, 2014) reclaims the pervasiveness, significance, and textuality of these as lowbrow but essential books.

20. Advertisement, *Advocate*, April 1970, 20–21. See also Ryan Powell, "Nowhere Home: Radical Gay Rurality in *Song of the Loon*," *Little Joe* 1 (2010): 63–68. Patricia Nell Warren, *The Front Runner* (New York: William Morrow, 1974).

21. Advertisement, *Advocate*, July 5, 1972, 23. The film *Sudden Rawhide*, also produced by Beehler, likewise seemed to capitalize on a brief vogue for gay erotic westerns; advertisement, *Advocate*, July 19, 1972, 23.

22. I examine *Boys in the Band* in more depth in Lucas Hilderbrand, "Queer Cinema, Queer Writing, Queer Criticism," in *The Cambridge Companion to Gay and Lesbian American Literature*, ed. Scott Herring (New York: Cambridge University Press, 2015), 73–86.

23. Jim Martin, "Out of the Closets and into the Bijous," *Take One* 4, no. 5 (May–June): 1973, 30.

24. Stevenson, "Bedroom to Bijou," 30.

25. John R. Burger's study of gay male video porn suggests that three trends emerged, surely in reaction to anxieties about HIV transmission and its associations with gay sex: first, gay porn increasingly promoted fantasies of "clean" and as-yet un-(sero)-converted straight men who performed as "gay-for-pay"; second, it increasingly featured solo masturbation scenes in contrast to coupled fuck scenes; and finally, it displayed a marked decrease in such previously common practices as deep kissing—further emphasizing not-gayness and anxiety about bodily fluids. John R. Burger, *One-Handed Histories: The Eroto-Politics of Gay Male Video Pornography* (New York: Hayworth Press, 1995): 27–28.

26. Harold Fairbanks, " '73's 10 Best, 10 Worst of Gay Pix," *Advocate*, January 16, 1974, 27.

27. See, for example, ads for *I Love You, I Kill You* (July 5, 1972); *Casey Is Cuming* (March 1, 1972); *Roundabouts* (October 25, 1972); *The Light from the Second Story Window* (September 26, 1973); and *The Night Before* (January 2, 1974).

28. Fairbanks' year-end ten best: *The Back Row, Brothers, The Crooked Arrangement, Erotikus, The Experiment, A Ghost of a Chance, Last Tango in Hollywood, The Night Before, Nights in Black Leather*, and *Sons of Satan* (horror satire). Ten worst: *Any Boy Can,*

Case of the Hooded Man, Country Chicken, Fantastic Heroes, Four More than Money, Greek Lightning, Hunk—A California Adventure, Letter Bond, Ramrod (3-D), and *Too Hot to Handle.*

29. Vito Russo, *The Celluloid Closet: Homosexuality in the Movies* (New York: Harper and Row, 1981); and Parker Tyler, *Screening the Sexes: Homosexuality in the Movies* (New York: Holt, Rinehart & Winston, 1972).

30. Advertisement, *Advocate*, May 23, 1973, center spread.

31. This history is culled from Turan and Zito, *Sinema*, 193–96, and a two-part interview with Barry Knight and Russell Moore, published as Jerry Douglas, "Jaguar Productions," *Manshots*, June 1996, 10–15, and Douglas, "Jaguar Productions, Part 2," *Manshots*, August 1996, 10–15 and 72. Joe Rubin has also significantly enriched my knowledge of Beehler and Jaguar Productions.

32. Harold Fairbanks, "*Nights* Gets Back to Basics, But It's a Good Movie, Too," *Advocate*, May 9, 1973, 30.

33. Harold Fairbanks, "Peter Burian: Joy in Life, Youth, and Beauty," *Advocate*, May 9, 1973, 30.

34. Joe Gage's *El Paso Wrecking Company* (1978) features scenes with even more extraordinary chromatic discontinuity and spatial disorientation, which effectively serve to locate its representations of working-class hypermasculinity in the realm of fantasy rather than purely making claims toward authenticity.

35. Laura Mulvey, "Visual Pleasure and Narrative Cinema," *Screen* 16, no. 3 (1975): 6–18.

36. My editors have helpfully alerted me to Edward D. Miller's analysis of Peter Berlin and his films, which makes a number of similar claims. Miller eloquently writes, "Peter Berlin reveled in an unabashed and excessive, self-conscious narcissism that both invited and rejected admirers and suitors and placed himself on the border between campy self-parody and ritualized erotic behavior. As much as he loved being a person in motion, he seemed to prefer being a statue in provocative stasis—his pleasure was found in being immobile as if in photographic suspension. He enjoyed restraint as much as release, and his wardrobe was more revealing than his nudity. . . . Within the narrative [of *That Boy*], these fantasy sex scenes provoke a longing for an event that never occurred and will never occur as Peter rebuffs all advances from those who can see him." Edward D. Miller, *Tomboys, Pretty Boys, and Outspoken Women: The Media Revolution of 1973* (Ann Arbor: University of Michigan Press, 2011), 175 and 193–94.

37. Daniel Harris, *The Rise and Fall of Gay Culture* (New York: Hyperion, 1997), 130–31. Harris makes a number of provocative, though questionable, historical claims about gay male porn aesthetics.

38. Don Teal, " 'No Degradation': Wakefield Poole Adds New Dimension to Porn," *Advocate*, March 1, 1972, 17. Quoted in Capino, "Seminal Fantasies," 156.

39. See Capino, "Seminal Fantasies"; and Powell, "Coming Together: Exhibition, Audience, and 'Early' Gay Art Porn," conference presentation at Sex, Media, Reception: New Approaches, University of Michigan, February 15, 2014.

Fading Flesh

*Personal Reflections on the Quest to Preserve
Hardcore Cinema*

JOE RUBIN

M ORE THAN TEN THOUSAND hardcore feature films were produced between the late 1960s and the late 1980s, the period during which such films were exhibited theatrically in the United States. While a few dozen have become cultural hallmarks, many enjoyed exhibition periods of no more than a few weeks, occasionally revived years later as the bottom portion of a triple feature, then only to then vanish into total obscurity. With the advent of home video, a sizable number of these films were made available once again, often copied from beat-up prints on primitive telecines, a film-to-tape transferring machine. There they remained: countless films viewable only in the lowest possible quality. Producers, assuming that the theatrical market was dead and VHS was the future, often discarded their prints and in some cases their negatives, preferring to hold on to the one-inch master videotape that made them so much cash in the early 1980s.

Now, as modern technology makes it possible to preserve these films more easily and in higher quality than ever before, archivists are confronted with a harsh reality: X-rated films are second only to silent movies in the number of titles that are totally lost or survive only in incomplete or severely deteriorated forms. As cofounder of the restoration lab OCN Digital and the X-rated film preservation and distribution company Vinegar Syndrome, I often ask myself, how could so many films that aren't very old have met such a dire fate? There are numerous answers to this question, and the predicament is nearly impossible to resolve.

To begin, very few archives, whether privately or publicly funded, have taken steps to actively preserve this material. Even UCLA and Indiana University's Kinsey Institute, which house some of the larger academic collections of hardcore cinema in the United States, do virtually nothing to properly preserve these films. Neither institution has even fully inventoried their collections. To be fair to UCLA, their archivists are perpetually inundated with new material, creating a backlog that may never be resolved. The biggest challenge at UCLA, however, involves political aspects of the fundraising operation that supports the UC system. To avoid controversy, the UC schools seem to accept donations of X-rated works to their various archives, but then downgrade those works for priority preservation status, moving other types of films in their possession to the head of the line. At Kinsey, a combination of poor funding for maintaining and preserving archival holdings, as well as a strange ambiguity regarding how X-rated films are approached within their academic framework, seem to be at play. But more on that later. Meanwhile, organizations that actively care for their collections of sexually explicit films struggle to find support. San Francisco's Institute for Advanced Studies of Human Sexuality (IASHS) has been trying to preserve its extensive archives of sexually explicit films for decades but has yet to find a donor willing to cover the costs.

Another obstacle to preserving these films is that many of the original producers and distributors are either long deceased or out of the film business. A notable exception is Distribpix, a New York–based production company that made over two hundred features between the 1960s and 1980s. Unlike so many other such companies, Distribpix not only retained all of their own negatives but also amassed a library of a couple hundred additional features made by other producers. Operated by Steven Morowitz, son of founder Arthur Morowitz, Distribpix is the only X-rated and sexploitation film production company determined to preserve its library and legacy. But without a steady and reliable cash flow, it has been unable to pursue many of its most pressing projects, which include preserving early films by Francis Ford Coppola (*Tonight For Sure,* 1961) and future horror filmmaker Danny Steinmann (*High Rise,* 1972).

The process of prioritizing what is most in need of preservation is never easy. The condition of the surviving elements must be weighed against the anticipated returns to be gained from commercially exploiting a restored version of the title in question. I am often forced to confront these issues myself when planning titles to release through Vinegar Syndrome. Films that are more financially viable are typically less in danger of being lost. The films in greatest need of restoration, most often due to decaying elements, have a harder time recouping the investments made in their preservation. But all of this, of course, presupposes the existence of complete elements on which a quality restoration can be performed.

At this point, thousands of films remain either completely lost or exist only as the video masters deemed more valuable than the negatives and prints of a few decades ago. These include many artistically and historically important works. Avant-garde filmmaker Jerry Abrams's 1970 documentary on San Francisco's sexual subcultures, *Sub Rosa Rising*, for example, exists only as copies of a low-quality telecine transfer made around 1980. The whereabouts of the negative and any surviving prints remain unknown. This film, and thousands of works like it, is currently destined to be seen only as a muddy, washed out and improperly framed video duplicate. Better elements may never be discovered.

Even if preprint elements exist, they may not be in any shape to be used in a preservation. Case in point is filmmaker Wakefield Poole's landmark features *Boys in the Sand* (1971) and *Bijou* (1972). Both were shot on one of the more popular formats for low-budget feature films of all genres in the late 1960s and early 1970s: 16 mm Ektachrome. Ektachrome (along with the less popular Eastman Commercial Original (ECO) and Agfachrome) was a camera positive stock often preferred by independent filmmakers over Eastman Color Negatives (ECN) because it allowed for easier editing and—of special interest to X-rated filmmakers, who often had neither the money nor the time for negative matching—avoided the need to make work prints. However, if a film became popular enough that many prints needed to be struck, a printing internegative was made, after which the Ekta originals were often discarded or abandoned in labs.

The most common Kodak stock used to make these internegatives was a cheap duping stock that went through the same developer bath sequence as a work print. It was essentially disposable, with a stable shelf life of no more than five years, at which time serious fade in the cyan layer started to set in. Thus, when Vinegar Syndrome set out to restore Poole's *Bijou*, we discovered that the surviving internegative was so faded that, in darker scenes, nearly 50 percent of the image detail was completely gone. Thankfully, other high-quality reversal materials were eventually recovered, allowing the film to be returned to its original visual splendor.

Poole's debut feature, *Boys in the Sand*, did not fare as well. Its internegative was equally faded and no superior elements could be located, rendering one of the most significant films of the 1970s involving homosexuality unable to be viewed as originally intended. Film historian Eric Schaefer has shown how 16 mm technology influenced the emergence of the hardcore pornographic feature; what we are realizing today is that it also shaped the degree to which these films are preserved.[1]

Returning to the IASHS—when I began working with them in 2010, they were primarily concerned with improving storage conditions for their film assets. After considering a number of options, we decided that it would be best to transport the bulk of their 35 mm materials to Vinegar Syndrome's climate-controlled storage facility, which would allow the films to be properly cared for, as well as slowly restored. To date, we have preserved over twenty feature films originating from the IASHS archives, including significant works from directors Alex de Renzy, Bob Chinn, and Harry Mohney, films central to any understanding of the erotic cinema landscape of the 1970s.

As an institute of higher learning, IASHS embodies many of the issues faced by academics and film archivists working on saving these films, who are sometimes pitted against each other due to overlapping goals but radically different methods of achieving them. During a recent chat with feminist porn scholar Laura Helen Marks, who writes in this volume about Shaun Costello's 1975 film *The Passions of Carol*, she jokingly bemoaned that the quality of my restorations has made her realize that the VHS-ported-to-DVD releases of X-rated films made available by gray market distributors look terrible. She hadn't realized it until she saw what these films are *supposed* to look like.

The fact that X-rated films were well photographed, professionally lit, and generally made with the same care and attention as any comparably budgeted feature film of the era seems lost on the vast majority of those who view them, scholars and members of the general public alike. And while the consumer sector cannot be faulted for having access only to low-quality, incorrectly framed, and often edited versions of these films, it is befuddling that, even among academics studying them, there isn't a stronger push to make X-rated films available in forms that reflect their creators' visions as accurately as possible. This unfortunate lack of interest seems at least partially rooted in the porn studies disciplinary rubric. The study of general cinematic qualities is often left by the wayside in favor of analysis of the representation of sexual acts and lifestyles. This is not to imply that scholars working in this field completely disregard the visual and stylistic components of films, but rather that these are often given minimal critical attention when compared to the analysis bestowed on the sex. This general attitude is flawed for a number of reasons, but most significantly because it speaks to an implicit intent: that filmmakers creating X-rated movies were motivated almost solely by a desire to depict sex acts and that all other aspects of the film were merely window dressing. Porn studies scholars have rarely approached their canon in the ways that earlier film scholars examined the work of such landmark directors as Douglas Sirk, Rainer Werner Fassbinder, or Orson Welles.

This, again, is where IASHS is unique. The institute values sexually explicit cinema as a representation of human sexuality, but also, in the words of its founder, Ted McIlvenna, as "erotic folk art." McIlvenna is adamant that students studying sexually explicit cinema recognize that the cinematic aspects of the film are just as significant as the sexual components, and that it is crucial to understand and appreciate both in order to properly analyze any work in the genre. It is this major distinction—that X rated films are *films* with sex in them, rather than sex acts documented on celluloid—that seems to be at the heart of why, even in the academic communities studying them, so little has been done to preserve and restore the physical materials on which they were photographed.

This deplorable failure to comprehend the artistic value of X-rated films is one of the primary reasons that I have placed such a great emphasis on the visual quality of the presentation in all of my releases through Vinegar Syndrome. For viewers, whether scholarly or not, experiencing the carefully composed and colorfully lit cinematography and the sometimes rhythmic editing in Sam Weston's 1977 films *Confessions* and *Expectations* allows them to appreciate these works in a new way, as cinematic art. This distinction forces viewers to reevaluate their perceived intent of the film and its maker. When understood through the same formal lens as any other low-budget, independent feature film, the viewer is obliged to pay attention to the basic formal aspects of its construction, rather than simply dwelling on the actions unfolding on screen. When the significance of cinematography, editing, lighting, production design, and even more basic narrative elements such as scripting and direction are glossed over, the need for the film to "look good" is by and large removed. A "viewable" copy does just fine if the only goal of the screening is merely to observe acts of coitus. When a work is considered *art*, it can be assumed to hold meaning and value that goes beyond the literal. It becomes crucial to be able to view the work in a form that mirrors the intended visual presentation of its creator. Thus, the imperative to preserve the physical elements (as well as restore them digitally) becomes paramount to the overall understood value of the work.

It is tangentially worth mentioning that, historically speaking, the usage of the term "art" to describe the nature of sexually explicit cinema has often carried along with it a tongue-in-cheek sensibility, simultaneously serving as a means to mock the crucial "redeeming social value" clauses put forth by the Supreme Court in the 1960s and justice Stewart Potter's infamous 1964 declaration regarding pornography—"I know it when I see it"—and a frequent methodology by which explicit films were defended from prosecution for their "artistic and cultural values." As evidenced in early explicit features, such as always-pseudonymous filmmaker Monroe Beehler's 1971 feature *Sexual Liberty Now* (often incorrectly attributed to its producer, John Lamb), which spends lengthy portions of its running time defending itself as not obscene and artistic, or the anonymously directed 1973 film *The Love Witch*, which interestingly comments on the frequent pastiche nature of obscenity trials by presenting itself as a film within a film in which Harry Reems literally plays a judge, jury, prosecutor, defendant, and lawyer in a bizarre courtroom comedy following the obscenity case of a rather ordinary sex film that must be defended as "artistic" in the most absurd of ways. As such, it is unfortunately difficult to engage in serious critical analysis of the actual *artistic* components of these films (subjectivity in what constitutes "art" aside), as very often the mere mention of the words "art" or "aesthetics" when describing sexually explicit cinema is met with a proverbial rolling of eyes.

At this point, the vast majority of the academic community, both those involved in porn studies as well as general film scholarship, has not acknowledged this imperative. Yet it is this acknowledgment that could greatly affect the future of this cinema for the better or, if no further positive strides are made, push it further down the path of deterioration and loss. Whereas Distribpix's work to preserve the hardcore films directed by auteur Radley Metzger (under the name Henry Paris) was met with praise from numerous critics and fans worldwide, including a nod from the British Film Institute, Metzger's hardcore titles were notably omitted from a recent summer 2014 retrospective of the director's work at the Film Society at Lincoln Center (though, to be fair, this was at least in part due to Metzger's personal wishes). Indeed, the series itself bore the curiously insistent title "This Is Softcore: The Art Cinema of Radley Metzger."[2]

The repertory cinema world has, unexpectedly, become one of the few popular venues to motivate public interest in experiencing these films in a context that places them on the same, or similar, cultural and artistic platform as other rare cinema in need of theatrical revival. Film historian Casey Scott's ongoing series at New York's Anthology Film Archives (which has been sponsored by both Vinegar Syndrome and Distribpix), titled "In The Flesh," has allowed hundreds of filmgoers the opportunity to see genre masterpieces in a theatrical environment, albeit from faded and well-used theatrical prints. These have included such classics as Jonas Middleton's *Through the Looking Glass* (1976) and Chuck Vincent's *Roommates* (1981). When discussions of restoring these films have come up during postscreening question-and-answer sessions, reactions have been positive and enthusiastic. It is also noteworthy that at the Anthology screenings, the age breakdown of the audience is evenly split between those under forty and those over forty, with the under-forty sector likely never having had the opportunity to have seen any of these films during their initial theatrical runs. Most of the questions regarding the restoration status of these films are brought up by younger audience members. It therefore may be events such as these that will some day serve as the catalysts by which a widespread push can be made for the urgency of saving these titles.

Many of these recently preserved works have not been discussed in academic porn studies journals or books, and without them the genre looks quite different. Both Linda Williams, looking at heterosexual porn, and Thomas Waugh, looking at gay porn, agree that male-male contact in heterosexual pornography was largely unheard of.[3] Yet Walt Davis's *Widow Blue*, which was made in December of 1970, thus ranking it among the earliest surviving fully hardcore narrative feature films, confounds these claims because of the strong presence of hardcore male-male content as well as another rarely integrated element in sexually explicit cinema: gory violence. While *Blue* was ostensibly created as a cheaply made one-day wonder, Davis's decision to both open this "heterosexual" film with an explicit homosexual coupling and later introduce graphic scenes of decapitation and castration renders it a landmark work. The film's pansexual view of hardcore sex beats such better-known bisexual films as Radley Metzger's *Score* (1973) and Jerry Douglas's *Both Ways* (1975) by a matter of years, and its mixing of unsimulated sexual content with scenes of gore more extreme than commonly found in mainstream horror films of the era makes the film a unique experiment.

Reflecting the crisis in pornographic preservation, until Vinegar Syndrome released *Widow Blue* (and two other fascinating Davis films) in 2014, it had been unavailable in its full form. This is but one example of the ways that access has shaped academic porn studies. Wakefield Poole is heralded everywhere as one of the major gay hardcore filmmakers of the 1970s, yet his expensive (and unsuccessful) 1973 *Bible!* featured straight-porn star Georgina Spelvin in a softcore spoof. Again, demarcations between gay/straight and softcore/hardcore were subverted, but the film remained absent from home video and effectively unseeable until the 2013 Vinegar Syndrome DVD release.

Without a means of viewing these early experimental ventures, many of which were never made available during the video age of the 1980s, both film scholars and those involved in porn studies are being deprived of significant examples of radically minded sex films, which will undoubtedly alter their perceptions of the state of hardcore cinema of the era. If these films do not become as easily accessible as better-known titles from Gerard Damiano, Metzger, and so on, porn studies risks becoming nothing more than an analysis of popular culture rather than of the extreme stylistic diversity employed by filmmakers in the first couple of decades of theatrical sex films.

At the moment, however, the future for preservation looks relatively bleak. Perhaps a bit less so in Europe, South America, and Asia, where the Danish Film Institute has at least actively sought out sexually explicit works, and in Brazil, where the Cinemateca Brasileira went as far as striking new prints of a handful of Boca do Lixo films, including such controversial and politically subversive films as Jean Garret's *Fuk Fuk a Brasileira* (1986), for a retrospective in Rotterdam that was curated by American film writer Gabe Klinger. The Japanese studio Nikatsu has restored a sizable percentage of their library, as has French production company Alpha France, although many of their DVD releases have been inexplicably edited for run times. But the United States, which produced more sexually explicit cinema between the late 1960s and mid-1980s than nearly all other countries combined, has yet to recognize the urgency of saving this significant portion of its artistic and cultural heritage.

And here we are: nearly three decades since the last first-run X-rated films flickered their ways across the screens of neighborhood cinemas, and nearly five decades since explicit sex first left its mark on the American film culture. We are still awaiting the day when hardcore sex is no longer deemed an acceptable reason for not protecting a work of cinematic art from turning to dust. The archival and restoration work performed and championed by Steven Morowitz, Ted McIlvenna, and me, as well as a select group of others, represents not only a sense of duty to work toward preserving a genre of film that has been both culturally and artistically maligned and dismissed since the era of its creation, but is also an imperative brought on by the unfortunate reality that if we do not obtain and protect as much of this material as possible, there is a great likelihood that no one else will. Film historians engaged with pornography need to realize that they cannot fully support their claims about the 1970s until they actually have access to the expansive cinematic landscape that stretches far beyond the common touchstones of the era.

NOTES

1. Eric Schaefer, "Gauging a Revolution: 16 mm Film and the Rise of the Pornographic Feature," *Cinema Journal* 41, no. 3 (Spring 2002): 3–26.
2. See "This Is Softcore: The Art Cinema of Radley Metzger" (online program guide), www.filmlinc.com.
3. See Linda Williams, *Hard Core: Power, Pleasure, and the "Frenzy of the Visible"* (Berkeley: University of California Press, 1989); and Thomas Waugh, *Hard to Imagine: Gay Male Eroticism in Photography and Film from Their Beginnings to Stonewall* (New York: Columbia University Press, 1996).

Notes on Contributors

PETER ALILUNAS is assistant professor and director of media studies in the School of Journalism and Communication at the University of Oregon. His research traces the transition of the adult film industry from celluloid to home video in the late 1970s. He is the author of *Smutty Little Movies: The Creation and Regulation of Adult Video* (2016). His work has been published in *Camera Obscura, Television & New Media, Film History,* and many other venues.

CAROLYN BRONSTEIN is Vincent de Paul Professor of Media Studies in the College of Communication at DePaul University. She is the author of *Battling Pornography: The American Feminist Anti-Pornography Movement, 1976–1986* (2011), winner of the 2012 Emily Toth Award of the Popular Culture Association / American Culture Association for the Best Single Work in Women's Studies. Her work on feminism, pornography, contemporary media culture, and representation of women has been featured in a wide range of academic journals, including *Feminist Media Studies, Camera Obscura, Journal of Popular Romance Studies, Violence Against Women, Feral Feminisms,* and *Journal of Mass Media Ethics,* as well as popular venues including *The Atlantic* and *Huffington Post.*

GILLIAN FRANK is a visiting fellow at the Center for the Study of Religion. He received a PhD in American studies at Brown University in 2009. From 2011 to 2013, Frank was an American Council of Learned Societies New Faculty Fellow in the Department of History at Stony Brook University. His research has appeared in publications such as *Gender and History, Journal of the History of Sexuality,* and *Journal of Religion and Popular Culture.* He is the author of the forthcoming book

Save Our Children: Sexual Politics and Cultural Conservatism in the United States, 1965–1990 and coeditor, with Bethany Moreton and Heather White, of the forthcoming anthology *Devotions: Histories of Sexuality and Religion in the Twentieth-Century United States.*

ELIZABETH FRATERRIGO is associate professor of history at Loyola University Chicago, where she teaches courses in public history, U.S. women's and gender history, twentieth-century popular culture, and material culture. Her first book, *Playboy and the Making of the Good Life in Modern America* (2009), examined transformations in gender, sexuality, and consumption in postwar America. She is currently working on a book project about the media activism of the National Organization for Women and other feminist groups in the 1960s and 1970s. Her work has appeared in the *Journal of Urban History, The Public Historian, Journal of Women's History,* and *American Historical Review.*

LUCAS HILDERBRAND is associate professor of film and media studies at the University of California, Irvine. He is the author of *Inherent Vice: Bootleg Histories of Videotape and Copyright* (2009) and *Paris Is Burning* (2013). He has also written widely on media and sexuality for such journals as *Camera Obscura, GLQ, Journal of the History of Sexuality, Film Quarterly, Jump Cut, Journal of Popular Music Studies, Women and Performance,* and *Sexualities.*

NANCY SEMIN LINGO received a PhD in American studies at the University of Texas and subsequently graduated from the Historic Preservation program at the Savannah College of Art and Design. She teaches American history at Austin Community College. Her research examines the life and career of Linda Lovelace, using extensive new interviews and archival research.

LAURA HELEN MARKS is a postdoctoral fellow at Tulane University in New Orleans. She earned a PhD in English from Louisiana State University. Her work on pornographic genre, adaptation, and neo-Victorian studies has appeared in *Sexualities, Phoebe,* and *Neo-Victorian Cities.* Marks is also a regular contributor to the adult film oral history podcast, *The Rialto Report.* She is currently completing a book manuscript, *Porning the Victorians: Erotic Adaptations and Gothic Desire.*

NICHOLAS MATTE teaches at the Mark S. Bonham Centre for Sexual Diversity Studies at the University of Toronto, where he also curates the Sexual Representation Collection and works on the LGBTQ Oral History Digital Collaboratory research project. His 2014 dissertation is titled "Historicizing Liberal American Transnormativities: Medicine, Media, Activism, 1960–1990," and his work has been published in *TSQ, GLQ, Transgender Studies Reader, Trans Activism in Canada, International Journal of Transgenderism*, and *Canadian Bulletin for the History of Medicine.*

JENNIFER C. NASH is associate professor of African American studies and gender and sexuality studies at Northwestern University. She is the author of *The Black Body in Ecstasy: Reading Race, Reading Pornography* (2014), which won the Alan Bray Memorial Book Prize from the GL/Q Caucus of the MLA. She is currently completing a book project titled *Black Feminism Remixed.*

JOE RUBIN is a film preservationist and co-owner of Vinegar Syndrome, a private DVD and Blu-ray label that focuses on preserving and releasing films from genres that might be otherwise lost, including low-budget horror, exploitation, and classic soft- and hardcore erotica. Vinegar Syndrome specializes in vintage grindhouse titles like *Vampire Hookers, The Phantom Gunslinger*, and *The Vixens of Kung Fu*, and Rubin is an expert on the films of such classic porn auteurs as Russ Meyer and Wakefield Poole.

WHITNEY STRUB is associate professor of history and director of the Women's and Gender Studies program at Rutgers University–Newark. His first book was *Perversion for Profit: The Politics of Pornography and the Rise of the New Right* (2011); his second book, *Obscenity Rules: Roth v. United States and the Long Struggle over Sexual Expression* (2013), won the 2013 David J. Langum, Sr. Prize in American Legal History. His articles on obscenity, pornography, and sexual politics have appeared in *American Quarterly, Radical History Review, Journal of the History of Sexuality, Journal of Women's History, Salon, Vice*, and *Temple of Schlock.*

ALEX WARNER received a PhD in history from Rutgers University. Her dissertation, "Where Angels Fear to Tread: Feminism, Sex, and the Problem of SM, 1969–1993," is a pioneering historical study of the lesbian SM community. Warner has taught at Rutgers, Seton Hall, and San Francisco State University, and has served on the board of the Committee on Lesbian, Gay, Bisexual, and Transgender History and as project historian for the Women's Leather History Project at the Leather Archives & Museum in Chicago.

LEIGH ANN WHEELER is professor of history at SUNY–Binghamton. She is author of *Against Obscenity: Reform and the Politics of Womanhood in America, 1873–1935* (2004) and *How Sex Became a Civil Liberty* (2013). Her articles have appeared in a range of journals, including the *Journal of the History of Sexuality, Journal of Women's History, Frontiers: A Journal of Women Studies,* and *Michigan Historical Review.* A former co-editor of the *Journal of Women's History,* she is currently a senior editor for the *Oxford Research Encyclopedia of American History.*

GREG YOUMANS is assistant professor of English and film studies at Western Washington University. His book on the 1977 documentary *Word Is Out: Stories of Some of Our Lives* appeared in 2011, and he has published articles in *Camera Obscura, eflux,* and *Millennium Film Journal.* He is currently at work on a book manuscript about queer filmmaking in the San Francisco Bay Area in the 1970s, as well as a project on lesbian poet Elsa Gidlow (1898–1986).

Index